AUTOBIOGRAPHY AND OTHER WRITINGS

BENJAMIN FRANKLIN was born in Boston, Massachusetts, in 1706, the son of a tallow chandler. At the age of 12 he was apprenticed to his brother James, a printer, who published Franklin's earliest writings. At 17 he resettled as a journeyman printer in Philadelphia. He worked at print shops in Philadelphia and London until 1728 when he set up as a printer on his own. In 1730 he married Deborah Read. Over the next twenty-five years he masterminded a series of civic improvements in Philadelphia. In 1732 he began publication of *Poor Richard's Almanack*. Success in his business and investments allowed him to retire from active management before turning 42. He performed a series of experiments on electricity (1746–50), leading to his invention of the lightning rod. He became a party leader in the Pennsylvania Assembly, and from 1757 he served in London as colonial agent. He began his *Autobiography* in 1771. In 1775 after negotiations to avert a rupture between Great Britain and the colonies had failed, he returned to Philadelphia and was elected to the Continental Congress, where he served on the committee to draft the Declaration of Independence and was designated American ambassador to France. As ambassador (1776–85), he negotiated French assistance for the United States and finally a peace accord with Great Britain. He returned to Philadelphia and was selected as a delegate to the Constitutional Convention of 1787. He died in April 1790, leaving his *Autobiography* completed only as far as 1758.

ORMOND SEAVEY is Professor of English at The George Washington University and the author of *Becoming Benjamin Franklin: The Autobiography and the Life* (1988).

THE WORLD'S CLASSICS

BENJAMIN FRANKLIN

Autobiography and Other Writings

Edited by
ORMOND SEAVEY

Oxford   New York
OXFORD UNIVERSITY PRESS

Oxford University Press, Great Clarendon Street, Oxford OX2 6DP

Oxford New York
Athens Auckland Bangkok Bogota Bombay
Buenos Aires Calcutta Cape Town Dar es Salaam
Delhi Florence Hong Kong Istanbul Karachi
Kuala Lumpur Madras Madrid Melbourne
Mexico City Nairobi Paris Singapore
Taipei Tokyo Toronto Warsaw

and associated companies in
Berlin Ibadan

Oxford is a trade mark of Oxford University Press

First published as a World's Classics paperback 1993

British Library Cataloguing in Publication Data

Data available

Library of Congress Cataloging in Publication Data
Franklin, Benjamin, 1706-1790.
Autobiography and other writings/Benjamin Franklin; edited by Ormond Seavey.
p. cm.—(World's classics)
Includes bibliographical references.
1. Franklin, Benjamin, 1706-1790. 2. Statesmen—United States—
Biography. I. Seavey, Ormond. II. Title. III. Series.
E302.6.F7A4 1993 973.3'092—dc20 92-14671
ISBN 0-19-282733-2

5 7 9 10 8 6

Printed in Great Britain by
Caledonian International Book Manufacturing Ltd
Glasgow

ACKNOWLEDGEMENTS

ANY editor of Franklin writings must acknowledge the labours of two centuries of Franklin students. In particular this edition is indebted to the work of the great uncompleted edition of *The Papers of Benjamin Franklin*, edited by Leonard W. Labaree, William B. Willcox, Barbara Oberg, and others (New Haven, Conn.: Yale University Press, 1959–). In addition, this volume includes various pieces recently identified as Franklin's by J. A. Leo Lemay in *The Canon of Benjamin Franklin 1722–1776: New Attributions and Reconsiderations* (Newark, Del.: University of Delaware Press, 1986), some of which appear for the first time in paperback form in this volume. The editors of the Library of America have assisted the preparation of this edition.

The following pieces are reprinted with permission from *The Papers of Benjamin Franklin*: the 'Epitaph'; the letter to Josiah and Abiah Franklin, dated 13 April 1738; 'Old Mistresses Apologue'; the letter to William Strahan, dated 5 July 1775. The text of the 'Internal State of America' is borrowed with grateful acknowledgement from *William and Mary Quarterly* (3rd ser. 15 (1958), 214–27). I am indebted to the helpful librarians of the Manuscript Division of the Library of Congress for their assistance in my preparation of the text of the 1726 journal. This edition reprints with permission *Benjamin Franklin's Memoirs: Parallel Text Edition*, edited by Max Farrand (Berkeley, Calif.: University of California Press, 1949). I am grateful to the Graduate School of Arts and Science and the English Department of the George Washington University for support in the preparation of the text of the *Autobiography*. In particular I thank Etsuko Taketani for her editorial work in that project. Harriet Levy and Catherine Clarke of Oxford University Press World's Classics have been consistently helpful.

O.S.

ACKNOWLEDGMENTS

ANY editor of Franklin writings must acknowledge the labours of two centuries of Franklin students. In particular this edition is indebted to the work of the great uncompleted edition of *The Papers of Benjamin Franklin*, edited by Leonard W. Labaree, William B. Willcox, Barbara Oberg, and others (New Haven, Conn., Yale University Press, 1959–). In addition, this volume includes various pieces recently identified as Franklin's by J. A. Leo Lemay in *The Canon of Benjamin Franklin, 1722–1776: New Attributions and Reconsideration* (Newark, Del., University of Delaware Press, 1986), some of which appear for the first time in paperback form in this volume. The editors of the Library of America have assisted the preparation of this edition.

The following pieces are reprinted with permission from *The Papers of Benjamin Franklin*: the 'Epitaph'; the letter to Josiah and Abiah Franklin, dated 13 April 1738; 'Old Mistresses Apologue'; the letter to William Strahan, dated 5 July 1775. The text of the 'Internal State of America' is borrowed with grateful acknowledgement from *William and Mary Quarterly* (3rd ser., 15 (1958), 214–27). I am indebted to the helpful librarians of the Manuscript Division of the Library of Congress for their assistance in my preparation of the text of the 1726 journal. This edition reprints with permission *Benjamin Franklin's Memoirs: Parallel Text Edition*, edited by Max Farrand (Berkeley, Calif., University of California Press, 1949). I am grateful to the Graduate School of Arts and Science and the English Department of the George Washington University for support in the preparation of the text of the 'autobiography'. In particular I thank Kristin Tabetan for her editorial work in that project. Harriet Levy and Catherine Clarke of Oxford University Press World's Classics have been consistently helpful.

O.S.

CONTENTS

GENERAL INTRODUCTION

BENJAMIN FRANKLIN may not appear at first to be a literary figure in the same way that Emerson, Stowe, Faulkner, or Stevens do. Instead, Franklin seems like a historical figure, known for his discoveries about electricity and his political activities during the American Revolution and later. But first of all Franklin was a writer. The most important stage of his education, as he later describes it, made him 'a tolerable English Writer, of which I was extreamly ambitious'. Franklin was a writer by profession to an extent equalled by no other colonial American. His advancement in business, his career as a statesman, even his acclaim as a scientist depended upon his writing abilities. The culmination of his writing career is his *Autobiography*, which he worked on intermittently during the last eighteen years of his long life.

Benjamin Franklin began writing his *Autobiography* in the summer of 1771 when he was 65, but in a sense he had already been working on his own self-portrait for fifty years. Though his *Autobiography* overshadows all his other works, the other writings prepared him to write his life story and were themselves a substantial part of that story. No American writer of the colonial period was so intensely conscious of himself as Franklin. But self-revelation in Franklin's case always took the route of indirection.

The earliest surviving published work by Franklin was written under the disguise of Silence Dogood, a proper but observant Puritan clergyman's widow, born on the Atlantic as her parents were crossing to New England. Prim Mistress Dogood takes note of the same social and cultural features that preoccupied the 16-year-old Franklin. Some years earlier, young Franklin had been withdrawn by his father from an education that would have prepared him for Harvard College; instead Benjamin was apprenticed to his brother

James, a Boston printer. Mistress Dogood contemplates Harvard College and describes a place filled with young fools. Thus, even early in his life, Franklin was disposed to reverse his own apparent disadvantages. In *Silence Dogood* 7 she comments extensively on the dull, formulaic quality of much of Puritan poetry. Though at the time he had lived only in Boston, young Franklin recognized that there existed a standard of wit and critical intelligence higher than that commonly accepted in New England.

While writing the *Dogood* letters, Franklin took over the management of his brother's newspaper while James Franklin was imprisoned for recklessly affronting the Massachusetts authorities. The emblem the Franklin brothers used for their newspaper *The New-England Courant* was Janus, the two-faced god. Franklin began early to define himself by alternative identities. He describes how he developed his own style of argumentation in imitation of Socrates, 'dropt my abrupt Contradiction, and positive Argumentation, and put on the humble Enquirer & Doubter'. It was always natural for Franklin to be trying on a fresh identity, as if he were putting on new clothes.

In writing under an assumed identity Franklin was doing what European writers of the eighteenth century characteristically did. But there was something more problematic about the disguises the adolescent Franklin assumed in Boston and Philadelphia. The Puritan belief in which Franklin had been raised valued one's own authentic feelings and expressions. So the masquerades in Franklin's early writings were adopted in defiance of a pervasive collective ethos. Swift was not hiding out as Lemuel Gulliver in the same way that Franklin was as Silence Dogood. The adoption of disguise had the effect of intensifying Franklin's self-consciousness. He was both himself and someone else as well.

The earliest surviving pages in which Franklin was writing truly on his own, with no aim of self-advancement or thought of audience, a journal he kept in 1726 on his voyage back to Philadelphia from London, reveal a young man intensely concerned with issues of society and solitude, right discipline, sincerity and reputation. He is very much a young man full of fun and pranks, getting into trouble and barely getting out. He is an excellent observer of the natural and social scene, noting the bird and fish species he has seen and performing a little experiment on the crabs which cling to gulf weed. And even at the age of 20 he is systematic and neat, making an entry for every day aboard the *Berkshire*. He even enters an explanatory footnote at one point. Another measure of Franklin's self-consciousness is that he preserved this journal into old age, even making reference to it in the *Autobiography*, suggesting that his reader will find the incidents of the voyage 'all minutely related'.

Purportedly the audience of the *Autobiography* is William Franklin, his 41-year-old illegitimate son, currently serving as royal governor of New Jersey. William Franklin had accompanied his father to England in 1757 and continued to serve as his father's ally and listening-post in America. By 1773, however, it was clear to the father that his son was leaning toward the British side in the conflicts which preceded the Revolution. William Franklin was never to read the manuscript of the autobiography addressed to him in 1771, and when Franklin finally began writing again, he addressed himself more explicitly to 'the Publick'.

The *Autobiography* provided Franklin with an opportunity in part to reveal achievements of his own which he had concealed earlier in his life out of a prudent concern for not showing his hand. As early as his first anonymous submission of a letter from Silence Dogood to his brother's newspaper, Franklin had hidden his own writings and activities, sometimes so that the credit might be shared more broadly, as in the case of his proposals for the first volunteer fire company or for the funding of the Pennsylvania Hospital. Franklin is candid about the vanity of retrieving credit for his past achievements, and in fact defends vanity in the first paragraph, 'being persuaded that it is often productive of Good to the Possessor & to others that are within his Sphere of Action'. Confident that his role would eventually be revealed, Franklin's anonymity ironically became the ultimate manifestation of vanity.

In fact Franklin avoids bragging in his own story, even pointing out occasions where credit had been given him that others deserved. It is clear from his own description that Franklin's relationships with other people and groups after his early twenties had been guarded and somewhat distant. He describes his wife Deborah as a safe refuge from the danger of venereal disease and as a 'good & faithful Helpmate, [who] assisted me much by attending the Shop'. Franklin advances in the world not through close friends but through collaborators, and his very notions of friendship after his youth are framed in terms of manipulation. He describes how he befriended a prominent Philadelphian who had formerly opposed his election as clerk of the Pennsylvania Assembly by asking to borrow a rare book and thanking the man for the loan.

Franklin exercises the same indirectness and wariness toward the reader of the *Autobiography* that he had exercised all his mature life in Philadelphia, London, and Paris. When he refers at the beginning to his vanity, he says, 'in many Cases it would not be quite absurd if a Man were to thank God for his Vanity among the other Comforts of Life'. Franklin knows that his contemporaries would still see vanity as a sin. But the very idea of sin is replaced by a term borrowed from the printing trade; sins are *errata*, typographical errors. More than forty years before beginning the *Autobiography*, in his fanciful 'Epitaph', he had first imagined himself as a text in need of authorial corrections. His 'bold and arduous Project of arriving at moral Perfection' is the most notable instance where Franklin combines playfulness and seriousness in relation to his reader. Franklin's reader knows that moral perfection is unattainable, and the young Franklin who undertakes the project reaches the same conclusion:

For something that pretended to be Reason was every now and then suggesting to me, that such extream Nicety as I exacted of my self might be a kind of Foppery in Morals, which if it were known would make me ridiculous; that a perfect Character might be attended with the Inconvenience of being envied and hated; and that a benevolent Man should allow a few Faults in himself, to keep his Friends in Countenance.

Moral perfection is less important than keeping one's friends in countenance. The admission of faults in the *Autobiography* is therefore not confessional but strategic in his campaign to ingratiate himself with his readers.

Franklin describes his own departure from the religion of his parents and his readiness to argue over religious questions without making any definite commitment of his own to any side. Yet his *Autobiography* shows him to be very much in a Puritan tradition of self-examination. Franklin's father had emigrated from England in the late seventeenth century because he could not exercise his Puritan beliefs freely there. Puritans set a special importance on self-consciousness, as the biographies and autobiographies they left behind demonstrate (Bercovitch, 17–25; Shea, 87–91, 234–48). Ironically, Franklin, who saw no need for regular church attendance while still in his teens, is the true successor of this tradition of Puritan self-consciousness.

Franklin also exemplified a long-standing tendency among Puritans to evolve toward a belief in the moral value of one's own goodness. The earliest Puritans, in the late sixteenth and early seventeenth centuries, had believed above all in the necessity of an undeserved spiritual regeneration accomplished by God. But lives spent in hopes of such miraculous regeneration, and in the endless soul-searching that was needed as well, produced anxieties that many Puritans wished to avoid. As a result, Puritans came more and more to hope that they could achieve righteousness through their own strenuous exertions. Max Weber and others have called this tendency the Puritan ethic, and Weber cites Franklin as a leading expositor of that ethic (Weber, 48–57). Though Franklin claimed to have found theological discussions unintelligible, he in fact exemplifies the beliefs of many of his more overtly religious contemporaries.

In fact, Franklin's defiance of religion is very qualified in all his descriptions of religious questions. He pauses at the beginning of the *Autobiography* to acknowledge the goodness of God to him, and when he introduces his Deistic creed in the third part of the *Autobiography*, he offers it as a statement shared by all believers everywhere. When he wrote in 1738 to his parents, who were concerned about his erroneous opinions, he was prepared to cite the Bible in defence of his beliefs. One of his last letters is a description of his religious convictions to the pious Ezra Stiles, a friend of long standing who had written to enquire about Franklin's beliefs about the divinity of Christ. In so far as he can, Franklin tries to placate Stiles, denying that his own position is really unorthodox. Franklin was determined to have both the freedom of action an unbeliever claims and the consensual security of the believer.

The Franklin who describes his youthful life in the *Autobiography* is a rather elderly man, who has undergone many important experiences after the ones he records. There is thus necessarily a distance between the old Franklin and the young one, creating several natural temptations for the writer. Old Franklin knows more than young Franklin did, so old Franklin might ignore the particular situations his younger version experienced. In an important sense, they are even different people: young Franklin is part of what old Franklin is, but young Franklin will not necessarily turn into the particular old Franklin who is his biographer. The temptation to judge the past or convert it into a series of purely instructive examples affects everyone of any age who has considered his or her past. 'I have lived some thirty years on this planet, and I have yet to hear the first syllable of valuable or even earnest advice from my seniors,' writes young Henry David Thoreau in *Walden*.

But old Franklin is actually quite generous and understanding toward his younger self. The faults of the young Franklin are only *errata*, and each is corrected as well as possible. Franklin is in turn careful not to give his young self too much credit. When his brother's friends discover his anonymous contribution, the first Silence Dogood letter, they commend it highly, but the older Franklin wonders whether their judgement was as good as he had thought at the time. Franklin does not describe himself as a child prodigy, though he can recall instances when he had been a leader as a youth, building a sort of wharf with stolen masonry or inspiring some of the London compositors in the print shop where he worked to reduce their beer drinking. Old Franklin still vividly remembers the feelings of his young self, to the point that he can recall every stage of his first journey from Boston to Philadelphia, how cold or hungry he felt at various points on the way.

The danger of detachment between author and character has been a persistent issue in American writing for which Franklin offers one of the earliest solutions. American writers have written about themselves since the seventeenth century. For the Puritans, writing about oneself came close to being a religious obligation. When Mary Rowlandson returned from captivity among the Indians, she saw it as her duty to describe her imperilled state as a captive. Puritans addressed a complex audience when they wrote about themselves: other humans would read their testimony, but the most important reader was God, to whom they were confessing their sins, their beliefs, and their praise. Franklin makes occasional honorific references to Providence in his life story, but it is clear that he has avoided entangling religious alliances. In the nineteenth and twentieth centuries, the American habit of self-description has taken on further complications. Emerson's essays depict the instants of insight of one potentially divine man. Detachment from one's true self becomes the root of all evil. Melville's Ishmael is so moody that he sets out on a suicidal whaling voyage. Whitman plants himself in the American soil and then grows out of it like leaves of grass. Henry Adams, after acknowledging Franklin as a predecessor in autobiography, describes a self-education which somehow avoids the crucial events of his adult life. Ralph Ellison's Invisible Man conceals himself in a room lit with 1,369 lights. Electricity, the power for those lights, was for Franklin an initially puzzling but finally familiar phenomenon: it was the source of lightning. Just as Franklin considered lightning as a problem to be solved rather than as a sign of the divine presence, he looked back at his younger self and saw not a divine or inspired being but a promising young fellow in need of good sense and a sound plan by which to organize his life. D. H. Lawrence, in a withering attack on Franklin in *Studies in Classic American Literature*, describes the result of Franklin's practical-minded avoidance of eternal considerations as 'a virtuous little automaton' (Lawrence, 16).

The *Autobiography* is incomplete, but probably even a longer version would not have satisfied Lawrence and others like him who find Franklin's life not emotionally adequate. In its concentration on the details of his early life, Franklin's life story significantly distorts his life as a whole. By itself, the *Autobiography* would not give the reader a clear sense of Franklin's political life or of the importance political questions had for him. Only toward the end, when he describes part of his role in the resistance to the Pennsylvania Proprietaries, does the political Franklin become more fully visible. The *Autobiography* even denies the importance of political issues in many cases, by stressing personal means around problems that could be perceived as public. His imagined solution to the problem of faction is a 'united Party for Virtue', but he sets aside the notion of organizing such a party and focuses on his own self-improvement. It is the same strategy urged in 'The Way to Wealth', Franklin's famous anthology of *Poor Richard* maxims on industry and frugality: there Father Abraham hears his neighbours grousing about taxes and replies with warnings that we impose the most serious taxation upon ourselves by idleness, pride, and folly.

Franklin's scientific interests get only passing attention in the *Autobiography*, not because they were unimportant to him but because he came to see his life story as a means to lead young people 'to equal the Industry & Temperance of thy early Youth', in the words of the letter from Abel James which Franklin inserts into the text. In fact, Franklin's scientific interests were important enough for him to supervise carefully five editions of *Experiments and Observations on Electricity*, a collection of his writings on a variety of subjects, primarily scientific. The lucidity of Franklin's writing on scientific subjects contributed in fact to the reputation he acquired in the Enlightenment. And electricity was only one of Franklin's scientific interests: included in this volume are his speculations about demography and anthropology. A larger collection of Franklin writings would display an even broader range of interests. For example, Franklin was the first person to chart the Gulf Stream; he studied convection physics to design the Pennsylvania fireplace (his name for what posterity has called the Franklin stove); he speculated on weather patterns; he served on a committee of the French *Académie des sciences* to investigate the scientific claims for mesmerism.

The significant concerns of Franklin's life beyond the fifty-one years chronicled in the *Autobiography* are present only through some of the emphases of the various stages of his writing that reflect the conditions not of his youth but of the times when he was writing. Thus he adds a footnote to his description of his quarrels with his brother James: 'I fancy his harsh & tyrannical Treatment of me, might be a means of impressing me with that Aversion to arbitrary Power that has stuck to me thro' my whole Life.' A family squabble turns into a prefiguration of Franklin's role as American advocate in England in the 1760s and 1770s.

But because the old Franklin still feels engaged in the conflicts of his youth, he is not diminishing the political issues of a later time by making such a comparison. His father's favourite verse from Proverbs (22: 29), which promises that the man diligent in his calling shall stand before kings, is cited while Franklin is serving as ambassador to the court of Louis XVI. After he had already served in the Constitutional Convention, he writes in Part 3 of the *Autobiography* of his service in the earliest constitutional convention, the Albany Congress of 1754, and laments that the plan he had advanced was never been put into effect: 'there would have been no need of Troops from England; of course the subsequent Pretence for Taxing America, and the bloody Contest it occasioned, would have been avoided'. In one way, the Albany Plan's failure seemed to exemplify the basic differences between the English and the Americans, since one saw the plan as too democratic, and the other saw it as too oriented towards English prerogatives. So the two rival perspectives led to war. But Franklin is not content to look back on a pattern consisting only of inevitabilities because his great theme is the possibility of altering one's fate, as he succeeded in altering the dubious prospects of the young man who arrived in Philadelphia from Boston with his pockets stuffed with shirts and stockings and great puffy rolls under each arm.

During his lifetime the model of behaviour Franklin advocated was the life devoted to industry and frugality, as most conspicuously depicted in the Preface to *Poor Richard Improved* for 1758. But this model of behaviour is not the model for Franklin's own success, as he describes in the *Autobiography*. To be sure, industry and frugality had played a part in his advancement, but risk-taking, partnerships, and currying favour at the right time had been just as important. Poor Richard, Franklin's spokesman in the almanac, however, says, '*He that lives upon Hope will die fasting*', and '*If you would have a faithful Servant, and one that you like, serve yourself*', and '*He that hath a Calling hath an Office of Profit and Honour*'. The ethic Poor Richard preaches is appropriate to maintaining oneself at a subsistence level. Franklin had more ambitious plans for himself. He wanted to stand before kings, or at least governors. Franklin's career and his guidance on careers thus exemplify a long-standing American paradox. In his valediction to America, 'The Internal State of America', he emphasizes resignation to the decrees of fate for his country; yet he shows himself in his life story continually trying to alter fate.

Franklin emphasizes the importance to his success of his abilities as a writer, abilities which also gave him an advant-

age over many colonial printers. As a publisher of the
Pennsylvania Gazette in Philadelphia, Franklin had the opportunity to attract attention in the largest and fastest-growing city in America. Newspaper writing was one of the earliest accesses for literary or imaginative writing in America. Franklin thus stands first in a distinguished line of American writers who first came to prominence through journalism: the list includes Walt Whitman, Mark Twain, Stephen Crane, Theodore Dreiser, Willa Cather, and Ernest Hemingway. As a printer Franklin was aware of what was being published in Europe as the Enlightenment dawned in the early years of the eighteenth century. So he could make familiar reference to writers like Dryden, Pope, Swift, Addison, Defoe, Richardson, and Voltaire, at a time when many other literate Americans knew little besides European religious writers.

Franklin excelled in an amazing variety of kinds of writing, as represented by the selections in this volume. Some of it is in the natural sciences, represented here by one of his essays about electricity. A significant portion of Franklin's writing was private and not originally meant for public consumption at all. Even some of his journalistic writings of the 1730s and 1740s were placed in other periodicals than his own *Pennsylvania Gazette*, including such items as the recently identified 'Apology for the Young Man in Goal [Jail]' or 'The Speech of Miss Polly Baker', whose authorship Franklin himself acknowledged as an old man in France.

Throughout his life Franklin was engaged in advocacy of various causes, from his early piece in favour of paper currency which he describes in the *Autobiography* to the extended campaign in defence of American interests in England in 1757–62 and 1764–75. Even his two short letters to the editor of *The Gazetteer and New Daily Advertiser* signed 'Homespun' which purport to discuss American eating preferences are attacks on British attempts to tax the colonies.

Franklin claimed in one letter to have been disgusted with the 'great uncertainty I found in metaphysical reasonings', but another category of his writings is, in the broad sense the eighteenth century understood, philosophical in character. In fact as one who engaged in what we would call natural science, Franklin was considered by the Enlightenment to be a philosopher. Men of letters such as Voltaire or Goethe performed experiments in their own laboratories, and the science which they explored was related to literary or political conceptions they advanced. Early in his life Franklin began assuming the authorial mask of the wise old man or describing wise old men, such as he does in *Busy-Body* 3, so the wise old man who narrates the *Autobiography* or discusses theology with Ezra Stiles in 1790 is a role Franklin deliberately grew into. In France he was expected to be a noble exemplar of republican simplicity, so he wrote his 'Remarks Concerning the Savages of North-America' to fulfil those expectations. To his friend Joseph Priestley, an English scientist and non-conformist clergyman, he writes a denunciation of war after he himself had just finished manœuvring to finance the American War for Independence. In his letter to Priestley he writes: 'Men I find to be a Sort of Beings very badly constructed, as they are generally more easily provok'd than reconcil'd, more disposed to do Mischief to each other than to make Reparation, much more easily deceiv'd than undeceiv'd, and having more Pride and even Pleasure in killing than in begetting one another.' The grim view of the natural human condition which his Puritan forebears had held stayed with the man who could also have enough optimism about the American condition to participate in the Revolution and help draft the Declaration of Independence and the Constitution.

Franklin's writings could, with a few significant exceptions, be described as a series of letters—the long letter purportedly addressed to his son which became his *Autobiography*, periodical letters like *Silence Dogood*, letters about his experiments to Englishmen interested in science, letters to the English press to advance American interests, and thousands of letters to friends on both sides of the Atlantic. The letter was actually Franklin's natural form (Lemay,

'Benjamin Franklin', 217–18); even the prefaces to *Poor Richard* are composed as letters to the courteous reader.

From the first, Franklin wrote with the possibility in mind of his letters appearing in print—a possibility which he knew was outside his control. The question of whether a public man's letters were rightly in the public domain when they dealt with public questions arose most strongly in Franklin's career during the early 1770s, when he discovered a correspondence carried on by Governor Thomas Hutchinson and Lieutenant-Governor Peter Oliver of Massachusetts with a prominently placed English civil servant in which Hutchinson and Oliver argued for the abridgement of civil liberties in the colony. Franklin forwarded copies of the Hutchinson–Oliver letters to the leaders of the Massachusetts Assembly, whose agent he was, warning that the letters should not be published. Before long, however, they were published by the Massachusetts radicals and became the grounds for a petition for Hutchinson's removal which Franklin was charged with presenting before the Privy Council. Franklin's role in the revelation of the letters came out, so the occasion of the presentation of the petition turned into a confrontation between Franklin and the crown's solicitor-general, Alexander Wedderburn, who denounced Franklin for an hour as a scoundrel before the petition was summarily rejected. Franklin had had his own role in the delivery and security of letters as deputy postmaster-general for America, a post he was removed from immediately afterwards. The Coercive Acts were soon passed in an effort to reduce Massachusetts to submission. Wedderburn denounced Franklin as the ultimate source of dissension in the colonies, when in fact Franklin was really caught in the middle, continually trying to conciliate extreme views in both England and America. Thereafter Franklin moved steadily toward an embrace of the most intransigent American position.

On another occasion Franklin wrote to his daughter from France expressing disapproval of the recently established Society of the Cincinnati, an organization of Revolutionary War officers and their descendants, on the grounds that the

Society might aim to establish itself as a new hereditary aristocracy. His daughter quickly had the letter published in America. Franklin then took steps to have the letter translated and published in France, but his friends there persuaded him that in a monarchy his arguments against hereditary honours would endanger the carefully preserved but fragile and recent Franco-American alliance, so he went no further with the project.

Letters from every period of Franklin's life have been included in this volume, reflecting the range of his interests and his versatility in addressing a variety of readers, from his own father in 1738 to Ezra Stiles, president of Yale College, in 1790. The writing of letters had earned Franklin his success and in time foiled his carefully contrived efforts at being a successful mediator between adversarial positions. For unlike the common pattern of old age bringing on a settled conservatism, Franklin's old age was spent as a revolutionary, organizing resistance and support against probably the most powerful nation in Europe.

But he was a wistful revolutionary also, since he had well-developed personal ties in England with both political and intellectual leaders. The story is told that not long after Franklin arrived in France as the American ambassador, he arrived at an inn where Edward Gibbon, the author of *The Decline and Fall of the Roman Empire*, was already staying. Franklin wrote a note inviting Gibbon to visit him, but Gibbon, an ardent Tory, replied that he could not justify having any conversation with 'a *revolted subject!*' Franklin supposedly responded that when Gibbon should turn to writing of the decline and fall of the British Empire, he 'would be happy to furnish him with *ample materials* which were in his possession' (William Cobbett, quoted in Zall, *Ben Franklin Laughing*, 108). Whether the story is true or not, it does accurately reflect the delicately balanced position Franklin had maintained in relation to the political and intellectual forces of his day.

NOTE ON REFERENCES

CITATIONS in the text of the General Introduction and the introductions to individual works are presented according to the current Modern Language Association system, so readers should look up citations in the Select Bibliography.

SELECT BIBLIOGRAPHY

Franklin's Writings

The Autobiography of Benjamin Franklin: A Genetic Text, ed. J. A. Leo Lemay and P. M. Zall (Knoxville, Tenn.: University of Tennessee Press, 1981).

Benjamin Franklin's Letters to the Press 1758–1775, ed. Verner W. Crane (Chapel Hill, NC: University of North Carolina Press, 1950).

The Papers of Benjamin Franklin, ed. Leonard W. Labaree, William B. Willcox, Barbara B. Oberg, *et al.*, vols. i–xxviii so far completed (New Haven, Conn.: Yale University Press, 1959–).

The Writings of Benjamin Franklin, ed. Albert H. Smyth, 10 vols. (Boston: Houghton Mifflin, 1905–7).

FRANKLIN, BENJAMIN, *Writings*, ed. J. A. Leo Lemay (New York: Library of America, 1987).

—— 'The Internal State of America', in Verner W. Crane, 'Franklin's "The Internal State of America" (1786)', *William and Mary Quarterly*, 3rd ser. 15 (1958), 223–7.

Critical Works

ADAMS, JOHN, *The Diary and Autobiography of John Adams*, ed. L. H. Butterfield (Cambridge, Mass.: Harvard University Press, 1961).

BERCOVITCH, SACVAN, *The Puritan Origins of the American Self* (New Haven, Conn.: Yale University Press, 1975).

BREITWIESER, MITCHELL R., *Cotton Mather and Benjamin Franklin: The Price of Representative Personality* (New York: Cambridge University Press, 1984).

CONNER, PAUL W., *Poor Richard's Politicks: Benjamin Franklin and His New American Order* (New York: Oxford University Press, 1965).

GARRETT, CLARKE, *Respectable Folly: Millenarians and the French Revolution in France and England* (Baltimore: Johns Hopkins University Press, 1975).

GRANGER, BRUCE I., *Benjamin Franklin: An American Man of Letters* (Ithaca, N.Y.: Cornell University Press, 1964).

HALL, MAX, *Benjamin Franklin & Polly Baker: The History of a Literary Deception* (Chapel Hill, NC: University of North Carolina Press, 1960).

HENINGER, S. K., Jr., *Touches of Sweet Harmony: Pythagorean Cosmology and Renaissance Poetics* (San Marino, Calif.: Huntington Library, 1974).

LAWRENCE, D. H., *Studies in Classic American Literature* (New York: Viking, 1961).

LEMAY, J. A. LEO, *The Canon of Benjamin Franklin, 1722–1776: New Attributions and Reconsiderations* (Newark, Del.: University of Delaware Press, 1986).

—— 'Benjamin Franklin', *Major Writers of Early American Literature*, ed. Everett Emerson (Madison: University of Wisconsin Press, 1972).

—— 'The Text, Rhetorical Strategies, and Themes of "The Speech of Miss Polly Baker" ', in Lemay, ed., *The Oldest Revolutionary* (Philadelphia: University of Pennsylvania Press, 1976).

LOPEZ, CLAUDE-ANNE, *Mon Cher Papa: Franklin and the Ladies of Paris* (New Haven, Conn.: Yale University Press, 1966).

LOVEJOY, ARTHUR O., *The Great Chain of Being* (Cambridge, Mass.: Harvard University Press, 1936).

POCOCK, J. G. A., *The Machiavellian Moment: Florentine Political Thought and the Atlantic Republican Tradition* (Princeton, NJ: Princeton University Press, 1975).

SEAVEY, ORMOND, *Becoming Benjamin Franklin: The Autobiography and the Life* (University Park, Pa.: Pennsylvania State University Press, 1988).

SHEA, DANIEL B., *Spiritual Autobiography in Early America* (Madison, Wisc.: University of Wisconsin Press, 1968).

SIMPSON, LEWIS P., 'The Printer As a Man of Letters: Franklin and the Symbolism of the Third Realm', in J. A. Leo Lemay, ed., *The Oldest Revolutionary* (Philadelphia: University of Pennsylvania Press, 1976).

WEBER, MAX, *The Protestant Ethic and the Spirit of Capitalism*, tr. Talcott Parsons (London: Allen & Unwin, 1930).

WOOD, GORDON S., *The Creation of the American Republic, 1776–1787* (Chapel Hill, NC: University of North Carolina Press, 1969).

ZALL, P. M., *Ben Franklin Laughing: Anecdotes from Original*

Sources by and about Benjamin Franklin (Berkeley: University of California Press, 1980).

—— *Franklin's Autobiography: A Model Life* (Boston: G. K. Hall, 1989).

—— 'A Portrait of the Autobiographer as an Old Artificer', in J. A. Leo Lemay, ed., *The Oldest Revolutionary* (Philadelphia: University of Pennsylvania Press, 1976).

A CHRONOLOGY OF
BENJAMIN FRANKLIN

1706   (17 Jan.) Born in Boston to Josiah and Abiah Folger Franklin.

1718–23   Apprenticed to his brother James Franklin; submits *Silence Dogood* letters anonymously to the *New-England Courant*; quarrels with his brother, and leaves for Philadelphia.

1724–6   After working briefly as a printer in Philadelphia for Samuel Keimer, sails for England having been misled by promises by Governor William Keith; once arrived in London, he works for two prominent printing houses.

1726–7   Returns to Philadelphia, working first as a clerk for Thomas Denham and then as a printer for Samuel Keimer; forms the Junto, a club of intellectually ambitious young tradesmen.

1728–32   Establishes his own printing press, initially in partnership; takes over publication of the *Pennsylvania Gazette*; son William born out of wedlock; marries Deborah Read; begins to publish *Poor Richard's Almanack*.

1733   Undertakes 'the bold and arduous Project of arriving at moral Perfection'.

1731–45   Involved in numerous civic improvements in Philadelphia, including the Library Company, service as clerk for the Pennsylvania Assembly and postmaster, organization of the Union Fire Company, design of the Pennsylvania fireplace, creation of the American Philosophical Society.

1746–51   Performs experiments on electricity; first edition of *Experiments and Observations on Electricity* published (1751); retires from active direction of his printing business; proposes establishment of the Philadelphia Academy (later called the University of Pennsylvania).

1754   Attends Albany Congress to form a colonial union in the face of imminent war with French Canada.

1757   Nominated to serve as colonial agent representing the Pennsylvania Assembly in disputes with the Proprietaries; travels to London with his son William, writes the Preface to *Poor Richard Improved*, 1758 (*The Way to Wealth*).

1762–4   Returns to Philadelphia after achieving no significant success in his negotiations with the Proprietaries; loses election of 1764 to the Assembly, but is chosen again as the Assembly's agent in London.

1765–6   Despite his opposition, the Stamp Act is passed by Parliament; arranges for a friend to serve as Pennsylvania stamp distributor, leading to rumours that he is insufficiently opposed to the unpopular tax; quells most of those rumours by his testimony against the act at the House of Commons.

1771   Begins the *Autobiography* while on a country vacation.

1772–4   Acquires a correspondence carried on by Massachusetts Governor Thomas Hutchinson and Lieutenant-Governor Andrew Oliver which advocated abridgement of rights in the colony; forwards copies of the letters to leaders of the Massachusetts Assembly, who ignore his instructions to keep the letters secret and petition for Hutchinson's removal; in presenting the Assembly's petition, Franklin is vitriolically denounced by Solicitor-General Alexander Wedderburn.

1774–5   Deborah Read Franklin dies in Philadelphia; Franklin engages in extensive negotiations to conciliate differences between Britain and the colonies involving William Pitt, Earl of Chatham, and others; despairing of conciliation, sails for America, where he is immediately named a delegate from Pennsylvania to the Second Continental Congress.

1776   Member of various committees of Congress including the committee to draft the Declaration of Independence; named one of three commissioners to France, arriving there just before the year's end.

1777–8   Negotiates a large loan from the French government and a treaty of alliance with France; becomes acquainted with leading *philosophes*.

1782–3   Along with John Adams and John Jay negotiates a peace treaty with England.

1784   Writes Part 2 of the *Autobiography*.

1785   Relieved by Thomas Jefferson as ambassador to France and sails home to Philadelphia.

1787   Serves as a Pennsylvania delegate to the Constitutional Convention.

1788   Resumes writing the *Autobiography*.

1790   Dies 17 April with the *Autobiography* uncompleted.

Autobiography

Franklin composed his autobiography at three different times in his life. As the introductory paragraph indicates, he began it while on a holiday with his friend Joseph Shipley, the Bishop of St Asaph, in southern England in the summer of 1771; at the time, Franklin was serving as colonial agent for the colonies of Pennsylvania, New Jersey, Georgia, and Massachusetts. Early in the writing he set down an outline for his life story to which he would later add further items. The outline is printed here following the end of the text of the *Autobiography*.

Though the first part of the *Autobiography* is explicitly addressed as a letter to his son, William Franklin never saw it, and the portion thus far completed accompanied Benjamin Franklin back to Philadelphia in 1775. When Franklin was chosen to serve as ambassador from the United States to France in 1777, Franklin left the manuscript and the notes with other papers of his in what he thought would be safekeeping. But after the British army captured Philadelphia in 1777, the trunk containing his papers was rifled. Eventually the manuscript of Part 1 of the autobiography and the notes came into the hands of Abel James, a Philadelphia Quaker merchant who was an old friend of Franklin's.

In 1782 James wrote to Franklin in Paris, providing a copy of the outline and urging him to continue the project. After receiving James's letter, Franklin conveyed a copy of it and of the *Autobiography* outline to his young English friend and editor, Benjamin Vaughan, with a request for comment. Franklin decided to include the letters he received from James and Vaughan in the text of his work. The two letters serve as a bridge from the first part to the remainder and also provide clues about how Franklin anticipated the work should be read. William Franklin had fought on the Loyalist side in the American Revolution and thus was no longer the designated audience for the book. Later in 1784, the year he received Vaughan's letter, Franklin wrote Part 2, which repeats the last episode of Part 1, which was then still in Philadelphia with Abel James.

Various other friends in Europe knew that Franklin was writing his life story, and he assured them that when he returned to

Philadelphia after his service as ambassador, he would resume the writing promptly. But further public service awaited him in America, and it was not until several terms as the chief executive for Pennsylvania and his service at the Constitutional Convention of 1787 had been completed that he finally returned to writing. By this time, Franklin was in his early eighties and somewhat encumbered by an abundance of his papers as well as by the fullness of his memory of the events of his mature years. In November 1789 Franklin had copies of the manuscript as thus far completed sent to two friends in Europe. While waiting for his friends' reactions Franklin continued with the writing (the brief Part 4), reaching the year 1758. For some years Franklin had been suffering from gout and a bladder stone, which combined to give him continual pain; he died in April 1790 with the *Autobiography* uncompleted.

It is clear that Franklin intended his autobiography to be published, but he did not live to oversee its printing, and the only surviving draft in his handwriting includes considerable rewriting: passages and words deleted or added. The text also includes occasional notes written to himself about material to be included later, which have been left out of this edition. Moreover, the punctuation in Franklin's manuscript does not conform to the standards of punctuation which Franklin observed in publications which he had printed himself. Frequently, for example, a colon is used as the end punctuation for a sentence or dashes are added to end punctuation. Where the manuscript indicates an ampersand (&), this text does not convert it into an 'and'. This edition does not presume to improve or correct the manuscript, or speculate about Franklin's final intentions if he had arranged for its printing. It is possible but not wholly likely that Franklin perceived the first part as a Franklin family document, intended for his son and later descendants, but even in that version there are directions (presumably to an editor or printer) for the inclusion of other materials, such as his Uncle Benjamin's poems and a note (not included in this text) on the possible derivation of the name Franklin. Both the text itself and references in his letters from the 1780s indicate clearly that he had publication in mind as he was composing parts 2, 3, and 4, but as he resumed writing for each part, his conventions of punctuation are not really different from his practice in the first part. The resulting text, like the poems of Edward Taylor or Emily Dickinson, which were also not prepared for publication, appears somewhat unusual in print. The

text used here, *Benjamin Franklin's Memoirs: Parallel Text Edition*,
edited by Max Farrand (Berkeley: University of California Press,
1949), has been revised by consultation with *The Autobiography of
Benjamin Franklin: A Genetic Text*, edited by J. A. Leo Lemay
and P. M. Zall (Knoxville, Tenn.: University of Tennessee Press,
1981), which prints all the corrections, deletions, and additions
which appear in the holograph manuscript of the *Autobiography*.

[PART 1]

> Twyford, at the Bishop
> of St Asaph's*
> 1771.

Dear Son,

I have ever had a Pleasure in obtaining any little Anecdotes of my Ancestors. You may remember the Enquiries I
made among the Remains of my Relations when you were
with me in England; and the Journey I took for that purpose.
Now imagining it may be equally agreable to you to know
the Circumstances of *my* Life, many of which you are yet
unacquainted with; and expecting a Weeks uninterrupted
Leisure in my present Country Retirement, I sit down to
write them for you. To which I have besides some other
Inducements. Having emerg'd from the Poverty & Obscurity
in which I was born & bred, to a State of Affluence & some
Degree of Reputation* in the World, and having gone so
far thro' Life with a considerable Share of Felicity, the
conducing Means I made use of, which, with the Blessing
of God, so well succeeded, my Posterity may like to know,
as they may find some of them suitable to their own
Situations, & therefore fit to be imitated.—That Felicity,
when I reflected on it, has induc'd me sometimes to say,
that were it offer'd to my Choice, I should have no Objection to a Repetition of the same Life from its Beginning,
only asking the Advantages Authors have in a second Edition to correct some Faults of the first. So would I if I
might, besides corr^g the Faults, change some sinister Accidents & Events of it for others more favourable, but tho'

this were deny'd, I should still accept the Offer. However, since such a Repetition is not to be expected, the Thing most like living one's Life over again, seems to be a *Recollection* of that Life; and to make that Recollection as durable as possible, the putting it down in Writing.——Hereby, too, I shall indulge the Inclination so natural in old Men, to be talking of themselves and their own past Actions, and I shall indulge it, without being troublesome to others who thro' respect to Age might think themselves oblig'd to give me a Hearing, since this may be read or not as any one pleases. And lastly, (I may as well confess it, since my Denial of it will be believ'd by no body) perhaps I shall a good deal gratify my own *Vanity*. Indeed I scarce ever heard or saw the introductory Words, *Without Vanity I may say*, &c. but some vain thing immediately follow'd. Most People dislike Vanity in others whatever Share they have of it themselves, but I give it fair Quarter wherever I meet with it, being persuaded that it is often productive of Good to the Possessor & to others that are within his Sphere of Action: And therefore in many Cases it would not be quite absurd if a Man were to thank God for his Vanity among the other Comforts of Life.——

And now I speak of thanking God, I desire with all Humility to acknowledge, that I owe the mention'd Happiness of my past Life to his kind Providence, which led me to the Means I us'd & gave them Success.——My Belief of This, induces me to *hope*, tho' I must not *presume*, that the same Goodness will still be exercis'd towards me in continuing that Happiness, or in enabling me to bear a fatal Reverso, which I may experience as others have done, the Complexion of my future Fortune being known to him only: and in whose Power it is to bless to us even our Afflictions.

The Notes one of my Uncles (who had the same kind of Curiosity in collecting Family Anecdotes) once put into my Hands, furnish'd me with several Particulars, relating to our Ancestors. From those Notes I learnt that the Family had liv'd in the same Village, Ecton in Northamptonshire, for 300 Years, & how much longer he knew not, perhaps from the Time when the Name *Franklin* that before was the Name of an Order of People, was assum'd by them for a Surname, when others took Surnames all over the Kingdom.—(Here a Note) on a Freehold of about 30 Acres, aided by the Smith's Business which had continued in the Family till his Time, the eldest Son being always bred to that Business. A Custom which he & my Father both followed as to their eldest Sons—When I search'd the Register at Ecton, I found an Account of their Births, Marriages and Burials, from the Year 1555 only, there being no Register kept in that Parish at any time preceding.—By that Register I perceiv'd that I was the youngest Son of the youngest Son for 5 Generations back. My Grandfather Thomas, who was born in 1598, lived at Ecton till he grew too old to follow Business longer, when he went to live with his Son John, a Dyer at Banbury in Oxfordshire, with whom my Father serv'd an Apprenticeship. There my Grandfather died and lies buried. We saw his Gravestone in 1758. His eldest Son Thomas liv'd in the House at Ecton, and left it with the Land to his only Child, a Daughter, who with her Husband, one Fisher of Wellingborough sold it to Mr Isted, now Lord of the Manor there. My Grandfather had 4 Sons that grew up, viz. Thomas, John, Benjamin and Josiah. I will give you what Account I can of them at this distance from my Papers, and if those are not lost in my Absence, you will among them find many more Particulars. Thomas was bred a Smith under his Father, but being ingenious, and encourag'd in Learning (as all his Brothers like wise werre,) by an Esquire Palmer then the principal Gentleman in that Parish, he qualify'd himself for the Business of Scrivener, became a considerable Man in the County Affairs, was a chief Mover of all publick Spirited Undertakings, for the County. or Town of Northampton & his own Village, of which many Instances were told us at Ecton, and he was much taken Notice of and patroniz'd by the then Lord Halifax. He died in 1702 Jan. 6. old Stile,* just 4 Years to a Day before I was born. The Account we receiv'd of his Life & Character from some old People at Ecton, I remember struck you as something extraordinary from its Similarity to what you knew of mine. Had he died on the same Day, you said one might have suppos'd a Transmigration.—John was bred a Dyer, I believe of Woollens. Benjamin, was bred a Silk Dyer, serving an Apprenticeship at London. He was an ingenious Man, I remember him well, for when I was a Boy he came over to my Father in Boston, and lived in the House with us some Years. He lived to a great Age. His Grandson Samuel Franklin now lives in Boston. He left behind him two Quarto Volumes, M. S. of his own Poetry, consisting of little occasional Pieces address'd to his Friends and Relations, of which the following sent to me, is a Specimen.

Sent to My Name upon a Report
of his Inclination to Martial affaires
7 July 1710

Beleeve me Ben. It is a Dangerous Trade
The Sword has Many Marr'd as well as Made
By it doe many fall Not Many Rise
Makes Many poor few Rich and fewer Wise
Fills Towns with Ruin, fields with blood beside
Tis Sloths Maintainer, And the Shield of pride
Fair Citties Rich to Day, in plenty flow
War fills with want, Tomorrow, & with woe
Ruin'd Estates, The Nurse of Vice, broke limbs & scarss
Are the Effects of Desolating Warrs

Sent to B. F. in N. E. 15 July 1710

B   e to thy parents an Obedient Son
E   ach Day let Duty constantly be Done
N   ever give Way to sloth or lust or pride
I   f free you'd be from Thousand Ills beside
A   bove all Ills be sure Avoide the shelfe
M   an's Danger lyes in Satan sin and selfe
I   n vertue Learning Wisdome progress Make
N   ere shrink at Suffering for thy saviours sake
F   raud and all Falshood in thy Dealings Flee
R   eligious Always in thy station be
A   dore the Maker of thy Inward part
N   ow's the Accepted time, Give him thy Heart
K   eep a Good Consceince 'tis a constant Frind

L ike Judge and Witness This Thy Acts Attend
I n Heart with bended knee Alone Adore
N one but the Three in One Forevermore.

He had form'd a Shorthand of his own, which he taught
me, but never practising it I have now forgot it. I was nam'd
after this Uncle, there being a particular Affection between
him and my Father. He was very pious, a great Attender
of Sermons of the best Preachers, which he took down in
his Shorthand and had with him many Volumes of them.—.
He was also much of a Politician, too much perhaps for his
Station. There fell lately into my Hands in London a
Collection he had made of all the principal Pamphlets
relating to Publick Affairs from 1641 to 1717. Many of the
Volumes are wanting, as appears by the Numbering, but
there still remains 8 Vols. Folio, and 24 in 4to & 8vo.—A
Dealer in old Books met with them, and knowing me by
my sometimes buying of him, he brought them to me. It
seems my Uncle must have left them here when he went
to America, which was above 50 Years since. There are
many of his Notes in the Margins.—

   This obscure Family of ours was early in the Reformation,
and continu'd Protestants thro' the Reign of Queen Mary,
when they were sometimes in Danger of Trouble on Account
of their Zeal against Popery. They had got an English Bible,
& to conceal & secure it, it was fastned open with Tapes
under & within the Frame of a Joint Stool. When my Great
Great Grandfather read in it to his Family, he turn'd up the
Joint Stool upon his Knees, turning over the Leaves then
under the Tapes. One of the Children stood at the Door to
give Notice if he saw the Apparitor coming, who was an
Officer of the Spiritual Court. In that Case the Stool was
turn'd down again upon its feet, when the Bible remain'd
conceal'd under it as before. This Anecdote I had from my
Uncle Benjamin.—The Family continu'd all of the Church
of England till about the End of Charles the 2^{ds} Reign, when
some of the Ministers that had been outed for Noncon-
formity, holding Conventicles in Northamptonshire, Benjamin

& Josiah adher'd to them, and so continu'd all their Lives.
The rest of the Family remain'd with the Episcopal Church

Josiah, my Father, married young, and carried his Wife
with three Children unto New England, about 1682. The
Conventicles having been forbidden by Law, & frequently
disturbed, induced some considerable Men of his Acquaintance to remove to that Country, and he was prevail'd with
to accompany them thither, where they expected to enjoy
their Mode of Religion with Freedom.—By the same Wife
he had 4 Children more born there, and by a second Wife
ten more, in all 17, of which I remember 13 sitting at one
time at his Table, who all grew up to be Men & Women,
and married;—I was the youngest Son and the youngest
Child but two, & was born in Boston, N. England.

My Mother the 2^d Wife was Abiah Folger, a Daughter of
Peter Folger, one of the first Settlers of New England, of
whom honourable mention is made by Cotton Mather, in his
Church History of that Country, (entitled Magnalia Christi
Americana) as a *godly learned Englishman*, if I remember the
Words rightly.—I have heard that he wrote sundry small
occasional Pieces, but only one of them was printed which
I saw now many Years since. It was written in 1675, in the
homespun Verse of that Time & People, and address'd to
those then concern'd in the Government there. It was in
favour of Liberty of Conscience, & in behalf of the Baptists,
Quakers, & other Sectaries, that had been under Persecution,
ascribing the Indian Wars & other Distresses, that had
befallen the Country to that Persecution, as so many Judgments of God, to punish so heinous an Offense; and exhort-
ing a Repeal of those uncharitable Laws. The whole appear'd
to me as written with a good deal of Decent Plainness &
manly Freedom. The six last concluding Lines I remember,
tho' I have forgotten the two first of the Stanza, but the
Purport of them was that his Censures proceeded from
Goodwill, & therefore he would be known as the Author,

because to be a Libeller, (says he)
I hate it with my Heart.

From Sherburne[†] Town where now I dwell,
My Name I do put here,
Without Offence, your real Friend,
It is Peter Folgier.

My elder Brothers were all put Apprentices to different Trades. I was put to the Grammar School at Eight Years of Age, my Father intending to devote me as the Tithe of his Sons to the Service of the Church. My early Readiness in learning to read (which must have been very early, as I do not remember when I could not read) and the Opinion of all his Friends that I should certainly make a good Scholar, encourag'd him in this Purpose of his. My Uncle Benjamin too approv'd of it, and propos'd to give me all his Shorthand Volumes of Sermons I suppose as a Stock to set up with, if I would learn his Character. I continu'd however at the Grammar School not quite one Year, tho' in that time I had risen gradually from the Middle of the Class of that Year to be the Head of it, and farther was remov'd into the next Class above it, in order to go with that into the third at the End of the Year. But my Father in the mean time, from a View of the Expence of a College Education which, having so large a Family, he could not well afford, and the mean Living many so educated were afterwards able to obtain, Reasons that he gave to his Friends in my Hearing, altered his first Intention, took me from the Grammar School, and sent me to a School for Writing & Arithmetic kept by a then famous Man, Mr Geo. Brownell, very successful in his Profession generally, and that by mild encouraging Methods. Under him I acquired fair Writing pretty soon, but I fail'd in the Arithmetic, & made no Progress in it.—At Ten Years old, I was taken home to assist my Father in his Business, which was that of a Tallow Chandler and Sope-Boiler. A Business he was not bred to, but had assumed on his Arrival in New England & on finding his Dying Trade would not maintain his

[†] In the Island of Nantucket.

Family, being in little Request. Accordingly I was employed in cutting Wick for the Candles, filling the Dipping Mold, & the Molds for cast Candles, attending the Shop, going of Errands, &c.—I dislik'd the Trade and had a strong Inclination for the Sea; but my Father declar'd against it; however, living near the Water, I was much in and about it, learnt early to swim well & to manage Boats, and when in a Boat or Canoe with other Boys I was commonly allow'd to govern, especially in any case of Difficulty; and upon other Occasions I was generally a Leader among the Boys, and sometimes led them into Scrapes, of wch I will mention one Instance, as it shows an early projecting public Spirit, tho' not then justly conducted. There was a Salt Marsh that bounded part of the Mill Pond, on the Edge of which at Highwater, we us'd to stand to fish for Minews. By much Trampling, we had made it a mere Quagmire. My Proposal was to build a Wharf there fit for us to stand upon, and I show'd my Comrades a large Heap of Stones which were intended for a new House near the Marsh, and which would very well suit our Purpose. Accordingly in the Evening when the Workmen were gone, I assembled a Number of my Playfellows, and working with them diligently like so many Emmets, sometimes two or three to a Stone, we brought them all away and built our little Wharff.—The next Morning the Workmen were surpriz'd at Missing the Stones; which were found in our Wharff; Enquiry was made after the Removers; we were discovered & complain'd of; several of us were corrected by our Fathers; and tho' I pleaded the Usefulness of the Work, mine convinc'd me that nothing was useful which was not honest.—

I think you may like to know something of his Person & Character. He had an excellent Constitution of Body, was of middle Stature, but well set and very strong. He was ingenious, could draw prettily, was skill'd a little in Music and had a clear pleasing Voice, so that when he play'd Psalm Tunes on his Violin & sung withal as he some times did in an Evening after the Business of the Day was over, it was extreamly agreable to hear. He had a mechanical Genius too, and on occasion was very handy in the Use of other Tradesmen's Tools. But his great Excellence lay in a sound Understanding, and solid Judgment in prudential Matters, both in private & publick Affairs. In the latter indeed he was never employed, the numerous Family he had to educate & the straitness of his Circumstances, keeping him close to his Trade, but I remember well his being frequently visited by leading People, who consulted him for his Opinion on Affairs of the Town or of the Church he belong'd to & show'd a good deal of Respect for his Judgment and Advice. He was also much consulted by private Persons about their Affairs when any Difficulty occur'd, & frequently chosen an Arbitrator between contending Parties.—At his Table he lik'd to have as often as he could, some sensible Friend or Neighbour, to converse with, and always took care to start some ingenious or useful Topic for Discourse, which might tend to improve the Minds of his Children. By this means he turn'd our Attention to what was good, just, & prudent in the Conduct of Life; and little or no Notice was ever taken of what related to the Victuals on the Table, whether it was well or ill drest, in or out of season, of good or bad flavour, preferable or inferior to this or that other thing of the kind;. so that I was bro't up in such a perfect Inattention to those Matters as to be quite Indifferent what kind of Food was set before me; and so unobservant of it, that to this Day, if I am ask'd I can scarce tell, a few Hours after Dinner, what I din'd upon.—This has been a Convenience to me in travelling, where my Companions have been sometimes very unhappy for want of a suitable Gratification of their more delicate because better instructed Tastes and Appetites.—

My Mother had likewise an excellent Constitution. She suckled all her 10 Children. I never knew either my Father or Mother to have any Sickness but that of which they dy'd, he at 89 & she at 85 Years of age. They lie buried together at Boston, where I some Years since plac'd a Marble stone over their Grave with this Inscription

Josiah Franklin
And Abiah his Wife

Lie here interred.
They lived lovingly together in Wedlock
Fifty-five Years.
Without an Estate or any gainful Employment,
By constant labour and Industry,
With God's Blessing,
They maintained a large Family
Comfortably;
And brought up thirteen Children,
And seven Grand Children
Reputably.
From this Instance, Reader,
Be encouraged to Diligence in thy Calling,
And distrust not Providence.
He was a pious & prudent Man,
She a discreet and virtuous Woman.
Their youngest Son,
In filial Regard to their Memory,
Places this Stone.
J. F. born 1655—Died 1744—Ætat 89
A. F. born 1667—died 1752————85

By my rambling Digressions I perceive my self to be
grown old. I us'd to write more methodically.—But one does
not dress for private Company as for a publick Ball. 'Tis
perhaps only Negligence.—

To return. I continu'd thus employ'd in my Father's
Business for two Years, that is till I was 12 Years old; and
my Brother John, who was bred to that Business having left
my Father, married and set up for himself at Rhodeisland,
there was all Appearance that I was destin'd to supply his
Place and be a Tallow Chandler. But my Dislike to the
Trade continuing, my Father was under Apprehensions that
if he did not find one for me more agreable, I should break
away and get to Sea, as his Son Josiah had done to his great
Vexation. He therefore sometimes took me to walk with him,
and see Joiners, Bricklayers, Turners, Braziers, &c. at their
Work, that he might observe my Inclination, & endeavour

to fix it on some Trade or other on Land.—It has ever since been a Pleasure to me to see good Workmen handle their Tools; and it has been useful to me, having learnt so much by it, as to be able to do little Jobs my self in my House, when a Workman could not readily be got; & to construct little Machines for my Experiments while the Intention of making the Experiment was fresh & warm in my Mind. My Father at last fix'd upon the Cutler's Trade, and my Uncle Benjamin's Son Samuel who was bred to that Business in London being about that time establish'd in Boston, I was sent to be with him some time on liking. But his Expectations of a Fee with me displeasing my Father, I was taken home again.—

From a Child I was fond of Reading, and all the little Money that came into my Hands was ever laid out in Books. Pleas'd with the Pilgrim's Progress, my first Collection was of John Bunyan's Works, in separate little Volumes. I afterwards sold them to enable me to buy R. Burton's Historical Collections; they were small Chapmen's Books and cheap, 40 or 50 in all.—My Father's little Library consisted chiefly of Books in polemic Divinity, most of which I read, and have since often regretted, that at a time when I had such a Thirst for Knowledge, more proper Books had not fallen in my Way, since it was now resolv'd I should not be a Clergyman. Plutarch's Lives there was, in which I read abundantly, and I still think that time spent to great Advantage. There was also a Book of Defoe's called an Essay on Projects and another of Dr Mather's* call'd Essays to do Good, which perhaps gave me a Turn of Thinking that had an Influence on some of the principal future Events of my Life.

This Bookish Inclination at length determin'd my Father to make me a Printer, tho' he had already one Son, (James) of that Profession. In 1717 my Brother James return'd from England with a Press & Letters to set up his Business in Boston. I lik'd it much better than that of my Father, but still had a Hankering for the Sea.—To prevent the apprehended Effect of such an Inclination, my Father was impatient to have me bound to my Brother. I stood out some time, but at last was persuaded and signed the Indentures, when I was yet but 12 Years old.—I was to serve as an Apprentice till I was 21 Years of Age, only I was to be allow'd Journeyman's Wages during the last Year. In a little time I made great Proficiency in the Business, and became a useful Hand to my Brother. I now had Access to better Books. An Acquaintance with the Apprentices of Booksellers, enabled me sometimes to borrow a small one, which I was careful to return soon & clean. Often I sat up in my Room reading the greatest Part of the Night, when the Book was borrow'd in the Evening & to be return'd early in the Morning lest it should be miss'd or wanted.—And after some time an ingenious Tradesman Mr Matthew Adams who had a pretty Collection of Books, & who frequented our Printing House, took Notice of me, invited me to his Library, & very kindly lent me such Books as I chose to read. I now took a Fancy to Poetry, and made some little Pieces. My Brother, thinking it might turn to account encourag'd me, & put me on composing two occasional Ballads. One was called the *Light House Tragedy*, & contain'd an Acc^t of the drowning of Capt. Worthilake with his Two Daughters; the other was a Sailor Song on the Taking of *Teach* or Blackbeard the Pirate. They were wretched Stuff, in the Grubstreet Ballad Stile, and when they were printed he sent me about the Town to sell them. The first sold wonderfully, the Event being recent, having made a great Noise. This flatter'd my Vanity. But my Father discourag'd me, by ridiculing my Performances, and telling me Verse-makers were generally Beggars; so I escap'd being a Poet, most probably a very bad one. But as Prose Writing has been of great Use to me in the Course of my Life, and was a principal Means of my Advancement, I shall tell you how in such a Situation I acquir'd what little Ability I have in that Way.

There was another Bookish Lad in the Town, John Collins by Name, with whom I was intimately acquainted. We sometimes disputed, and very fond we were of Argument, & very desirous of confuting one another. Which disputacious Turn, by the way, is apt to become a very bad Habit, making People often extreamly disagreable in Company, by the Contradiction that is necessary to bring it into Practice, & thence, besides souring & spoiling the Conversation, is productive of Disgusts & perhaps Enmities where you may have occasion for Friendship. I had caught it by reading my Father's Books of Dispute about Religion. Persons of good Sense, I have since observ'd, seldom fall into it, except Lawyers, University Men, and Men of all Sorts that have been bred at Edinborough. A Question was once some how or other started between Collins & me, of the Propriety of educating the Female Sex in Learning, & their Abilities for Study. He was of Opinion that it was improper; & that they were naturally unequal to it. I took the contrary Side, perhaps a little for Dispute sake. He was naturally more eloquent, had a ready Plenty of Words, and sometimes as I thought bore me down more by his Fluency than by the Strength of his Reasons. As we parted without settling the Point, & were not to see one another again for some time, I sat down to put my Arguments in Writing, which I copied fair & sent to him. He answer'd & I reply'd. Three or four Letters of a Side had pass'd, when my Father happen'd to find my Papers, and read them. Without entring into the Discussion, he took occasion to talk to me about the Manner of my Writing, observ'd that tho' I had the Advantage of my Antagonist in correct Spelling & pointing (which I ow'd to the Printing House) I feel far short in elegance of Expression, in Method and in Perspicuity, of which he convinc'd me by several Instances. I saw the Justice of his Remarks, & thence grew more attentive to the *Manner* in Writing, and determin'd to endeavour at Improvement.——

About this time I met with an odd Volume of the Spectator.* I had never before seen any of them. I bought it, read it over and over, and was much delighted with it. I thought the Writing excellent, & wish'd if possible to imitate it. With that View, I took some of the Papers, & making short Hints of the Sentiment in each Sentence, laid them by a few Days, and then without looking at the Book, try'd to compleat the Papers again, by expressing each hinted Sentiment at length & as fully as it had been express'd before, in any suitable Words that should come to hand.

Then I compar'd my Spectator with the Original, discover'd some of my Faults & corrected them. But I found I wanted—a Stock of Words or a Readiness in recollecting & using them, which I thought I should have acquir'd before that time, if I had gone on making Verses, since the continual Occasion for Words of the same Import but of different Length, to suit the Measure, or of different Sound for the Rhyme, would have laid me under a constant Necessity of searching for Variety, and also have tended to fix that Variety in my Mind, & make me a Master of it. Therefore I took some of the Tales & turn'd them into Verse: And after a time, when I had pretty well forgotten the Prose, turn'd them back again. I also sometimes jumbled my Collections of Hints into Confusion, and after some Weeks, endeavour'd to reduce them into the best Order, before I began to form the full Sentences, & compleat the Paper. This was to teach me Method in the Arrangement of Thoughts. By comparing my Work afterwards with the original, I discover'd many faults and amended them; but I sometimes had the Pleasure of Fancying that in certain Particulars of small Import, I had been lucky enough to improve the Method or the Language and this encourag'd me to think I might possibly in time come to be a tolerable English Writer, of which I was extreamly ambitious

My Time for these Exercises & for Reading, was at Night after Work, or before Work began in the Morning; or on Sundays, when I contrived to be in the Printing House alone, evading as much as I could the common Attendance on publick Worship, which my Father used to exact of me when I was under his Care:—And which indeed I still thought a Duty; tho' I could not as it seemed to me, afford the Time to practise it.

When about 16 Years of Age, I happen'd to meet with a Book written by one Tryon, recommending a Vegetable

Diet. I determined to go into it. My Brother being yet unmarried, did not keep House, but boarded himself & his Apprentices in another Family. My refusing to eat Flesh occasioned an Inconveniency, and I was frequently chid for my singularity. I made my self acquainted with Tryon's Manner of preparing some of his Dishes, such as Boiling Potatoes, or Rice, making Hasty Pudding, & a few others, and then propos'd to my Brother, that if he would give me Weekly half the Money he paid for my Board, I would board my self. He instantly agreed to it, and I presently found that I could save half what he paid me. This was an additional Fund for buying Books: But I had another Advantage in it. My Brother and the rest going from the Printing House to their Meals, I remain'd there alone, and dispatching presently my light Repast, (which often was no more than a Bisket or a Slice of Bread, a Handful of Raisins or a Tart from the Pastry Cook's, & a Glass of Water) had the rest of the Time till their Return, for Study, in which I made the greater Progress from that greater Clearness of Head & quicker Apprehension which usually attend Temperance in Eating & Drinking. And now it was that being on some Occasion made asham'd of my Ignorance in Figures, which I had twice fail'd in learning when at School, I took Cocker's Book of Arithmetick, & went thro' the whole by my self with great Ease.—I also read Seller's & Sturmy's Books of Navigation, & became acquainted with the little Geometry they contain, but never proceeded far in that Science.—And I read about this Time Locke on Human Understanding. and the Art of Thinking by Messrs du Port Royal.

While I was intent on improving my Language, I met with an English Grammar (I think it was Greenwood's) at the End of which there were two little Sketches of the Arts of Rhetoric and Logic, the latter finishing with a Specimen of a Dispute in the Socratic Method. And soon after I procur'd Xenophon's Memorable Things of Socrates, wherein there are many Instances of the same Method. I was charm'd with it, adopted it, dropt my abrupt Contradiction, and positive Argumentation, and put on the humble

Enquirer. & Doubter. And being then, from reading Shaftsbury & Collins, become a real Doubter in many Points of our Religious Doctrine, I found this Method safest for my self & very embarassing to those against whom I used it, therefore I took a Delight in it, practis'd it continually & grew very artful & expert in drawing People even of superior Knowledge into Concessions the Consequences of which they did not foresee, entangling them in Difficulties out of which they could not extricate themselves, and so obtaining Victories that neither my self nor my Cause always deserved.—I continu'd this Method some few Years, but gradually left it, retaining only the Habit of expressing my self in Terms of modest Diffidence, never using when I advance any thing that may possibly be disputed, the Words, *Certainly*, *undoubtedly*, or any others that give the Air of Positiveness to an Opinion; but rather say, *I conceive*, or *I apprehend* a Thing to be so or so, *It appears to me*, or *I think it so or so for such & such Reasons*, or *I imagine* it to be so, or *it is so if I am not mistaken*.—This Habit I believe has been of great Advantage to me, when I have had occasion to inculcate my Opinions & persuade Men into Measures that I have been from time to time engag'd in promoting.—And as the chief Ends of Conversation are to *inform*, or to be *informed*, to *please* or to *persuade*, I wish well meaning sensible Men would not lessen their Power of doing Good by a Positive assuming Manner that seldom fails to disgust, tends to create Opposition, and to defeat every one of those Purposes for which Speech was given us, to wit, giving or receiving Information, or Pleasure: For If you would *inform*, a positive dogmatical Manner in advancing your Sentiments, may provoke Contradiction & prevent a candid Attention. If you wish Information & Improvement from the Knowledge of others and yet at the same time express your self as firmly fix'd in your present Opinions, modest sensible Men, who do not love Disputation, will probably leave you undisturb'd in the Possession of your Error; and by such a Manner you can seldom hope to recommend your self in *pleasing* your Hearers, or to persuade those whose Concurrence you desire.——Pope says, judiciously,

> *Men should be taught as if you taught them not,*
> *And things unknown propos'd as things forgot,——*

farther recommending, it to us,

> *To speak tho' sure, with seeming Diffidence.*

And he might have couple'd with this Line that which he has coupled with another, I think less properly,

> *For want of Modesty is want of Sense.*

If you ask why *less properly*, I must repeat the Lines;

> "Immodest Words admit of *no* Defence;
> "*For* Want of Modesty is Want of Sense."

Now is not *Want of Sense* (where a Man is so unfortunate as to want it) some Apology for his *Want of Modesty?* and would not the Lines stand more justly thus?

> Immodest Words admit *but this* Defence,
> That Want of Modesty is Want of Sense.

This however I should submit to better Judgments.——

My Brother had in 1720 or 21, begun to print a Newspaper. It was the second that appear'd in America, & was called *The New England Courant*. The only one before it, was *the Boston News Letter*. I remember his being dissuaded by some of his Friends from the Undertaking, as not likely to succeed, one Newspaper being in their Judgment enough for America.——At this time 1771 there are not less than five & twenty.——He went on however with the Undertaking, and after having work'd in composing the Types & printing off the Sheets I was employ'd to carry the Papers thro' the Streets to the Customers.——He had some ingenious Men among his Friends who amus'd themselves by writing little Pieces for this Paper, which gain'd it Credit, & made it more in Demand; and these Gentlemen often visited us.—— Hearing their Conversations, and their Accounts of the

Approbation their Papers were receiv'd with, I was excited
to try my Hand among them. But being still a Boy, &
suspecting that my Brother would object to printing any
Thing of mine in his Paper if he knew it to be mine, I
contriv'd to disguise my Hand, & writing an anonymous
Paper I put it in at Night under the Door of the Printing
House. It was found in the Morning & communicated to
his Writing Friends when they call'd in as Usual. They read
it, commented on it in my Hearing, and I had the exquisite
Pleasure, of finding it met with their Approbation, and that
in their different Guesses at the Author none were named
but Men of some Character among us for Learning &
Ingenuity.—I suppose now that I was rather lucky in my
Judges: And that perhaps they were not really so very good
ones as I then esteem'd them. Encourag'd however by this,
I wrote and convey'd in the same Way to the Press several
more Papers, which were equally approv'd, and I kept my
Secret till my small Fund of Sense for such Performances
was pretty well exhausted, & then I discovered it; when I
began to be considered a little more by my Brother's
Acquaintance, and in a manner that did not quite please
him, as he thought, probably with reason, that it tended to
make me too vain. And perhaps this might be one Occasion
of the Differences that we began to have about this Time.
Tho' a Brother, he considered himself as my Master, & me
as his Apprentice; and accordingly expected the same Services from me as he would from another; while I thought
he demean'd me too much in some he requir'd of me, who
from a Brother expected more Indulgence. Our Disputes
were often brought before our Father, and I fancy I was
either generally in the right, or else a better Pleader, because
the Judgment was generally in my favour: But my Brother
was passionate & had often beaten me, which I took extreamly amiss; and thinking my Apprenticeship very tedious,
I was continually wishing for some Opportunity of shorten-
ing it, which at length offered in a manner unexpected.
Note. I fancy his harsh & tyrannical Treatment of me, might

be a means of impressing me with that Aversion to arbitrary Power that has stuck to me thro' my whole Life

One of the Pieces in our News-Paper, on some political Point which I have now forgotten, gave Offence to the Assembly. He was taken up, censur'd and imprison'd for a Month by the Speaker's Warrant, I suppose because he would not discover his Author. I too was taken up & examin'd before the Council; but tho' I did not give them any Satisfaction, they contented themselves with admonishing me, and dismiss'd me; considering me perhaps as an Apprentice who was bound to keep his Master's Secrets. During my Brother's Confinement, which I resented a good deal, notwithstanding our private Differences, I had the Management of the Paper, and I made bold to give our Rulers some Rubs in it, which my Brother took very kindly, while others began to consider me in an unfavourable Light, as a young Genius that had a Turn for Libelling & Satyr. My Brother's Discharge was accompany'd with an Order of the House, (a very odd one) *that James Franklin should no longer print the Paper called the New England Courant.* There was a Consultation held in our Printing House among his Friends what he should do in this Case. Some propos'd to evade the Order by changing the Name of the Paper; but my Brother seeing Inconveniences in that, it was finally concluded on as a better Way, to let it be printed for the future under the Name of *Benjamin Franklin.* And to avoid the Censure of the Assembly that might fall on him, as still printing it by his Apprentice, the Contrivance was, that my old Indenture should be return'd to me with a full Discharge on the Back of it, to be shown on Occasion; but to secure to him the Benefit of my Service I was to sign new Indentures for the Remainder of the Term, wch were to be kept private. A very flimsy Scheme it was, but however it was immediately executed, and the Paper went on accordingly under my Name for several Months. At length a fresh Difference arising between my Brother and me, I took upon me to assert my Freedom, presuming that he would not venture to produce the new Indentures. It was not fair in me to take this Advantage, and this I therefore reckon one of the first Errata of my Life: But the Unfairness of it weigh'd little with me, when under the Impressions of Resentment, for the Blows his Passion too often urg'd him to bestow upon me. Tho' He was otherwise not an ill-natur'd Man: Perhaps I was too saucy & provoking.—

When he found I would leave him, he took care to prevent my getting Employment in any other Printing-House of the Town, by going round & speaking to every Master, who accordingly refus'd to give me Work. I then thought of going to New York as the nearest Place where there was a Printer: and I was the rather inclin'd to leave Boston, when I reflected that I had already made my self a little obnoxious, to the governing Party; & from the arbitrary Proceedings of the Assembly in my Brother's Case it was likely I might if I stay'd soon bring my self into Scrapes; and farther that my indiscrete Disputations about Religion began to make me pointed at with Horror by good People, as an Infidel or Atheist; I determin'd on the Point: but my Father now siding with my Brother, I was sensible that if I attempted to go openly, Means would be used to prevent me. My Friend Collins therefore undertook to manage a little for me. He agreed with the Captain of a New York Sloop for my Passage, under the Notion of my being a young Acquaintance of his that had got a naughty Girl with Child, whose Friends would compel me to marry her, and therefore I could not appear or come away publickly. So I sold some of my Books to raise a little Money, Was taken on board privately, and as we had a fair Wind, in three Days I found my self in New York near 300 Miles from home, a Boy of but 17, without the least Recommendation to or Knowledge of any Person in the Place, and with very little Money in my Pocket.—

My Inclinations for the Sea, were by this time worne out, or I might now have gratify'd them.—But having a Trade, & supposing my self a pretty good Workman, I offer'd my Service to the Printer of the Place, old Mr Wm Bradford.— He could give me no Employment, having little to do, and

Help enough already: But, says he, my Son at Philadelphia has lately lost his principal Hand, Aquila Rose, by Death. If you go thither I believe he may employ you.—Philadelphia was 100 Miles farther. I set out, however, in a Boat for Amboy; leaving my Chest and Things to follow me round by Sea. In crossing the Bay we met with a Squall that tore our rotten Sails to pieces, prevented our getting into the Kill, and drove us upon Long Island. In our Way a drunken Dutchman, who was a Passenger too, fell over board; when he was sinking I reach'd thro' the Water to his shock Pate & drew him up so that we got him in again.—His Ducking sober'd him a little, & he went to sleep, taking first out of his Pocket a Book which he desir'd I would dry for him. It prov'd to be my old favourite Author Bunyan's Pilgrim's Progress in Dutch, finely printed on good Paper with copper Cuts, a Dress better than I had ever seen it wear in its own Language. I have since found that it has been translated into most of the Languages of Europe, and suppose it has been more generally read than any other Book except perhaps the Bible.—Honest John was the first that I know of who mix'd Narration & Dialogue, a Method of Writing very engaging to the Reader, who in the most interesting Parts finds himself as it were brought into the Company, & present at the Discourse. De foe in his Cruso, his Moll Flanders, Religious Courtship, Family Instructor, & other Pieces, has imitated it with Success. And Richardson has done the same in his Pamela, &c.——

When we drew near the Island we found it was at a Place where there could be no Landing, there being a great Surff on the stony Beach. So we dropt Anchor & swung round towards the Shore. Some people came down to the Water Edge & hallow'd to us as we did to them. But the Wind was so high & the Surff so loud, that we could not hear so as to understand each other. There were Canoes on the Shore, & we made Signs & hallow'd that they should fetch us, but they either did not understand us, or thought it impracticable. So they went away, and Night coming on, we had no Remedy but to wait till the Wind should abate, and in the mean time the Boatman & I concluded to sleep if we could, and so crouded into the Scuttle with the Dutchman who was still wet, and the Spray beating over the Head of our Boat, leak'd thro' to us, so that we were soon almost as wet as he. In this Manner we lay all Night with very little Rest. But the Wind abating the next Day, we made a Shift to reach Amboy before Night, having been 30 Hours on the Water without Victuals, or any Drink but a Bottle of filthy Rum:—The Water we sail'd on being salt.—

In the Evening I found my self very feverish, & went ill to Bed. But having read somewhere that cold Water drank plentifully was good for a Fever, I follow'd the Prescription, sweat plentifully most of the Night, my Fever left me, and in the Morning crossing the Ferry, I proceeded on my Journey, on foot, having 50 Miles to Burlington, where I was told I should find Boats that would carry me the rest of the Way to Philadelphia.

It rain'd very hard all the Day, I was thoroughly soak'd, and by Noon a good deal tir'd, so I stopt at a poor Inn, where I staid all Night, beginning now to wish I had never left home. I cut so miserable a Figure too, that I found by the Questions ask'd me I was suspected to be some runaway Servant, and in danger of being taken up on that Suspicion.—However I proceeded the next Day, and got in the Evening to an Inn within 8 or 10 Miles of Burlington, kept by one Dr Brown.—

He entred into Conversation with me while I took some Refreshment, and finding I had read a little, became very sociable and friendly. Our Acquaintance continu'd as long as he liv'd. He had been, I imagine, an itinerant Doctor, for there was no Town in England, or Country in Europe, of which he could not give a very particular Account. He had some Letters, & was ingenious, but much of an Unbeliever, & wickedly undertook some Years after to travesty the Bible in doggrel Verse as Cotton had done Virgil.—By this means he set many of the Facts in a very ridiculous Light, & might have hurt weak minds if his Work had been

publish'd:—but it never was.—At his House I lay that
Night, and the next Morning reach'd Burlington.—But had
the Mortification to find that the regular Boats were gone,
a little before my coming, and no other expected to go till
Tuesday, this being Saturday. Wherefore I return'd to an
old Woman in the Town of whom I had bought Gingerbread
to eat on the Water, & ask'd her Advice; she invited me to
lodge at her House till a Passage by Water should offer; &
being tired with my foot Travelling, I accepted the Invita-
tion. She understanding I was a Printer, would have had
me stay at that Town & follow my Business, being ignorant
of the Stock necessary to begin with. She was very hospit-
able, gave me a Dinner of Ox Cheek with great Goodwill,
accepting only of a Pot of Ale in return. And I tho't my
self fix'd till Tuesday should come. However walking in the
Evening by the Side of the River a Boat came by, which I
found was going towards Philadelphia, with several People
in her. They took me in, and as there was no Wind, we
row'd all the Way; and about Midnight not having yet seen
the City, some of the Company were confident we must
have pass'd it, and would row no farther, the others knew
not where we were, so we put towards the Shore, got into
a Creek, landed near an old Fence with the Rails of which
we made a Fire, the Night being cold, in October, and there
we remain'd till Daylight. Then one of the Company knew
the Place to be Cooper's Creek a little above Philadelphia,
which we saw as soon as we got out of the Creek, and arriv'd
there about 8 or 9 a Clock, on the Sunday morning, and
landed at the Market street Wharff.—

I have been the more particular in this Description of my
Journey, & shall be so of my first Entry into that City, that
you may in your Mind compare such unlikely Beginning
with the Figure I have since made there. I was in my
working Dress, my best Cloaths being to come round by
Sea. I was dirty from my Journey; my Pockets were stuff'd
out with Shirts & Stockings; I knew no Soul, nor where to
look for Lodging I was fatigu'd with Travelling, Rowing &
Want of Rest. I was very hungry, and my whole Stock of

Cash consisted of a Dutch Dollar and about a Shilling in
Copper. The latter I gave the People of the Boat for my
Passage, who at first refus'd it on Acc^t of my Rowing; but
I insisted on their taking it, a Man being sometimes more
generous when he has but a little Money than when he has
plenty, perhaps thro' Fear of being thought to have but
little. Then I walk'd up the Street, gazing about, till near
the Market House I met a Boy with Bread. I had made
many a Meal on Bread, & inquiring where he got it, I went
immediately to the Baker's he directed me to in second
Street; and ask'd for Bisket, intending such as we had in
Boston, but they it seems were not made in Philadelphia,
then I ask'd for a threepenny Loaf, and was told they had
none such: so not considering or knowing the Difference of
Money & the greater Cheapness nor the Names of his Bread,
I bad him give me three pennyworth of any sort. He gave
me accordingly three great Puffy Rolls. I was surpriz'd at
the Quantity, but took it, and having no Room in my
Pockets, walk'd off, with a Roll under each Arm, & eating
the other. Thus I went up Market Street as far as fourth
Street, passing by the Door of Mr Read, my future Wife's
Father, when she standing at the Door saw me, & thought
I made as I certainly did a most awkward ridiculous Appearance. Then I turn'd and went down Chestnut Street
and part of Walnut Street, eating my Roll all the Way, and
coming round found my self again at Market street Wharff,
near the Boat I came in, to which I went for a Draught of
the River Water, and being fill'd with one of my Rolls, gave
the other two to a Woman & her Child that came down the
River in the Boat with us and were waiting to go farther.
Thus refresh'd I walk'd again up the Street, which by this
time had many clean dress'd People in it who were all
walking the same Way; I join'd them, and thereby was led
into the great Meeting House of the Quakers near the
Market. I sat down among them, and after looking round a
while & hearing nothing said, being very drowzy thro'
Labour & want of Rest the preceding Night, I fell fast
asleep, and continu'd so till the Meeting broke up, when

one was kind enough to rouse me. This was therefore the first House I was in or slept in, in Philadelphia.——

Walking again down towards the River, & looking in the Faces of People, I met a young Quaker Man whose Countenance I lik'd, and accosting him requested he would tell me where a Stranger could get Lodging. We were then near the Sign of the Three Mariners. Here, says he, is one Place that entertains Strangers, but it is not a reputable House; if thee wilt walk with me, I'll show thee a better. He brought me to the Crooked Billet in Water-Street. Here I got a Dinner. And while I was eating it, several sly Questions were ask'd me, as it seem'd to be suspected from my youth & Appearance, that I might be some Runaway. After Dinner my Sleepiness return'd: and being shown to a Bed, I lay down without undressing, and slept till Six in the Evening; was call'd to Supper; went to Bed again very early and slept soundly till the next Morning. Then I made my self as tidy as I could, and went to Andrew Bradford the Printer's.——I found in the Shop the old Man his Father, whom I had seen at New York, and who travelling on horse back had got to Philadelphia before me.——He introduc'd me to his Son, who receiv'd me civilly, gave me a Breakfast, but told me he did not at present want a Hand, being lately supply'd with one. But there was another Printer in town lately set up, one Keimer, who perhaps might employ me; if not, I should be welcome to lodge at his House, & he would give me a little Work to do now & then till fuller Business should offer.

The old Gentleman said, he would go with me to the new Printer: And when we found him, Neighbour, says Bradford, I have brought to see you a young Man of your Business, perhaps you may want such a One. He ask'd me a few Questions, put a Composing Stick in my Hand to see how I work'd, and then said he would employ me soon, tho' he had just then nothing for me to do. And taking old Bradford whom he had never seen before, to be one of the Towns People that had a Good Will for him, enter'd into a Conversation on his present Undertaking & Prospects; while

Bradford not discovering that he was the other Printer's Father; on Keimer's Saying he expected soon to get the greatest Part of the Business into his own Hands, drew him on by artful Questions and starting little Doubts, to explain all his Views, what Interest he rely'd on, & in what manner he intended to proceed.—I who stood by & heard all, saw immediately that one of them was a crafty old Sophister, and the other a mere Novice. Bradford left me with Keimer, who was greatly surpriz'd when I told him who the old Man was.

Keimer's Printing House I found, consisted of an old shatter'd Press, and one small worn-out Fount of English, which he was then using himself, composing in it an Elegy on Aquila Rose before-mentioned, an ingenious young Man of excellent Character much respected in the Town, Clerk of the Assembly, & a pretty Poet. Keimer made Verses, too, but very indifferently.—He could not be said to write them, for his Manner was to compose them in the Types directly out of his Head; so there being no Copy, but one Pair of Cases, and the Elegy likely to require all the Letter, no one could help him.—I endeavour'd to put his Press (which he had not yet us'd, & of which he understood nothing) into Order fit to be work'd with; & promising to come & print off his Elegy as soon as he should have got it ready, I return'd to Bradford's who gave me a little Job to do for the present, & there I lodged & dieted. A few Days after Keimer sent for me to print off the Elegy. And now he had got another Pair of Cases, and a Pamphlet to reprint, on which he set me to work.—

These two Printers I found poorly qualified for their Business. Bradford had not been bred to it, & was very illiterate; and Keimer tho' something of a Scholar, was a mere Compositor, knowing nothing of Presswork. He had been one of the French Prophets and could act their enthusiastic Agitations.* At this time he did not profess any particular Religion, but something of all on occasion, was very ignorant of the World, & had, as I afterwards found, a good deal of the Knave in his Composition. He did not like my Lodging at Bradford's while I work'd with him. He had a House indeed, but without Furniture, so he could not lodge me: But he got me a Lodging at Mr Read's beforementioned, who was the Owner of his House. And my Chest & Clothes being come by this time, I made rather a more respectable Appearance in the Eyes of Miss Read, than I had done when she first happen'd to see me eating my Roll in the Street.—

I began now to have some Acquaintance among the young People of the Town, that were Lovers of Reading with whom I spent my Evenings very pleasantly and gaining Money by my Industry & Frugality, I lived very agreably, forgetting Boston as much as I could, and not desiring that any there should know where I resided.—except my Friend Collins who was in my Secret, & kept it when I wrote to him. At length an Incident happened that sent me back again much sooner than I had intended.—

I had a Brother-in-law, Robert Holmes, Master of a Sloop, that traded between Boston and Delaware. He being at New Castle* 40 Miles below Philadelphia, heard there of me, and wrote me a Letter, mentioning the Concern of my Friends in Boston at my abrupt Departure, assuring me of their Goodwill to me, and that every thing would be accommodated to my Mind if I would return, to which he exhorted me very earnestly.—I wrote an Answer to his Letter, thank'd him for his Advice, but stated my Reasons for quitting Boston fully, & in such a Light as to convince him I was not so wrong as he had apprehended.—Sir William Keith Governor of the Province, was then at New Castle, and Capt. Holmes happening to be in Company with him when my Letter came to hand, spoke to him of me, and show'd him the Letter. The Governor read it, and seem'd surpriz'd when he was told my Age. He said I appear'd a young Man of promising Parts, and therefore should be encouraged: The Printers at Philadelphia were wretched ones, and if I would set up there, he made no doubt I should succeed; for his Part, he would procure me the publick Business, & do me every other Service in his Power. This my Brother-in-Law afterwards told me in Boston. But I knew as yet nothing of it; when one Day Keimer and I being at Work together near the Window, we saw the Governor and another Gentleman (which prov'd to be Col. French, of New Castle) finely dress'd, come directly across the Street to our House, & heard them at the Door. Keimer ran down immediately, thinking it a Visit to him. But the Governor enquir'd for me, came up, & with a Condescension & Politeness I had been quite unus'd to, made me many Compliments, desired to be acquainted with me, blam'd me kindly for not having made my self known to him when I first came to the Place, and would have me away with him to the Tavern where he was going with Col. French to taste as he said some excellent Madeira. I was not a little surpriz'd, and Keimer star'd like a Pig poison'd. I went however with the Governor & Col. French, to a Tavern the Corner of Third Street, and over the Madeira he propos'd my Setting up my Business, laid before me the Probabilities of Success, & both he & Col French, assur'd me I should have their Interest & Influence in procuring the Publick Business of both Governments. On my doubting whether my Father would assist me in it, Sir William said he would give me a Letter to him, in which he would state the Advantages,—and he did not doubt of prevailing with him. So it was concluded I should return to Boston in the first Vessel with the Governor's Letter recommending me to my Father. In the mean time the Intention was to be kept secret, and I went on working with Keimer as usual, the Governor sending for me now & then to dine with him, a very great Honour I thought it, and conversing with me in the most affable, familiar, & friendly manner imaginable. About the End of April 1724, a little Vessel offer'd for Boston. I took Leave of Keimer as going to see my Friends. The Governor gave me an ample Letter, saying many flattering things of me to my Father, and strongly recommending the Project of my setting up at Philadelphia, as a Thing that must make my Fortune.—We struck on a Shoal in going down the Bay & sprung a Leak, we had a blustring time at Sea, and were oblig'd to pump

almost continually, at which I took my Turn.—We arriv'd
safe however at Boston in about a Fortnight.—I had been
absent Seven Months and my Friends had heard nothing of
me, for my Br. Holmes was not yet return'd; and had not
written about me. My unexpected Appearance surpriz'd the
Family; all were however very glad to see me and made me
Welcome, except my Brother. I went to see him at his
Printing-House: I was better dress'd than ever while in his
Service, having a genteel new Suit from Head to foot, a
Watch, and my Pockets lin'd with near Five Pounds Sterling
in Silver. He receiv'd me not very frankly, look'd me all
over, and turn'd to his Work again. The Journey-Men were
inquisitive where I had been, what sort of a Country it was,
and how I lik'd it? I prais'd it much, & the happy Life I
led in it; expressing strongly my Intention of returning to
it; and one of them asking what kind of Money we had
there, I produc'd a handful of Silver and spread it before
them, which was a kind of Raree-Show they had not been
us'd to, Paper being the Money of Boston. Then I took an
Opportunity of letting them see my Watch: and lastly, (my
Brother still grum* & sullen) I gave them a Piece of Eight
to drink & took my Leave.—This Visit of mine offended
him extreamly. For when my Mother some time after spoke
to him of a Reconciliation, & of her Wishes to see us on
good Terms together, & that we might live for the future
as Brothers, he said, I had insulted him in such a Manner
before his People that he could never forget or forgive
it.—In this however he was mistaken.—

My Father receiv'd the Governor's Letter with some
apparent Surprize; but said little of it to me for some Days;
when Capt. Homes returning, he show'd it to him, ask'd if
he knew Keith, and what kind of a Man he was: Adding
his Opinion that he must be of small Discretion, to think
of setting a Boy up in Business who wanted yet 3 Years of
being at Man's Estate. Homes said what he could in fav^r
of the Project; but my Father was clear in the Impropriety
of it; and at last gave a flat Denial to it. Then he wrote a
civil Letter to Sir William thanking him for the Patronage

he had so kindly offered me, but declining to assist me as yet in Setting up, I being in his Opinion too young to be trusted with the Management of a Business so important; & for which the Preparation must be so expensive.—

My Friend & Companion Collins, who was a Clerk at the Post-Office, pleas'd with the Account I gave him of my new Country, determin'd to go thither also:—And while I waited for my Fathers Determination, he set out before me by Land to Rhodeisland, leaving his Books which were a pretty Collection of Mathematicks & Natural Philosophy, to come with mine & me to New York where he propos'd to wait for me. My Father, tho' he did not approve of Sir William's Proposition was yet pleas'd that I had been able to obtain so advantageous a Character from a Person of such Note where I had resided, and that I had been so industrious & careful as to equip my self so handsomely in so short a time: therefore seeing no Prospect of an Accommodation between my Brother & me, he gave his Consent to my Returning again to Philadelphia, advis'd me to behave respectfully to the People there, endeavour to obtain the general Esteem, & avoid lampooning & libelling to which he thought I had too much Inclination;—telling me, that by steady Industry and a prudent Parsimony, I might save enough by the time I was One and Twenty to set me up, & that if I came near the Matter he would help me out with the Rest.—This was all I could obtain, except some small Gifts as Tokens of his & my Mother's Love, when I embark'd again for New-York, now with their Approbation & their Blessing.—

The Sloop putting in at Newport, Rhodeisland, I visited my Brother John, who had been married & settled there some Years. He received me very affectionately, for he always lov'd me.—A Friend of his, one Vernon, having some Money due to him in Pensilvania, about 35 Pounds Currency, desired I would receive it for him, and keep it till I had his Directions what to remit it in. Accordingly he gave me an Order.—This afterwards occasion'd me a good deal of Uneasiness.—At Newport we took in a Number of Passengers for New York: Among which were two young Women, Companions, and a grave, sensible Matron-like Quaker-Woman with her Attendants.—I had shown an obliging Readiness to do her some little Services which impress'd her I suppose with a degree of Good-will towards me.—Therefore when she saw a daily growing Familiarity between me & the two Young Women, which they appear'd to encourage, she took me aside & said, Young Man, I am concern'd for thee, as thou has no Friend with thee, and seems not to know much of the World, or of the Snares Youth is expos'd to; depend upon it those are very bad Women, I can see it in all their Actions, and if thee art not upon thy Guard, they will draw thee into some Danger: they are Strangers to thee,—and I advise thee in a friendly Concern for thy Welfare, to have no Acquaintance with them.—As I seem'd at first not to think so ill of them as she did, she mention'd some Things she had observ'd & heard that had escap'd my Notice; but now convinc'd me she was right. I thank'd her for her kind Advice, and promis'd to follow it.—When we arriv'd at New York, they told me where they liv'd, & invited me to come and see them: but I avoided it. And it was well I did: For the next Day, the Captain miss'd a Silver Spoon & some other Things that had been taken out of his Cabbin, and knowing that these were a Couple of Strumpets, he got a Warrant to search their Lodgings, found the stolen Goods, and had the Thieves punish'd.—So tho' we had escap'd a sunken Rock which we scrap'd upon in the Passage, I thought this Escape of rather more Importance to me. At New York I found my Friend Collins, who had arriv'd there some Time before me. We had been intimate from Children, and had read the same Books together. But he had the Advantage of more time for Reading, & Studying and a wonderful Genius for Mathematical Learning in which he far outstript me. While I liv'd in Boston most of my Hours of Leisure for Conversation were spent with him, & he continu'd a sober as well as an industrious Lad; was much respected for his Learning by several of the Clergy & other Gentlemen, &

seem'd to promise making a good Figure in Life: but during my Absence he had acquir'd a Habit of Sotting with Brandy; and I found by his own Account & what I heard from others, that he had been drunk every day since his Arrival at New York, & behav'd very oddly. He had gam'd too and lost his Money, so that I was oblig'd to discharge his Lodgings, & defray his Expences to and at Philadelphia:—Which prov'd extreamly inconvenient to me.—The then Governor of N York, Burnet, Son of Bishop Burnet hearing from the Captain that a young Man, one of his Passengers, had a great many Books, desired he would bring me to see him. I waited upon him accordingly, and should have taken Collins with me but that he was not sober. The Gov.ʳ treated me with great Civility, show'd me his Library, which was a very large one, & we had a good deal of Conversation about Books & Authors. This was the second Governor who had done me the Honour to take Notice of me, which to a poor Boy like me was very pleasing.—We proceeded to Philadelphia. I received on the Way Vernon's Money, without which we could hardly have finished our Journey.—Collins wish'd to be employ'd in some Counting House; but whether they discover'd his Dramming by his Breath, or by his Behaviour, tho' he had some Recommendations, he met with no Success in any Application, and continu'd Lodging & Boarding at the same House with me & at my Expence. Knowing I had that Money of Vernon's he was continually borrowing of me, still promising Repayment as soon as he should be in Business. At length he had got so much of it, that I was distress'd to think what I should do, in case of being call'd on to remit it.—His Drinking continu'd, about which we sometimes quarrel'd, for when a little intoxicated he was very fractious. Once in a Boat on the Delaware with some other young Men, he refused to row in his Turn: I will be row'd home, says he. We will not row you, says I. You must says he, or stay all Night on the Water, just as you please. The others said, Let us row; What signifies it? But my Mind being soured with his other Conduct, I continu'd to refuse. So he swore he would make me row, or throw me overboard; and coming along stepping on the Thwarts towards me, when he came up & struck at me, I clapt my Hand under his Crutch, and rising pitch'd him head-foremost into the River. I knew he was a good Swimmer, and so was under little Concern about him; but before he could get round to lay hold of the Boat, we had with a few Strokes pull'd her out of his Reach.—And ever when he drew near the Boat, we ask'd if he would row, striking a few Strokes to slide her away from him.—He was ready to die with Vexation, & obstinately would not promise to row; however seeing him at last beginning to tire, we lifted him in; and brought him home dripping wet in the Evening. We hardly exchang'd a civil Word afterwards; and a A West India Captain who had a Commission to procure a Tutor for the Sons of a Gentleman at Barbadoes, happening to meet with him, agreed to carry him thither. He left me then, promising to remit me the first Money he should receive in order to discharge the Debt. But I never heard of him after.—The Breaking into this Money of Vernon's was one of the first great Errata of my Life. And this Affair show'd that my Father was not much out in his Judgment when he suppos'd me too Young to manage Business of Importance But Sir William, on reading his Letter, said he was too prudent. There was great Difference in Persons, and Discretion did not always accompany Years, nor was Youth always without it. And since he will not set you up, says he, I will do it my self. Give me an Inventory of the Things necessary to be had from England, and I will send for them. You shall repay me when you are able; I am resolv'd to have a good Printer here, and I am sure you must succeed. This was spoken with such an Appearance of Cordiality, that I had not the least doubt of his meaning what he said.—I had hitherto kept the Proposition of my Setting up a Secret in Philadelphia, & I still kept it. Had it been known that I depended on the Governor, probably some Friend that knew him better would have advis'd me not to rely on him, as I afterwards heard it as his known Character to be liberal of Promises which he never meant to keep.—Yet unsolicited as he was by me, how could I think his generous Offers insincere? I believ'd him one of the best Men in the World.—

I presented him an Inventory of a little Print.[g] House, amounting by my Computation to about 100£ Sterling. He lik'd it, but ask'd me if my being on the Spot in England to chuse the Types & see that every thing was good of the kind, might not be of some Advantage. Then, says he, when there, you may make Acquaintances & establish Correspondencies in the Bookselling, & Stationary Way. I agreed that this might be advantageous. Then says he, get yourself ready to go with Annis; which was the annual Ship, and the only one at that Time usually passing between London and Philadelphia. But it would be some Months before Annis sail'd, so I continu'd working with Keimer, fretting about the Money Collins had got from me, and in daily Apprehensions of being call'd upon by Vernon, which however did not happen for some Years after.—

I believe I have omitted mentioning that in my first Voyage from Boston, being becalm'd off Block Island, our People set about catching Cod & hawl'd up a great many. Hitherto I had stuck to my Resolution of not eating animal Food; and on this Occasion, I consider'd with my Master Tryon, the taking every Fish as a kind of unprovok'd Murder, since none of them had or ever could do us any Injury that might justify the Slaughter..—All this seem'd very reasonable.—But I had formerly been a great Lover of Fish, & when this came hot out of the Frying Pan, it smelt admirably well. I balanc'd some time between Principle & Inclination: till I recollected, that when the Fish were opened, I saw smaller Fish taken out of their Stomachs:—Then, thought I, if you eat one another, I don't see why we mayn't eat you. So I din'd upon Cod very heartily and continu'd to eat with other People, returning only now & then occasionally to a vegetable Diet. So convenient a thing it is to be a *reasonable Creature*, since it enables one to find or make a Reason for every thing one has a mind to do.—

Keimer & I liv'd on a pretty good familiar Footing & agreed tolerably well: for he suspected nothing of my Setting up. He retain'd a great deal of his old Enthusiasms, and lov'd an Argumentation.. We therefore had many Disputations. I us'd to work him so with my Socratic Method, and had trapann'd him so often by Questions apparently so distant from any Point we had in hand, and yet by degrees led to the Point, and brought him into Difficulties & Contradictions, that at last he grew ridiculously cautious, and would hardly answer me the most common Question, without asking first, *What do you intend to infer from that?* However it gave him so high an Opinion of my Abilities in the Confuting Way, that he seriously propos'd my being his Colleague in a Project he had of setting up a new Sect. He was to preach the Doctrines, and I was to confound all Opponents. When he came to explain with me upon the Doctrines, I found several Conundrums which I objected to, unless I might have my Way a little too, and introduce some of mine. Keimer wore his Beard at full Length, because somewhere in the Mosaic Law it is said, *thou shalt not mar the Corners of thy Beard.* He likewise kept the seventh day Sabbath; and these two Points were Essentials with him.——I dislik'd both, but agreed to admit them upon Condition of his adopting the Doctrine of using no animal Food. I doubt, says he, my Constitution will not bear that. I assur'd him it would, & that he would be the better for it. He was usually a great Glutton, and I promis'd my self some Diversion in half-starving him. He agreed to try the Practice if I would keep him Company. I did so and we held it for three Months. We had our Victuals dress'd and brought to us regularly by a Woman in the Neighbourhood, who had from me a List of 40 Dishes to be prepar'd for us at different times, in all which there was neither Fish Flesh nor Fowl, and the Whim suited me the better at this time from the Cheapness of it, not costing us above 18^d Sterling each, per Week.——I have since kept several Lents most strictly, Leaving the common Diet for that, and that for the common, abruptly, without the least Inconvenience: So that

I think there is little in the Advice of making those Changes
by easy Gradations.—I went on pleasantly, but Poor Keimer
suffer'd grievously, tir'd of the Project, long'd for the Flesh
Pots of Egypt, and order'd a roast Pig; He invited me &
two Women Friends to dine with him, but it being brought
too soon upon table, he could not resist the Temptation,
and ate it all up before we came.—

I had made some Courtship during this time to Miss
Read, I had a great Respect & Affection for her, and had
some Reason to believe she had the same for me: but as I
was about to take a long Voyage, and we were both very
young, only a little above 18. it was thought most prudent
by her Mother to prevent our going too far at present, as
a Marriage if it was to take place would be more convenient
after my Return, when I should be as I expected set up in
my Business. Perhaps too she thought my Expectations not
so well founded as I imagined them to be.—

My chief Acquaintances at this time were, Charles Osborne, Joseph Watson, & James Ralph; All Lovers of Reading. The two first were Clerks to an eminent Scrivener or
Conveyancer in the Town, Charles Brogden; the other was
Clerk to a Merchant. Watson was a pious sensible young
Man, of great Integrity.—The others rather more lax in
their Principles of Religion, particularly Ralph, who as well
as Collins had been unsettled by me, for which they both
made me suffer.—Osborne was sensible, candid, frank, sincere, and affectionate to his Friends; but in litterary Matters
too fond of criticising. Ralph, was ingenious, genteel in his
Manners, & extreamly eloquent; I think I never knew a
prettier Talker.—Both of them great Admirers of Poetry,
and began to try their Hands in little Pieces. Many pleasant
Walks we four had together, on Sundays into the Woods
near Skuylkill, where we read to one another & conferr'd
on what we read. Ralph was inclin'd to pursue the Study
of Poetry, not doubting but he might become eminent in it
and make his Fortune by it, alledging that the best Poets
must when they first began to write, make as many Faults
as he did.—Osborne dissuaded him, assur'd him he had no

Genius for Poetry, & advis'd him to think of nothing beyond the Business he was bred to; that in the mercantile way tho' he had no Stock, he might by his Diligence & Punctuality recommend himself to Employment as a Factor, and in time acquire wherewith to trade on his own Account. I approv'd the amusing one's Self with Poetry now & then, so far as to improve one's Language, but no farther. On this it was propos'd that we should each of us at our next Meeting produce a Piece of our own Composing, in order to improve by our mutual Observations, Criticisms & Corrections. As Language & Expression was what we had in View, we excluded all Considerations of Invention, by agreeing that the Task should be a Version of the 18th Psalm, which describes the Descent of a Deity. When the Time of our Meeting drew nigh, Ralph call'd on me first, & let me know his Piece was ready. I told him I had been busy, & having little Inclination had done nothing.—He then show'd me his Piece for my Opinion; and I much approv'd it, as it appear'd to me to have great Merit. Now, says he, Osborne never will allow the least Merit in any thing of mine, but makes 1000 Criticisms out of mere Envy. He is not so jealous of you. I wish therefore you would take this Piece, & produce it as yours. I will pretend not to have had time, & so produce nothing: We shall then see what he will say to it.—It was agreed, and I immediately transcrib'd it that it might appear in my own hand. We met. Watson's Performance was read: there were some Beauties in it: but many Defects. Osborne's was read: It was much better. Ralph did it Justice, remark'd some Faults, but applauded the Beauties. He himself had nothing to produce. I was backward, seem'd desirous of being excus'd, had not had sufficient Time to correct: &c. but no Excuse could be admitted, produce I must. It was read and repeated; Watson and Osborne gave up the Contest; and join'd in applauding it immoderately. Ralph only made some Criticisms & propos'd some Amendments, but I defended my Text. Osborne was against, Ralph, & told him he was no better a Critic than Poet; so he dropt the Argument. As they two went home together, Osborne express'd himself still more strongly in favour of what he thought my Production, having restrain'd himself before as he said, lest I should think it Flattery. But who would have imagin'd, says he, that Franklin had been capable of such a Performance; such Painting, such Force! such Fire! he has even improv'd the Original! In his common Conversation, he seems to have no Choice of Words; he hesitates and blunders; and yet, good God, how he writes!—When we next met, Ralph discover'd the Trick, we had plaid him, and Osborne was a little laught at. This Transaction fix'd Ralph in his Resolution of becoming a Poet. I did all I could to dissuade him from it, but. He continu'd scribbling Verses, till *Pope* cur'd him.—He became however a pretty good Prose Writer. More of him hereafter. But as I may not have occasion again to mention the other two, I shall just remark here, that Watson died in my Arms a few Years after, much lamented, being the best of our Set. Osborne went to the West Indies, where he became an eminent Lawyer & made Money, but died young. He and I had made a serious Agreement, that the one who happen'd first to die, should if possible make a friendly Visit to the other, and acquaint him how he found things in that separate State. But he never fulfill'd his Promise.

The Governor, seeming to like my Company, had me frequently to his House; & his Setting me up was always mention'd as a fix'd thing. I was to take with me Letters recommendatory to a Number of his Friends, besides the Letter of Credit, to furnish me with the necessary Money for purchasing the Press & Types, Paper, &c. For these Letters I was appointed to call at different times, when they were to be ready, but a future time was still named.—Thus we went on till the Ship whose Departure too had been several times postponed was on the Point of sailing. Then when I call'd to take my Leave & receive the Letters, his Secretary, Dr Bard, came out to me and said the Governor was extreamly busy, in writing, but would be down at New-castle before the Ship, & there the Letters would be delivered to me.

Ralph, tho' married & having one Child, had determined to accompany me in this Voyage. It was thought he intended to establish a Correspondence, & obtain Goods to sell on Commission. But I found afterwards, that thro' some Discontent with his Wifes, Relations, he purposed to leave her on their Hands, & never return again.——Having taken leave of my Friends, & interchang'd some Promises with Miss Read, I left Philadelphia in the Ship, which anchor'd at Newcastle. The Governor was there. But when I went to his Lodging, the Secretary came to me from him with the civillest Message in the World, that he could not then see me being engag'd in Business of the utmost Importance, but should send the Letters to me on board, wish'd me heartily a good Voyage and a speedy Return, &c. I return'd on board, a little puzzled, but still not doubting.——

Mr Andrew Hamilton, a famous Lawyer of Philadelphia, had taken Passage in the same Ship for himself and Son: and with Mr Denham a Quaker Merchant, & Messrs Onion & Russel Masters of an Iron Work in Maryland, had engag'd the Great Cabin; so that Ralph and I were forc'd to take up with a Birth in the Steerage:——And none on board knowing us, were considered as ordinary Persons.——But Mr Hamilton & his Son (it was James, since Governor) return'd from New Castle to Philadelphia, the Father being recall'd by a great Fee to plead for a seized Ship.——And just before we sail'd Col. French coming on board, & showing me great Respect, I was more taken Notice of, and with my Friend Ralph invited by the other Gentlemen to come into the Cabin, there being now Room. Accordingly we remov'd thither.

Understanding that Col. French had brought on board the Governor's Dispatches, I ask'd the Captain for those Letters that were to be under my Care. He said all were put into the Bag together; and he could not then come at them; but before we landed in England, I should have an Opportunity of picking them out. So I was satisfy'd for the present, and we proceeded on our Voyage. We had a sociable Company in the Cabin, and lived uncommonly well, having the Addition of all Mr Hamilton's Stores, who had laid in plentifully. In this Passage Mr Denham contracted a Friendship for me that continued during his Life. The Voyage was otherwise not a pleasant one, as we had a great deal of bad Weather.——

When we came into the Channel, the Captain kept his Word with me, & gave me an Opportunity of examining the Bag for the Governor's Letters. I found none upon which my Name was put, as under my Care; I pick'd out 6 or 7 that by the Handwriting I thought might be the promis'd Letters, especially as one of them was directed to Basket the King's Printer, and another to some Stationer. We arriv'd in London the 24th of December, 1724.——I waited upon the Stationer who came first in my Way, delivering the Letter as from Gov. Keith. I don't know such a Person, says he: but opening the Letter, O, this is from Riddlesden; I have lately found him to be a compleat Rascal, and I will have nothing to do with him, nor receive any Letters from him. So putting the Letter into my Hand, he turn'd on his Heel & left me to serve some Customer.——I was surprized to find these were not the Governor's Letters. And after recollecting and comparing Circumstances, I began to doubt his Sincerity.——I found my Friend Denham, and opened the whole Affair to him. He let me into Keith's Character, told me there was not the least Probability that he had written any Letters for me, that no one who knew him had the smallest Dependance on him, and he laught at the Notion of the Governor's giving me a Letter of Credit, having as he said no Credit to give.——On my expressing some Concern about what I should do: He advis'd me to endeavour getting some Employment in the Way of my Business. Among the Printers here, says he, you will improve yourself; and when you return to America, you will set up to greater Advantage.——

We both of us happen'd to know, as well as the Stationer, that Riddlesden the Attorney, was a very Knave. He had half ruin'd Miss Read's Father by drawing him in to be bound for him. By his Letter it appear'd, there was a secret

Scheme on foot to the Prejudice of Hamilton, (Suppos'd to be then coming over, with us,) and that Keith was concern'd in it with Riddlesden. Denham, who was a Friend of Hamilton's, thought he should ought to be acquainted with it. So when he arriv'd in England, which was soon after, partly from Resentment & Ill-Will to Keith & Riddlesden, & partly from Good Will to him: I waited on him, and gave him the Letter. He thank'd me cordially, the Information being of Importance to him. And from that time he became my Friend, greatly to my Advantage afterwards on many Occasions.

But what shall we think of a Governor's playing such pitiful Tricks, & imposing so grossly on a poor ignorant Boy! It was a Habit he had acquired. He wish'd to please every body; and having little to give, he gave Expectations.—He was otherwise an ingenious sensible Man, a pretty good Writer, & a good Governor for the People, tho' not for his Constituents the Proprietaries, whose Instructions he sometimes disregarded.—Several of our best Laws were of his Planning, and pass'd during his Administration.—

Ralph and I were inseparable Companions. We took Lodgings together in Little Britain at 3/6 per Week, as much as we could then afford.—He found some Relations, but they were poor & unable to assist him. He now let me know his Intentions of remaining in London, and that he never meant to return to Philad.[a]—He had brought no Money with him, the whole he could muster having been expended in paying his Passage.—I had 15 Pistoles: So he borrowed occasionally of me, to subsist while he was looking out for Business.—He first endeavoured to get into the Playhouse, believing himself qualify'd for an Actor; but Wilkes, to whom he apply'd, advis'd him candidly not to think of that, Employment, as it was impossible he he should succeed in it.—Then he propos'd to Roberts, a Publisher in Paternoster Row, to write for him a Weekly Paper like the Spectator, on certain Conditions, which Roberts did not approve. Then he endeavour'd to get Employm.[t] as a Hackney Writer to copy for the Stationers & Lawyers about the Temple: but could find no Vacancy.—

I immediately got into Work at Palmer's then a famous Printing House in Bartholomew Close; and here I continu'd near a Year. I was pretty diligent; but spent with Ralph a good deal of my Earnings in going to Plays & other Places of Amusement. We had together consum'd all my Pistoles, and now just rubb'd on from hand to mouth. He seem'd quite to forget his Wife & Child, and I by degrees my Engagements wth Miss Read, to whom I never wrote more than one Letter, & that was to let her know I was not likely soon to return. This was another of the great Errata of my Life, which I should wish to correct if I were to live it over again.—In fact, by our Expences, I was constantly kept unable to pay my Passage.

At Palmer's I was employ'd in Composing for the second Edition of Woollaston's Religion of Nature. Some of his Reasonings not appearing to me well-founded, I wrote a little metaphysical Piece, in which I made Remarks on them. It was entitled, *A Dissertation on Liberty & Necessity, Pleasure and Pain.*—I inscrib'd it to my Friend Ralph.—I printed a small Number. It occasion'd my being more consider'd by Mr Palmer, as a young Man of some Ingenuity, tho' he seriously expostulated with me upon the Principles of my Pamphlet which to him appear'd abominable, My printing this Pamphlet was another Erratum.

While I lodg'd in Little Britain I made an Acquaintance with one Wilcox a Bookseller, whose Shop was at the next Door. He had an immense Collection of second-hand Books. Circulating Libraries were not then in Use; but we agreed that on certain reasonable Terms which I have now forgotten, I might take, read & return any of his Books. This I esteem'd a great Advantage, & I made as much Use of it as I could.—

My Pamphlet by some means falling into the Hands of one Lyons, a Surgeon, Author of a Book intituled *The Infallibility of Human Judgment*, it occasioned an Acquaintance between us; he took great Notice of me, call'd on me often, to converse on these Subjects, carried me to the Horns a pale Ale-House in   Lane, Cheapside,* and introduc'd me to Dr Mandevile, Author of the Fable of the Bees who had a Club there, of which he was the Soul, being a most facetious entertaining Companion. Lyons too introduc'd me to Dr Pemberton, at Batson's Coffee House, who promis'd to give me an Opportunity some time or other of seeing Sir Isaac Newton, of which I was extreamly desirous; but this never happened.

I had brought over a few Curiosities among which the principal was a Purse made of the Asbestos, which purifies by Fire. Sir Hans Sloane heard of it, came to see me, and invited me to his House in Bloomsbury Square; where he show'd me all his Curiosities, and persuaded me to let him add that to the Number, for which he paid me handsomely.—

In our House there lodg'd a young Woman; a Millener, who I think had a Shop in the Cloisters. She had been genteelly, bred; was sensible & lively, and of most pleasing Conversation.—Ralph read Plays to her in the Evenings, they grew intimate, she took another Lodging, and he follow'd her. They liv'd together some time, but he being still out of Business, & her Income not sufficient to maintain them with her Child, he took a Resolution of going from London, to try for a Country School, which he thought himself well qualify'd to undertake, as he wrote an excellent Hand, & was a Master of Arithmetic & Accounts.—This however he deem'd a Business below him, & confident of future better Fortune when he should be unwilling to have it known that he once was so meanly employ'd, he chang'd his Name, & did me the Honour to assume mine.—For I soon after had a Letter from him, acquainting me, that he was settled in a small Village in Berkshire, I think it was, where he taught reading & writing to 10 or a dozen Boys at 6 pence each per Week, recommending Mrs T. to my Care, and desiring me to write to him directing for Mr Franklin Schoolmaster at such a Place. He continu'd to write frequently, sending me large Specimens of an Epic Poem,

which he was then composing, and desiring my Remarks &
Corrections.—These I gave him from time to time, but
endeavour'd rather to discourage his Proceeding. One of
Young's Satires was then just publish'd. I copy'd & sent
him a great Part, of it, which set in a strong Light the Folly
of pursuing the Muses with any Hope of Advancement by
them. All was in vain. Sheets of the Poem continu'd to come
by every Post In the mean time Mrs T. having on his
Account lost her Friends & Business, was often in Distresses, & us'd to send for me, and borrow what I could
spare to help her out of them. I grew fond of her Company,
and being at this time under no Religious Restraints, &
presuming on my Importance to her, I attempted Familiar-
ities, (another Erratum) which she repuls'd with a proper
Resentment, and acquainted him with my Behaviour. This
made a Breach between us, & when he return'd again to
London, he let me know he thought I had cancel'd all the
Obligations he had been under to me.—So I found I was
never to expect his Repaying me what I lent to him or
advan'd for him. This was however not then of much
Consequence, as he was totally unable.—And in the Loss
of his Friendship. I found my self reliev'd from a Burthen.
I now began to think of getting a little Money beforehand;
and expecting better Work, I left Palmer's to work at
Watts's near Lincoln's Inn Fields, a still greater Printing
House. Here I continu'd all the rest of my Stay in London.

At my first Admission into this Printing House, I took
to working at Press, imagining I felt a Want of the Bodily
Exercise I had been us'd to in America, where Presswork is
mix'd with Composing. I drank only Water; the other
Workmen, near 50 in Number, were great Guzzlers of Beer.
On occasion I carried up & down Stairs a large Form of
Types in each hand, when others carried but one in both
Hands. They wonder'd to see from this & several Instances
that the Water-American as they call'd me was *stronger* than
themselves who drunk *strong* Beer. We had an Alehouse Boy
who attended always in the House to supply the Workmen.
My Companion at the Press, drank every day a Pint before

Breakfast, a Pint at Breakfast with his Bread and Cheese; a Pint between Breakfast and Dinner; a Pint at Dinner; a Pint in the Afternoon about Six o'clock, and another when he had done his Day's-Work. I thought it a detestable Custom.—But it was necessary, he suppos'd, to drink *strong* Beer that he might be *strong* to labour. I endeavour'd to convince him that the Bodily Strength afforded by Beer could only be in proportion to the Grain or Flour of the Barley dissolved in the Water of which it was made; that there was more Flour in a Penny-worth of Bread, and therefore if he would eat that with a Pint of Water, it would give him more Strength than a Quart of Beer.—He drank on however, & had 4 or 5 Shillings to pay out of his Wages every Saturday Night for that muddling Liquor; an Expence I was free from.—And thus these poor Devils keep themselves always under.

Watts after some Weeks desiring to have me in the Composing-Room, I left the Pressmen. A new *Bienvenu* or Sum for Drink, being 5/, was demanded of me by the Compostors. I thought it an Imposition, as I had paid below. The Master thought so too, and forbad my Paying it. I stood out two or three Weeks, was accordingly considered as an Excommunicate, and had so many little Pieces of private Mischief done me, by mixing my Sorts, transposing my Pages, breaking my Matter, &c. &c. if I were ever so little out of the Room, & all ascrib'd to the Chapel Ghost, which they said ever haunted those not regularly admitted, that notwithstanding the Master's Protection, I found myself oblig'd to comply and pay the Money; convinc'd of the Folly of being on ill Terms with those one is to live with continually. I was now on a fair Footing with them, and soon acquir'd considerable Influence. I propos'd some reasonable Alterations in their Chapel[†] Laws, and carried them against all Opposition. From my Example a great Part of them, left their muddling Breakfast of Beer & Bread & Cheese, finding they could with me be supply'd from a

[†] A Printing House is always called a Chappel by the Workmen.—

neighbouring House with a large Porringer of hot Water-gruel, sprinkled with Pepper, crumb'd with Bread, & a Bit of Butter in it, for the Price of a Pint of Beer, viz, three halfpence. This was a more comfortable as well as cheaper Breakfast, & kept their Heads clearer.—Those who conti-nu'd sotting with Beer all day, were often, by not paying, out of Credit at the Alehouse, and us'd to make Interest with me to get Beer, *their Light*, as they phras'd it, *being out*. I watch'd the Pay table on Saturday Night, & collected what I stood engag'd for them, having to pay some times near Thirty Shillings a Week on their Accounts.—This, and my being esteem'd a pretty good Riggite,* that is a jocular verbal Satyrist, supported my Consequence in the Society.— My constant Attendance, (I never making a St. Monday), recommended me to the Master; and my uncommon Quick-ness at composing, occasion'd my being put upon all Work of Dispatch which was generally better paid. So I went on now very agreably.—

My Lodging in Little Britain being too remote, I found another in Duke-street opposite to the Romish Chapel. It was two pair of Stairs backwards at an Italian Warehouse. A Widow Lady kept the House; she had a Daughter & a Maid Servant, and a Journey-man who attended the Ware-house, but lodg'd abroad.—After sending to enquire my character at the House where I last lodg'd, she agreed to take me in at the same Rate 3/6 per Week, cheaper as she said from the Protection she expected in having a Man lodge in the House. She was a Widow, an elderly Woman had been bred a Protestant, being a Clergyman's Daughter, but was converted to the Catholic Religion by her Husband, whose Memory she much revered had lived much among People of Distinction, and knew a 1000 Anecdotes of them. as far back as the Times of Charles the second. She was lame in her Knees with the Gout, and therefore seldom stirr'd out of her Room, so sometimes wanted Company; and hers was so highly amusing to me; that I was sure to spend an Evening with her whenever she desired it. Our Supper was only half an Anchovy each, on a very little Strip of Bread & Butter, and half a Pint of Ale between us.—But the Entertainment was in her Conversation. My always keeping good Hours, and giving little Trouble in the Family, made her unwilling to part with me; so that when I talk'd of a Lodging I had heard of, nearer my Business, for 2/ a Week, which, intent as I now was on saving Money, made some Difference; she bid me not think of it, for she would abate me two Shillings a Week for the future, so I remain'd with her at 1/6 as long as I staid in London.—

In a Garret of her House there lived a Maiden Lady of 70 in the most retired Manner, of whom my Landlady gave me this Account, that she was a Roman-Catholic, had been sent abroad when young & lodg'd in a Nunnery with an Intent of becoming a Nun: but the Country not agreeing with her, she return'd to England, where there being no Nunnery, she had vow'd to lead the Life of a Nun as near as might be done in those Circumstances: Accordingly She had given all her Estate to charitable Uses, reserving only Twelve Pounds a Year to live on, and out of this Sum she still gave a great deal in Charity, living her self on Water-gruel only, & using no Fire but to boil it.—She had lived many Years in that Garret, being permitted to remain there gratis by successive catholic Tenants of the House below, as they deem'd it a Blessing to have her there. A Priest visited her, to confess her every Day. I have ask'd her, says my Landlady, how she, as she liv'd, could possibly find so much Employment for a Confessor? O, says she, it is impossible to avoid *vain Thoughts*. I was permitted once to visit her: She was chearful & polite, & convers'd pleasant-ly. The Room was clean, but had no other Furniture than a Matras, a Table with a Crucifix & Book, a Stool, which she gave me to sit on, and a Picture over the Chimney of St. *Veronica*, displaying her Handkerchief with the miracu-lous Figure of Christ's bleeding Face on it, which she explain'd to me with great Seriousness. She look'd pale, but was never sick, and I give it as another Instance on how small an Income Life & Health may be supported.—

At Watts's Printinghouse I contracted an Acquaintance with an ingenious young Man, one Wygate. who having wealthy Relations, had been better educated than most Printers, was a tolerable Latinist, spoke French, & lov'd Reading. I taught him, & a Friend of his, to swim, at twice going into the River, & they soon became good Swimmers. They introduc'd me to some Gentlemen from the Country who went to Chelsea by Water to see the College and Don Saltero's Curiosities.* In our Return, at the Request of the Company, whose Curiosity Wygate had excited, I stript & leapt into the River, & swam from near Chelsea to Blackfryars, performing on the Way many Feats of Activity both upon & under Water, that surpriz'd & pleas'd those to whom they were Novelties.——I had from a Child been ever delighted with this Exercise, had studied & practis'd all Thevenot's Motions & Positions, added some of my own, aiming at the graceful & easy, as well as the Useful.——All these I took this Occasion of exhibiting to the Company, & was much flatter'd by their Admiration.——And Wygate, who was desirous of becoming a Master, grew more & more attach'd to me, on that account, as well as from the Similarity of our Studies. He at length propos'd to me travelling all over Europe together, supporting ourselves every where by working at our Business. I was once inclin'd to it. But mentioning it to my good Friend Mr Denham, with whom I often spent an Hour, when I had Leisure. He dissuaded me from it; advising me to think only of return.[g] to Pensilvania, which he was now about to do.——

I must record one Trait of this good Man's Character. He had formerly been in Business at Bristol, but fail'd in Debt to a Number of People, compounded and went to America. There, by a close Application to Business as a Merchant, he acquir'd a plentiful Fortune in a few Years. Returning to England in the Ship with me, He invited his old Creditors to an Entertainment, at which he thank'd them for the easy Composition they had favour'd him with, & when they expected nothing but the Treat, every Man at the first Remove, found under his Plate an Order on a

Banker for the full Amount of the unpaid Remainder with Interest.

He now told me he was about to return to Philadelphia, and should carry over a great Quantity of Goods in order to open a Store there: He propos'd to take me over as his Clerk, to keep his Books (in which he would instruct me) copy his Letters, and attend the Store. He added, that as soon as I should be acquainted with mercantile Business he would promote me by sending me with a Cargo of Flour & Bread &c to the West Indies, and procure me Commissions from others; which would be profitable, & if I manag'd well, would establish me handsomely. The Thing pleas'd me, for I was grown tired of London, remember'd with Pleasure the happy Months I had spent in Pennsylvania, and wish'd again to see it Therefore I immediately agreed, on the Terms of Fifty Pounds a Year Pensylvania Money; less indeed than my then present Gettings as a Compostor, but affording a better Prospect.—

I now took Leave of Printing, as I thought for ever, and was daily employ'd in my new Business; going about with Mr Denham among the Tradesmen, to purchase various Articles, & seeing them pack'd up, doing Errands, calling upon Workmen to dispatch, &c. and when all was on board, I had a few Days Leisure. On one of these Days I was to my Surprize sent for by a great Man I knew only by Name, a Sir William Wyndham and I waited upon him. He had heard by some means or other of my Swimming from Chelsey to Blackfryars, and of my teaching Wygate and another young Man to swim in a few Hours. He had two Sons about to set out on their Travels; he wish'd to have them first taught Swimming; and propos'd to gratify me handsomely if I would teach them.—They were not yet come to Town and my Stay was uncertain, so I could not undertake it. But from this Incident I thought it likely, that if I were to remain in England and open a Swimming School, I might get a good deal of Money.—And it struck me so strongly, that had the Overture been sooner made me, probably I should not so soon have returned to America.—

After Many Years, you & I had something of more Importance to do with one of these Sons of Sir William Wyndham, become Earl of Egremont, which I shall mention in its Place.—

Thus I spent about 18 Months in London. Most Part of the Time, I work'd hard at my Business, & spent but little upon my self except in seeing Plays, & in Books.—My Friend Ralph had kept me poor. He owed me about 27 Pounds; which I was now never likely to receive; a great Sum out of my small Earnings. I lov'd him notwithstanding, for he had many amiable Qualities.—tho' I had by no means improv'd my Fortune.—, But I had pick'd up some very ingenious Acquaintance whose Conversation was of great Advantage to me, and I had read considerably.

We sail'd from Gravesend on the 23^d of July 1726.—For The Incidents of the Voyage, I refer you to my Journal, where you will find them all minutely related. Perhaps the most important Part of that Journal is the *Plan* to be found in it which I formed at Sea, for regulating my future Conduct in Life. It is the more remarkable, as being form'd when I was so young, and yet being pretty faithfully adhered to quite thro' to old Age.—We landed in Philadelphia the 11th of October, where I found sundry Alterations. Keith was no longer Governor, being superceded by Major Gordon: I met him walking the Streets as a common Citizen. He seem'd a little asham'd at seeing me, but pass'd without saying any thing. I should have been as much asham'd at seeing Miss Read, had not her Fr.^{ds} despairing with Reason of my Return, after the Receipt of my Letter, persuaded her to marry another, one Rogers, a Potter, which was done in my Absence. With him however she was never happy, and soon parted from him, refusing to cohabit with him, or bear his Name It being now said that he had another Wife. He was a worthless Fellow tho' an excellent Workman which was the Temptation to her Friends.. He got into Debt, and ran away in 1727 or 28. went to the West Indies, and died there. Keimer had got a better House, a Shop well supply'd with Stationary plenty of new Types, a number of

Hands tho' none good, and seem'd to have a great deal of Business.

Mr Denham took a Store in Water Street, where we open'd our Goods. I attended the Business diligently, studied Accounts, and grew in a little Time expert at selling.— We lodg'd and boarded together, he counsell'd me as a Father, having a sincere Regard for me: I respected & lov'd him: and we might have gone on together very happily: But in the Beginning of Feby 1726/7 when I had just pass'd my 21st Year, we both were taken ill. My Distemper was a Pleurisy, which very nearly carried me off:—I suffered a good deal, gave up the Point in my own mind, & was rather disappointed when I found my self recovering; regretting in some degree that I must now sometime or other have all that disagreable Work to do over again.—I forget what his Distemper was. It held him a long time, and at length carried him off. He left me a small Legacy in a nuncupative Will,* as a Token of his Kindness for me, and he left me once more to the wide World. For the Store was taken into the Care of his Executors, and my Employment under him ended:—My Brother-in-law Homes, being now at Philadelphia, advis'd my Return to my Business. And Keimer tempted me with an Offer of large Wages by the Year to come & take the Management of his Printing-House. that he might better attend his Stationer's Shop.—I had heard a bad Character of him in London, from his Wife & her Friends, & was not fond of having any more to do with him. I try'd for farther Employment as a Merchant's Clerk; but not readily meeting with any, I clos'd again with Keimer.—

I found in *his* House these Hands; Hugh Meredith a Welsh-Pensilvanian, 30 Years of Age, bred to Country Work honest, sensible, had a great deal of solid Observation, was something of a Reader, but given to drink:—Stephen Potts, a young Country Man of full Age, bred to the Same:—of uncommon natural Parts, & great Wit & Humour, but a little idle.—These he had agreed with at extream low Wages, per Week, to be rais'd a Shilling every 3 Months, as they would deserve by improving in their Business, & the Expectation of these high Wages to come on hereafter was what he had drawn them in with.—Meredith was to work at Press, Potts at Bookbinding, which he by Agreement, was to teach them, tho' he knew neither one nor t'other. John——a wild Irishman brought up to no Business, whose Service for 4 Years Keimer had purchas'd from the Captain of a Ship. He too was to be made a Pressman. George Webb, an Oxford Scholar, whose Time for 4 Years he had likewise bought, intending him for a Compositor: of whom more presently. And David Harry, a Country Boy, whom he had taken Apprentice. I soon perceiv'd that the Intention of engaging me at Wages so much higher than he had been us'd to give, was to have these raw cheap Hands form'd thro' me, and as soon as I had instructed them, then, they being all articled to him, he should be able to do without me.—I went on however, very chearfully; put his Printing House in Order, which had been in great Confusion, and brought his Hands by degrees to mind their Business and to do it better.

It was an odd Thing to find an Oxford Scholar in the Situation of a bought Servant. He was not more than 18 Years of Age, & gave me this Account of himself; that he was born in Gloucester, educated at a Grammar School there, had been distinguish'd among the Scholars for some apparent Superiority in performing his Part when they exhibited Plays; belong'd to the Witty Club there, and had written some Pieces in Prose & Verse which were printed in the Goucester Newspapers.—Thence he was sent to Oxford; there he continu'd about a Year, but not well-satisfy'd, wishing of all things to see London & become a Player. At length receiving his Quarterly Allowance of 15 Guineas, instead of discharging his Debts, he walk'd out of Town, hid his Gown in a Furz Bush, and footed it to London, where having no Friend to advise him, he fell into bad Company, soon spent his Guineas, found no means of being introduc'd among the Players, grew necessitous, pawn'd his Cloaths & wanted Bread. Walking the Street very hungry, & not knowing what to do with himself, a Crimp's Bill was put into his Hand, offering immediate Entertainment & Encouragement to such as would bind themselves to serve in America. He went directly, sign'd the Indentures, was put into the Ship & came over; never writing a Line to acquaint his Friends what was become of him. He was lively, witty, good-natur'd and a pleasant Companion,; but idle, thoughtless & imprudent to the last Degree.

John the Irishman soon ran away. With the rest I began to live very agreably; for they all respected me, the more as they found Keimer incapable of instructing them, and that from me they learnt something daily. We never work'd on a Saturday, that being Keimer's Sabbath. So I had two Days for Reading. My Acquaintance with ingenious People in the Town, increased. Keimer himself treated me with great Civility & apparent Regard; and nothing now made me uneasy but my Debt to Vernon, which I was yet unable to pay. being hitherto but a poor Oeconomist.—He however kindly made no Demand of it.

Our Printing-House often wanted Sorts, and there was no Letter Founder in America. I had seen Types cast at James's in London, but without much Attention to the Manner: However I now contriv'd a Mould, made use of the Letters we had, as Puncheons, struck the Matrices in Lead, and thus supply'd in a pretty tolerable way all Deficiencies. I also engrav'd several Things on occasion. I made the Ink, I was Warehouse-man & every thing, in short quite a Factotum.—

But however serviceable I might be, I found that my Services became every Day of less Importance, as the other Hands improv'd in the Business. And when Keimer paid my second Quarter's Wages, he let me know that he felt them too heavy, and thought I should make an Abatement. He grew by degrees less civil, put on more of the Master, frequently found Fault, was captious and seem'd ready for an Out-breaking. I went on nevertheless with a good deal of Patience, thinking that his incumber'd Circumstances were partly the Cause. At length a Trifle snapt our Connexion. For a great Noise happening near the Courthouse, I put my Head out of the Window to see what was the Matter. Keimer being in the Street look'd up & saw me, call'd out to me in a loud Voice and angry Tone to mind my Business, adding some reproachful Words, that nettled me the more for their Publicity, all the Neighbours who were looking out on the same Occasion being Witnesses how I was treated. He came up immediately into the Printing-House, continu'd the Quarrel, high Words pass'd on both Sides, he gave me the Quarter's Warning we had stipulated, expressing a Wish that he had not been oblig'd to so long a Warning: I told him his Wish was unnecessary for I would leave him that Instant; and so taking my Hat walk'd out of Doors; desiring Meredith whom I saw below to take care of some Things I left, & bring them to my Lodging.—

Meredith came accordingly in the Evening, when we talk'd my Affair over. He had conceiv'd a great Regard for me, & was very unwilling that I should leave the House while he remain'd in it. He dissuaded me from returning to my native Country which I began to think of. He reminded me that Keimer was in debt for all he possess'd, that his Creditors began to be uneasy, that he kept his Shop miserably, sold often without Profit for ready Money, and often trusted without keeping Account. That he must therefore fail; which would make a Vacancy I might profit of.—I objected my Want of Money. He then let me know, that his Father had a high Opinion of me, and from some Discourse that had pass'd between them, he was sure would advance Money to set us up, if I would enter into Partnership with him.—My Time, says he, will be out with Keimer in the Spring. By that time we may have our Press & Types in from London:—I am sensible I am no Workman. If you like it, Your Skill in the Business shall be set against the Stock I furnish; and we will share the Profits equally.—The Proposal was agreable, and I consented. His Father was in Town, and approv'd of it, the more as he saw I had great Influence with his Son, had prevail'd on him to abstain long from, Dramdrinking, and he hop'd might break him of that wretched Habit entirely, when we came to be so closely connected. I gave an Inventory to the Father, who carry'd it to a Merchant; the Things were sent for; the Secret was to be kept till they should arrive, and in the mean time I was to get Work if I could at the other Printing House.—But I found no Vacancy there, and so remain'd idle a few Days, when Keimer, on a Prospect of being employ'd to print some Paper-money, in New Jersey, which would require Cuts & various Types that I only could supply, and apprehending Bradford might engage me & get the Jobb from him, sent me a very civil Message, that old Friends should not part for a few Words the Effect of sudden Passion, and wishing me to return. Meredith persuaded me to comply, as it would give more Opportunity for his Improvement under my daily Instructions.—So I return'd, and we went on more smoothly than for some time before.—The New Jersey Jobb was obtain'd. I contriv'd a Copper-Plate Press for it, the first that had been seen in the Country.—I cut several Ornaments and Checks for the Bills. We went together to Burlington, where I executed the Whole to Satisfaction, & he received so large a Sum for the Work, as to be enabled thereby to keep his Head much longer above Water.—

At Burlington I made an Acquaintance with many principal People of the Province. Several of them had been appointed by the Assembly a Committee to attend the Press, and take Care that no more Bills were printed than the Law directed. They were therefore by Turns constantly with us, and generally he who attended brought with him a Friend or two for Company. My Mind having been much more improv'd by Reading than Keimer's, I suppose it was for that Reason my Conversation seem'd to be more valu'd. They had me to their Houses, introduc'd me to their Friends and show'd me much Civility, while he, tho' the Master, was a little neglected. In truth he was an odd Fish, ignorant of common Life, fond of rudely opposing receiv'd Opinions, slovenly to extream dirtiness, enthusiastic in some

Points of Religion, and a little Knavish withal. We continu'd
there near 3 Months, and by that time I could reckon among
my acquired Friends, Judge Allen, Samuel Bustill, the
Secretary of the Province, Isaac Pearson, Joseph Cooper &
several of the Smiths, Members of Assembly, and Isaac
Decow the Surveyor General. The latter was a shrewd
sagacious old Man, who told me that he began for himself
when young by wheeling Clay for the Brickmakers, learnt
to write after he was of Age, carry'd the Chain for Sur-
veyors, who taught him Surveying, and he had now by his
Industry acquir'd a good Estate; and says he, I foresee, that
you will soon work this Man out of his Business & make a
Fortune in it at Philadelphia. He had not then the least
Intimation of my Intention to set up there or any where.—
These Friends were afterwards of great Use to me, as I
occasionally was to some of them.—They all continued their
Regard for me as long as they lived.—

Before I enter upon my public Appearance in Business,
it may be well to let you know the then State of my Mind,
with regard to my Principles and Morals, that you may see
how far those influenc'd the future Events of my Life. My
Parent's had early given me religious Impressions, and
brought me through my Childhood piously in the Dissenting
Way. But I was scarce 15 when, after doubting by turns of
several Points as I found them disputed in the different
Books I read, I began to doubt of Revelation it self. Some
Books against Deism fell into my Hands; they were said to
be the Substance of Sermons preached at Boyle's Lectures.
It happened that they wrought an Effect on me quite
contrary to what was intended by them: For the Arguments
of the Deists which were quoted to be refuted, appeared to
me much Stronger than the Refutations. In short I soon
became a thorough Deist. My Arguments perverted some
others, particularly Collins & Ralph: but each of them
having afterwards wrong'd me greatly without the least
Compunction, and recollecting Keith's Conduct towards me,
(who was another Freethinker) and my own towards Vernon
& Miss Read which at Times gave me great Trouble, I

began to suspect that this Doctrine tho' it might be true, was not very useful.—My London Pamphlet, which had for its Motto those Lines of Dryden

> ———*Whatever is, is right.*
> *Tho' purblind Man/ Sees but a Part of*
> *The Chain, the nearest Link,*
> *His Eyes not carrying to the equal Beam,*
> *That poizes all, above.**

And from the Attributes of God, his infinite Wisdom, Goodness & Power concluded that nothing could possibly be wrong in the World, & that Vice & Virtue were empty Distinctions, no such Things existing: appear'd now not so clever a Performance as I once thought it; and I doubted whether some Error had not insinuated itself unperceiv'd, into my Argument, so as to infect all that follow'd, as is common in metaphysical Reasonings.—I grew convinc'd that *Truth, Sincerity & Integrity* in Dealings between Man & Man, were of the utmost Importance to the Felicity of Life, and I form'd written Resolutions, (wch still remain in my Journal Book) to practise them ever while I lived. Revelation had indeed no weight with me as such; but I entertain'd an Opinion, that tho' certain Actions might not be bad *because* they were forbidden by it, or good *because* it commanded them; yet probably those Actions might be forbidden *because* they were bad for us, or commanded *because* they were beneficial to us, in their own Natures, all the Circumstances of things considered. And this Persuasion, with the kind hand of Providence, or some guardian Angel, or accidental favourable Circumstances & Situations, or all together, preserved me, (thro' this dangerous Time of Youth & the hazardous Situations I was sometimes in among Strangers, remote from the Eye & Advice of my Father,) without any *wilful* gross Immorality or Injustice that might have been expected from my Want of Religion.—I say *wilful*, because the Instances I have mentioned, had something of *Necessity* in them, from my Youth, Inexperience, & the Knavery of others.—I had therefore a tolerable Character to begin the

World with, I valued it properly, & determin'd to preserve it.—

We had not been long return'd to Philadelphia, before the New Types arriv'd from London.—We settled with Keimer, & left him by his Consent before he heard of it.—We found a House to hire near the Market, and took it. To lessen the Rent, (which was then but 24£ a Year tho' I have since known it to let for 70) We took in Tho⁵ Godfrey a Glazier & his Family, who were to pay a considerable Part of it. to us, and we to board with them. We had scarce opened our Letters & put our Press in Order, before George House, an Acquaintance of mine, brought a Countryman to us; whom he had met in the Street enquiring for a Printer. All our Cash was now expended in the Variety of Particulars we had been obliged to procure, & this Countryman's Five Shillings, being our first Fruits & coming so seasonably, gave me more Pleasure than any Crown I have since earn'd; and from the Gratitude I felt towards House, has made me often more ready than perhaps I should otherwise have been to assist young Beginners.—

There are Croakers in every Country always boding its Ruin. Such a one then lived in Philadelphia, a Person of Note, an elderly Man, with a wise Look and very grave Manner of Speaking. His Name was Samuel Mickle. This Gentleman, a Stranger to me, stopt one Day at my Door, and ask'd me if I was the young Man who had lately opened a new Printing-house: Being answer'd in the Affirmative; He said he was sorry for me; because it was an expensive Undertaking, & the Expence would be lost, for Philadelphia was a sinking Place, the People already half Bankrupts or near being so; all Appearances of the contrary such as new Buildings & the Rise of Rents, being to his certain Knowledge fallacious, for they were in fact among the Things that would soon ruin us. And he gave me such a Detail of Misfortunes now existing or that were soon to exist, that he left me half-melancholy. Had I known him before I engag'd in this Business, probably I never should have done it.—This Man continu'd to live in this decaying Place, &

to declaim in the same Strain, refusing for many Years to buy a House there, because all was going to Destruction, and at last I had the Pleasure of seeing him give five times as much for one as he might have bought it for when he first began his Croaking.——

I should have mention'd before, that in the Autumn of the preceding Year, I had form'd most of my ingenious Acquaintance into a Club, for mutual Improvement, which we call'd the Junto. We met on Friday Evenings. The Rules I drew up, requir'd that every Member in his Turn should produce one or more Queries on any Point of Morals, Politics or Natural Philosophy, to be discuss'd by the Company, and once in three Months produce and read an Essay of his own Writing on any Subject he pleased. Our Debates were to be under the Direction of a President, and to be conducted in the sincere Spirit of Enquiry after Truth, without fondness for Dispute, or Desire of Victory; and to prevent Warmth, all Expressions of Positiveness in Opinion, or of direct Contradiction, were after some time made contraband & prohibited under small pecuniary Penalties. The first Members were, Joseph Brientnal, a Copyer of Deeds for the Scriveners; a good-natur'd friendly middle-ag'd Man, a great Lover of Poetry, reading all he could meet with, & writing some that was tolerable; very ingenious in many little Nicknackeries, & of sensible Conversation. Thomas Godfrey, a self-taught Mathematician, great in his Way, & afterwards Inventor of what is now call'd Hadley's Quadrant. But he knew little out of his way, and was not a pleasing Companion, as like most Great Mathematicians I have met with, he expected unusual Precision in every thing said, or was forever denying or distinguishing upon Trifles, to the Disturbance of all Conversation.——He soon left us.——Nicholas Scull, a Surveyor, afterwards Surveyor-General, Who lov'd Books, & sometimes made a few Verses. William Parsons, bred a Shoemaker, but loving Reading, had acquir'd a considerable Share of Mathematics, which he first studied with a View to Astrology that he afterwards laught at. He also became Surveyor General.——William

Maugridge, a Joiner, & a most exquisite Mechanic, & a solid sensible Man. Hugh Meredith, Stephen Potts, & George Webb, I have Characteris'd before. Robert Grace, a young Gentleman of some Fortune, generous, lively & witty, a Lover of Punning and of his Friends. And William Coleman, then a Merchant's Clerk, about my Age, who had the coolest clearest Head, the best Heart, and the exactest Morals, of almost any Man I ever met with. He became afterwards a Merchant of great Note, and one of our Provincial Judges: Our Friendship continued without Interruption to his Death, upwards of 40 Years. And the Club continu'd almost as long. and was the best School of Philosophy, Morals & Politics that then existed in the Province; for our Queries which were read the Week preceding their Discussion, put us on reading with Attention upon the several Subjects, that we might speak more to the purpose: and here too we acquired better Habits of Conversation, every thing being studied in our Rules which might prevent our disgusting each other. From hence the long Continuance of the Club, which I shall have frequent Occasion to speak farther of hereafter; But my giving this Account of it here, is to show something of the Interest I had, every one of these exerting themselves in recommending Business to us.—Brientnal particularly procur'd us from the Quakers, the Printing 40 Sheets of their History, the rest being to be done by Keimer: and upon this·we work'd exceeding hard, for the Price was low. It was a Folio, Pro Patria Size, in Pica with Long Primer Notes. I compos'd of it a Sheet a Day, and Meredith work'd it off at Press. It was often 11 at Night and sometimes later, before I had finish'd my Distribution for the next days Work: For the little Jobbs sent in by our other Friends now & then put us back. But so determin'd I was to continue doing a Sheet a Day of the Folio, that one Night when having impos'd my Forms, I thought my Days Work over, one of them by accident was broken and two Pages reduc'd to Pie, I immediately distributed & compos'd it over again before I went to bed. And this Industry visible to our Neighbours began to give us Character and Credit; particularly I was told, that mention being made of the new Printing Office at the Merchants Every-night-Club, the general Opinion was that it must fail, there being already two Printers in the Place, Keimer & Bradford; but Doctor Baird (whom you and I saw many Years after at his native Place, St. Andrews in Scotland) gave a contrary Opinion; for the Industry of that Franklin, says he, is superior to any thing I ever saw of the kind: I see him still at work when I go home from Club; and he is at Work again before his Neighbours are out of bed. This struck the rest, and we soon after had Offers from one of them to supply us with Stationary. But as yet we did not chuse to engage in Shop Business.

I mention this Industry the more particularly and the more freely, tho' it seems to be talking in my own Praise, that those of my Posterity who shall read it, may know the Use of that Virtue, when they see its Effects in my Favour throughout this Relation.—

George Webb, who had found a Friend that lent him wherewith to purchase his Time of Keimer, now came to offer himself as a Joureyman to us. We could not then imploy him, but I foolishly let him know, as a Secret, that I soon intended to begin a Newspaper, & might then have Work for him.—My Hopes of Success as I told him were founded on this, that the then only Newspaper, printed by Bradford was a paltry thing, wretchedly manag'd, no way entertaining; and yet was profitable to him.—I therefore thought a good Paper could scarcely fail of good Encouragem^t I requested Webb not to mention it, but he told it to Keimer, who immediately, to be beforehand with me, published Proposals for Printing one himself,—on which Webb was to be employ'd.—I resented this, and to counteract them, as I could not yet begin our Paper, I wrote several Pieces of Entertainm^t for Bradford's Paper, under the Title of the Busy Body which Breintnal continu'd some Months. By this means the Attention of the Publick was fix'd on that Paper, & Keimers Proposals which we burlesqu'd & ridicul'd, were disregarded. He began his Paper however,

and after carrying it on three Quarters of a Year, with at
most only 90 Subscribers, he offer'd it to me for a Trifle,
& I having been ready some time to go on with it, took it
in hand directly. and it prov'd in a few Years extreamly
profitable to me—

I perceive that I am apt to speak in the singular Number,
though our Partnership still continu'd. The Reason may be,
that in fact the whole Management of the Business lay upon
me. Meredith was no Compostor, a poor Pressman, &
seldom sober. My Friends lamented my Connection with
him, but I was to make the best of it.

Our first Papers made a quite different Appearance from
any before in the Province, a better Type & better printed:
but some spirited Remarks of my Writing on the Dispute
then going on between Govr Burnet and the Massachusetts
Assembly, struck the principal People, occasion'd the Paper
& the Manager of it to be much talk'd of, & in a few Weeks
brought them all to be our Subscribers. Their Example was
follow'd by many, and our Number went on growing continually.—This was one of the first good Effects of my
having learnt a little to scribble.—Another was, that the
leading Men, seeing a News Paper now in the hands of one
who could also handle a Pen, thought it convenient to oblige
& encourage me.—Bradford still printed the Votes & Laws
& other Publick Business. He had printed an Address of the
House to the Governor in a coarse blundering manner; We
reprinted it elegantly & correctly, and sent one to every
Member. They were sensible of the Difference, it
strengthen'd the Hands of our Friends in the House, and
they voted us their Printers for the Year ensuing.

Among my Friends in the House I must not forget Mr
Hamilton before mentioned, who was now then returned
from England & had a Seat in it. He interested himself for
me strongly in that Instance, as he did in many others
afterwards, continuing his Patronage till his Death. I got his
Son once 500£ Mr Vernon about this time put me in mind
of the Debt I ow'd him:—but did not press me.—I wrote
him an ingenuous Letter of Acknowledgements, crav'd his

Forbearance a little longer which he allow'd me, & as soon as I was able I paid the Principal with Interest & many Thanks.—So that *Erratum* was now in some degree corrected.—

But now another Difficulty came upon me, which I had never the least Reason to expect. Mr. Meredith's Father, who was to have paid for our Printing House according to the Expectations given me, was able to advance only one Hundred Pounds, Currency, which had been paid, & a Hundred more was due to the Merchant; who grew impatient & su'd us all. We gave Bail, but saw that if the Money could not be rais'd in time, the Suit must come to a Judgment & Execution, & our hopeful Prospects must with us be ruined, as the Press & Letters must be sold for Payment, perhaps at half-Price.—In this Distress two true Friends whose Kindness I have never forgotten nor ever shall I forget while I can remember any thing, came to me separately unknown to each other, and without any Application from me, offering each of them to advance me all the Money that should be necessary to enable me to take the whole Business upon my self if that should be practicable, but they did not like my continuing the Partnership with Meredith, who as they said was often seen drunk in the Streets, & playing at low Games in Alehouses, much to our Discredit. These two Friends were *William Coleman & Robert Grace.* I told them I could not propose a Separation while any Prospect remain'd of the Merediths fulfilling their Part of our Agreement. Because I thought my self under great Obligations to them for what they had done & would do if they could. But if they finally fail'd in their Performance, & our Partnership must be dissolv'd, I should then think myself at Liberty to accept the Assistance of my Friends. Thus the matter rested for some time. When I said to my Partner, perhaps your Father is dissatisfied at the Part you have undertaken in this Affair of ours, and is unwilling to advance for you & me what he would for you alone: If that is the Case, tell me, and I will resign the whole to you & go about my Business. No—says he, my

Father has really been disappointed and is really unable; and I am unwilling to distress him farther. I see this is a Business I am not fit for. I was bred a Farmer, and it was a Folly in me to come to Town & put my self at 30 Years of Age an Apprentice to learn a new Trade. Many of our Welsh People are going to settle in North Carolina where Land is cheap: I am inclin'd to go with them, & follow my old Employment. You may find Friends to assist you. If you will take the Debts of the Company upon you, return to my Father the hundred Pound he has advanc'd, pay my little personal Debts, and give me Thirty Pounds & a new Saddle, I will relinquish the Partnership & leave the whole in your Hands. I agreed to this Proposal. It was drawn up in Writing, sign'd & seal'd immediately. I gave him what he demanded & he went soon after to Carolina; from whence he sent me next Year two long Letters, containing the best Account that had been given of that Country, the Climate, Soil, Husbandry, &c. for in those Matters he was very judicious. I printed them in the Papers, and they gave grate Satisfaction to the Publick.

As soon as he was gone, I recurr'd to my two Friends; and because I would not give an unkind Preference to either, I took half what each had offered & I wanted, of one, & half of the other; paid off the Company Debts, and went on with the Business in my own Name, advertising that the Partnership was dissolved. I think this was in or about the Year 1729.——

About this Time there was a Cry among the People for more Paper-Money, only 15,000£ being extant in the Province & that soon to be sunk. The wealthy Inhabitants oppos'd any Addition, being against all Paper Currency, from an Apprehension that it would depreciate as it had done in New England to the Prejudice of all Creditors.——We had discuss'd this Point in our Junto, where I was on the Side of an Addition, being persuaded that the first small Sum struck in 1723 had done much good, by increasing the Trade Employment, & Number of Inhabitants in the Province, since I now saw all the old Houses inhabited, & many

new ones building, where as I remember'd well, that when
I first walk'd about the Streets of Philadelphia, eating my
Roll, I saw most of the Houses in Walnut street between
Second & Front streets with Bills on their Doors, to be let;
and many likewise in Chesnut Street, & other Streets; which
made me then think the Inhabitants of the City were one
after another deserting it.—Our Debates possess'd me so
fully of the Subject, that I wrote and printed an anonymous
Pamphlet on it, entituled, *The Nature & Necessity of a Paper
Currency*. It was well receiv'd by the common People in
general; but the Rich Men dislik'd it; for it increas'd and
strengthen'd the Clamour for more Money; and they happening to have no Writers among them that were able to
answer it, their Opposition slacken'd, & the Point was
carried by a Majority in the House. My Friends there, who
conceiv'd I had been of some Service, thought fit to reward
me, by employing me in printing the Money, a very profitable Jobb, and a great Help to me.—This was another
Advantage gain'd by my being able to write The Utility of
this Currency became by Time and Experience so evident,
as never afterwards to be much disputed, so that it grew
soon to 55,000£ and in 1739 to 80,000£ since which it arose
during War to upwards of 350,000£. Trade, Building &
Inhabitants all the while increasing. Tho' I now think there
are Limits beyond which the Quantity may be hurtful.—

I soon after obtain'd, thro' my Friend Hamilton, the
Printing of the NewCastle Paper Money, another profitable
Jobb, as I then thought it; small Things appearing great to
those in small Circumstances. And these to me were really
great Advantages, as they were great Encouragements.—He
procured me also the Printing of the Laws and Votes of
that Government which continu'd in my Hands as long as
I follow'd the Business.—

I now open'd a little Stationer's Shop. I had in it Blanks
of all Sorts the correctest that ever appear'd among us, being
assisted in that by my Friend Brientnal; I had also Paper,
Parchment, Chapmen's Books, &c. One Whitemash a Compositor I had known in London, an excellent Workman now

came to me & work'd with me constantly & diligently, and I took an Apprentice the Son of Aquila Rose. I began now gradually to pay off the Debt I was under for the Printing-House.—In order to secure my Credit and Character as a Tradesman, I took care not only to be in *Reality* Industrious & frugal, but to avoid all *Appearances* of the Contrary. I drest plainly; I was seen at no Places of idle Diversion; I never went out a-fishing or shooting; a Book, indeed, sometimes debauch'd me from my Work; but that was seldom, snug, & gave no Scandal: and to show that I was not above my Business, I sometimes brought home the Paper I purchas'd at the Stores, thro' the Streets on a Wheelbarrow. Thus being esteem'd an industrious thriving young Man, and paying duly for what I bought, the Merchants who imported Stationary solicited my Custom, others propos'd supplying me with Books, & I went on swimmingly.—In the mean time Keimer's Credit & Business declining daily, he was at last forc'd to sell his Printing-house to satisfy his Creditors. He went to Barbadoes, & there lived some Years, in very poor Circumstances.

His Apprentice David Harry, whom I had instructed while I work'd with him, set up in his Place at Philadelphia having bought his Materials. I was at first apprehensive of a powerful Rival in, Harry, as his Friends were very able, & had a good deal of Interest. I therefore propos'd a Partnership to him; which he, fortunately for me, rejected with Scorn. He was very proud, dress'd like a Gentleman, liv'd expensively, took much Diversion & Pleasure abroad, ran in debt, & neglected his Business, upon which all Business left him; and finding nothing to do, he follow'd Keimer to Barbadoes; taking the Printinghouse with him There this Apprentice employ'd his former Master as a Journeyman. They quarrel'd often. Harry went continually behind-hand, and at length was forc'd to sell his Types, and return to his Country Work in Pensilvania. The Person that bought them, employ'd Keimer to use them, but in a few Years he died. There remain'd now no Competitor with me in Philadelphia, but the old one, Bradford, who was rich & easy, did a little Printing now & then by straggling Hands, but was not very anxious about the Business. However, as he kept the Post Office, it was imagined he had better Opportunities of obtaining News, his Paper was thought a better Distributer of Advertisements than mine, & therefore had many more, which was a profitable thing to him & a Disadvantage to me. For tho' I did indeed receive & send Papers by the Post, yet the publick Opinion was otherwise; for what I did send was by Bribing the Riders who took them privately: Bradford being unkind enough to forbid it: which occasion'd some Resentment on my Part; and I thought so meanly of him for it, that when I afterwards came into his Situation, I took care never to imitate it.

I had hitherto continu'd to board with Godfrey who lived in Part of my House with his Wife & Children, & had one Side of the Shop for his Glazier's Business, tho' he work'd little, being always absorb'd in his Mathematics.—Mrs Godfrey projected a Match for me with a Relation's Daughter, took Opportunities of bringing us often together, till a serious Courtship on my Part ensu'd the Girl being in herself very deserving. The old Folks encourag'd me by continual Invitations to Supper, & by leaving us together, till at length it was time to explain. Mrs Godfrey manag'd our little Treaty. I let her know that I expected as much Money with their Daughter as would pay off my Remaining Debt for the Printing-house, which I believe was not then above a Hundred Pounds. She brought me Word they had no such Sum to spare. I said they might mortgage their House in the Loan Office.—The Answer to this after some Days was, they did not approve the Match; that on Enquiry of Bradford they had been inform'd the Printing Business was not a profitable one, the Types would soon be worn out & more wanted, that S. Keimer & D. Harry had fail'd one after the other, and I should probably soon follow them; and therefore I was forbidden the House, & the Daughter shut up.—Whether this was a real Change of Sentiment, or only Artifice, on a Supposition of our being too far engag'd in Affection to retract, & therefore that we should steal a

Marriage, which would leave them at Liberty to give or withold what they pleas'd, I know not: But I suspected the latter, resented it, and went no more. Mrs Godfrey brought me afterwards some more favourable Accounts of their Disposition, & would have drawn me on again: But I declared absolutely my Resolution to have nothing more to do with that Family. This was resented by the Godfreys, we differ'd, and they removed, leaving me the whole House, and I resolved to take no more Inmates. But this Affair having turn'd my Thoughts to Marriage, I look'd round me, and made Overtures of Acquaintance in other Places; but soon found that the Business of a Printer being generally thought a poor one, I was not to expect Money with a Wife unless with such a one, as I should not otherwise think agreable.—In the mean time, that hard-to-be-govern'd Passion of Youth, had hurried me frequently into Intrigues with low Women that fell in my Way, which were attended with some Expence & great Inconvenience, besides a continual Risque to my Health by a Distemper which of all Things I dreaded, tho' by great good Luck I escaped it.—

A friendly Correspondence as Neighbours & old Acquaintances, had continued between me & Mrs Read's Family who all had a Regard for me from the time of my first Lodging in their House. I was often invited there and consulted in their Affairs, wherein I sometimes was of Service.—I pity'd poor Miss Read's unfortunate Situation who was generally dejected, seldom chearful, and avoided Company. I consider'd my Giddiness & Inconstancy when in London as in a great degree the Cause of her Unhappiness.; tho' the Mother was good enough to think the Fault more her own than mine, as she had prevented our Marrying before I went thither, and persuaded the other Match in my Absence, . Our mutual Affection was revived, but there were now great Objections to our Union. That Match was indeed look'd upon as invalid a preceding Wife being said to be living in England; but this could not easily be prov'd, because of the Distance &c. And tho' there was a Report of his Death, it was not certain. Then, tho' it should be true, he had left many Debts which his Successor might be call'd upon to pay. We ventured however, over all these Difficulties, and I took her to Wife Sept. 1. 1730. None of the Inconveniencies happened that we had apprehended, she prov'd a good & faithful Helpmate, assisted me much by attending the Shop, we throve together, and have ever mutually endeavour'd to make each other happy.—Thus I corrected that great *Erratum* as well as I could.

About this Time our Club meeting, not at a Tavern, but in a little Room of Mr Grace's set apart for that Purpose; a Proposition was made by me, that since our Books were often referr'd to in our Disquisitions upon the Queries, it might be convenient to us to have them all together where we met, that upon Occasion they might be consulted; and By thus clubbing our Books to a common Library, we should, while we lik'd to keep them together, have each of us the Advantage of using the Books of all the other Members, which would be nearly as beneficial as if each owned the whole. It was lik'd and agreed to, & we fill'd one End of the Room with such Books as we could best spare. The Number was not so great as we expected; and tho' they had been of great Use, yet some Inconveniencies occurring for want of due Care of them, the Collection after about a Year was separated, & each took his Books home again.

And now I set on foot my first Project of a public Nature, that for a Subscription Library. I drew up the Proposals, got them put into Form by our great Scrivener Brockden, and by the help of my Friends in the Junto, procur'd Fifty Subscribers of 40/ each to begin with & 10/ a Year for 50 Years, the Term our Company was to continue. We afterwards obtain'd a Charter, the Company being increas'd to 100. This was the Mother of all the N American Subscription Libraries now so numerous. It is become a great thing itself, & continually increasing.—These Libraries have improv'd the general Conversation of the Americans, made the common Tradesmen & Farmers as intelligent as most Gentlemen from other Countries, and perhaps have contributed in some degree to the Stand so generally made throughout the Colonies in Defence of their Privileges.—*

[PART 2]

Mem:º

Thus far was written with the Intention express'd in the Beginning. and therefore contains several little family Anecdotes of no Importance to others. What follows was written many Years after in compliance with the Advice contain'd in these Letters, and accordingly intended for the Publick. The Affairs of the Revolution occasion'd the Interruption.

Letter from Mr Abel James with Notes of my Life, to be here inserted. Also—

Letter from Mr Vaughan to the same purpose

My dear & honored Friend.

I have often been desirous of writing to thee, but could not be reconciled to the Thought that the Letter might fall into the Hands of the British, lest some Printer or busy Body should publish some Part of the Contents & give our Friends Pain & myself Censure.

Some Time since there fell into my Hands to my great Joy about 23 Sheets in thy own hand-writing containing an Account of the Parentage & Life of thyself, directed to thy Son ending in the Year 1730 with which there were Notes likewise in thy writing, a Copy of which I inclose in Hopes it may be a means if thou continuedst it up to a later period, that the first & latter part may be put together; & if it is not yet continued, I hope thou wilt not delay it, Life is uncertain as the Preacher tells us, and what will the World say if kind, humane & benevolent Ben Franklin should leave his Friends & the World deprived of so pleasing & profitable a Work, a Work which would be useful & entertaining not only to a few, but to millions.

The Influence Writings under that Class have on the Minds of Youth is very great, and has no where appeared so plain as in our public Friends' Journals. It almost insensibly leads the Youth into the Resolution of endeavouring to become as good and as eminent as the Journalist. Should thine for Instance when published, and I think it could not fail of it, lead the Youth to equal the Industry & Temperance of thy early Youth, what a Blessing with that Class would such a Work be. I know of no Character living nor many of them put together, who has so much in his Power as Thyself to promote a greater Spirit of Industry & early Attention to Business, Frugality and Temperance with the American Youth. Not that I think the Work would have no other Merit & Use in the World, far from it, but the first is of such vast Importance, that I know nothing that can equal it.

The foregoing letter and the minutes accompanying it being shewn to a friend, I received from him the following:

LETTER FROM MR. BENJAMIN VAUGHAN.

Paris, January 31, 1783.

"MY DEAREST SIR,

"When I had read over your sheets of minutes of the principal incidents of your life, recovered for you by your Quaker acquaintance; I told you I would send you a letter expressing my reasons why I thought it would be useful to complete and publish it as he desired. Various concerns have for some time past prevented this letter being written, and I do not know whether it was worth any expectation: happening to be at leisure however at present, I shall by writing at least interest and instruct myself; but as the terms I am inclined to use may tend to offend a person of your manners, I shall only tell you how I would address any other person, who was as good and as great as yourself, but less diffident. I would say to him, Sir, I *solicit* the history of your life from the following motives.

"Your history is so remarkable, that if you do not give it, somebody else will certainly give it; and perhaps so as nearly to do as much harm, as your own management of the thing might do good.

"It will moreover present a table of the internal circumstances of your country, which will very much tend to invite to it settlers of virtuous and manly minds. And considering the eagerness with which such information is sought by them, and the extent of your reputation, I do not know of a more efficacious advertisement than your Biography would give.

"All that has happened to you is also connected with the detail of the manners and situation of *a rising* people; and in this respect I do not think that the writings of Ceasar and Tacitus can be more interesting to a true judge of human nature and society.

"But these, Sir, are small reasons in my opinion, compared with the chance which your life will give for the forming of future great men; and in conjunction with your *Art of Virtue*, (which you design to publish) of improving the features of private character, and consequently of aiding all happiness both public and domestic.

"The two works I allude to, Sir, will in particular give a noble rule and example of *self-education*. School and other education constantly proceed upon false principles, and shew a clumsy apparatus pointed at a false mark; but your apparatus is simple, and the mark a true one; and while parents and young persons are left destitute of other just means of estimating and becoming prepared for a reasonable course in life, your discovery that the thing is in many a man's private power, will be invaluable!

"Influence upon the private character late in life, is not only an influence late in life, but a weak influence. It is in *youth* that we plant our chief habits and prejudices; it is in youth that we take our party as to profession, pursuits, and matrimony. In youth therefore the turn is given; in youth the education even of the next generation is given; in youth the private and public character is determined; and the term of life extending but from youth to age, life ought to begin well from youth; and more especially *before* we take our party as to our principal objects.

"But your Biography will not merely teach self-education, but the education of *a wise man*; and the wisest man will receive lights and improve his progress, by seeing detailed the conduct of another wise man. And why are weaker men to be deprived of such helps, when we see our race has been blundering on in the dark, almost without a guide in this particular, from the farthest trace of time. Shew then, Sir, how much is to be done, *both to sons and fathers*; and invite all wise men to become like yourself; and other men to become wise.

"When we see how cruel statesmen and warriors can be to the humble race, and how absurd distinguished men can be to their acquaintance, it will be instructive to observe the instances multiply of pacific acquiescing manners; and to find how compatible it is to be great and *domestic*; enviable and yet *good-humoured*.

"The little private incidents which you will also have to relate, will have considerable use, as we want above all things, *rules of prudence in ordinary affairs*; and it will be curious to see how you have acted in these. It will be so far a sort of key to life, and explain many things that all men ought to have once explained to them, to give them a chance of becoming wise by foresight.

"The nearest thing to having experience of one's own, is to have other people's affairs brought before us in a shape that is interesting; this is sure to happen from your pen. Your affairs and management will have an air of simplicity or importance that will not fail to strike; and I am convinced you have conducted them with as much originality as if you had been conducting discussions in politics or philosophy; and what more worthy of experiments and system, (its importance and its errors considered) than human life!

"Some men have been virtuous blindly, others have speculated fantastically, and others have been shrewd to bad purposes; but you, Sir, I am sure, will give under your hand, nothing but what is at the same moment, wise, practical, and good.

"Your account of yourself (for I suppose the parallel I am drawing for Dr. Franklin, will hold not only in point of character but of private history), will shew that you are ashamed of no origin; a thing the more important, as you prove how little necessary all origin is to happiness, virtue, or greatness.

"As no end likewise happens without a means, so we shall find, Sir, that even you yourself framed a plan by which you became considerable; but at the same time we may see that though the event is flattering, the means are as simple as wisdom could make them; that is depending upon nature, virtue, thought, and habit.

"Another thing demonstrated will be the propriety of every man's waiting for his time for appearing upon the stage of the world. Our sensations being very much fixed to the moment, we are apt to forget that more moments are to follow the first, and consequently that man should arrange his conduct so as to suit the *whole* of a life. Your attribution appears to have been applied to your *life*, and the passing moments of it have been enlivened with content and enjoyment, instead of being tormented with foolish impatience or regrets. Such a conduct is easy for those who make virtue and themselves their standard, and who try to keep themselves in countenance by examples of other truly great men, of whom patience is so often the characteristic.

"Your Quaker correspondent, Sir, (for here again I will suppose the subject of my letter resembling Dr. Franklin,) praised your frugality, diligence, and temperance, which he considered as a pattern for all youth: but it is singular that he should have forgotten your modesty, and your disinterestedness, without which you never could have waited for your advancement, or found your situation in the mean time comfortable; which is a strong lesson to shew the poverty of glory, and the importance of regulating our minds.

"If this correspondent had known the nature of your reputation as well as I do, he would have said; your former writings and measures would secure attention to your Biography, and Art of Virtue; and your Biography and Art of Virtue, in return, would secure attention to them. This is an advantage attendant upon a various character, and which brings all that belongs to it into greater play; and it is the more useful, as perhaps more persons are at a loss for the *means* of improving their minds and characters, than they are for the time or the inclination to do it.

"But there is one concluding reflection, Sir, that will shew the use of your life as a mere piece of biography. This style of writing seems a little gone out of vogue, and yet it is a very useful one; and your specimen of it may be particularly serviceable, as it will make a subject of comparison with the lives of various public cut-throats and intriguers, and with absurd monastic self-tormentors, or vain literary triflers. If it encourages more writings of the same kind with your own, and induces more men to spend lives fit to be written; it will be worth all Plutarch's Lives put together.

"But being tired of figuring to myself a character of which every feature suits only one man in the world, without giving him the praise of it; I shall end my letter, my dear Dr. Franklin, with a personal application to your proper self.

"I am earnestly desirous then, my dear Sir, that you should let the world into the traits of your genuine character, as civil broils may otherwise tend to disguise or traduce it. Considering your great age, the caution of your character, and your peculiar style of thinking, it is not likely that any one besides yourself can be sufficiently master of the facts of your life, or the intentions of your mind.

"Besides all this, the immense revolution of the present period, will necessarily turn our attention towards the author of it; and when virtuous principles have been pretended in it, it will be highly important to shew that such have really influenced; and, as your own character will be the principal one to receive a scrutiny, it is proper (even for its effects upon your vast and rising country, as well as upon England and upon Europe), that it should stand respectable and eternal. For the furtherance of human happiness, I have always maintained that it is necessary to prove that man is not even at present a vicious and detestable animal; and still more to prove that good management may greatly amend him; and it is for much the same reason, that I am anxious to see the opinion established, that there are fair characters existing among the individuals of the race; for the moment that all men, without exception, shall be conceived abandoned, good people will cease efforts deemed to be hopeless, and perhaps think of taking their share in the scramble of life, or at least of making it comfortable principally for themselves.

"Take then, my dear Sir, this work most speedily into hand: shew yourself good as you are good, temperate as you are temperate; and above all things, prove yourself as one who from your infancy have loved justice, liberty, and concord, in a way that has made it natural and consistent for you to have acted, as we have seen you act in the last seventeen years of your life. Let Englishmen be made not only to respect, but even to love you. When they think well of individuals in your native country, they will go nearer to thinking well of your country; and when your countrymen see themselves well thought of by Englishmen, they will go nearer to thinking well of England. Extend your views even further; do not stop at those who speak the English tongue, but after having settled so many points in nature and politics, think of bettering the whole race of men.

"As I have not read any part of the life in question, but know only the character that lived it, I write somewhat at hazard. I am sure however, that the life, and the treatise I allude to (on the *Art of Virtue*), will necessarily fulfil the chief of my expectations; and still more so if you take up the measure of suiting these performances to the several views above stated. Should they even prove unsuccessful in all that a sanguine admirer of yours hopes from them, you will at least have framed pieces to interest the human mind; and whoever gives a feeling of pleasure that is innocent to man, has added so much to the fair side of a life otherwise too much darkened by anxiety, and too much injured by pain.

"In the hope therefore that you will listen to the prayer addressed to you in this letter, I beg to subscribe myself, my dearest Sir, &c. &c.

"Signed   BENJ. VAUGHAN."

Continuation of the
Account of my Life. Begun at Passy 1784

It is some time since I receiv'd the above Letters, but I have been too busy till now to think of complying with the Request they contain. It might too be much better done if I were at home among my Papers, which would aid my Memory, & help to ascertain Dates. But my Return being uncertain, and having just now a little Leisure, I will endeavour to recollect & write what I can; If I live to get home, it may there be corrected and improv'd

Not having any Copy here of what is already written, I know not whether an Account is given of the means I used to establish the Philadelphia publick Library, which from a small Beginning is now become so considerable. though I remember to have come down to near the Time of that Transaction., 1730. I will therefore begin here, with an Account of it, which may be struck out if found to have been already given.—

At the time I establish'd my self in Pensylvania, there was not a good Bookseller's Shop in any of the Colonies to the Southward of Boston. In New-York & Philad^a the Printers were indeed Stationers, they sold only Paper, &c. Almanacks, Ballads, and a few common School Books. Those who lov'd Reading were oblig'd to send for their Books from England.—The Members of the Junto had each a few. We had left the Alehouse where we first met, and hired a Room to hold our Club in. I propos'd that we should all of us bring our Books to that Room, where they would not only be ready to consult in our Conferences, but become a common Benefit, each of us being at Liberty to borrow such as he wish'd to read at home. This was accordingly done, and for some time contented us. Finding the Advantage of this little Collection, I propos'd to render the Benefit from Books more common by commencing a Public Subscription Library. I drew a Sketch of the Plan and Rules that would be necessary, and got a skilful Conveyancer Mr Charles Brockden to put the whole in Form of Articles of Agreement to be subscribed, by which each Subscriber engag'd to pay a certain Sum down for the first Purchase of Books and an annual Contribution for encreasing them.—So few were the Readers at that time in Philadelphia, and the Majority of us so poor, that I was not able with great Industry to find more than Fifty Persons, mostly young Tradesmen, willing to pay down for this purpose Forty shillings each, & Ten Shillings per Annum. On this little Fund we began. The Books were imported. The Library was open one Day in the Week for lending them to the Subscribers, on their Promisory Notes to pay Double the Value if not duly returned. The Institution soon manifested its Utility, was imitated by other Towns and in other Provinces, the Librarys were augmented by Donations, Reading became fashionable, and our People having no publick Amusements to divert their Attention from Study became better acquainted with Books, and in a few Years were observ'd by Strangers to be better instructed & more intelligent than People of the same Rank generally are in other Countries.—

When we were about to sign the above-mentioned Articles, which were to be binding on us, our Heirs, &c for fifty Years, Mr Brockden, the Scrivener, said to us, "You are young Men, but it is scarce probable that any of you will live to see the Expiration of the Term fix'd in this Instrument." A Number of us, however, are yet living: But the Instrument was after a few Years rendred null by a Charter that incorporated & gave Perpetuity to the Company.—

The Objections, & Reluctances I met with in Soliciting the Subscriptions, made me soon feel the Impropriety of presenting one's self as the Proposer of any useful Project that might be suppos'd to raise one's Reputation in the smallest degree above that of one's Neighbours, when one has need of their Assistance to accomplish that Project. I therefore put my self as much as I could out of sight, and stated it as a Scheme of *a Number of Friends*, who had requested me to go about and propose it to such as they thought Lovers of Reading. In this way my Affair went on more smoothly, and I ever after practis'd it on such Occasions; and from my frequent Successes, can heartily recommend it. The present little Sacrifice of your Vanity will afterwards be amply repaid. If it remains a while uncertain to whom the Merit belongs, some one more vain than yourself will be encourag'd to claim it, and then even Envy will be dispos'd to do you Justice, by plucking those assum'd Feathers, & restoring them to their right Owner.

This Library afforded me the Means of Improvement by constant Study, for which I set apart an Hour or two each Day; and thus repair'd in some Degree the Loss of the Learned Education my Father once intended for me. Reading was the only Amusement I allow'd my self. I spent no time in Taverns, Games, or Frolicks of any kind. And my Industry in my Business continu'd as indefatigable as it was necessary. I was in debt for my Printing-house, I had a young Family coming on to be educated, and I had to contend with for Business two Printers who were establish'd in the Place before me,.. My Circumstances however grew daily easier,: my original Habits of Frugality continuing. And My Father having among his Instructions to me when a Boy, frequently repeated a Proverb of Solomon, *"Seest thou a Man diligent in his Calling, he shall stand before Kings, he shall not stand before mean Men."** I from thence consider'd Industry as a Means of obtaining Wealth and Distinction, which encourag'd me; tho' I did not think that I should ever literally stand before Kings, which however has since happened.—for I have stood before five, & even had the honour of sitting down with one, the King of Denmark, to Dinner.

We have an English Proverb that says,

> He that would thrive
> Must ask his Wife;

it was lucky for me that I had one as much dispos'd to Industry & Frugality as my self. She assisted me chearfully in my Business, folding & stitching Pamphlets, tending Shop, purchasing old Linen Rags for the Paper-makers, &c &c. We kept no idle Servants, our Table was plain & simple, our Furniture of the cheapest. For instance my Breakfast was a long time Bread & Milk, (no Tea,) and I ate it out of a twopenny earthen Porringer with a Pewter Spoon. But mark how Luxury will enter Families, and make a Progress, in Spite of Principle. Being Call'd one Morning to Breakfast, I found it in a China Bowl with a Spoon of Silver. They had been bought for me without my Knowledge by my Wife, and had cost her the enormous Sum of three and twenty Shillings, for which she had no other Excuse or Apology to make, but that she thought *her* Husband deserv'd a Silver Spoon & China Bowl as well as any of his Neighbours. This was the first Appearance of Plate & China in our House, which afterwards in a Course of Years as our Wealth encreas'd, augmented gradually to several Hundred Pounds in Value.—

I had been religiously educated as a Presbyterian; and tho' some of the Dogmas of that Persuasion, such as the Eternal Decrees of God, Election, Reprobation, &c. appear'd to me unintelligible, others doubtful, & I early absented myself from the Public Assemblies of the Sect, Sunday being my Studying-Day, I never was without some religious Principles; I never doubted, for instance, the Existance of the Deity, that he made the World, & govern'd it by his Providence; that the most acceptable Service of God was the doing Good to Man; that our Souls are immortal; and that all Crime will be punished & Virtue rewarded either here or hereafter; these I esteem'd the Essentials of every Religion, and being to be found in all the Religions we had in our Country I respected them all, tho' with different degrees of Respect as I found them more or less mix'd with other Articles which without any Tendency to inspire, promote or confirm Morality, serv'd principally to divide us & make us unfriendly to one another.—This Respect to all, with an Opinion that the worst had some good Effects, induc'd me to avoid all Discourse that might tend to lessen the good Opinion another might have of his own Religion; and as our Province increas'd in People and new Places of worship were continually wanted, & generally erected by voluntary Contribution, my Mite for such purpose, whatever might be the Sect, was never refused.——

Tho' I seldom attended any Public Worship, I had still an Opinion of its Propriety, and of its Utility when rightly conducted, and I regularly paid my annual Subscription for the Support of the only Presbyterian Minister or Meeting we had in Philadelphia. He us'd to visit me sometimes as a Friend, and admonish me to attend his Administrations, and I was now and then prevail'd on to do so, once for five Sundays successively. Had he been, *in my Opinion*, a good Preacher perhaps I might have continued, notwithstanding the occasion I had for the Sunday's Leisure in my Course of Study: But his Discourses were chiefly either polemic, Arguments, or Explications of the peculiar Doctrines of our Sect, and were all to me very dry, uninteresting and unedifying, since not a single moral Principle was inculcated or enforc'd, their Aim seeming to be rather to make us Presbyterians than good Citizens. At length he took for his Text that Verse of the 4th Chapter of Philippians, *Finally, Brethren, Whatsoever Things are true, honest, just, pure, lovely, or of good report, if there be any virtue, or any praise, think on these Things*;* & I imagin'd in a Sermon on such a Text, we could not miss of having some Morality: But he confin'd himself to five Points only as meant by the Apostle, viz. 1. Keeping holy the Sabbath Day. 2. Being diligent in Reading the Holy Scriptures. 3. Attending duly the Publick Worship. 4. Partaking of the Sacrament. 5. Paying a due Respect to God's Ministers.——These might be all good Things, but as they were not the kind of good Things that I expected from that Text, I despaired of ever meeting with them from any other, was disgusted, and attended his Preaching no more.—— I had some Years before compos'd a little Liturgy or Form of Prayer for my own private Use, viz, in 1728. entitled, *Articles of Belief & Acts of Religion*. I return'd to the Use of this, and went no more to the public Assemblies.——My Conduct might be blameable, but I leave it without attempting farther to excuse it, my present purpose being to relate Facts, and not to make Apologies for them.——

It was about this time that I conceiv'd the bold and arduous Project of arriving at moral Perfection. I wish'd to live without committing any Fault at any time; I would conquer all that either Natural Inclination, Custom, or Company might lead me into. As I knew, or thought I knew, what was right and wrong, I did not see why I might not *always* do the one and avoid the other. But I soon found I had undertaken a Task of more Difficulty than I had imagined: While my *Attention was taken up* Care was employ'd in guarding against one Fault, I was often surpriz'd by another. Habit took the Advantage of Inattention. Inclination was sometimes too strong for Reason. I concluded at length, that the mere speculative Conviction that it was our Interest to be compleatly virtuous, was not sufficient to prevent our Slipping, and that the contrary Habits must be broken and good Ones acquired and established, before we can have any Dependance on a steady uniform Rectitude of Conduct. For this purpose I therefore contriv'd the following Method.—

In the various Enumerations of the moral Virtues I had met with in my Reading, I found the Catalogue more or less numerous, as different Writers included more or fewer Ideas under the same Name. Temperance, for Example, was by some confin'd to Eating & Drinking, while by others it was extended to mean the moderating every other Pleasure, Appetite, Inclination or Passion, bodily or mental, even to our Avarice & Ambition. I propos'd to myself, for the sake of Clearness, to use rather more Names with fewer Ideas annex'd to each, than a few Names with more Ideas; and I included under Thirteen Names of Virtues all that at that time occurr'd to me as necessary or desirable, and annex'd to each a short Precept, which fully express'd the Extent I gave to its Meaning.—

These Names of Virtues with their Precepts were

1. TEMPERANCE.

Eat not to Dulness
Drink not to Elevation.

2. SILENCE.

Speak not but what may benefit others or your self. Avoid trifling Conversation.

3. ORDER.

Let all your Things have their Places. Let each Part of your Business have its Time.

4. RESOLUTION.

Resolve to perform what you ought. Perform without fail what you resolve.

5. FRUGALITY.

Make no Expence but to do good to others or yourself: i. e. Waste nothing.

6. INDUSTRY.

Lose no Time.—Be always employ'd in something useful.—Cut off all unnecessary Actions.—

7. SINCERITY.

Use no hurtful Deceit.
Think innocently and justly; and, if you speak; speak accordingly.

8. JUSTICE.

Wrong none, by doing Injuries or omitting the Benefits that are your Duty.

9. MODERATION.

Avoid Extreams. Forbear resenting Injuries so much as you think they deserve.

10. CLEANLINESS

Tolerate no Uncleanness in Body, Cloaths or Habitation.—

11. TRANQUILITY

Be not disturbed at Trifles, or at Accidents common or unavoidable.

12. CHASTITY.

Rarely use Venery but for Health or Offspring; Never to Dulness, Weakness, or the Injury of your own or another's Peace or Reputation.—

13. HUMILITY.
Imitate Jesus and Socrates.——

My intention being to acquire the *Habitude* of all these
Virtues, I judg'd it would be well not to distract my
Attention by attempting the whole at once, but to fix it on
one of them at a time, and when I should be Master of
that, then to proceed to another, and so on till I should
have gone thro' the thirteen. And as the previous Acquisition of some might facilitate the Acquisition of certain
others, I arrang'd them with that View as they stand above.
Temperance first, as it tends to procure that Coolness &
Clearness of Head, which is so necessary where constant
Vigilance was to be kept up, and Guard maintained, against
the unremitting Attraction of ancient Habits, and the Force
of perpetual Temptations. This being acquir'd & establish'd,
Silence would be more easy, and my Desire being to gain
Knowledge at the same time that I improv'd in Virtue, and
considering that in Conversation it was obtain'd rather by
the Use of the Ears than of the Tongue, & therefore wishing
to break a Habit I was getting into of Prattling, Punning &
Joking, which only made me acceptable to trifling Company,
I gave *Silence* the second Place. This, and the next, *Order*,
I expected would allow me more Time for attending to my
Project and my Studies; RESOLUTION once become habitual, would keep me firm in my Endeavours to obtain all the
subsequent Virtues; *Frugality & Industry*, by, freeing me
from my remaining Debt, & producing Affluence & Independance would make more easy the Practice of *Sincerity*
and *Justice*, &c. &c. Conceiving then that agreeable to the
Advice of Pythagoras in his Golden Verses,* daily Examination would be necessary, I contriv'd the following Method
for conducting that Examination.

I made a little Book in which I allotted a Page for each
of the Virtues. I rul'd each Page with red Ink, so as to have
seven Columns, one for each Day of the Week, marking
each Column with a Letter for the Day. I cross'd these
Columns with thirteen red Lines, marking the Beginning of

each Line with the first Letter of one of the Virtues, on which Line & in its proper Column I might mark by a little black Spot every Fault I found upon Examination, to have been committed respecting that Virtue upon that Day.

Form of the Pages

TEMPERANCE.

Eat not to Dulness
Drink not to Elevation.

	S	M	T	W	T	F	S
T							
S	••	•		•		•	
O	•	•	•			•	•
R			•			•	
F		•			•		
I			•				
S							
J							
M							
Cl.							
T							
Ch.							
H							

I determined to give a Week's strict Attention to each of the Virtues successively. Thus in the first Week my great Guard was to avoid every the least Offence against Temperance, leaving the other Virtues to their ordinary Chance, only marking every Evening the Faults of the Day. Thus if in the first Week I could keep my first Line marked T clear of Spots, I suppos'd the Habit of that Virtue so much strengthen'd and its opposite weaken'd, that I might venture

extending my Attention to include the next, and for the
following Week keep both Lines clear of Spots. Proceeding
thus to the last, I could go thro' a Course compleat in
Thirteen Weeks, and four Courses in a Year.—And like him
who having a Garden to weed, does not attempt to eradicate
all the bad Herbs at once, which would exceed his Reach
and his Strength, but works on one of the Beds at a time,
& having accomplish'd the first proceeds to a second; so I
should have, (I hoped) the encouraging Pleasure of seeing
on my Pages the Progress I made in Virtue, by clearing
successively my Lines of their Spots, till in the End by a
Number of Courses, I should be happy in viewing a clean
Book after a thirteen Weeks daily Examination

This my little Book had for its Motto these Lines from
Addison's Cato;

> *Here will I hold: If there is a Pow'r above us,*
> *(And that there is, all Nature cries aloud*
> *Thro' all her Works) he must delight in Virtue,*
> *And that which he delights in must be happy.*

Another from *Cicero*.

O Vitae Philosophia Dux! O Virtutum indagatrix, expultrix-
que vitiorum! Unus dies bene, & ex preceptis tuis actus, peccanti
immortalitati est anteponendus. *

Another from the Proverbs of Solomon speaking of Wisdom or Virtue;

Length of Days is in her right hand, and in her Left
Hand Riches and Honours; Her Ways are Ways of Pleas-
antness, and all her Paths are Peace.   III, 16, 17.

And conceiving God to be the Fountain of Wisdom, I
thought it right and necessary to solicit his Assistance for
obtaining it; to this End I form'd the following little Prayer,
which was prefix'd to my Tables of Examination; for daily
Use.

O Powerful Goodness! bountiful Father! merciful Guide!
Increase in me that Wisdom which discovers my truest Interests;

Strengthen my Resolutions to perform what that Wisdom dictates. Accept my kind Offices to thy other Children, as the only Return in my Power for thy continual Favours to me.

I us'd also sometimes a little Prayer which I took from *Thomson's* Poems. viz

> *Father of Light and Life, thou Good supreme,*
> *O teach me what is good, teach me thy self!*
> *Save me from Folly, Vanity and Vice,*
> *From every low Pursuit, and fill my Soul*
> *With Knowledge, conscious Peace, & Virtue pure,*
> *Sacred, substantial, neverfading Bliss!*

The Precept of *Order* requiring that *every Part of my Business should have its allotted Time*, one Page in my little Book contain'd the following Scheme of Employment for the Twenty-four Hours of a natural Day,

The Morning Question, What Good shall I do this Day?	5 6 7	Rise, wash and address Powerful Goodness; contrive Day's Business and take the Resolution of the Day;
	8 9 10 11	prosecute the present Study: and breakfast?— Work
	12 1	Read, or overlook my Accounts, and dine.
	2 3 4 5	Work
	6 7 8	Put Things in their Places, Supper, Musick, or Diversion, or Conversation
	9	Examination of the Day.
Evening Question, What Good have I done to day?	10 11 12	
	1	Sleep.—
	2 3 4	

I enter'd upon the Execution of this Plan for Self Examination, and continu'd it with occasional Intermissions for some time. I was surpriz'd to find myself so much fuller of Faults than I had imagined, but I had the Satisfaction of

seeing them diminish. To avoid the Trouble of renewing
now & then my little Book, which by scraping out the Marks
on the Paper of old Faults to make room for new Ones in
a new Course, became full of Holes: I transferr'd my Tables
& Precepts to the Ivory Leaves of a Memorandum Book,
on which the Lines were drawn with red Ink that made a
durable Stain, and on those Lines I mark'd my Faults with
a black Lead Pencil, which Marks I could easily wipe out
with a wet Sponge. After a while I went thro' one Course
only in a Year, and afterwards only one in several Years;
till at length I omitted them entirely, being employ'd in
Voyages & Business abroad with a Multiplicity of Affairs,
that interfered. but I always carried my little Book with me.
My Scheme of ORDER, gave me the most Trouble, and I
found that tho' it might be practicable where a Man's
Business was such as to leave him the Disposition of his
Time, that of a Journeyman Printer for instance, it was not
possible to be exastly observ'd by a Master, who must mix
with the World, and often receive People of Business at
their own Hours.—*Order* too, with regard to Places for
Things, Papers, &c. I found extreamly difficult to acquire.
I had not been early accustomed to *Method*, & having an
exceeding good Memory, I was not so sensible of the
Inconvenience attending Want of Method. This Article
therefore cost me so much painful Attention & my Faults
in it vex'd me so much, and I made so little Progress in
Amendment, & had such frequent Relapses, that I was
almost ready to give up the Attempt, and content my self
with a faulty Character in that respect. Like the Man who
in buying an Ax of a Smith my Neighbour, desired to have
the whole of its Surface as bright as the Edge; the Smith
consented to grind it bright for him if he would turn the
Wheel. He turn'd while the Smith press'd the broad Face
of the Ax hard & heavily on the Stone, which made the
Turning of it very fatiguing. The Man came every now &
then from the Wheel to see how the Work went on; and at
length would take his Ax as it was without farther Grinding.
No, says the Smith, Turn on, turn on; we shall have it

bright by and by; as yet 'tis only speckled. Yes, says the Man; but—*I think I like a speckled Ax best.*—And I believe this may have been the Case with many who having for want of some such Means as I employ'd found the Difficulty of obtaining good, & breaking bad Habits, in other Points. of Vice & Virtue, have given up the Struggle, & concluded that *a speckled Ax was best.* For something that pretended to be Reason was every now and then suggesting to me, that such extream Nicety as I exacted of my self might be a kind of Foppery in Morals, which if it were known would make me ridiculous; that a perfect Character might be attended with the Inconveninence of being envied and hated; and that a benevolent Man should allow a few Faults in himself, to keep his Friends in Countenance. In Truth I found myself incorrigible with respect to *Order*; and now I am grown old, and my Memory bad, I feel very sensibly the want of it. But on the whole, tho' I never arrived at the Perfection I had been so ambitious of obtaining, but fell far short of it, yet I was by the Endeavour made a better and a happier Man than I otherwise should have been, if I had not attempted it; As those who aim at perfect Writing by imitating the engraved Copies, tho' they never reach the wish'd for Excellence of those Copies, their Hand is mended by the Endeavour, and is tolerable while it continues fair & legible.—

And it may be well my Posterity should be informed, that to this little Artifice, with the Blessing of God, their Ancestor ow'd the constant Felicity of his Life down to his 79th Year in which this is written. What Reverses may attend the Remainder is in the Hand of Providence: But if they arrive the Reflection on past Happiness enjoy'd ought to help his Bearing them with more Resignation. To *Temperance.* he ascribes his long-continu'd Health, & what is still left to him of a good Constitution. To *Industry* and *Frugality* the early Easiness of his Circumstances, & Acquisition of his Fortune, with all that Knowledge which enabled him to be an useful Citizen, and obtain'd for him some Degree of Reputation among the Learned   To

Sincerity & *Justice* the Confidence of his Country, and the honourable Employs it conferr'd upon him. And to the joint Influence of the whole Mass of the Virtues, even in their imperfect State he was able to acquire them, all that Evenness of Temper, & that Chearfulness in Conversation which makes his Company still sought for, & agreable even to his younger Acquaintance. I hope therefore that some of my Descendants may follow the Example & reap the Benefit.—

It will be remark'd that, tho' my Scheme was not wholly without Religion there was in it no Mark of any of the distinguishing Tenets of any particular Sect.—I had purposely avoided them; for being fully persuaded of the Utility and Excellency of my Method, and that it might be serviceable to People in all Religions, and intending some time or other to publish it, I would not have any thing in it that should prejudice any one of any Sect against it.—I purposed writing a little Comment on each Virtue, in which I would have shown the Advantages of possessing it, & the Mischiefs attending its opposite Vice; and I should have called my Book the ART *of Virtue*, because it would have shown the *Means* & *Manner* of obtaining Virtue, which would have distinguish'd it from the mere Exhortation to be good, that does not instruct & indicate the Means; but is like the Apostle's Man of verbal Charity, who only, without showing to the Naked & the Hungry *how* or where they might get Cloaths or Victuals, exhorted them to be fed & clothed. *James* II, 15, 16.—*

But it so happened that my Intention of writing & publishing this Comment was never fulfilled. I did indeed, from time to time put down short Hints of the Sentiments, Reasonings, &c. to be made use of in it; some of which I have still by me: But the necessary close Attention to private Business in the earlier part of Life, and public Business since, have occasioned my postponing it. For it being connected in my Mind with a *great and extensive Project* that required the whole Man to execute, and which an unforeseen Succession of Employs prevented my attending to, it has hitherto remain'd unfinish'd.——

In this Piece it was my Design to explain and enforce this Doctrine, that vicious Actions are not hurtful because they are forbidden, but forbidden because they are hurtful, the Nature of Man alone consider'd: That it was therefore every ones Interest to be virtuous, who wish'd to be happy even in this World. And I should from this Circumstance, there being always in the World a Number of rich Merchants, Nobility, States and Princes, who have need of honest Instruments for the Management of their Affairs, and such being so rare have endeavoured to convince young Persons, that no Qualities were so likely to make a poor Man's Fortune as those of Probity & Integrity.

My List of Virtues contain'd at first but twelve: But a Quaker Friend having kindly inform'd me that I was generally thought proud; that my Pride show'd itself frequently in Conversation; that I was not content with being in the right when discussing any Point, but was overbearing & rather insolent; of which he convinc'd me by mentioning several Instances;——I determined endeavouring to cure myself if I could of this Vice or Folly among the rest, and I added *Humility* to my List, giving an extensive Meaning to the Word.——I cannot boast of much Success in acquiring the *Reality* of this Virtue; but I had a good deal with regard to the *Appearance* of it.——I made it a Rule to forbear all direct Contradiction to the Sentiments of others, and all positive Assertion of my own. I even forbid myself agreable to the old Laws of our Junto, the Use of every Word or Expression in the Language that imported a fix'd Opinion; such as *certainly, undoubtedly*, &c. and I adopted instead of them, *I conceive, I apprehend,* or *I imagine* a thing to be so or so, or it so appears to me at present.——When another asserted something that I thought an Error, I deny'd myself the Pleasure of contradicting him abruptly, and of showing immediately some Absurdity in his Proposition; and in answering I began by observing that in certain Cases or

Circumstances his Opinion would be right, but that in the present case there *appear'd* or *seem'd* to me some Difference, &c. I soon found the Advantage of this Change in my Manners. The Conversations I engag'd in went on more pleasantly. The modest way in which I propos'd my Opinions, procur'd them a readier Reception and less Contradiction; I had less Mortification when I was found to be in the wrong, and I more easily prevail'd with others to give up their Mistakes & join with me when I happen'd to be in the right. And this Mode, which I at first put on, with some violence to natural Inclination, became at length so easy & so habitual to me, that perhaps for these Fifty Years past no one has ever heard a dogmatical Expression escape me. And to this Habit (after my Character of Integrity) I think it principally owing, that I had early so much Weight with my Fellow Citizens, when I proposed new Institutions, or Alterations in the old; and so much Influence in public Councils when I became a Member. For I was but a bad Speaker, never eloquent, subject to much Hesitation in my choice of Words, hardly correct in Language, and yet I generally carried my Points.—

In reality there is perhaps no one of our natural Passions so hard to subdue as *Pride*. Disguise it, struggle with it, beat it down, stifle it, mortify it as much as one pleases, it is still alive, and will every now and then peep out and show itself. You will see it perhaps often in this History. For even if I could conceive that I had compleatly overcome it, I should probably by proud of my Humility.—

Thus far written at Passy 1784

[PART 3]

I am now about to write at home, Augt 1788.—but cannot have the help expected from my Papers, many of them being lost in the War. I have however found the following.

Having mentioned *a great & extensive Project* which I had conceiv'd, it seems proper that some Account should be here given of that Project and its Object. Its first Rise in my

Mind appears in the following little Paper, accidentally preserv'd, viz.

OBSERVATIONS on my Reading History in Library, May 9. 1731.

"That the great Affairs of the World, the Wars, Revolutions, &c. are carried on and effected by Parties.—

"That the View of these Parties is their present general Interest, or what they take to be such.—

"That the different Views of these different Parties, occasion all Confusion.

"That while a Party is carrying on a general Design, each Man has his particular private Interest in View.

"That as soon as a Party has gain'd its general Point, each Member becomes intent upon his particular Interest, which thwarting others, breaks that Party into Divisions, and occasions more Confusion.

"That few in Public Affairs act from a meer View of the Good of their Country, whatever they may pretend; and tho' their Actings bring real Good to their Country, yet Men primarily consider'd that their own and their Country's Interest was united, and did not act from a Principle of Benevolence.

"That fewer still in public Affairs act with a View to the Good of Mankind.

"There seems to me at present to be a great Occasion for raising an united Party for Virtue, by forming the Virtuous and good Men of all Nations into a regular Body, to be govern'd by suitable good and wise Rules, which good and wiss Men may probably be more unanimous in their Obedience to, than common People are to common Laws

"I at present think, that whoever attempts this aright, and is well qualified, cannot fail of pleasing God, & of meeting with Success.—

B F.—

Revolving this Project in my Mind, as to be undertaken hereafter when my Circumstances should afford me the necessary Leisure, I put down from time to time on Pieces of Paper such Thoughts as occur'd to me respecting it. Most of these are lost; but I find one purporting to be the Substance of an intended Creed, containing as I thought the Essentials of every known Religion, and being free of every thing that might shock the Professors of any Religion. It is express'd in these Words. viz.

"That there is one God who made all things.

"That he governs the World by his Providence.—

"That he ought to be worshipped by Adoration, Prayer & Thanksgiving.

"But that the most acceptable Service of God is doing Good to Man.

"That the Soul is immortal.

"And that God will certainly reward Virtue and punish Vice either here or hereafter."—

My Ideas at that time were, that the Sect should be begun & spread at first among young and single Men only; that each Person to be initiated should not only declare his Assent to such Creed, but should have exercis'd himself with the Thirteen Weeks Examination and Practice of the Virtues as in the before-mention'd Model; that the Existence of such a Society should be kept a Secret till it was become considerable, to prevent Solicitations for the Admission of improper Persons; but that the Members should each of them search among his Acquaintance for ingenuous well-disposed Youths, to whom with prudent Caution the Scheme should be gradually communicated: That the Members should engage to afford their Advice Assistance and Support to each other in promoting one another's Interest Business and Advancement in Life: That for Distinction we should be call'd the Society of the *Free and Easy*; Free, as being by the general Practice and Habit of the Virtues, free from the Dominion of Vice, and particularly by the Practice of Industry & Frugality, free from Debt, which exposes a Man to Confinement and a Species of Slavery to his Creditors. This is as much as I can now recollect of the Project, except that I communicated it in part to two young Men, who adopted it with some Enthusiasm. But my then narrow Circumstances, and the Necessity I was under of sticking close to my Business, occasion'd my Postponing the farther Prosecution of it at that time, and my multifarious Occu-papations public & private induc'd me to continue postpon-ing, so that it has been omitted till I have no longer Strength or Activity left sufficient for such an Enterprize: Tho' I am still of Opinion that it was a practicable Scheme, and might have been very useful, by forming a great Num-ber of good Citizens: And I was not discourag'd by the seeming Magnitude of the Undertaking, as I have always thought that one Man of tolerable Abilities may work great Changes, & accomplish great Affairs among Mankind, if he first forms a good Plan, and, cutting off all Amusements or other Employments that would divert his Attention, makes the Execution of that same Plan his sole Study and Busi-ness.—

In 1732 I first published my Almanack, under the Name of *Richard Saunders*; it was continu'd by me about 25 Years, commonly call'd *Poor Richard's* Almanack. I endeavour'd to make it both entertaining and useful, and it accordingly came to be in such Demand that I reap'd considerable Profit from it, vending annually near ten Thousand. And observing that it was generally read, scarce any Neighbourhood in the Province being without it, I consider'd it as a proper Vehicle for conveying Instruction among the common People, who bought scarce any other Books. I therefore filled all the little Spaces that occurr'd between the Remarkable Days in the Calendar, with Proverbial Sentences, chiefly such as incul-cated Industry and Frugality, as the Means of procuring Wealth and thereby securing Virtue, it being more difficult for a Man in Want to act always honestly, as (to use here one of those Proverbs) *it is hard for an empty Sack to stand upright*. These Proverbs, which contained the Wisdom of many Ages and Nations, I assembled and form'd into a connected Discourse prefix'd to the Almanack of 1757, as the Harangue of a wise old Man to the People attending an

Auction. The bringing all these scatter'd Counsels thus into a Focus, enabled them to make greater Impression. The Piece being universally approv^{ed} was copied in all the Newspapers of the Continent, reprinted in Britain on a Broadside to be stuck up in Houses, two Translations were made of it in French, and great Numbers bought by the Clergy & Gentry to distribute gratis among their poor Parishioners and Tenants. In Pennsylvania, as it discouraged useless Expence in foreign Superfluities, some thought it had its share of Influence in producing that growing Plenty of Money which was observable for several Years after its Publication.——

I consider'd my Newspaper also as another Means of communicating Instruction, & in that View frequently reprinted in it Extracts from the Spectator and other moral Writers, and sometimes publish'd little Pieces of my own which had been first compos'd for Reading in our Junto. Of these are a Socratic Dialogue tending to prove, that, whatever might be his Parts and Abilities, a vicious Man could not properly be called a Man of Sense. And a Discourse on Self denial, showing that Virtue was not Secure, till its Practice became a Habitude, & was free from the Opposition of contrary Inclinations.——These may be found in the Papers about the beginning of 1735.——In the Conduct of my Newspaper I carefully excluded all Libelling and Personal Abuse, which is of late Years become so disgraceful to our Country. Whenever I was solicited to insert any thing of that kind, and the Writers pleaded as they generally did, the Liberty of the Press, and that a Newspaper was like a Stage Coach in which any one who would pay had a Right to a Place, my Answer was, that I would print the Piece separately if desired, and the Author might have as many Copies as he pleased to distribute himself, but that I would not take upon me to spread his Detraction, and that having contracted with my Subscribers to furnish them with what might be either useful or entertaining, I could not fill their Papers with private Altercation in which they had no Concern without doing them manifest

Injustice. Now many of our Printers make no scruple of gratifying the Malice of Individuals by false Accusations of the fairest Characters among ourselves, augmenting Animosity even to the producing of Duels, and are moreover so indiscreet as to print scurrilous Reflections on the Government of neighbouring States, and even on the Conduct of our best national Allies, which may be attended with the most pernicious Consequences.—These Things I mention as a Caution to young Printers, & that they may be encouraged not to pollute their Presses and disgrace their Profession by such infamous Practices, but refuse steadily; as they may see by my Example, that such a Course of Conduct will not on the whole be injurious to their Interests.—

In 1733, I sent one of my Journeymen to Charleston South Carolina where a Printer was wanting. I furnish'd him with a Press and Letters, on an Agreement of Partnership, by which I was to receive One Third of the Profits of the Business, paying One Third of the Expence. He was a Man of Learning and honest, but ignorant in Matters of Account; and tho' he sometimes made me Remittances, I could get no Account from him, nor any satisfactory State of our Partnership while he lived. On his Decease, the Business was continued by his Widow, who being born & bred in Holland, where as I have been inform'd the Knowledge of Accompts makes a Part of Female Education, she not only sent me as clear a State as she could find of the Transactions past, but continu'd to account with the greatest Regularity & Exactitude every Quarter afterwards; and manag'd the Business with such Success that she not only brought up reputably a Family of Children, but at the Expiration of the Term was able to purchase of me the Printing-House and establish her Son in it. I mention this Affair chiefly for the Sake of recommending that Branch of Education for our young Females, as likely to be of more Use to them & their Children in Case of Widowhood than either Music or Dancing, by preserving them from Losses by Imposition of crafty Men, and enabling them to continue perhaps a profitable mercantile House with establish'd Correspondence till a Son is grown up fit to undertake and go on with it, to the lasting Advantage and enriching of the Family.—

About the Year 1734. there arrived among us from Ireland, a young Presbyterian Preacher named Hemphill, who delivered with a good Voice, & apparently extempore, most excellent Discourses, which drew together considerable Numbers of different Persuasions, who join'd in admiring them. Among the rest I became one of his constant Hearers, his Sermons pleasing me as they had little of the dogmatical kind, but inculcated strongly the Practice of Virtue, or what in the religious Stile are called Good Works. Those however, of our Congregation, who considered themselves as orthodox Presbyterians, disapprov'd his Doctrine, and were join'd by most of the old Clergy, who arraign'd him of Heterodoxy before the Synod, in order to have him silenc'd. I became his zealous Partisan, and contributed all I could to raise a Party in his Favour; and we combated for him a while with some Hopes of Success. There was much Scribbling pro & con upon the Occasion; and finding that tho' an elegant Preacher he was but a poor Writer, I lent him my Pen and wrote for him two or three Pamphlets, and one Piece in the Gazette of April 1735. Those Pamphlets, as is generally the Case with controversial Writings, tho' eagerly read at the time, were soon out of Vogue, and I question whether a single Copy of them now exists. During the Contest an unlucky Occurrence hurt his Cause exceedingly. One of our Adversaries having heard him preach a Sermon that was much admired, thought he had somewhere read that Sermon before, or at least a part of it. On Search he found that Part quoted at length in one of the British Reviews, from a Discourse of Dr Forster's. This Detection gave many of our Party Disgust, who accordingly abandoned his Cause, and occasion'd our more speedy Discomfiture in the Synod. I stuck by him, however, as I rather approv'd his giving us good Sermons compos'd by others, than bad ones of his own Manufacture; tho' the latter was the Practice of our common Teachers. He afterwards acknowledg'd to me that none of those he preach'd were his own; adding that his Memory was such as enabled him to retain and repeat any Sermon after one Reading only.—On our Defeat he left us, in search elsewhere of better Fortune, and I quitted the Congregation, never joining it after, tho' I continu'd many Years my Subscription for the Support of its Ministers.—

I had begun in 1733 to study Languages. I soon made myself so much a Master of the French as to be able to read the Books with Ease. I then undertook the Italian. An Acquaintance who was also learning it, us'd often to tempt me to play Chess with him. Finding this took up too much of the Time I had to spare for Study, I at length refus'd to play any more, unless on this Condition, that the Victor in every Game, should have a Right to impose a Task, either in Parts of the Grammar to be got by heart, or in Translation, &c. which Tasks the Vanquish'd was to perform upon Honour before our next Meeting. As we play'd pretty equally we thus beat one another into that Language.—I afterwards with a little Pains-taking acquir'd as much of the Spanish as to read their Books also. I have already mention'd that I had only one Years Instruction in a Latin School, and that when very young, after which I neglected that Language entirely.—But when I had attained an Acquaintance with the French, Italian and Spanish, I was surpriz'd to find, on looking over a Latin Testament, that I understood so much more of that Language than I had imagined; which encouraged me to apply my self again to the Study of it, & I met with the more Success, as those preceding Languages had greatly smooth'd my Way. From these Circumstances I have thought, that there is some Inconsistency in our common Mode of Teaching Languages. We are told that it is proper to begin first with the Latin, and having acquir'd that it will be more easy to attain those modern Languages which are deriv'd from it; and yet we do not begin with the Greek in order more easily to acquire the Latin. It is true, that if you can clamber & get to the Top of a Stair-Case without using the Steps, you will more easily gain them in descending: but certainly if you begin with the lowest you will with more Ease ascend to the Top. And I would therefore offer it to the Consideration of those who superintend the Eduting of our Youth, whether, since many of those who begin with the Latin, quit the same after spending some Years, without having made any great Proficiency, and what they have learnt becomes almost useless, so that their time has been lost, it would not have been better to have begun them with the French, proceeding to the Italian &c. for tho' after spending the same time they should quit the Study of Languages, & never arrive at the Latin, they would however have acquir'd another Tongue or two that being in modern Use might be serviceable to them in common Life.

After ten Years Absence from Boston, and having become more easy in my Circumstances, I made a Journey thither to visit my Relations, which I could not sooner well afford. In returning I call'd at Newport, to see my Brother then settled there with his Printing-House. Our former Differences were forgotten, and our Meeting was very cordial and affectionate. He was fast declining in his Health, and requested of me that in case of his Death which he apprehended not far distant, I would take home his Son, then but 10 Years of Age, and bring him up to the Printing Business. This I accordingly perform'd, sending him a few Years to School before I took him into the Office. His Mother carry'd on the Business till he was grown up, when I assisted him with an Assortment of new Types, those of his Father being in a Manner worn out.—Thus it was that I made my Brother ample Amends for the Service I had depriv'd him of by leaving him so early.—

In 1736 I lost one of my Sons a fine Boy of 4 Years old, by the Small Pox taken in the common way. I long regretted bitterly & still regret that I had not given it to him by Inoculation; This I mention for the Sake of Parents, who omit that Operation on the Supposition that they should never forgive themselves if a Child died under it; my Example showing that the Regret may be the same either way, and that therefore the safer should be chosen.—

Our Club, the Junto, was found so useful, & afforded such Satisfaction to the Members, that several were desirous of introducing their Friends, which could not well be done without exceeding what we had settled as a convenient Number, viz. Twelve. We had from the Beginning made it a Rule to keep our Institution a Secret, which was pretty well observ'd. The Intention was, to avoid Applications of improper Persons for Admittance, some of whom perhaps we might find it difficult to refuse. I was one of those who were against any Addition to our Number, but instead of it made in Writing a Proposal, that every Member separately should endeavour to form a subordinate Club, with the same Rules respecting Queries, &c. and without informing them of the Connexion with the Junto. The Advantages propos'd were the Improvement of so many more young Citizens by the Use of our Institutions; Our better Acquaintance with the general Sentiments of the Inhabitants on any Occasion, as the Junto-Member might propose what Queries we should desire, and was to report to Junto what pass'd in his separate Club; the Promotion of our particular Interests in Business by more extensive Recommendations; and the Increase of our Influence in public Affairs & our Power of doing Good by spreading thro' the several Clubs the Sentiments of the Junto. The Project was approv'd, and every Member undertook to form his Club: but they did not all succeed. Five or six only were compleated, which were call'd by different Names, as the Vine, the Union, the Band, &c. they were useful to themselves, & afforded us a good deal of Amusement, Information & Instruction, besides answering in some considerable Degree our Views of influencing the public Opinion on particular Occasions, of which I shall give some Instances in course of time as they happened.—

My first Promotion was my being chosen in 1736 Clerk of the General Assembly. The Choice was made that Year without Opposition; but the Year following when I was again propos'd (the Choice, like that of the Members being annual) a new Member made a long Speech against me in order to favour some other Candidate. I was however chosen; which was the more agreable to me, as besides the Pay for immediate Service as Clerk, the Place gave me a better Opportunity of keeping up an Interest among the Members, which secur'd to me the Business of Printing the Votes, Laws, Paper Money, and other occasional Jobbs for the Public, that on the whole were very profitable. I therefore did not like the Opposition of this new Member, who was a Gentleman of Fortune, & Education, with Talents that were likely to give him in time great Influence in the House, which indeed afterwards happened. I did not however aim at gaining his Favour by paying any servile Respect to him, but after some time took this other Method. Having heard that he had in his Library a certain very scarce & curious Book, I wrote a Note to him expressing my Desire of perusing that Book, and requesting he would do me the Favour of lending it to me for a few Days. He sent it immediately; and I return'd it in about a Week, with another Note expressing strongly my Sense of the Favour. When we next met in the House he spoke to me, (which he had never done before) and with great Civility. And he ever afterwards manifested a Readiness to serve me on all Occasions, so that we became great Friends, & our Friendship continu'd to his Death. This is another Instance of the Truth of an old Maxim I had learnt, which says, *He that has once done you a Kindness will be more ready to do you another, than he whom you yourself have obliged.* And it shows how much more profitable it is prudently to remove, than to resent, return & continue inimical Proceedings.—

In 1737, Col. Spotswood, late Governor of Virginia, & then Post-master, General, being dissatisfied with the Conduct of his Deputy at Philadelphia, respecting some Negligence in rendering, & Inexactitude of his Accounts, took from him the Commission & offered it to me. I accepted it readily, and found it of great Advantage; for tho' the Salary was small, it facilitated the Correspondence that improv'd my Newspaper, encreas'd the Number demanded, as well as the Advertisements to be inserted, so that it came to afford me a very considerable Income. My old Competitor's

Newspaper declin'd proportionably, and I was satisfy'd without retaliating his Refusal, while Postmaster, to permit my Papers being carried by the Riders. Thus He suffer'd greatly from his Neglect in due Accounting; and I mention it as a Lesson to those young Men who may be employ'd in managing Affairs for others that they should always render Accounts & make Remittances, with Great Clearness and Punctuality.—The Character of observing Such a Conduct is the most powerful of all Recommendations to new Employments & Increase of Business.

I began now to turn my Thoughts a little to public Affairs, beginning however with small Matters. The City Watch was one of the first Things that I conceiv'd to want Regulation. It was managed by the Constables of the respective Wards in Turn. The Constable warn'd a Number of Housekeepers to attend him for the Night. Those who chose never to attend paid him Six Shillings a Year to be excus'd, which was suppos'd to be for hiring Substitutes; but was in Reality much more than was necessary for that purpose, and made the Constableship a Place of Profit. And the Constable for a little Drink often got such Ragamuffins about him as a Watch, that reputable Housekeepers did not chuse to mix with. Walking the Rounds too was often neglected, and most of the Night spent in Tippling. I thereupon wrote a Paper to be read in Junto, representing these Irregularities, but insisting more particularly on the Inequality of this Six Shilling Tax of the Constables, respecting the Circumstances of those who paid it, since a poor Widow Housekeeper, all of whose Property to be guarded by the Watch did not perhaps exceed the Value of Fifty Pounds, paid as much as the wealthiest Merchant who had Thousands of Pounds-worth of Goods in his Stores. On the whole I proposed as a more effectual Watch, the Hiring of proper Men to serve constantly in that Business; and as a more equitable Way of supporting the Charge, the levying a Tax that should be proportion'd to Property. This Idea being approv'd by the Junto, was communicated to the other Clubs, but as arising in each of them. And tho' the Plan was not immediately carried into Execution, yet by preparing the Minds of People for the Change, it paved the Way for the Law obtain'd a few Years after, when the Members of our Clubs were grown into more Influence.——

About this time I wrote a Paper, (first to be read in Junto but it was afterwards publish'd) on the different Accidents and Carelessnesses by which Houses were set on fire, with Cautions against them, and Means proposed of avoiding them. This was much spoken of as a useful Piece, and gave rise to a Project, which soon followed it, of forming a Company for the more ready Extinguishing of Fires, and mutual Assistance in Removing & Securing of Goods when in Danger. Associates in this Scheme were presently found amounting to Thirty. Our Articles of Agreement oblig'd every Member to keep always in good Order and fit for Use, a certain Number of Leather Buckets, with strong Bags & Baskets (for packing & transporting of Goods), which were to be brought to every Fire; and we agreed to meet once a Month & spend a social Evening together, in discoursing, and communicating such Ideas as occur'd to us upon the Subject of Fires as might be useful in our Conduct on such Occasions. The Utility of this Institution soon appeard, and many more desiring to be admitted than we thought convenient for one Company, they were advised to form another; which was accordingly done. And this went on, one new Company being formed after another, till they became so numerous as to include most of the Inhabitants who were Men of Property; and now at the time of my Writing this, tho' upwards of Fifty Years since its Establishment, that which I first formed, called the Union Fire Company, still subsists and flourishes, tho' the first Members are all deceas'd but myself & one who is older by a Year than I am.——The small Fines that have been paid by Members for Absence at the Monthly Meetings, have been apply'd to the Purchase of Fire Engines, Ladders, Firehooks, and other useful Implements for each Company, so that I question whether there is a City in the World better provided with the Means of putting a Stop to beginning

Conflagrations; and in fact since these Institutions, the City has never lost by Fire more than one or two Houses at a time, and the Flames have often been extinguish'd before the House in which they began has been half consumed.—

In 1739 arriv'd among us from England the Rev. Mr Whitefiel, who had made himself remarkable there as an itinerant Preacher. He was at first permitted to preach in some of our Churches; but the Clergy taking a Dislike to him, soon refus'd him their Pulpits and he was oblig'd to preach in the Fields. The Multitudes of all Sects and Denominations that attended his Sermons were enormous and it was matter of Speculation to me who was one of the Number, to observe the extraordinary Influence of his Oratory on his Hearers, and how much they admir'd & respected him, notwithstanding his common Abuse of them, by assuring them they were naturally *half Beasts and half Devils*. It was wonderful to see the Change soon made in the Manners of our Inhabitants; from being thoughtless or indifferent about Religion, it seem'd as if all the World were growing Religious; so that one could not walk thro' the Town in an Evening without Hearing Psalms sung in different Families of every Street. And it being found inconvenient to assemble in the open Air, subject to its Inclemencies, the Building of a House to meet-in was no sooner propos'd and Persons appointed to receive Contributions, but sufficient Sums were soon receiv'd to procure the Ground and erect the Building which was 100 feet long & 70 broad, about the Size of Westminster-hall; and the Work was carried on with such Spirit as to be finished in a much shorter time than could have been expected. Both House and Ground were vested in Trustees, expressly for the Use of any Preacher of any religious Persuasion who might desire to say something to the People of Philadelphia, the Design in building not being to accommodate any particular Sect, but the Inhabitants in general, so that even if the Mufti of Constantinople were to send a Missionary to preach Mahometanism to us, he would find a Pulpit to his Service.—

Mr Whitfield, in leaving us, went preaching all the Way thro' the Colonies to Georgia. The Settlement of that Province had lately been begun; but instead of being made with hardy industrious Husbandmen accustomed to Labour, the only People fit for such an Enterprise, it was with Families of broken Shopkeepers and other insolvent Debtors, many of indolent & idle habits, taken out of the Goals, who being set down in the Woods, unqualified for clearing Land, & unable to endure the Hardships of a new Settlement, perished in Numbers, leaving many helpless Children unprovided for. The Sight of their miserable Situation inspired the benevolent Heart of Mr Whitefield with the Idea of building an Orphan House there, in which they might be supported and educated. Returning northward he preach'd up this Charity, & made large Collections;—for his Eloquence had a wonderful Power over the Hearts & Purses of his Hearers, of which I myself was an Instance. I did not disapprove of the Design, but as Georgia was then destitute of Materials & Workmen, and it was propos'd to send them from Philadelphia at a great Expence, I thought it would have been better to have built the House here & brought the Children to it. This I advis'd, but he was resolute in his first Project, and rejected my Counsel, and I thereupon refus'd to contribute. I happened soon after to attend one of his Sermons, in the Course of which I perceived he intended to finish with a Collection, & I silently resolved he should get nothing from me. I had in my Pocket a Handful of Copper, Money, three or four silver Dollars, and five Pistoles in Gold. As he proceeded I began to soften, and concluded to give the Coppers. Another Stroke of his Oratory made me asham'd of that, and determin'd me to give the Silver; & he finish'd so admirably, that I empty'd my Pocket wholly into the Collector's Dish, Gold and all. At this Sermon there was also one of our Club, who being of my Sentiments respecting the Building in Georgia, and suspecting a Collection might be intended, had by Precaution emptied his Pockets before he came from home; towards the Conclusion of the Discourse however, he felt a strong

Desire to give, and apply'd to a Neighbour who stood near
him to borrow some Money for the Purpose. The Application was unfortunately to perhaps the only Man in the
Company who had the firmness not to be affected by the
Preacher. His Answer was, *At any other time, Friend Hop-
kinson, I would lend to thee freely; but not now; for thee seems
to be out of thy right Senses.*—

Some of Mr Whitfield's Enemies affected to suppose that
he would apply these Collections to his own private Emolument; but I, who was intimately acquainted with him,
(being employ'd in printing his Sermons and Journals, &c.)
never had the least Suspicion of his Integrity, but am to
this day decidedly of Opinion that he was in all his Conduct,
a perfectly *honest Man.* And methinks my Testimony in his
Favour ought to have the more Weight, as we had no
religious Connection. He us'd indeed sometimes to pray for
my Conversion, but never had the Satisfaction of believing
his Prayers were heard. Ours was a mere civil Friendship,
sincere on both Sides, and lasted to his Death.

The following Instance will show something of the Terms
on which we stood.: Upon one of his Arrivals from England
at Boston, he wrote to me that he should come soon to
Philadelphia, but knew not where he could lodge when there,
as he understood his old kind Host Mr Benezet was remov'd
to Germantown. My Answer was; You know my House, if
you can make shift with its scanty Accommodations you will
be most heartily welcome. He reply'd, that if I made that
kind Offer for Christ's sake, I should not miss of a Reward.—
And I return'd, *Don't let me be mistaken; it was not for Christ's
sake, but for your sake.* One of our common Acquaintance
jocosely remark'd, that knowing it to be the Custom of the
Saints, when they receiv'd any favour, to shift the Burthen
of the Obligation from off their own Shoulders, and place
it; in Heaven, I had contriv'd to fix it on Earth.—

The last time I saw Mr Whitefield was in London, when
he consulted me about his Orphan House Concern, and his
Purpose of appropriating it to the Establishment of a College.

He had a loud and clear Voice, and articulated his Words & Sentences so perfectly that he might be heard and understood at a great Distance, especially as his Auditories, however numerous, observ'd the most exact Silence. He preach'd one Evening from the Top of the Court House Steps, which are in the Middle of Market Street, and on the West Side of Second Street which crosses it at right angles. Both Streets were fill'd with his Hearers to a considerable Distance. Being among the hindmost in Market Street, I had the Curiosity to learn how far he could be heard, by retiring backwards down the Street towards the River, and I found his Voice distinct till I came near Front-Street, when some Noise in that Street, obscur'd it. Imagining then a Semi-Circle, of which my Distance should be the Radius, and that it were fill'd with Auditors, to each of whom I allow'd two square feet, I computed that he might well be heard by more than Thirty-Thousand. This reconcil'd me to the Newspaper Accounts of his having preach'd to 25000 People in the Fields, and to the antient Histories of Generals haranguing whole Armies, of which I had sometimes doubted.——

By hearing him often I came to distinguish easily between Sermons newly compos'd, & those which he had often preach'd in the Course of his Travels. His Delivery of the latter was so improv'd by frequent Repetitions, that every Accent, every Emphasis, every Modulation of Voice, was so perfectly well turn'd and well plac'd, that without being interested in the Subject, one could not help being pleas'd with the Discourse, a Pleasure of much the same kind with that receiv'd from an excellent Piece of Musick. This is an Advantage itinerant Preachers have over those who are stationary: as the latter cannot well improve their Delivery of a Sermon by so many Rehearsals.——

His Writing and Printing from time to time gave great Advantage to his Enemies. Unguarded Expressions and even erroneous Opinions del^d in Preaching might have been afterwards explain'd, or qualify'd by supposing others that might have accompany'd them; or they might have been deny'd; But *litera scripta manet*.* Critics attack'd his Writings violently, and with so much Appearance of Reason as to diminish the Number of his Votaries, and prevent their Encrease: So that I am of Opinion, if he had never written any thing he would have left behind him a much more numerous and important Sect. And his Reputation might in that case have been still growing, even after his Death; as there being nothing of his Writing on which to found a Censure; and give him a lower Character, his Proselites would be left at Liberty to feign for him as great a Variety of Excellencies, as their enthusiastic Admiration might wish him to have possessed.

My Business was now continually augmenting, and my Circumstances growing daily easier, my Newspaper having become very profitable, as being for a time almost the only one in this and the neighbouring Provinces.—I experienc'd too the Truth of the Observation, that *after getting the first hundred Pound, it is more easy to get the second*: Money itself being of a prolific Nature: The Partnership at Carolina having succeeded, I was encourag'd to engage in others, and to promote several of my Workmen who had behaved well, by establishing them with Printing-Houses in different Colonies, on the same Terms with that in Carolina. Most of them did well, being enabled at the End of our Term, Six Years, to purchase the Types of me; and go on working for themselves, by which means several Families were raised. Partnerships often finish in Quarrels, but I was happy in this, that mine were all carry'd on and ended amicably; owing I think a good deal to the Precaution of having very explicitly settled in our Articles every thing to be done by or expected from each Partner, so that there was nothing to dispute, which Precaution I would therefore recommend to all who enter into Partnerships, for whatever Esteem Partners may have for & Confidence in each other at the time of the Contract, little Jealousies and Disgusts may arise, with Ideas of Inequality in the Care & Burthen of the Business, &c. which are attended often with Breach of

Friendship & of the Connection, perhaps with Lawsuits and other disagreable Consequences

I had on the whole abundant Reason to be satisfied with my being established in Pennsylvania. There were however two things that I regretted: There being no Provision for Defence, nor for a compleat Education of Youth. No Militia nor any College. I therefore in 1743, drew up a Proposal for establishing an Academy; & at that time thinking the Rev^d Mr Peters, who was out of Employ, a fit Person to superintend such an Institution, I communicated the Project to him. But he having more profitable Views in the Service of the Proprietor, which succeeded, declin'd the Undertaking. And not knowing another at that time suitable for such a Trust, I let the Scheme lie a while dormant.—I succeeded better the next Year, 1744, in proposing and establishing a Philosophical Society. The Paper I wrote for that purpose will be found among my Writings when collected.—

With respect to Defence, Spain having been several Years at War against Britain, and being at length join'd by France, which brought us into greater Danger; and the laboured & long-continued Endeavours of our Governor Thomas to prevail with our Quaker Assembly to pass a Militia Law, & make other Provisions for the Security of the Province having proved abortive, I determined to try what might be done by a voluntary Association of the People. To promote this I first wrote & published a Pamphlet, intitled, PLAIN TRUTH, in which I stated our defenceless Situation in strong Lights, with the Necessity of Union & Discipline for our Defence, and promis'd to propose in a few Days an Association to be generally signed for that purpose. The Pamphlet had a sudden & surprizing Effect. I was call'd upon for the Instrument of Association: And having settled the Draft of it with a few Friends, I appointed a Meeting of the Citizens in the large Building before mentioned. The House was pretty full. I had prepared a Number of printed Copies, and provided Pens and Ink dispers'd all over the Room. I harangu'd them a little on the Subject, read the Paper & explain'd it, and then distributed the Copies which

were eagerly signed, not the least Objection being made.
When the Company separated, & the Papers were collected
we found above Twelve hundred Hands; and other Copies
being dispers'd in the Country the Subscribers amounted at
length to upwards of Ten Thousand. These all furnish'd
themselves as soon as they could with Arms; form'd themselves into Companies, and Regiments, chose their own
Officers, & met every Week to be instructed in the manual
Exercise, and other Parts of military Discipline. The
Women, by Subscriptions among themselves, provided Silk
Colours, which they presented to the Companies, painted
with different Devices and Motto's which I supplied. The
Officers of the Companies composing the Philadelphia Regiment, being met, chose me for their Colonel; but conceiving
myself unfit, I declin'd that Station, & recommended Mr
Lawrence, a fine Person and Man of Influence, who was
accordingly appointed. I then propos'd a Lottery to defray
the Expence of Building a Battery below the Town, and
furnishing it with Cannon. It filled expeditiously and the
Battery was soon erected, the Merlons being fram'd of Logs
& fill'd with Earth. We bought some old Cannon from
Boston, but these not being sufficient, we wrote to England
for more, soliciting at the same Time our Proprietaries for
some Assistance, tho' without much Expectation of obtaining it. Mean while Colonel Lawrence, William Allen, Abraham Taylor, Esquires, and myself were sent to New York
by the Associators, commission'd to borrow some Cannon
of Governor Clinton. He at first refus'd us peremptorily:
but at a Dinner with his Council where there was great
Drinking of Madeira Wine, as the Custom at that Place then
was, he soften'd by degrees, and said he would lend us Six.
After a few more Bumpers he advanc'd to Ten. And at
length he very good-naturedly conceded Eighteen. They
were fine Cannon, 18 pounders, with their Carriages, which
we soon transported and mounted on our Battery, where
the Associators kept a nightly Guard while the War lasted:
And among the rest I regularly took my Turn of Duty there
as a common Soldier.——

My Activity in these Operations was agreable to the Governor and Council; they took me into Confidence, & I was consulted by them in every Measure wherein their Concurrence was thought useful to the Association. Calling in the Aid of Religion, I propos'd to them the Proclaiming a Fast, to promote Reformation, & implore the Blessing of Heaven on our Undertaking. They embrac'd the Motion, but as it was the first Fast ever thought of in the Province, the Secretary had no Precedent from which to draw the Proclamation. My Education in New England, where a Fast is proclaim'd every Year, was here of some Advantage. I drew it in the accustomed Stile, it was translated into German, printed in both Languages and divulg'd thro' the Province. This gave the Clergy of the different Sects an Opportunity of Influencing their Congregations to join in the Association; and it would probably have been general among all but Quakers if the Peace had not soon interven'd.

It was thought by some of my Friends that by my Activity in these Affairs, I should offend that, Sect, and thereby lose my Interest in the Assembly where they were a great Majority. A young Gentleman who had likewise some Friends in the House, and wish'd to succeed me as their Clerk, acquainted me that it was decided to displace me at the next Election, and he therefore in good Will advis'd me to resign, as more consistent with my Honour than being turn'd out. My Answer to him was, that I had read or heard of some Public Man, who made it a Rule never to ask for an Office, and never to refuse one when offer'd to him. I approve, says I, of his Rule, and will practise it with a small Addition; I shall never *ask*, never *refuse*, nor ever *resign* an Office. If they will have my Office of Clerk to dispose of to another, they shall take it from me. I will not by giving it up, lose my Right of some time or other making Reprisals on my Adversaries. I heard however no more of this. I was chosen again, unanimously as usual, at the next Election. Possibly as they dislik'd my late Intimacy with the Members of Council, who had join'd the Governors in all the Disputes about military Preparations with which the House had long been harass'd, they might have been pleas'd if I would voluntarily have left them; but they did not care to displace me on Account merely of my Zeal for the Association; and they could not well give another Reason.—Indeed I had some Cause to believe, that the Defence of the Country was not disagreeable to any of them, provided they were not requir'd to assist in it. And I found that a much greater Number of them than I could have imagined, tho' against offensive War, were clearly for the defensive. Many Pamphlets *pro & con.* were publish'd on the Subject, and some by good Quakers in favour of Defence, which I believe convinc'd most of their younger People. A Transaction in our Fire Company gave me some Insight into their prevailing Sentiments. It had been propos'd that we should encourage the Scheme for building a Battery by laying out the present Stock, then about Sixty Pounds, in Tickets of the Lottery. By our Rules no Money could be dispos'd of but at the next Meeting after the Proposal. The Company consisted of Thirty Members, of which Twenty-two were Quakers, & Eight only of other Persuasions. We eight punctually attended the Meeting; but tho' we thought that some of the Quakers would join us, we were by no means sure of a Majority. Only one Quaker, Mr James Morris, appear'd to oppose the Measure: He express'd much Sorrow that it had ever been propos'd, as he said *Friends* were all against it, and it would create such Discord as might break up the Company. We told him, that we saw no Reason for that; we were the Minority, and if *Friends* were against the Measure and outvoted us, we must and should, agreable to the Usage of all Societies, submit. When the Hour for Business arriv'd, it was mov'd to put the Vote. He allow'd we might then do it by the Rules, but as he could assure us that a Number of Members intended to be present for the purpose of opposing it, it would be but candid to allow a little time for their appearing. While we were disputing this, a Waiter came to tell me two Gentlemen below desir'd to speak with me. I went down, and found they were two of our Quaker Members. They told me there were eight of them assembled at a Tavern just by; that they were determin'd to come and vote with us if there should be occasion, which they hop'd would not be the Case; and desir'd we would not call for their Assistance if we could do without it, as their Voting for such a Measure might embroil them with their Elders & Friends; Being thus secure of a Majority, I went up, and after a little seeming Hesitation, agreed to a Delay of another Hour. This Mr Morris allow'd to be extreamly fair. Not one of his opposing Friends appear'd, at which he express'd great Surprize; and at the Expiration of the Hour, we carry'd the Resolution Eight to one; And as of the 22 Quakers, Eight were ready to vote with us and, Thirteen by their Absence manifested that they were not inclin'd to oppose the Measure, I afterwards estimated the Proportion of Quakers sincerely against Defence as one to twenty one only. For these were all regular Members, of that Society, and in good Reputation among them, and had due Notice of what was propos'd at that Meeting.

The honourable & learned Mr Logan,* who had always been of that Sect, was one who wrote an Address to them, declaring his Approbation of defensive War, and supporting his Opinion by many strong Arguments: He put into my Hands Sixty Pounds, to be laid out in Lottery Tickets for the Battery, with Directions to apply what Prizes might be drawn wholly to that Service. He told me the following Anecdote of his old Master Wm Penn. respecting Defence. He came over from England, when a young Man, with that Proprietary, and as his Secretary. It was War Time, and their Ship was chas'd by an armed Vessel suppos'd to be an Enemy. Their Captain prepar'd for Defence, but told Wm Penn and his Company of Quakers, that he did not expect their Assistance, and they might retire into the Cabin; which they did, except James Logan, who chose to stay upon Deck, and was quarter'd to a Gun. The suppos'd Enemy prov'd a Friend; so there was no Fighting. But when the Secretary went down to communicate the Intelligence, Wm Penn rebuk'd him severely for staying upon Deck and undertaking to assist in defending the Vessel, contrary to the Principles of *Friends*, especially as it had not been required by the Captain. This Reproof being before all the Company, piqu'd the Secretary, who answer'd, *I being thy Servant, why did thee not order me to come down: but thee was willing enough that I should stay and help to fight the Ship when thee thought there was Danger.*

My being many Years in the Assembly, the Majority of which were constantly Quakers, gave me frequent Opportunities of seeing the Embarassment given them by their Principle against War, whenever Application was made to them by Order of the Crown to grant Aids for military Purposes. They were unwilling to offend Government on the one hand, by a direct Refusal, and their Friends the Body of Quakers on the other, by a Compliance contrary to their Principles. Hence a Variety of Evasions to avoid Complying, and Modes of disguising the Compliance when it became unavoidable. The common Mode at last was to grant Money under the Phrase of its being *for the King's Use*, and never to enquire how it was applied. But if the Demand was not directly from the Crown, that Phrase was found not so proper, and some other was to be invented. As when Powder was wanting, (I think it was for the Garrison at Louisburg,) and the Government of New England solicited a Grant of some from Pensilvania, which was much urg'd on the House by Governor Thomas,[†] they could not grant Money to buy Powder, because that was an Ingredient of War, but they voted an Aid to New England, of Three Thousand Pounds, to be put into the hands of the Governor, and appropriated it for the Purchasing of Bread, Flour, Wheat, or *other Grain*. Some of the Council desirous of giving the House still farther Embarassment, advis'd the Governor not to accept Provision, as not being the Thing he had demanded. But he reply'd, "I shall, take the Money, for I understand very well their Meaning; *Other Grain*, is Gunpowder;" which he accordingly bought; and they never

---

[†] See the Votes

objected to it. It was in Allusion to this Fact, that when in our Fire Company we feared the Success of our Proposal in favour of the Lottery, & I had said to my Friend Mr Syng, one of our Members, if we fail, let us move the Purchase of a Fire Engine with the Money; the Quakers can have no Objection to that: and then if you nominate me, and I you, as the Committee for that purpose, we will buy a great Gun, which is certainly a *Fire-Engine*: I see, says he, you have improv'd by being so long in the Assembly; your equivocal Project would be just a Match for their Wheat *or other Grain*.

These Embarassments that the Quakers suffer'd from having establish'd & published it as one of their Principles, that no kind of War was lawful, and which being once published, they could not afterwards, however they might change their minds, easily get rid of, reminds me of what I think a more prudent Conduct in another Sect among us; that of the Dunkers. I was acquainted with one of its Founders, Michael Welfare,* soon after it appear'd.—He complain'd to me that they were grievously calumniated by the Zealots of other Persuasions, and charg'd with abominable Principles and Practices to which they were utter Strangers. I told him this had always been the case with new Sects; and that to put a Stop to such Abuse, I imagin'd it might be well to publish the Articles of their Belief and the Rules of their Discipline. He said that it had been propos'd among them, but not agreed to, for this Reason; "When we were first drawn together as a Society, says he, it had pleased God to inlighten our Minds so far, as to see that some Doctrines which we once esteemed Truths were Errors, & that others which we had esteemed Errors were real Truths. From time to time he has been pleased to afford us farther Light, and our Principles have been improving, & our Errors diminishing. Now we are not sure that we are arriv'd at the End of this Progression, and at the Perfection of Spiritual or Theological Knowledge; and we fear that if we should once print our Confession of Faith, we should feel ourselves as if bound & confin'd by it, and perhaps be unwilling to receive farther Improvement; and our Successors still more so, as conceiving what we their Elders & Founders had done, to be something sacred, never to be departed from."—This Modesty in a Sect is perhaps a singular Instance in the History of Mankind, every other Sect supposing itself in Possession of all Truth, and that those who differ are so far in the Wrong: Like a Man travelling in foggy Weather: Those at some Distance before him on the Road he sees wrapt up in the Fog, as well as those behind him, and also the People in the Fields on each side; but neer him all appears clear.—Tho' in truth he is as much in the Fog as any of them. To avoid this kind of Embarassment the Quakers have of late Years been gradually declining the public Service in the Assembly & in the Magistracy. Chusing rather to quit their Power than their Principle.

In order of Time I should have mentioned before, that having in 1742 invented an open Stove, for the better warming of Rooms and at the same time saving Fuel, as the fresh Air admitted was warmed in Entring, I made a Present of the Model to Mr Robert Grace, one of my early Friends, who having an Iron Furnace, found the Casting of the Plates for these Stoves a profitable Thing, as they were growing in Demand. To promote that Demand I wrote and published a Pamphlet Intitled, *An Account of the New-Invented* PENN-SYLVANIA FIRE PLACES: *Wherein their Construction & manner of Operation is particularly explained; their Advantages above every other Method of warming Rooms demonstrated; and all Objections that have been raised against the Use of them answered & obviated, &c.* This Pamphlet had a good Effect, Gov.ʳ Thomas was so pleas'd with the Construction of this Stove, as describ'd in it that he offer'd to give me a Patent for the sole Vending of them for a Term of Years; but I declin'd it from a Principle which has ever weigh'd with me on such Occasions, viz. *That as we enjoy great Advantages from the Inventions of others, we should be glad of an Opportunity to serve others by any Invention of ours, and this we should do freely and generously.* An Ironmonger in London, however, after assuming a good deal of my Pamphlet & working it up into his own, and making some small Changes in the Machine, which rather hurt its Operation, got a Patent for it there, and made as I was told a little Fortune by it.—And this is not the only Instance of Patents taken out for my Inventions by others, tho' not always with the same Success:—which I never contested, as having no Desire of profiting by Patents my self, and hating Disputes.—The Use of these Fireplaces in very many Houses both of this and the neighbouring Colonies, has been and is a great Saving of Wood to the Inhabitants.—

Peace being concluded, and the Association Business therefore at an End, I turn'd my Thoughts again to the Affair of establishing an Academy. The first Step I took was to associate in the Design a Number of active Friends, of whom the Junto furnished a good Part; the next was to write and publish a Pamphlet intitled, *Proposals relating to the Education of Youth in Pennsylvania*.—This I distributed among the principal Inhabitants gratis; and as soon as I could suppose their Minds a little prepared by the Perusal of it, I set on foot a Subscription for Opening and Supporting an Academy; it was to be paid in Quotas yearly for Five Years; by so dividing it I judg'd the Subscription might be larger, and I believe it was so, amounting to no less (if I remember right) than Five thousand Pounds.—In the Introduction to these Proposals, I stated their Publication not as an Act of mine, but of some *publick-spirited Gentlemen*; avoiding as much as I could, according to my usual Rule, the presenting myself to the Publick as the Author of any Scheme for their Benefit.—

The Subscribers, to carry the Project into immediate Execution chose out of their Number Twenty-four Trustees, and appointed Mr Francis, then Attorney General, and myself, to draw up Constitutions for the Government of the Academy, which being done and signed, an House was hired, Masters engag'd and the Schools opened I think in the same Year 1749. The Scholars encreasing fast, the House was soon found too small, and we were looking out for a

Piece of Ground properly situated, with Intention to build, when Providence threw into our way a large House ready built, which with a few Alterations might well serve our purpose, this was the Building before mentioned erected by the Hearers of Mr Whitefield, and was obtain'd for us in the following Manner.

It is to be noted, that the Contributions to this Building being made by People of different Sects, Care was taken in the Nomination of Trustees, in whom the Building & Ground was to be vested, that a Predominancy should not be given to any Sect, lest in time that Predominancy might be a means of appropriating the whole to the Use of such Sect, contrary to the original Intention; it was therefore that one of each Sect was appointed, viz. one Church-of-England-man, one Presbyterian, one Baptist, one Moravian, &c. Those in case of Vacancy by Death were to fill it by Election from among the Contributors. The Moravian happen'd not to please his Colleagues, and on his Death, they resolved to have no other of that Sect. The Difficulty then was, how to avoid having two of some other Sect, by means of the new Choice. Several Persons were named and for that Reason not agreed to. At length one mention'd me, with the Observation that I was merely an honest Man, & of no Sect at all; which prevail'd with them to chuse me. The Enthusiasm which existed when the House was built, had long since abated, and its Trustees had not been able to procure fresh Contributions for paying the Ground Rent, and discharging some other Debts the Building had occa-sion'd, which embarrass'd them greatly. Being now a Member of both Sets of Trustees, that for the Building & that for the Academy, I had good Opportunity of negociating with both, & brought them finally to an Agreement, by which the Trustees of the Building were to cede it to those of the Academy, the latter undertaking to discharge the Debt, to keep forever open in the Building a large Hall for occasional Preachers according to the original Intention, and maintain a Free School for the Instruction of poor Children. Writings were accordingly drawn, and on paying the Debts the Trustees of the Academy were put in Possession of the Premises, and by dividing the great & lofty Hall into Stories, and different Rooms above & below for the several Schools, and purchasing some additional Ground, the whole was soon made fit for our purpose, and the Scholars remov'd into the Building. The Care and Trouble of agreeing with the Work men, purchasing Materials, and superintending the Work fell upon me, and I went thro' it the more chearfully, as it did not then interfere with my private Business, having the Year before taken a very able, industrious & honest Partner, Mr David Hall, with whose Character I was well acquainted, as he had work'd for me four Years. He took off my Hands all Care of the Printing-Office, paying me punctually my Share of the Profits. This Partnership continued Eighteen Years, successfully for us both.—

The Trustees of the Academy after a while were incorporated by a Charter from the Governor; their Funds were increas'd by Contributions in Britain, and Grants of Land from the Proprietaries, to which the Assembly has since made considerable Addition, and thus was established the present University of Philadelphia. I have been continued one of its Trustees from the Beginning, now near forty Years, and have had the very great Pleasure of seeing a Number of the Youth who have receiv'd their Education in it, distinguish'd by their improv'd Abilities, serviceable in public Stations, and Ornaments to their Country.

When I disengag'd myself as above mentioned from private Business, I flatter'd myself that, by the sufficient tho' moderate Fortune I had acquir'd, I had secur'd Leisure during the rest of my Life, for Philosophical Studies and Amusements; I purchas'd all Dr Spence's Apparatus, who had come from England to lecture here; and I proceeded in my Electrical Experiments with great Alacrity; but the Publick now considering me as a Man of Leisure, laid hold of me for their Purposes; every Part of our Civil Government, and almost at the same time, imposing some Duty upon me. The Governor put me into the Commission of the Peace; the Corporation of the City chose me of the

Common Council, and soon after an Alderman; and the
Citizens at large chose me a Burgess to represent them in
Assembly. This latter Station was the more agreable to me,
as I was at length tired with sitting there to hear Debates
in which as Clerk I could take no part, and which were
often so unentertaining, that I was induc'd to amuse myself
with making magic Squares, or Circles, or any thing to avoid
Weariness. And I conceiv'd my becoming a Member would
enlarge my Power of doing Good. I would not however
insinuate that my Ambition was not flatter'd by all these
Promotions. It certainly was. For considering my low Beginning they were great Things to me. And they were still
more pleasing, as being so many spontaneous Testimonies
of the public's good Opinion, and by me entirely unsolicited.

The Office of Justice of the Peace I try'd a little, by
attending a few Courts, and sitting on the Bench to hear
Causes. But finding that more Knowledge of the Common
Law than I possess'd, was necessary to act in that Station
with Credit, I gradually withdrew from it, excusing myself
by my being oblig'd to attend the higher Dutys of a
Legislator in the Assembly. My Election to this Trust was
repeated every Year for Ten Years, without my ever asking
any Elector for his Vote, or signifying either directly or
indirectly any Desire of being chosen.—On taking my Seat
in the House, my Son was appointed their Clerk.

The Year following, a Treaty being to be held with the
Indians at Carlisle, the Governor sent a Message to the
House, proposing that they should nominate some of their
Members to be join'd with some Members of Council as
Commissioners for that purpose.[†] The House nam'd the
Speaker (Mr Norris) and my self; and being commission'd
we went to Carlisle, and met the Indians accordingly.—As
those People are extreamly apt to get drunk, and when so
are very quarrelsome & disorderly, we strictly forbad the
selling any Liquor to them; and when they complain'd of
this Restriction, we told them that if they would continue

[†] See the Votes to have this more correctly

sober during the Treaty, we would give them Plenty of Rum when Business was over. They promis'd this; and they kept their Promise—because they could get no Liquor—and the Treaty was conducted very orderly, and concluded to mutual Satisfaction. They then claim'd and receiv'd the Rum. This was in the Afternoon. They were near 100 Men, Women & Children, and were lodg'd in temporary Cabins built in the Form of a Square. just without the Town. In the Evening, hearing a great Noise among them, the Commission.^{rs} walk'd out to see what was the Matter. We found they had made a great Bonfire in the Middle of the Square. They were all drunk Men and Women, quarrelling and fighting. Their dark-colour'd Bodies, half naked, seen only by the gloomy Light of the Bonfire, running after and beating one another with Firebrands, accompanied by their horrid Yellings, form'd a Scene the most resembling our Ideas of Hell that could well be imagin'd. There was no appeasing the Tumult, and we retired to our Lodging. At Midnight a Number of them came thundering at our Door, demanding more Rum; of which we took no Notice. The next Day, sensible they had misbehav'd in giving us that Disturbance, they sent three of their old Counsellors to make their Apology. The Orator acknowledg'd the Fault, but laid it upon the Rum; and then endeavour'd to excuse the Rum, by saying, "*The great Spirit who made all things made every thing for some Use, and whatever Use he design'd any thing for, that Use it should always be put to; Now, when he made Rum, he said,* LET THIS BE FOR INDIANS TO GET DRUNK WITH. *And it must be so.*—And indeed if it be the Design of Providence to extirpate these Savages in order to make room for the Cultivators of the Earth, it seems not improbable that Rum may be the appointed Means. It has already annihilated all the Tribes who formerly inhabited the Seacoast.—

In 1751. Dr Thomas Bond, a particular Friend of mine, conceiv'd the Idea of establishing a Hospital in Philadelphia, for the Reception and Cure of poor sick Persons, whether Inhabitants of the Province or Strangers. A very beneficent

Design, which has been ascrib'd to me, but was originally his. He was zealous & active in endeavouring to procure Subscriptions towards for it; but the Proposal being a Novelty in America, and at first not well understood, he met with small Success. At length he came to me, with the Compliment that he found there was no such thing as carrying a public Spirited Project through, without my being concern'd in it; "for, says he, I am often ask'd by those to whom I propose Subscribing, Have you consulted Franklin upon this Business? and what does he think of it?—And when I tell them that I have not, (supposing it rather out of your Line,) they do not subscribe, but say they will consider of it." I enquir'd into the Nature, & probable Utility of his Scheme, and receiving from him a very satisfactory Explanation, I not only subscrib'd to it myself, but engag'd heartily in the Design of Procuring Subscriptions from others. Previous however to the Solicitation, I endeavoured to prepare the Minds of the People by writing on the Subject in the Newspapers, which was my usual Custom in such Cases, but which he had omitted. The Subscriptions afterwards were more free and generous, but beginning to flag, I saw they would be insufficient without some Assistance from the Assembly, and therefore propos'd to petition for it, which was done. The Country Members did not at first relish the Project. They objected that it could only be serviceable to the City, and therefore the Citizens should alone be at the Expence of it; and they doubted whether the Citizens themselves generally approv'd of it: My Allegation on the contrary, that it met with such Approbation as to leave no doubt of our being able to raise 2000£ by voluntary Donations, they considered as a most extravagant Supposition, and utterly impossible. On this I form'd my Plan; and asking Leave to bring in a Bill, for incorporating the Contributors, according to the Prayers of their Petition, and granting them a blank Sum of Money, which Leave was obtain'd chiefly on the Consideration that the House could throw the Bill out if they did not like it, I drew it so as to make the important Clause a conditional

One, viz. "And be it enacted by the Authority aforesaid That when the said Contributors shall have met and chosen their Managers and Treasurer, *and shall have raised by their Contributions a Capital Stock of* 2000£ *Value*, (the yearly Interest of which is to be applied to the Accommodating of the Sick Poor in the said Hospital, free of Charge for Diet, Attendance, Advice and Medicines) and *shall make the same appear to the Satisfaction of the Speaker of the Assembly* for the time being; that *then* it shall and may be lawful for the said Speaker, and he is hereby required to sign an Order on the Provincial Treasurer for the Payment of Two Thousand Pounds in two yearly Payments, to the Treasurer of the said Hospital, to be applied to the Founding, Building and Finishing of the same."—This Condition carried the Bill through; for the Members who had oppos'd the Grant, and now conceiv'd they might have the Credit of being charitable without the Expence, agreed to its Passage; And then in soliciting Subscriptions among the People we urg'd the conditional Promise of the Law as an additional Motive to give, since every Man's Donation would be doubled. Thus the Clause work'd both ways. The Subscriptions accordingly soon exceeded the requisite Sum, and we claim'd and receiv'd the Public Gift, which enabled us to carry the Design into Execution. A convenient and handsome Building was sooon erected, the Institution has by constant Experience been found useful, and flourishes to this Day.—And I do not remember any of my political Maneuvres, the Success of which gave me at the time more Pleasure. Or that in after-thinking of it, I more easily excus'd my-self for having made some Use of Cunning.—

It was about this time that another Projector, the Revd Gilbert Tennent, came to me, with a Request that I would assist him in procuring a Subscription for erecting a new Meeting-house. It was to be for the Use of a Congregation he had gathered among the Presbyterians who were originally Disciples of Mr Whitefield. Unwilling to make myself disagreable to my fellow Citizens, by too frequently soliciting their Contributions, I absolutely refus'd. He then desir'd I would furnish him with a List of the Names of Persons I knew by Experience to be generous and public-spirited. I thought it would be unbecoming in me, after their kind Compliance with my Solicitations, to mark them out to be worried by other Beggars, and therefore refus'd also to give such a List.—He then desir'd I would at leas give him my Advice. That I will readily do, said I; and, in the first Place, I advise you to apply to all those whom you know will give something; next to those whom you are uncertain whether they will give any thing or not; and show them the List of those who have given: and lastly, do not neglect those who you are sure will give nothing; for in some of them you may be mistaken.—He laugh'd, and thank'd me, and said he would take my Advice. He did so, for he ask'd of *every body*; and he obtain'd a much larger Sum than he expected, with which he erected the capacious and very elegant Meeting-house that stands in Arch Street.—

Our City, tho' laid out with a beautiful Regularity, the Streets large, strait, and crossing each other at right Angles, had the Disgrace of suffering those Streets to remain long unpav'd, and in wet Weather the Wheels of heavy Carriages plough'd them into a Quagmire, so that it was difficult to cross them. And in dry Weather the Dust was offensive. I had liv'd near what was call'd the Jersey Market, and saw with Pain the Inhabitants wading in Mud while purchasing their Provisions. A Strip of Ground down the middle of that Market was at length pav'd with Brick, so that being once in the Market they had firm Footing, but were often over Shoes in Dirt to get there.—By talking and writing on the Subject, I was at length instrumental in getting the Street pav'd with Stone between the Market and the brick'd Foot-Pavement that was on each Side next the Houses. This for some time gave an easy Access to the Market, dry-shod. But the rest of the Street not being pav'd, whenever a Carriage came out of the Mud upon this Pavement, it shook off and left its Dirt on it, and it was soon cover'd with Mire, which was not remov'd, the City as yet having no

Scavengers.—After some Enquiry I found a poor industrious Man, who was willing to undertake keeping the Pavement clean, by sweeping it twice a week & carrying off the Dirt from before all the Neighbours Doors, for the Sum of Sixpence per Month, to be paid by each House. I then wrote and printed a Paper, setting forth the Advantages to the Neighbourhood that might be obtain'd by this small Expence; the greater Ease in keeping our Houses clean, so much Dirt not being brought in by People's Feet; the Benefit to the Shops by more Custom, as Buyers could more easily get at them, and by not having in windy Weather the Dust blown in upon their Goods, &c. &c. I sent one of these Papers to each House, and in a Day or two went round to see who would subscribe an Agreement to pay these Sixpences. It was unanimously sign'd, and for a time well executed. All the Inhabitants of the City were delighted with the Cleanliness of the Pavement that surrounded the Market; it being a Convenience to all; and this rais'd a general Desire to have all the Streets paved; & made the People more willing to submit to a Tax for that purpose. After some time I drew a Bill for Paving the City, and brought it into the Assembly.[†] It was just before I went to England in 1757. and did not pass till I was gone, and then with an Alteration in the Mode of Assessment, which I thought not for the better, but with an additional Provision for lighting as well as Paving the Streets, which was a great Improvement.—It was by a private Person, the late Mr John Clifton, his giving a Sample of the Utility of Lamps by placing one at his Door, that the People were first impress'd with the Idea of enlightning all the City. The Honour of this public Benefit has also been ascrib'd to me, but it belongs truly to that Gentleman. I did but follow his Example; and have only some Merit to claim respecting the Form of our Lamps as differing from the Globe Lamps we at first were supply'd with from London. Those we found inconvenient in these respects; they admitted no Air, below, the Smoke therefore

[†] See Votes

did not readily go out above, but circulated in the Globe, lodg'd on its Inside, and soon obstructed the the Light they were intended to afford; giving, besides, the daily Trouble of wiping them clean: and an accidental Stroke on one of them would demolish it, & render it totally useless. I therefore suggested the composing them of four flatt flat Panes, with a long Funnel above to draw up the Smoke, and Crevices admitting Air below, to facilitate the Ascent of the Smoke. By this means they were kept clean, and did not grow dark in a few Hours as the London Lamps do, but continu'd bright till Morning; and an accidental Stroke would generally break but a single Pane, easily repair'd. I have sometimes wonder'd that the Londoners did not, from the Effect Holes in the Bottom of the Globe Lamps us'd at Vauxhall, have in keeping them clean, learn to have such Holes in their Street Lamps. But those Holes being made for another purpose, viz. to communicate Flame more suddenly to the Wick, by a little Flax hanging down thro' them, the other Use of letting in Air seems not to have been thought of.—And therefore, after the Lamps have been lit a few Hours, the Streets of London are very poorly illuminated.—

The Mention of these Improvements puts me in mind of one I propos'd when in London, to Dr Fothergill, who was among the best Men I have known, and a great Promoter of useful Projects. I had observ'd that the Streets when dry were never swept and the light Dust carried away, but it was suffer'd to accumulate till wet Weather reduc'd it to Mud, and then after lying some Days so deep on the Pavement that there was no Crossing but in Paths kept clean by poor People with Brooms, it was with great Labour rak'd together & thrown up into Carts open above, the Sides of which suffer'd some of the Slush at every jolt on the Pavement to shake out and fall, some times to the Annoyance of Foot-Passengers. The Reason given for not sweeping the dusty Streets was, that the Dust would fly into the Windows of Shops and Houses. An accidental Occurrence had instructed me how much Sweeping might be done in a little Time. I found at my Door in Craven Street one Morning a poor Woman sweeping my Pavement with a birch Broom. She appeared very pale & feeble as just come out of a Fit of Sickness. I ask'd who employ'd her to sweep there. She said, "Nobody; but I am very poor and in Distress, and I sweeps before Gentlefolkeses Doors, and hopes they will give me something." I bid her sweep the whole Street clean and I would give her a Shilling. This was at 9 aClock. At 12 she came for the Shilling. From the Slowness I saw at first in her Working, I could scarce believe that the Work was done so soon, and sent my Servant to examine it, who reported that the whole Street was swept perfectly clean, and all the Dust plac'd in the Gutter which was in the Middle. And the next Rain wash'd it quite away, so that the Pavement & even the Kennel were perfectly clean.—I then judg'd that if that feeble Woman could sweep such a Street in 3 Hours, a strong active Man might have done it in half the time. And here let me remark the Convenience of having but one Gutter in such a narrow Street, running down its Middle, instead of two, one on each Side near the Footway. For Where all the Rain that falls on a Street runs from the Sides and meets in the middle, it forms there a Current strong enough to wash away all the Mud it meets with: But when divided into two Channels, it is often too weak to cleanse either, and only makes the Mud it finds more fluid, so that the Wheels of the Carriages and Feet of Horses throw and dash it up on the Foot Pavement which is thereby rendred foul and slippery, and sometimes splash it upon those who are walking.—My Proposal communicated to the good Doctor, was as follows.

"For the more effectual cleaning and keeping clean the Streets of London and Westminster, it is proposed,

"That the several Watchmen be contracted with to have the Dust swept up in dry Seasons, and the Mud rak'd up at other Times, each in the several Streets & Lanes of his Round.

"That they be furnish'd with Brooms and other proper Instruments for these purposes, to be kept at their respective Stands, ready to furnish the poor People they may employ in the Service.

"That in the dry Summer Months the Dust be all swept up into Heaps at proper Distances, before the Shops and Windows of Houses are usually opened: when the Scavengers with close-covered Carts shall also carry it all away.——

"That the Mud when rak'd up be not left in Heaps to be spread abroad again by the Wheels of Carriages & Trampling of Horses; but that the Scavengers be provided with Bodies of Carts, not plac'd high upon Wheels, but low upon Sliders; with Lattice Bottoms, which being cover'd with Straw, will retain the Mud thrown into them, and permit the Water to drain from it, whereby it will become much lighter, Water making the greatest Part of its Weight. These Bodies of Carts to be plac'd at convenient Distances, and the Mud brought to them in Wheelbarrows, they remaining where plac'd till the Mud is drain'd, and then Horses brought to draw them away."——

I have since had Doubts of the Practicability of the latter Part of this Proposal, on Account of the Narrowness of some Streets, and the Difficulty of placing the Draining Sleds so as not to encumber too much the Passage: But I am still of Opinion that the former, requiring the Dust, to be swept up & carry'd away before the Shops are open, is very practicable in the Summer, when the Days are long. For in walking thro' the Strand and Fleet street one Morning at 7 aClock I observ'd there was not one shop open tho' it had been Day-light & the Sun up above three Hours. The Inhabitants of London chusing voluntarily to live much by Candle Light, and sleep by Sunshine; and yet often complain a little absurdly, of the Duty on Candles and the high Price of Tallow.——

Some may think these trifling Matters not worth minding or relating.: But when they consider, that tho' Dust blown into the Eyes of a single Person or into a single Shop on a windy Day, is but of small Importance, yet the great Number of the Instances in a populous City, and its frequent Repetitions give it Weight & Consequence; perhaps they will not censure very severely those who bestow some of Attention to Affairs of this seemingly low Nature. Human Felicity is produc'd not so much by great Pieces of good Fortune that seldom, happen, as by little Advantages that occur every day. Thus if you teach a poor young Man to shave himself and keep his Razor in order, you may contribute more to the Happiness of his Life than in giving him a 1000 Guineas. The Money may be soon spent, and the Regret only remaining of having foolishly consum'd it. But in the other Case he escapes the frequent Vexation of waiting for Barbers, & of their sometimes, dirty Fingers, offensive Breaths and dull Razors. He shaves when most convenient to him, and enjoys daily the Pleasure of its being done with a good Instrument.—With these Sentiments I have hazarded the few preceding Pages, hoping they may afford Hints which some time or other may be useful to a City I love, having lived many Years in it very happily; and perhaps to some of our Towns in America.—

Having been for some time employed by the Postmaster General of America, as his Comptroller, in regulating the several Offices, and bringing the Officers to account, I was upon his Death in 1753 appointed jointly with Mr William Hunter to succeed him. by a Commission from the Postmaster General in England. The American Office had never hitherto paid any thing to that of Britain. We were to have 600£ a Year between us if we could make that Sum out of the Profits of the Office. To do this, a Variety of Improvements were necessary; some of these were inevitably at first expensive; so that in the first four Years the Office became above 900£ in debt to us.—But it soon after began to repay us, and before I was displac'd, by a Freak of the Minister's, of which I shall speak hereafter, we had brought it to yield *three times* as much clear Revenue to the Crown as the Post-Office of Ireland. Since that imprudent Transaction, they have receiv'd from it,—Not one Farthing.—

The Business of the Post-Office occasion'd my taking a Journey this Year to New England, where the College of Cambridge of their own Motion, presented me with the Degree of Master of Arts. Yale College in Connecticut, had before made me a similar Compliment. Thus without studying in any College I came to partake of their Honours. They were confer'd in Consideration of my Improvements & Discoveries in the electric Branch of Natural Philosophy.—

In 1754, War with France being again apprehended, a Congress of Commissioners from the different Colonies, was by an Order of the Lords of Trade, to be assembled at Albany, there to confer with the Chiefs of the Six Nations, concerning the Means of defending both their Country and ours. Governor Hamilton, having receiv'd this Order, acquainted the House with it, requesting they would furnish proper Presents for the Indians to be given on this Occasion; and naming the Speaker (Mr Norris) and my self, to join Mr Thomas Penn & Mr Secretary Peters, as Commissioners to act for Pennsylvania. The House approv'd the Nomination, and provided the Goods for the Present, tho' they did not much like treating out of the Province, and we met the other Commissioners and met at Albany about the Middle of June. In our Way thither, I projected and drew up a Plan for the Union of all the Colonies, under one Government so far as might be necessary for Defence, and other important general Purposes. As we pass'd thro' New York, I had there shown my Project to Mr James Alexander & Mr Kennedy, two Gentlemen of great Knowledge in public Affairs, and being fortified by their Approbation I ventur'd to lay it before the Congress. It then appear'd that several of the Commissioners had form'd Plans of the same kind. A previous Question was first taken whether a Union should be established, which pass'd in the Affirmative unanimously. A Committee was then appointed. One Member from each Colony, to consider the several Plans and report. Mine happen'd to be prefer'd, and with a few Amendments was accordingly reported. By this Plan, the general Government was to be administred by a President General appointed and supported by the Crown, and a Grand Council to be chosen by the Representatives of the People of the several Colonies met in their respective Assemblies. The Debates upon it in Congress went on daily hand in hand with the Indian Business. Many Objections and Difficulties were started, but at length they were all overcome, and the Plan was unanimously agreed to, and Copies ordered to be transmitted to the Board of Trade and to the Assemblies of the several Provinces. Its Fate was singular. The Assemblies did not adopt it, as they all thought there was too much *Prerogative* in it; and in England it was judg'd to have too much of the Democratic: The Board of Trade therefore did not approve of it; nor recommend it for the Approbation of his Majesty; but another Scheme was form'd (suppos'd better to answer the same Purpose) whereby the Governors of the Provinces with some Members of their respective Councils were to meet and order the raising of Troops, building of Forts, &c. &c to draw on the Treasury of Great Britain for the Expence, which was afterwards to be refunded by an Act of Parliament laying a Tax on America. My Plan, with my Reasons in suppport of it, is to be found among my political Papers that are printed. Being the Winter following in Boston, I had much Conversation with Gov' Shirley upon both the Plans. Part of what pass'd between us on the Occasion may also be seen among those Papers.—The different & contrary Reasons of dislike to my Plan, makes me suspect that it was really the true Medium; & I am still of Opinion it would have been happy for both Sides the Water if it had been adopted. The Colonies so united would have been sufficiently strong to have defended themselves; there would then have been no need of Troops from England; of course the subsequent Pretence for Taxing America, and the bloody Contest it occasioned, would have been avoided. But such Mistakes are not new; History is full of the Errors of States & Princes.

> "*Look round the habitable World, how few*
> *Know their own Good, or knowing it pursue.**

Those who govern, having much Business on their hands, do not generally like to take the Trouble of considering and carrying into Execution new Projects. The best public Measures are therefore seldom *adopted from previous Wisdom*, but *forc'd by the Occasion*.

The Governor of Pennsylvania in sending it down to the Assembly, express'd his Approbation of the Plan "as appearing to him to be drawn up with great Clearness & Strength of Judgment, and therefore recommended it as well worthy their closest & most serious Attention" The House however, by the Managem^t of a certain Member, took it up when I happen'd to be absent, which I thought not very fair, and reprobated it without paying any Attention to it at all, to my no small Mortification.

In my Journey to Boston this Year I met at New York with our new Governor, Mr Morris, just arriv'd there from England, with whom I had been before intimately acquainted. He brought a Commission to supersede Mr Hamilton, who, tir'd with the Disputes his Proprietary Instructions subjected him to, had resigned. Mr Morris ask'd me, if I thought he must expect as uncomfortable an Administration. I said, No; you may on the contrary have a very comfortable one, if you will only take care not to enter into any Dispute with the Assembly; "My dear Friend, says he, pleasantly, how can you advise my avoiding Disputes. You know I love Disputing; it is one of my greatest Pleasures: However, to show the Regard I have for your Counsel, I promise you I will if possible avoid them." He had some Reason for loving to dispute, being eloquent, an acute Sophister, and therefore generally successful in argumentative Conversation. He had been brought up to it from a Boy, his Father (as I have heard) accustoming his Children to dispute with one another for his Diversion while siting at Table after Dinner. But I think the Practice was not wise, for in the Course of my Observation, these disputing, contradicting & confuting People are generally unfortunate in their Affairs. They get Victory sometimes, but they never get Good Will, which would be of more use to them. We parted, he going to Philadelphia, and I to Boston. In returning, I met at New York with the Votes of the Assembly, by which it appear'd that notwithstanding his Promise to me, he and the House were already in high Contention, and it was a continual Battle between them, as long as he retain'd the Government. I had my Share of it; for as soon as I got back to my Seat in the Assembly, I was put on every Committee for answering his Speeches and Messages, and by the Committees always desired to make the Drafts. Our Answers as well as his Messages were often tart, and sometimes indecently abusive. And as he knew I wrote for the Assembly, one might have imagined that when we met we could hardly avoid cutting Throats. But he was so good-natur'd a Man, that no personal Difference between him and me was occasion'd by the Contest, and we often din'd together. One Afternoon in the height of this public Quarrel, we met in the Street. "Franklin, says he, you must go home with me and spend the Evening. I am to have some Company that you will like;" and taking me by the Arm he led me to his House. In gay Conversation over our Wine after Supper he told us Jokingly that he much admir'd the Idea of Sancho Panza, who when it was propos'd to give him a Government, requested it might be a Government of *Blacks*, as then, if he could not agree with his People he might sell them. One of his Friends who sat next me, says, "Franklin, why do you continue to side with these damn'd Quakers? had not you better sell them? the Proprietor would give you a good Price." The Governor, says I, has not yet *black'd* them enough. He had indeed labour'd hard to blacken the Assembly in all his Messages, but they wip'd off his Colouring as fast as he laid it on, and plac'd it in return thick upon his own Face; so that finding he was likely to be negrify'd himself, he as well as Mr Hamilton, grew tir'd of the Contest, and quitted the Government.

These public Quarrels were all at bottom owing to the Proprietaries, our hereditary Governors; who when any Expence was to be incurr'd for the Defence of their Province, with incredible Meanness instructed their Deputies to pass no Act for levying the necessary Taxes, unless their vast Estates were in the same Act expresly excused; and they had even taken Bonds of those Deputies to observe such Instructions. The Assemblies for three Years held out against this Injustice, Tho' constrain'd to bend at last. At length Capt. Denny, who was Governor Morris's Successor, ventur'd to disobey those instructions; how that was brought about I shall show hereafter.

But I am got forward too fast with my Story; there are still some Transactions to be mentioned that happened during the Administration of Governor Morris.—

War being, in a manner, commenced with France, the Government of Massachusets Bay projected an Attack upon Crown Point, and sent Mr Quincy to Pennsylvania, and Mr Pownall, afterwards Govr Pownall, to N. York to sollicit Assistance. As I was in the Assembly, knew its Temper, & was Mr Quincy's Countryman, he apply'd to me for my Influence & Assistance. I dictated his Address to them which was well receiv'd. They voted an Aid of Ten Thousand Pounds, to be laid out in Provisions. But the Governor refusing his Assent to their Bill, (which included this with other Sums granted for the Use of the Crown) unless a Clause were inserted exempting the Proprietary Estate from bearing any Part of the Tax that would be necessary, the Assembly, tho' very desirous of making their Grant to New England effectual, were at a Loss how to accomplish it. Mr Quincy laboured hard with the Governor to obtain his Assent, but he was obstinate. I then suggested a Method of doing the Business without the Governor, by Orders on the Trustees of the Loan-Office, which by Law the Assembly had the Right of Drawing. There was indeed little or no Money at that time in the Office, and therefor I propos'd that the Orders should be payable in a Year and to bear an Interest of Five percent. With these Orders I suppos'd the Provisions might easily be purchas'd. The Assembly with very little Hesitation adopted the Proposal. The Orders were immediately printed, and I was one of the Committee directed to sign and dispose of them. The Fund for Paying them was the Interest of all the Paper Currency then extant in the Province upon Loan, together with the Revenue arising from the Excise which being known to be more than sufficient, they obtain'd instant Credit, and were not only receiv'd in Payment for the Provisions, but many money'd People who had Cash lying by them, vested it in those Orders, which they found advantageous, as they bore Interest while upon hand, and might on any Occasion be used as Money: So that they were eagerly all bought up, and in a few Weeks none of them were to be seen. Thus this important Affair was by my means compleated, Mr Quincy return'd Thanks to the Assembly in a handsome Memorial, went home highly pleas'd with the Success of his Embassy, and ever after bore for me the most cordial and affectionate Friendship.——

The British Government not chusing to permit the Union of the Colonies, as propos'd at Albany, and to trust that Union with their Defence, lest they should thereby grow too military, and feel their own Strength, Suspicions & Jealousies at this time being entertain'd of them; sent over General Braddock* with two Regiments of Regular English Troops for that purpose. He landed at Alexandria in Virginia, and thence march'd to Frederic Town in Maryland, where he halted for Carriages. Our Assembly apprehending, from some Information, that he had conceived violent Prejudices against, them, as averse to the Service, wish'd me to wait upon him, not as from them, but as Postmaster General, under the guise of proposing to settle with him the Mode of conducting with most Celerity and Certainty the Dispatches between him and the Governors of the several Provinces, with whom he must necessarily have continual Correspondence, and of which they propos'd to pay the Expence. My Son accompanied me on this Journey. We found the General at Frederic Town, waiting impatiently for the Return of those he had sent thro' the back Parts of Maryland & Virginia to collect Waggons. I staid with him several Days, Din'd with him daily, and had full Opportunity of removing all his Prejudices, by the Information of what the Assembly had before his Arrival actually done and were still willing to do to facilitate his Operations. When I was about to depart, the Returns of Waggons to be obtain'd were brought, in, by which it appear'd that they amounted only to twenty-five, and not all of those were in serviceable Condition. The General and all the Officers were surpriz'd, declar'd the Expedition was then at an End, being impossible, and exclaim'd against the Ministers for ignorantly landing them in a Country destitute of the Means of conveying their Stores, Baggage. &c. not less than 150 Waggons being necessary. I happen'd to say, I thought it was pity they had not been landed rather in Pennsylvania, as in that Country almost every Farmer had his Waggon. The General eagerly laid hold of my Words, and said, "Then you, Sir, who are a Man of Interest there, can probably procure them for us; and I beg you will undertake it." I ask'd what Terms were to be offer'd the Owners of the Waggons; and I was desir'd to put on Paper the Terms that appear'd to me necessary. This I did, and they were agreed to, and a Commission and Instructions accordingly prepar'd immediately. What those Terms were will appear in the Advertisement I publish'd as soon as I arriv'd at Lancaster; which being, from the great and sudden Effect it produc'd, a Piece of some Curiosity, I shall insert at length, as follows.

ADVERTISEMENT.

Lancaster, April 26, 1755.

WHEREAS 150 Waggons, with 4 Horses to each Waggon, and 1500 Saddle or Pack-Horses are wanted for the Service of his Majesty's Forces now about to rendezvous at *Wills*'s Creek; and his Excellency General *Braddock* hath been pleased to impower me to contract for the Hire of the same; I hereby give Notice, that I shall attend for that Purpose at *Lancaster* from this Time till next *Wednesday* Evening; and at *York* from next *Thursday* Morning 'till *Friday* Evening; where I shall be ready to agree for Waggons and Teams, or single Horses, on the following Terms, *viz.*

1st. That there shall be paid for each Waggon with 4 good Horses and a Driver, *Fifteen Shillings* per *Diem*: And for each able Horse with a Pack-Saddle or other Saddle and Furniture, *Two Shillings* per *Diem*. And for each able Horse without a Saddle, *Eighteen Pence* per *Diem*.

2dly, That the Pay commence from the Time of their joining the Forces at *Wills*'s Creek (which must be on or before the twentieth of *May* ensuing) and that a reasonable Allowance be made over and above for the Time necessary for their travelling to *Wills*'s Creek and home again after their Discharge.

3dly, Each Waggon and Team, and every Saddle or Pack Horse is to be valued by indifferent Persons, chosen between me and the Owner, and in Case of the Loss of any Waggon, Team or other Horse in the Service, the Price according to such Valuation, is to be allowed and paid.

4thly, Seven Days Pay is to be advanced and paid in hand by me to the Owner of each Waggon and Team, or Horse, at the Time of contracting, if required; and the Remainder to be paid by General *Braddock*, or by the Paymaster of the Army, at the Time of their Discharge, or from time to time as it shall be demanded.

5thly, No Drivers of Waggons, or Persons taking care of the hired Horses, are on any Account to be called upon to do the Duty of Soldiers, or be otherwise employ'd than in conducting or taking Care of their Carriages and Horses.

6thly, All Oats, Indian Corn or other Forage, that Waggons or Horses bring to the Camp more than is necessary for the Subsistence of the Horses, is to be taken for the Use of the Army, and a reasonable Price paid for it.

Note. My Son *William Franklin*, is impowered to enter into like Contracts with any Person in *Cumberland* County.

B. FRANKLIN.

To the Inhabitants of the Counties of
Lancaster, York, *and* Cumberland.

Friends and Countrymen,

BEING occasionally at the Camp at *Frederic* a few Days
since, I found the General and Officers of the Army extreamly exasperated, on Account of their not being supply'd
with Horses and Carriages, which had been expected from
this Province as most able to furnish them; but thro' the
Dissensions between our Governor and Assembly, Money
had not been provided nor any Steps taken for that Purpose.

It was proposed to send an armed Force immediately into
these Counties, to seize as many of the best Carriages and
Horses as should be wanted, and compel as many Persons
into the Service as would be necessary to drive and take
care of them.

I apprehended that the Progress of a Body of Soldiers
thro' these Counties on such an Occasion, especially considering the Temper they are in, and their Resentment
against us, would be attended with many and great Inconveniencies to the Inhabitants; and therefore more willingly
undertook the Trouble of trying first what might be done
by fair and equitable Means.

The People of these back Counties have lately complained
to the Assembly that a sufficient Currency was wanting; you
have now an Opportunity of receiving and dividing among
you a very considerable Sum; for if the Service of this
Expedition should continue (as it's more than probable it
will) for 120 Days, the Hire of these Waggons and Horses will amount to upwards of *Thirty thousand Pounds*, which
will be paid you in Silver and Gold of the King's Money.

The Service will be light and easy, for the Army will
scarce march above 12 Miles per Day, and the Waggons and
Baggage Horses, as they carry those Things that are absolutely necessary to the Welfare of the Army, must march
with the Army and no faster, and are, for the Army's sake,
always plac'd where they can be most secure, whether on a
March or in Camp.

If you are really, as I believe you are, good and loyal
Subjects to His Majesty, you may now do a most acceptable
Service, and make it easy to yourselves; for three or four

of such as cannot separately spare from the Business of their Plantations a Waggon and four Horses and a Driver, may do it together, one furnishing the Waggon, another one or two Horses, and another the Driver, and divide the Pay proportionably between you. But if you do not this Service to your King and Country voluntarily, when such good Pay and reasonable Terms are offered you, your Loyalty will be strongly suspected; the King's Business must be done; so many brave Troops, come so far for your Defence, must not stand idle, thro' your backwardness to do what may be reasonably expected from you; Waggons and Horses must be had; violent Measures will probably be used; and you will be to seek for a Recompence where you can find it, and your Case perhaps be little pitied or regarded.

I have no particular Interest in this Affair; as (except the Satisfaction of endeavouring to do Good and prevent Mischief) I shall have only my Labour for my Pains. If this Method of obtaining the Waggons and Horses is not like to succeed, I am oblig'd to send Word to the General in fourteen Days; and I suppose Sir *John St. Clair* the Hussar, with a Body of Soldiers, will immediately enter the Province, for the Purpose aforesaid, of which I shall be sorry to hear, because

I am,   *very sincerely and truly*
        your Friend and Well-wisher,

B. FRANKLIN

I receiv'd of the General about 800£ to be disburs'd in Advance-money to the Waggon-Owners &c: but that Sum being insufficient, I advanc'd upwards of 200£ more, and in two Weeks, the 150 Waggons with 259 carrying Horses were on their March for the Camp.—The Advertisement promised Payment according to the Valuation, in case any Waggon or Horse should be lost. The Owners however, alledging they did not know General Braddock, or what Dependance might be had on his Promise, insisted on my Bond for the Performance, which I accordingly gave them.

While I was at the Camp, supping one Evening with the officers of Col. Dunbar's Regiment, he represented to me his Concern for the Subalterns, who he said were generally not in Affluence, and could ill afford in this dear Country to lay in the Stores that might be necessary in so long a March thro' a Wilderness where nothing was to be purchas'd. I commisserated their Case, and resolved to endeavour procuring them some Relief. I said nothing however to him of my Intention, but wrote the next Morning to the Committee of Assembly, who had the Disposition of some public Money, warmly recommending the Case of these Officers to their Consideration, and proposing that a Present should be sent them of Necessaries & Refreshments. My Son, who had had some Experience of a Camp Life, and of its Wants, drew up a List for me, which I inclos'd in my Letter. The Committee approv'd, and used such Diligence, that conducted by my Son, the Stores arrived at the Camp as soon as the Waggons. They consisted of 20 Parcels, each containing

6 lb Loaf Sugar
6 lb good Muscovado D^o—
1 lb good Green Tea
1 lb good Bohea D^o
6 lb good ground Coffee
6 lb Chocolate
1/2 C.^{wt} best white Biscuit
1/2 lb Pepper
1 Quart best white Wine Vinegar
1 Gloucester Cheese
1 Kegg cont.^{g} 20 lb good Butter
2 Doz. old Madeira Wine
2 Gallons Jamaica Spirits
1 Bottle Flour of Mustard
2 Well-cur'd Hams
1/2 Doz dry'd Tongues
6 lb Rice
6 lb Raisins.

These 20 Parcels well pack'd were plac'd on as many Horses, each Parcel with the Horse, being intended as a Present for one Officer. They were very thankfully receiv'd, and the Kindness acknowledg'd by Letters to me from the Colonels of both Regiments in the most grateful Terms. The General too was highly satisfied with my Conduct in procuring him the Waggons, &c. and readily paid my Acc^t of Disbursements; thanking me repeatedly and requesting my farther Assistance in sending Provisions after him. I undertook this also, and was busily employ'd in it till we heard of his Defeat, advancing, for the Service, of my own Money, upwards of 1000£ Sterling, of which I sent him an Account. It came to his Hands luckily for me a few Days before the Battle, and he return'd me immediately an Order on the Paymaster for the round Sum of 1000£ leaving the Remainder to the next Account. I consider this Payment as good Luck; having never been able to obtain that Remainder; of which more hereafter.

This General was I think a brave Man, and might probably have made a Figure as a good Officer in some European War. But he had too much self-confidence, too high an Opinion of the Validity of Regular Troops, and too mean a One of both Americans and Indians. George Croghan, our Indian Interpreter, join'd him on his March with 100 of those People, who might have been of great Use to his Army as Guides, Scouts, &c. if he had treated them kindly;—but he slighted & neglected them, and they gradually left him. In Conversation with him one day, he was giving me some Account of his intended Progress. "After taking Fort Du Quesne, says he, I am to proceed to Niagara; and having taken that, to Frontenac, if the Season will allow time; and I suppose it will; for Duquesne can hardly detain me above three or four Days; and then I see nothing that can obstruct my March to Niagara." —Having before revolv'd in my Mind the long Line his Army must make in their March, by a very narrow Road to be cut for them thro' the Woods & Bushes; & also what I had read of a former Defeat of 1500 French who invaded the Iroquois Country, I had conceiv'd some Doubts,—& some Fears for the Event: of the Campaign. But I ventur'd only to say, To be sure, Sir, if you arrive well before, Duquesne, with these fine Troops so well provided with Artillery, that Place, not yet compleatly fortified, and as we hear with no very strong Garrison, can probably make but a short Resistance. The only Danger I apprehend of Obstruction to your March, is from Ambuscades of Indians, who by constant Practice are dextrous in laying & executing them. And the slender Line near four Miles long, which your Army must make, may expose it to be attack'd by Surprize in its Flanks, and to be cut like a Thread into several Pieces, which from their Distance cannot come up in time to support each other. He smil'd at my Ignorance, & reply'd, "These Savages may indeed be a formidable Enemy to your raw American Militia; but, upon the King's regular & disciplin'd Troops, Sir, it is impossible they should make any Impression." I was conscious of an Impropriety in my Disputing with a military Man in Matters of his Profession, and said no more.—The Enemy however did not take the Advantage of his Army which I apprehended its long Line of March expos'd it to, but let it advance without Interruption till within 9 Miles of the Place; and then when more in a Body, (for it had just pass'd a River, where the Front had halted till all were come over) & in a more open Part of the Woods than any it had pass'd, attack'd its advanc'd Guard, by a heavy Fire from behind Trees & Bushes; which was the first Intelligence the General had of an Enemy's being near him. This Guard being disordered, the General hurried the Troops up to their Assistance, which was done in great Confusion thro' Waggons, Baggage and Cattle; and presently the Fire came upon their Flank; the Officers being on Horseback were more easily distinguish'd, pick'd out as Marks, and fell very fast; and the Soldiers were crowded together in a Huddle, having or hearing no Orders, and standing to be shot at till two thirds of them were killed, and then being seiz'd with a Pannick the whole fled with Precipitation. The Waggoners took each a Horse out of his Team, and scamper'd; their

Example was immediately follow'd by others, so that all the Waggons, Provisions, Artillery and Stores were left to the Enemy. The General being wounded was brought off with Difficulty, his Secretary Mr Shirley was killed by his Side, and out of 86 Officers 63 were killed or wounded, and 714 Men killed out of 1100. These 1100 had been picked Men, from the whole Army, the Rest had been left behind with Col. Dunbar, who was to follow with the heavier Part of the Stores, Provisions and Baggage. The Flyers, not being pursu'd, arriv'd at Dunbar's Camp, and the Pannick they brought with them instantly seiz'd him and all his People. And tho' he had now above 1000 Men, and the Enemy who had beaten Braddock did not at most exceed 400, Indians and French together; instead of Proceeding and endeavouring to recover some of the lost Honour, he order'd all the Stores Ammunition, &c to be destroy'd, that he might have more Horses to assist his Flight towards the Settlements. and less Lumber to remove. He was there met with Requests from the Governor's of Virginia, Maryland and Pennsylvania, that he would post his Troops on the Frontiers so as to afford some Protection to the Inhabitants; but he continu'd his hasty March thro' all the Country, not thinking himself safe till he arriv'd at Philadelphia, where the Inhabitants could protect him. This whole Transaction gave us Americans the first Suspicion that our exalted Ideas of the Prowess of British Regulars had not been well founded.—

In their first March too, from their Landing till they got beyond the Settlements, they had plundered and stript the Inhabitants, totally ruining some poor Families, besides insulting, abusing & confining the People if they remonstrated.—This was enough to put us out of Conceit of such Defenders if we had really wanted any. How different was the Conduct of our French Friends in 1781, who during a March thro' the most inhabited Part of our Country, from Rhodeisland to Virginia, near 700 Miles, occasion'd not the smallest Complaint, for the Loss of a Pig, a Chicken, or even an Apple!

Capt. Orme, who was one of the General's Aid de Camps, and being grievously wounded was brought off with him, and continu'd with him to his Death, which happen'd in a few Days, told me, that he was totally silent, all the first Day, and at Night only said, *Who'd have thought it*? that he was silent again the following Days, only saying at last, *We shall better know how to deal with them another time*; and dy'd a few Minutes after.

The Secretary's Papers with all the General's Orders, Instructions and Correspondence falling into the Enemy's Hands, they selected and translated into French a Number of the Articles, which they printed to prove the hostile Intentions of the British Court before the Declaration of War. Among these I saw some Letters of the General to the Ministry speaking highly of the great Service I had rendred the Army, & recommending me to their Notice. David Hume too, who was some Years after Secretary to Lord Harcourt when Minister in France, and afterwards to Gen.[1] Conway when Secretary of State, told me he had seen among the Papers in that Office Letters from Braddock highly recommending me. But the Expedition having been unfortunate, my Service it seems was not thought of much Value, for those Recommendations were never of any Use to me.——

As to Rewards from himself, I ask'd only one, which was, that he would give Orders to his Officers not to enlist any more of our bought Servants, and that he would discharge such as had been already enlisted. This he readily granted, and several were accordingly return'd to their Masters on my Application.——Dunbar, when the Command devolv'd on him, was not so generous. He Being at Philadelphia on his Retreat, or rather Flight, I apply'd to him for the Discharge of the Servants of three poor Farmers of Lancaster County that he had inlisted, reminding him of the late General's Orders on that head. He promis'd me, that if the Masters would come to him at Trenton, where he should be in a few Days on his March to New York, he would there deliver their Men to them. They accordingly were at the Expence

& Trouble of going to Trenton,—and there he refus'd to perform his Promise, to their great Loss & Disappointment.—

As soon as the Loss of the Waggons and Horses was generally known, all the Owners came upon me for the Valuation wch I had given Bond to pay. Their Demands gave me a great deal of Trouble, my acquainting them that the Money was ready in the Paymaster's Hands, but that Orders for pay^g it must first be obtained from General Shirley,* and my assuring them that I had apply'd to that General by Letter, but he being at a Distance an Answer could not soon be receiv'd, and they must have Patience; all this was not sufficient to satisfy, and some began to sue me. General Shirley at length reliev'd me from this terrible Situation, by appointing Commissioners to examine the Claims and ordering Payment. They amounted to near twenty Thousand Pound, which to pay would have ruined me.

Before we had the News of this Defeat, the two Doctors Bond came to me with a Subscription Paper, for raising Money to defray the Expence of a grand Fire Work, which it was intended to exhibit at a Rejoicing on receipt of the News of our Taking Fort Duquesne. I looked grave and said, "it would, I thought, be time enough to prepare for the Rejoicing when we knew we should have occasion to rejoice."—They seem'd surpriz'd that I did not immediately comply with their Proposal. "Why, the D——l, says one of them, "you surely don't suppose that the Fort will not be taken? "I don't know that it will not be taken; but I know that the Events of War are subject to great Uncertainty.—I gave them the Reasons of my doubting. The Subscription was dropt, and the Projectors thereby miss'd the Mortification they would have undergone if the Firework had been prepared.—Dr Bond on some other Occasions afterwards said, that he did not like Franklin's forebodings.—

Governor Morris who had continually worried the Assembly wth Message after Message before the Defeat of Braddock, to beat them into the making of Acts to raise Money for the Defence of the Province without Taxing among others the Proprietary Estates, and had rejected all their Bills for not having such an exempting Clause, now redoubled his Attacks, with more hope of Success, the Danger & Necessity being greater. The Assembly however continu'd firm, believing they had Justice on their side, and that it would be giving up an essential Right, if they suffered the Governor to amend their Money-Bills. In one of the last, indeed, which was for granting 50,000£ his propos'd Amendment was only of a single Word; the Bill express'd that all Estates real and personal were to be taxed, those of the Proprietaries *not* excepted. His Amendment was; For *not* read *only*. A small but very material Alteration!—However, when the News of this Disaster reach'd England, our Friends there whom we had taken care to furnish with all the Assembly's Answers to the Governor's Messages, rais'd a Clamour against the Proprietaries for their Meanness & Injustice in giving their Governor such Instructions, some going so far as to say that by obstructing the Defence of their Province, they forfeited their Right to it. They were intimidated by this, and sent Orders to their Receiver General to add 5000£ of their Money to whatever Sum might be given by the Assembly, for such Purpose. This being notified to the House, was accepted in Lieu of their Share of a general Tax, and a new Bill was form'd with an exempting Clause which pass'd accordingly. By this Act I was appointed one of the Commissioners for disposing of the Money, 60,000£. I had been active in modelling it, and procuring its Passage: and had at the same time drawn a Bill for establishing and disciplining a voluntary Militia, which I carried thro' the House without much Difficulty, as Care was taken in it, to leave the Quakers at their Liberty. To promote the Association necessary to form the Militia, I wrote a Dialogue,[†] stating and answering all the Objections I could think of to such a Militia, which was printed & had

---

[†] This Dialogue and the Militia Act, are in the Gent Magazine for Feb[y] & March 1756—

as I thought great Effect. While the several Companies in the City & Country were forming and learning their Exercise, the Governor prevail'd with me to take Charge of our Northwestern Frontier, which was infested by the Enemy, and provide for the Defence of the Inhabitants by raising Troops, & building a Line of Forts. I undertook this military Business, tho' I did not conceive myself well-qualified for it. He gave me a Commission with full Powers and a Parcel of blank Commissions for Officers. to be given to whom I thought fit. I had but little Difficulty in raising Men, having soon 560 under my Command. My Son who had in the preceding War been an Officer in the Army rais'd against Canada, was my Aid de Camp, and of great Use to me. The Indians had burnt Gnadenhut, a Village settled by the Moravians,* and massacred the Inhabitants, but the Place was thought a good Situation for one of the Forts. In order to march thither, I assembled the Companies at Bethlehem, the chief Establishment of those People. I was surprized to find it in so good a Posture of Defence. The Destruction of Gnadenhut had made them apprehend Danger. The principal Buildings were defended by a Stockade: They had purchased a Quantity of Arms & Ammunition from New York, and had even plac'd Quantities of small Paving Stones between the Windows of their high Stone Houses, for their Women to throw down upon the Heads of any Indians that should attempt to force into them. The armed Bretheren too, kept Watch, and reliev'd as methodically as in any Garrison Town. In Conversation with Bishop Spangenberg, I mention'd this my Surprize; for knowing they had obtain'd an Act of Parliament exempting them from military Duties in the Colonies, I had suppos'd they were conscienciously scrupulous of bearing Arms. He answer'd me, "That it was not one of their establish'd Principles; but that at the time of their obtaining that Act, it was thought to be a Principle with many of their People. On this Occasion, however, they to their Surprize found it adopted by but a few." It seems they were either deceiv'd in themselves, or deceiv'd the Parliament. But Common

Sense aided by present Danger, will sometimes be too strong for whimsicll Opinions.

It was the Beginning of January when we set out upon this Business of Building Forts. I sent one Detachment towards the Minisinks, with Instructions to erect one for the Security of that upper Part of the Country; and another to the lower Part, with similar Instructions. And I concluded to go myself with the rest of my Force to Gnadenhut, where a Fort was tho't more immediately necessary. The Moravians procur'd me five Waggons for our Tools, Stores, Baggage, &c. Just before we left Bethlehem, Eleven Farmers who had been driven from their Plantations by the Indians, came to me, requesting a supply of Fire Arms, that they might go back and fetch off their Cattle. I gave them each a Gun with suitable Ammunition. We had not march'd many Miles before it began to rain, and it continu'd raining all Day. There were no Habitations on the Road, to shelter us, till we arriv'd near Night, at the House of a German, where and in his Barn we were all huddled together as wet as Water could make us. It was well we were not attack'd in our March, for Our Arms were of the most ordinary Sort and our Men could not keep their Gunlocks dry. The Indians are dextrous in Contrivances for that purpose, which we had not. They met that Day the eleven poor Farmers above-mentioned & kill'd Ten of them. The one who escap'd inform'd that his & his Companions Guns would not go off, the Priming being wet with the Rain. The next Day being fair, we continu'd our March and arriv'd at the desolated Gnadenhut. There was a Saw Mill near, round which were left several Piles of Boards, with which we soon hutted ourselves; an Operation the more necessary at that inclement Season, as we had no Tents. Our first Work was to bury more effectually the Dead we found there, who had been half interr'd by the Country People. The next Morning our Fort was plann'd and mark'd out, the Circumference measuring 455 feet, which would require as many Palisades to be made of Trees one with another of a Foot Diameter each. Our Axes, of which we had 70 were immediately set to work, to cut down Trees; and our Men being dextrous in the Use of them, great Dispatch was made. Seeing the Trees fall so fast, I had the Curiosity to look at my Watch when two Men began to cut at a Pine. In 6 Minutes they had it upon the Ground; and I found it of 14 Inches Diameter. Each Pine made three Palisades of 18 Feet long, pointed at one End. While these were preparing, our other Men, dug a Trench all round of three feet deep in which the Palisades were to be planted, and our Waggons, the Body being taken off, and the fore and hind Wheels separated by taking out the Pin which united the two Parts of the Perch, we had 10 Carriages with two Horses each, to bring the Palisades from the Woods to the Spot. When they were set up, our Carpenters built a Stage of Boards all round within, about 6 Feet high, for the Men to stand on when to fire thro' the Loopholes. We had one swivel Gun which we mounted on one of the Angles; and fired it as soon as fix'd, to let the Indians know, if any were within hearing, that we had such Pieces, and thus our Fort, (if such a magnificent Name may be given to so miserable a Stockade) was finished in a Week, tho' it rain'd so hard every other Day that the Men could not work.

This gave me occasion to observe, that when Men are employ'd they are best contented. For on the Days they work'd they were good-natur'd and chearful; and with the consciousness of having done a good Days work they spent the Evenings jollily; but on the idle Days they were mutinous and quarrelsome, finding fault with their Pork, the Bread, &c. and in continual ill-humour: which put me in mind of a Sea-Captain, whose Rule it was to keep his Men constantly at Work; and when his Mate once told him that they had done every thing, and there was nothing farther to employ them about; O, says he, *make them scour the Anchor.*

This kind of Fort, however contemptible is a sufficient Defence against Indians who have no Cannon. Finding our selves now posted securely, and having a Place to retreat to on Occasion, we ventur'd out in Parties to scour the adjacent

Country. We met with no Indians, but we found the Places
on the neighbouring Hills where they had lain to watch our
Proceedings. There was an Art in their Contrivance of these
Places that seems worth mention. It being Winter, a Fire
was necessary for them. But a common Fire on the Surface
of the Ground would by its Light have discover'd their
Position at a Distance. They had therefore dug Holes in the
Ground about three feet Diameter, and some what deeper.
We saw where they had with their Hatchets cut off the
Charcoal from th Sides of burnt Logs lying in the Woods.
With these Coals they had made small Fires in the Bottom
of the Holes, and we observ'd among the Weeds & Grass
the Prints of their Bodies made by their laying all round
with their Legs hanging down in the Holes to keep their
Feet warm, which with them is an essential Point. This kind
of Fire, so manag'd, could not discover them either by its
Light, Flame; Sparks or evon Smoke. It appear'd that their
Number was not great, and it seems they saw we were too
many to be attack'd by them with Prospect of Advantage.

We had for our Chaplain a zealous Presbyterian Minister,
Mr Beatty, who complain'd to me that the Men did not
generally attend his Prayers & Exhortations. When they
enlisted, they were promis'd, besides Pay & Provisions, a
Gill of Rum a Day, which was puctually serv'd out to them
half in the Morning and the other half in the Evening, and
I observ'd they were as punctual in attending to receive it.
Upon which I said to Mr. Beatty, "It is perhaps below the
Dignity of your Profession to act as Steward of the Rum.
But if you were to deal it out, and only just after Prayers,
you would have them all about you." He lik'd the Thought,
undertook the Office, and with the help of a few hands to
measure out the Liquor executed it to Satisfaction; and
never were Prayers more generally & more punctually at-
tended. So that I thought this Method preferable to the
Punishments inflicted by some military Laws for Non-
Attendance on Divine Service.

I had hardly finish'd this Business, and got my Fort well
stor'd with Provisions, when I receiv'd a Letter from the

Governor, acquainting me that he had called the Assembly, and wish'd my Attendance there, if the Posture of Affairs on the Frontiers was such that my remaining there was no longer necessary. My Friends too of the Assembly pressing me by their Letters to be if possible at the Meeting, and my three intended Forts being now compleated, and the Inhabitants contented to remain on their Farms under that Protection, I resolved to return. The more willingly as a New England Officer, Col. Clapham, experienc'd in Indian War, being on a Visit to our Establishment, consented to accept the Command. I gave him a Commission, and parading the Garrison had it read before them, and introduc'd him to them as an Officer who from his Skill in Military Affairs was much more fit to command them than myself; and giving them a little Exhortation took my Leave. I was escorted as far as Bethlehem, where I rested a few Days, to recover from the Fatigue I had undergone. The first Night being in a good Bed, I could hardly sleep, it was so different from my hard Lodging on the Floor of our Hut at Gnaden, wrapt only in a Blanket or two.——

While at Bethlehem, I enquir'd a little into the Practices of the Moravians. Some of them had accompanied me, and all were very kind to me. I found they work'd for a common Stock, eat at common Tables, and slept in common Dormitorys, great Numbers together. In the Dormitories I observ'd Loopholes at certain Distances all along just under the Cieling, which I thought judiciously plac'd for Change of Air. I was at their Church, where I was entertain'd with good Musick, the Organ being accompanied with Violins, Hautboys,* Flutes, Clarinets, &c I understood that their Sermons were not usually preached to mix'd Congregations; of Men Women and Children, as is our common Practice; but that they assembled sometimes the married Men, at other times their Wives, then the Young Men, the young Women, and the little Children, each Division by itself. The Sermon I heard was to the latter, who came in and were plac'd in Rows on Benches, the Boys under the Conduct of a young Man their Tutor, and the Girls conducted by a

young Woman. The Discourse seem'd well adapted to their
Capacities, and was delivered in a pleasing familiar Manner,
coaxing them as it were to be good. They behav'd very
orderly, but look'd pale and unhealthy, which made me
suspect they were kept too much within-doors, or not
allow'd sufficient Exercise. I enquir'd concerning the Moravian Marriages, whether the Report was true that they
were by Lot? I was told that Lots were us'd only in
particular Cases. That generally when a young Man found
himself dispos'd to marry, he inform'd the Elders of his
Class, who consulted the Elder Ladies that govern'd the
young Women. As these Elders of the different Sexes were
well acquainted with the Tempers & Dispositions of their
respective Pupils, they could best judge what Matches were
suitable, and their Judgments were generally acquiesc'd in.
But if for example it should happen that two or three young
Women were found to be *equally* proper for the young Man,
the Lot was then recurr'd to. I objected, If the Matches are
not made by the mutual Choice of the Parties, some of them
may chance to be very unhappy. And so they may, answer'd
my Informer, if you let the Parties chuse for themselves.—
Which indeed I could not deny.

Being return'd to Philadelphia, I found the Association
went on swimmingly, the Inhabitants that were not Quakers
having pretty generally come into it, form'd themselves into
Companies, and chosen their Captains, Lieutenants and
Ensigns according to the new Law. Dr B. visited me, and
gave me an Account of the Pains he had taken to spread a
general good Liking to the Law, and ascrib'd much to those
Endeavours. I had had the Vanity to ascribe all to my
Dialogue; However, not knowing but that he might be in
the right, I let him enjoy his Opinion. which I take to be
generally the best way in such Cases—The Officers meeting
chose me to be Colonel of the Regiment;—which I this time
accepted. I forget how many Companies we had, but We
paraded about 1200 well-looking Men, with a Company of
Artillery who had been furnish'd with 6 brass Field Pieces,
which they had become so expert in the Use of as to fire

twelve times in a Minute. The first Time I review'd my Regiment, they accompanied me to my House, and would salute me with some Rounds fired before my Door, which shook down and broke several Glasses of my Electrical Apparatus. And my new Honour prov'd not much less brittle; for all our Commissions were soon after broke by a Repeal of the Law in England.——

During the short time of my Colonelship, being about to set out on a Journey to Virginia, the Officers of my Regiment, took it into their heads that it would be proper for them to escort me out of town as far as the Lower Ferry. Just as I was getting on Horseback, they came to my door, between 30 & 40, mounted, and all in their Uniforms. I had not been previously acquainted with the Project, or I should have prevented it, being naturally averse to the assuming of State on any Occasion, & I was a good deal chagrin'd at their Appearance, as I could not avoid their accompanying me. What made it worse, was, that as soon as we began to move, they drew their Swords, and rode with them naked all the way. Somebody wrote an Account of this to the Proprietor, and it gave him great Offence. No such Honour had been paid him when in the Province; nor to any of his Governors; and he said it was only proper to Princes of the Blood Royal; which may be true for aught I know, who was, and still am, ignorant of the Etiquette, in such Cases. This silly Affair, however greatly increas'd his Rancour against me, which was before considerable, not a little, on account of my Conduct in the Assembly, respecting the Exemption of his Estate from Taxation, which I had always oppos'd very warmly, & not without severe Reflections on his Meanness & Injustice in contending for it. He accus'd me to the Ministry as being the great Obstacle to the King's Service, preventing by my Influence in the House the proper Forming of the Bills for raising Money; and he instanc'd this Parade with my Officers as a Proof of my having an Intention to take the Government of the Province out of his Hands by Force. He also apply'd to Sir Everard Fauckener, then Post Master General, to deprive me of my

Office. But this had no other Effect, than to procure from Sir Everard a gentle Admonition.

Notwithstanding the continual Wrangle between the Governor and the House, in which I as a Member had so large a Share, there still subsisted a civil Intercourse between that Gentleman & myself, and we never had any personal Difference. I have sometimes since thought that his little or no Resentment against me for the Answers it was known I drew up to his Messages, might be the Effect of professional Habit, and that, being bred a Lawyer, he might consider us both as merely Advocates for contending Clients in a Suit, he for the Proprietaries & I for the Assembly, He would therefore sometimes call in a friendly way to advise with me on difficult Points, and sometimes, tho' not often, take my Advice. We acted in Concert to supply Braddock's Army with Provisions, and When the shocking News arriv'd of his Defeat, the Govern.ʳ sent in haste for me, to consult with him on Measures for preventing the Desertion of the back Counties. I forget now the Advice I gave, but I think it was, that Dunbar should be written to and prevail'd with if possible to post his Troops on the Frontiers for their Protection, till by Reinforcements from the Colonies he might be able to proceed on the Expedition.—And after my Return from the Frontier, he would have had me undertake the Conduct of such an Expedition with Provincial Troops, for the Reduction of Fort Duquesne, Dunbar & his Men being otherwise employ'd; and he propos'd to commission me as General. I had not so good an Opinion of my military Abilities as he profess'd to have; and I believe his Professions must have exceeded his real Sentiments: but probably he might think that my Popularity would facilitate the Raising of the Men, and my Influence in Assembly the Grant of Money to pay them;—and that perhaps without taxing the Proprietary Estate. Finding me not so forward to engage as he expected, the Project was dropt: and he soon after left the Government, being superseded by Capt. Denny.—

Before I proceed in relating the Part I had in public Affairs under this new Governor's Administration, it may not be amiss here to give some Account of the Rise & Progress of my Philosophical Reputation.——

In 1746 being at Boston, I met there with a Dr Spence, who was lately arrived from Scotland, and show'd me some electric Experiments. They were imperfectly perform'd, as he was not very expert; but being on a Subject quite new to me, they equally surpriz'd and pleas'd me. Soon after my Return to Philadelphia, our Library Company receiv'd from Mr Peter Colinson, F.R.S. of London a Present of a Glass Tube, with some Account of the Use of it in making such Experiments. I eagerly seiz'd the Opportunity of repeating what I had seen at Boston, and by much Practice acquir'd great Readiness in performing those also which we had an Account of from England, adding a Number of new Ones.——I say much Practice, for my House was continually full for some time, with People who came to see these new Wonders. To divide a little this Incumbrance among my Friends, I caused a Number of similar Tubes to be blown at our Glass-House, with which they furnish'd themselves, so that we had at length several Performers. Among these the principal was Mr Kinnersley, an ingenious Neighbour, who being out of Business, I encouraged to undertake showing the Experiments for Money, and drew up for him two Lectures, in which the Experiments were rang'd in such Order and accompanied with Explanations, in such Method, as that the foregoing should assist in Comprehending the following. He procur'd an elegant Apparatus for the purpose, in which all the little Machines that I had roughly made for myself, were nicely form'd by Instrument-makers. His Lectures were well attended and gave great Satisfaction; and after some time he went thro' the Colonies exhibiting them in every capital Town, and pick'd up some Money. In the West India Islands indeed it was with Difficulty the Experim.[ts] could be made, from the general Moisture of the Air.

Oblig'd as we were to Mr Colinson for his Present of the Tube, &c. I thought it right he should be inform'd of our

Success in using it, and wrote him several Letters containing Accounts of our Experiments. He got them read in the Royal Society, where they were not at first thought worth so much Notice as to be printed in their Transactions. One Paper which I wrote for Mr. Kinnersley, on the Sameness of Lightning with Electricity, I sent to Dr. Mitchel, an Acquaintance of mine, and one of the Members also of that Society; who wrote me word that it had been read but was laught at by the Connoisseurs: The Papers however being shown to Dr Fothergill,* he thought them of too much value to be stifled, and advis'd the Printing of them. Mr Collinson then gave them to *Cave* for publication in his Gentleman's Magazine;* but he chose to print them separately in a Pamphlet, and Dr Fothergill wrote the Preface. *Cave* it seems judg'd rightly for his Profit; for by the Additions that arriv'd afterwards they swell'd to a Quarto Volume, which has had five Editions, and cost him nothing for Copy-money.

It was however some time before those Papers were much taken Notice of in England. A Copy of them happening to fall into the Hands of the Count de Buffon,* a Philosopher deservedly of great Reputation in France, and indeed all over Europe he prevail'd with M. Dalibard to translate them into French; and they were printed at Paris. The Publication offended the Abbé Nollet,* Preceptor in Natural Philosophy to the Royal Family, and an able Experimenter, who had form'd and publish'd a Theory of Electricity, which then had the general Vogue. He could not at first believe that such a Work came from America, & said it must have been fabricated by his Enemies at Paris, to oppose decry his System. Afterwards having been assur'd that there really existed such a Person as Franklin of Philadelphia, which he had doubted, he wrote and published a Volume of Letters, chiefly address'd to me, defending his Theory, & denying the Verity of my Experiments and of the Positions deduc'd from them. I once purpos'd answering the Abbé, and actually began the Answer. But on Consideration that my Writings contain'd only a Description of Experiments, which any one might repeat & verify, and if not to be verify'd could not be defended; or of Observations, offer'd as Conjectures, & not deliverd dogmatically, therefore not laying me under any Obligation to defend them; and reflecting that a Dispute between two Persons writing in different Languages might be lengthend greatly by mis-translations, and thence misconceptions of one anothers Meaning, much of one of the Abbe's Letters being founded on an Error in the Translation; I concluded to let my Papers shift for themselves; believing it was better to spend what time I could spare from public Business in making new Experiments, than in Disputing about those already made. I therefore never answer'd M. Nollet; and the Event gave me no Cause to repent my Silence; for my friend M. le Roy of the Royal Academy of Sciences took up my Cause & refuted him, my Book was translated into the Italian, German and Latin Languages, and the Doctrine it contain'd was by degrees universally adopted by the Philosophers of Europe in preference to that of the Abbé, so that he liv'd to see himself the last of his Sect,: except Mr B——* his Eleve & immediate Disciple.

What gave my Book the more sudden and general Celebrity, was the Success of one of its propos'd Experiments, made by Messrs Dalibard & Delor, at Marly; for drawing Lightning from the Clouds. This engag'd the public Attention every where. M. Delor, who had an Apparatus for experimental Philosophy, and lectur'd in that Branch of Science, undertook to repeat what he call'd the *Philadelphia Experiments*, and after they were performed before the King & Court, all the Curious of Paris flock'd to see them. I will not swell this Narrative with an Account of that capital Experiment, nor of the infinite Pleasure I receiv'd in the Success of a similar one I made soon after with a Kite at Philadelphia, as both are to be found in the Histories of Electricity.——Dr Wright, an English Physician then at Paris, wrote to a Friend who was of the Royal Society an Account of the high Esteem my Experiments were in among the Learned abroad, and of their Wonder that my Writings had been so little noticed in England. The Society on this resum'd the Consideration of the Letters that had been read to them, and the celebrated Dr Watson* drew up a summary Acc^t of them, & of all I had afterwards sent to England on the Subject, which he accompanied with some Praise of the Writer. This Summary was then printed in their Transactions: And some Members of the Society in London, particularly the very ingenious Mr Canton,* having verified the Experiment of procuring Lightnin from the Clouds by a Pointed Rod, and acquainting them with the Success, they soon made me more than Amends for the Slight with which they had before treated me. Without my having made any Application for that Honour, they chose me a Member, and voted that I should be excus'd the customary Payments, which would have amounted to twenty-five Guineas, and ever since have given me their Transactions gratis.—They also presented me with the Gold Medal of Sir Godfrey Copley for the Year 1753, the Delivery of which was accompanied by a very handsome Speech of the President Lord Macclesfield,* wherein I was highly honoured.—

Our new Governor, Capt. Denny, brought over for me the before mentioned Medal from the Royal Society, which he presented to me at an Entertainment given him by the City. He accompanied it with very polite Expressions of his Esteem for me, having, as he said been long acquainted with my Character. After Dinner, when the Company as was customary at that time, were engag'd in Drinking, he took me aside into another Room, and acquainted me that he had been advis'd by his Friends in England to cultivate a Friendship with me, as one who was capable of giving him the best Advice, & of contributing most effectually to the making his Administration easy. That he therefore desired of all things to have a good Understanding with me; and he begg'd me to be assur'd of his Readiness on all Occasions to render me every Service that might be in his Power. He said much to me also of the Proprietor's good Dispositions towards the Province, and of the Advantage it might be to us all, and to me in particular, if the Opposition that had been so long continu'd to his Measures, were dropt, and Harmony restor'd between him and the People, in effecting which it was thought no one could be more serviceable than my self, and I might depend on adequate Acknowledgements & Recompences, &c. &c. The Drinkers finding we did not return immediately to the Table, sent us a Decanter of Madeira, which the Governor made liberal Use of, and in proportion became more profuse of his Solicitations and Promises. My Answers were to this purpose, that my Circumstances, Thanks to God, were such as to make Proprietary Favours unnecessary to me; and that being a Member of the Assembly I could not possibly accept of any; that however I had no personal Enmity to the Proprietary, and that whenever the public Measures he propos'd should appear to be for the Good of the People, no one should espouse and forward them more zealously than myself, my past Opposition having been founded on this, that the Measures which had been urg'd were evidently intended to serve the Proprietary Interest with great Prejudice to that of the People. That I was much obliged to him (the Governor) for his Professions of Regard to me, and that he might rely on every thing in my Power to make his Administration as easy to him as possible, hoping at the same time that he had not brought with him the same unfortunate Instructions his Predecessor had been hamper'd with. On this he did not then explain himself. But when he afterwards came to do Business with the Assembly they appear'd again, the Disputes were renewed, and I was as active as ever in the Opposition, being the Penman first of the Request to have a Communication of the Instructions, and then of the Remarks upon them, which may be found in the Votes of the Time, and in the Historical Review I afterwards publish'd; but between us personally no Enmity arose; we were often together, he was a Man of Letters, had seen much of the World, and was very entertaining & pleasing in Conversation. He gave me the first Information that my old Friend Ja^s Ralph was still alive, that he was esteem'd one of the best political Writers in England, had been employ'd in the

Dispute between Prince Frederic and the King,* and had obtain'd a Pension of Three Hundred a Year; that his Reputation was indeed small as Poet, *Pope* having damn'd his Poetry in the Dunciad,* but his Prose was thought as good as any Man's.—

The Assembly finally, finding the Proprietaries obstinately persisted in manacling their Deputies with Instructions inconsistent not only with the Privileges of the People, but with the Service of the Crown, resolv'd to petition the King against them, and appointed me their Agent to go over to England to present & support the Petition. The House had sent up a Bill to the Governor granting a Sum of Sixty Thousand Pounds for the King's Use, (10,000£ of which was subjected to the Orders of the then General Lord Loudon,*) which the Governor absolutely refus'd to pass in Compliance with his Instructions. I had agreed with Captain Morris of the Packet at New York for my Passage, and my Stores were put on board, when Lord Loudon arriv'd at Philadelphia, expresly, as he told me to endeavour an Accomodation between the Governor and Assembly, that his Majesty's Service might not be obstructed by their Dissensions: Accordingly he desir'd the Governor & myself to meet him, that he might hear what was to be said on both sides. We met and discuss'd the Business. In behalf of the Assembly I urg'd all the Arguments that may be found in the publick Papers of that Time, which were of my Writing, and are printed with the Minutes of the Assembly & the Governor pleaded his Instructions, the Bond he had given to observ them, and his Ruin if he disobey'd: Yet seem'd not unwilling to hazard himself if Lord Loudon would advise it. This his Lordship did not chuse to do, tho' I once thought I had nearly prevail'd with him to do it; but finally he rather chose to urge the Compliance of the Assembly; and he intreated me to use my Endeavours with them for that purpose; declaring he could spare none of the King's Troops for the Defence of our Frontiers, and that if we did not continue to provide for that Defence ourselves they must remain expos'd to the Enemy. I acquainted the House with what had pass'd, and presenting them with a Set of Resolutions I had drawn up, declaring our Rights, & that we did not relinquish our Claim to those Rights but only suspended the Exercise of them on this Occasion thro' *Force*, against which we protested, they at length agreed to drop that Bill and frame another agreable conformable to the Proprietary Instructions. This of course the Governor pass'd, and I was then at Liberty to proceed on my Voyage: but in the meantime the Pacquet had sail'd with my Sea-Stores, which was some Loss to me, and my only Recompence was his Lordship's Thanks for my Service, all the Credit of obtaining the Accommodation falling to his Share.

He set out for New York before me; and as the Time for dispatching the Pacquet Boats, was in his Disposition, and there were two then remaining there, one of which he said was to sail very soon, I requested to know the precise time, that I might not miss her by any Delay of mine. His Answer was, I have given out that she is to sail on Saturday next, but I may let you know *entre nous*, that if you are there by Monday morning you will be in time, but do not delay longer. By some Accidental Hindrance at a Ferry, it was Monday Noon before I arrived, and I was much afraid she might have sailed as the Wind was fair, but I was soon made easy by the Information that she was still in the Harbour, and would not move till the next Day.——

One would imagine that I was now on the very point of Departing for Europe. I thought so; but I was not then so well acquainted with his Lordship's Character, of which *Indecision* was one of the Strongest Features. I shall give some Instances. It was about the Beginning of April that I came to New York, and I think it was near the End of June before we sail'd. There were then two of the Pacquet Boats which had been long in Port, but were detain'd for the General's Letters, which were always to be ready to-morrow. Another Pacquet arriv'd, and she too was detain'd. and before we sail'd a fourth was expected. Ours was the first to be dispatch'd, as having been there longest. Passengers were engag'd in all, & some extreamly impatient to be gone, and the Merchants uneasy about their Letters, & the Orders they had given for Insurance. (it being War-time) & for Fall Goods, But their Anxiety avail'd nothing; his Lordships Letters were not ready. And yet whoever waited on him found him always at his Desk, Pen in hand, and concluded he must needs write abundantly. Going my self one Morning to pay my Respects, I found in his Antechamber one Innis, a Messenger of Philadelphia, who had come from thence express, with a Pacquet from Governor Denny for the General. He deliver'd to me some Letters from my Friends there, which occasion'd my enquiring when he was to return & where he lodg'd, that I might send some Letters by him. He told me he was order'd to call to-morrow at nine for the General's Answer to the Governor, and should set off immediately. I put my Letters into his Hands the same Day. A Fortnight after I met him again in the same Place. So you are soon return'd, Innis! *Return'd*; No, I am not *gone* yet. —How so? —I have call'd here by Order every Morning these two Weeks past for his Lordship's Letter, and it is not yet ready.—Is it possible, when he is so great a Writer, for I see him constantly at his Scritore. Yes, says Innis, but he is like St. George on the Signs, *always on horseback, and never rides on.* This Observation of the Messenger was it seems well founded; for when in England, I understood that Mr Pitt* gave it as one Reason for Removing this General, and sending Amherst & Wolf,* *that the Ministers never heard from him, and could not know what he was doing.*

This daily Expectation of Sailing, and all thr three Packets going down Sandy hook, to join the Fleet there the Passengers, thought it best to be on board, lest by a sudden Order the Ships should sail, and they be left behind. There if I remember right we were about Six Weeks, consuming our Sea Stores, and oblig'd to procure more. At length the Fleet sail'd, the General and all his Army on board, bound to Lewisburg with Intent to beseige and take that Fortress; all the Packet-Boats in Company, ordered to attend the General's Ship, ready to receive his Dispatches when those should be ready. We were out 5 Days before we got a Letter with Leave to part; and then our Ship quitted the Fleet and steered for England. The other two Packets he still detain'd, carry'd them with him to Halifax, where he staid some time to exercise the Men in sham Attacks upon sham Forts, then alter'd his Mind as to besieging Louisburg, and return'd to New York with all his Troops, together with the two Packets abovementioned and all their Passengers. During his Absence the French and Savages had taken Fort George on the Frontier of that Province, and the Savages had massacred many of the Garrison after Capitulation. I saw afterwards in London, Capt. Bonnell, who commanded one of those Packets. He told me, that when he had been detain'd a Month, he acquainted his Lordship that his Ship was grown foul, to a degree that must necessarily hinder her fast Sailing, a Point of consequence for a Packet Boat, and requested an Allowance of Time to heave her down and clean her Bottom. He was ask'd how long time that would require. He answer'd Three Days. The General reply'd, If you can do it in one Day, I give leave; otherwise not; for you must certainly sail the Day after tomorrow. So he never obtain'd leave tho' detain'd afterwards from day to day during full three Months. I saw also in London one of Bonell's Passengers, who was so enrag'd against his Lordship for deceiving and detaining him so long at New-York, and then carrying him to Halifax, and back again, that he swore he would sue him for Damages. Whether he did or not I never heard; but as he represented the Injury to his Affairs it was very considerable. On the whole I then wonder'd much, how such a Man came to be entrusted with so important a Business as the Conduct of a great Army: but having since seen more of the great World, and the means of obtaining & Motives for giving Places, & Employments my Wonder is diminished. General Shirley, on whom the Command of the Army devolved upon the Death of Braddock, would in my Opinion if continued in Place, have made a much better Campaign than that of Loudon in 1757, which was frivolous, expensive and disgraceful to our Nation beyond Conception: For tho' Shirley was not a bred Soldier, he was sensible and sagacious in himself, and attentive to good Advice from others. capable of forming judicious Plans, quick and active in carrying them into Execution. Loudon, instead of defending the Colonies with his great Army, left them totally expos'd while he paraded it idly at Halifax, by which means Fort George was lost;—besides he derang'd all our mercantile Operations, & distress'd our Trade by a long Embargo on the Exportation of Provisions, on pretence of keeping Supplies from being obtain'd by the Enemy, but in Reality for beating down their Price in Favour of the Contractors, in whose Profits it was said, perhaps from Suspicion only, he had a Share. And when at length the Embargo was taken off, by neglecting to send Notice of it to Charlestown, the Carolina Fleet was detain'd near three Months longer, whereby their Bottoms were so much damag'd by the Worm, that a great Part of them founder'd in the Passage home. Shirley was I believe sincerely glad of being reliev'd from so burthensom a Charge. as the Conduct of an Army must be to a Man unacquainted with military Business. I was at the Entertainment given by the City of New York, to Lord Loudon on his taking upon him the Command. Shirley, tho' thereby superseded, was present also. There was a great Company of Officers, Citizens and Strangers, and some Chairs having been borrowed in the Neighbourhood, there was one among them very low which fell to the Lot of Mr Shirley. Perceiving it as I sat by him, I said, they have given you, Sir, too low a Seat.—No Matter, says he; Mr Franklin; I find *a low Seat* the easiest!

While I was, as aforemention'd, detain'd at New York, I receiv'd all the Accounts of the Provisions, &c. that I had furnish'd to Braddock, some of which Acc^{ts} could not sooner be obtain'd from the different Persons I had employ'd to assist in the Business. I presented them to Lord Loudon, desiring to be paid the Ballance. He caus'd them to be regularly examin'd by the proper Officer, who, after comparing every Article with its Voucher, certified them to be right, and the Ballance due, for which his Lordship promis'd to give me an Order on the Paymaster. This, however, was put off from time to time, and tho' I called often for it by Appointment, I did not get it. At length, just before my Departure, he told me he had on better Consideration concluded not to mix his Accounts with those of his Predecessors. And you, says he, when in England, have only to exhibit your Accounts at the Treasury, and you will be paid immediately. I mention'd, but without Effect, the great & unexpected Expence I had been put to by being detain'd so long at N York, as a Reason for my desiring to be presently paid; and On my observing that it was not right I should be put to any farther Trouble or Delay in obtaining the Money I had advanc'd, as I charg'd no Commissions for my Service. O, Sir, says he, you must not think of persuading us that you are no Gainer. We understand better those Affairs, and know that every one concern'd in supplying the Army finds means in the doing it to fill his own Pockets. I assur'd him that was not my Case, and that I had not pocketed a Farthing: but he appear'd clearly not to believe me; and indeed I have since learnt that immense Fortunes are often made in such Employments.—As to my Ballance, I am not paid it to this Day, of which more hereafter.—

Our Captain of the Pacquet had boasted much before we sail'd, of the Swiftness of his Ship. Unfortunately when we came to Sea, she proved the dullest of 96 Sail, to his no small Mortification. After many Conjectures respecting the Cause, when we were near another Ship almost as dull as ours, which however gain'd upon us, the Captain order'd all hands to come aft and stand as near the Ensign Staff as possible. We were, Passengers included, about forty Persons. While we stood there the Ship mended her Pace, and soon left our Neighbour far behind, which prov'd clearly what our Captain suspected, that she was loaded too much by the Head. The Casks of Water it seems had been all plac'd forward. These he therefore order'd to be remov'd farther aft; on which the Ship recover'd her Character, and prov'd the best Sailer in the Fleet. The Captain said she had once gone at the Rate of 13 Knots, which is accounted 13 Miles per hour. We had on board as a Passenger Captain Kennedy of the Navy, who contended that it was impossible, that no Ship ever sailed so fast, and that there must have been some Error in the Division of the Log-Line,* or some Mistake in heaving the Log. A Wager ensu'd between the two Captains, to be decided when there should be sufficient Wind. Kennedy thereupon examin'd rigorously the Log-line, and being satisfy'd with that he determin'd to throw the Log himself. Accordingly some Days after when the Wind blew very fair & fresh, and the Captain of the Packet (Lutwidge) said he believ'd she then went at the Rate of 13 Knots, Kennedy made the Experiment, and own'd his Wager lost. The above Fact I give for the sake of the following Observation. It has been remark'd as an Imperfection in the Art of Ship-building, that it can never be known 'till she is try'd, whether a new Ship will or will not be a good Sailer; for that the Model of a good sailing Ship has been exactly follow'd in a new One, which has prov'd on the contrary remarkably dull. I apprehend this may be partly occasion'd by the different Opinions of Seamen respecting the Modes of lading, rigging & sailing of a Ship. Each has his System. And the same Vessel laden by the Judgment & Orders of one Captain shall sail better or worse than when by the Orders of another. Besides, it scarce ever happens that a Ship is form'd, fitted for the Sea, & sail'd by the same Person. One Man builds the Hull, another riggs her, a third lades and sails her. No one of these has the Advantage of knowing all the Ideas & Experience of the others, & therefore cannot draw just Conclusions from a Combination of the whole. Even in the simple Operation of Sailing when at Sea, I have often observ'd different Judgments in the Officers who commanded the successive Watches, the Wind being the same, One would have the Sails trimm'd sharper or flatter than another, so that they seem'd to have no certain Rule to govern by. Yet I think a Set of Experiments might be instituted, first to determine the most proper Form of the Hull; for swift sailing; next the best Dimensions & properest Place for the Masts; then the Form & Quantity of Sail, and their Position as the Winds may be; and lastly the Disposition of her Lading. This is the Age of Experiments; and such a Set accurately made & combin'd would be of great Use. I am therefore persuaded that ere long some ingenious Philosopher will undertake it:—to whom I wish Success—

We were several times chas'd on our Passage, but outsail'd every thing, and in thirty Days had Soundings. We had a good Observation, and the Captain judg'd himself so near our Port, (Falmouth) that if we made a good Run in the Night we might be off the Mouth of that Harbour in the Morning, and by running in the Night might escape the Notice of the Enemy's Privateers, who often cruis'd near the Entrance of the Channel. Accordingly all the Sail was set that we could possibly make, and the Wind being very fresh & fair, we went right before it, & made great Way. The Captain after his Observation, shap'd his Course as he thought so as to pass wide of the Scilly Isles: but it seems there is sometimes a strong Indraught setting up St. George's Channel which deceives Seamen, and caus'd the Loss of Sir Cloudsley Shovel's Squadron. This Indraught was probably the Cause of what happen'd to us. We had a Watchman plac'd in the Bow to whom they often call'd, *Look well out befor'e, there*; and he as often answer'd *Aye, Aye!* But perhaps had his Eyes shut, and was half asleep at the time: they sometimes answering as is said mechanically: For he did not see a Light just before us, which had been hid by the Studding Sails from the Man at Helm & from the rest of the Watch; but by an accidental Yaw of the Ship was discover'd, & occasion'd a great Alarm, we being very near it, the light appearing to me as big as a Cart Wheel. It was Midnight, & Our Captain fast asleep. But Capt. Kennedy jumping upon Deck, & seeing the Danger, ordered the Ship to wear round, all Sails standing. An Operation dangerous to the Masts, but it carried us clear, and we escap'd Shipwreck, for we were running right upon the Rocks on which the Lighthouse was erected. This Deliverance impress'd me strongly with the Utility of Lighthouses, and made me resolve to encourage the building more of them in America, if I should live to return there.—

In the Morning it was found by the Soundings, &c. that we were near our Port, but a thick Fog hid the Land from our Sight. About 9 aclock the Fog began to rise, and seem'd to be lifted up from the Water like the Curtain at a Play-house, discovering underneath the Town of Falmouth, the Vessels in its Harbour, & the Fields that surrounded it. A most pleasing Spectacle to those who had been so long without any other Prospects, than the uniform View of a vacant Ocean!—And it gave us the more Pleasure, as we were now freed from the Anxieties which the State of War accosion'd.—

I set out immediately w.th my Son for London, and we only stopt a little by the Way to view Stonehenge on Salisbury Plain, and Lord Pembroke's House and Gardens, with his very curious Antiquities at Wilton.

We arriv'd in London the 27th of July 1757. [PART 4] As soon as I was settled in a Lodging Mr Charles had provided for me, I went to visit Dr Fothergill, to whom I was strongly recommended, and whose Counsel respecting my Proceedings I was advis'd to obtain. He was against an immediate Complaint to Governm.t, and thought the Proprietaries should first be personally apply'd to, who might possibly be induc'd by the Interposition & Persuasion of some private Friends to accommodate Matters amicably. I then waited on my old Friend and Correspondent Mr Peter Collinson,* who told me that John Hanbury,* the great Virginia Merchant, had requested to be informed when I should arrive, that he might carry me to Lord Granville's,* who was then President of the Council,, and wish'd to see me as soon as possible. I agreed to go with him the next Morning. Accordingly Mr Hanbury called for me and took me in his Carriage to that Nobleman's, who receiv'd me with great Civility; and after some Questions respecting the present State of Affairs in America, & Discourse thereupon, he said to me, "You Americans have wrong Ideas of the

Nature of your Constitution; you contend that the King's Instructions to his Governors are not Laws, and think yourselves at Liberty to regard or disregard them at your own Discretion. But those Instructions are not like the Pocket Instructions given to a Minister going abroad, for regulating his Conduct in some trifling Point of Ceremony. They are first drawn up by Judges learned in the Laws; they are then considered, debated & perhaps amended in Council, after which they are signed by the King. They are then so far as relates to you, the *Law of the Land*; for THE KING IS THE LEGISLATOR OF THE COLONIES." I told his Lordship this was new Doctrine to me. I had always understood from our Charters, that our Laws were to be made by our Assemblies, to be presented indeed to the King for his Royal Assent, but that being once given the King could not repeal or alter them. And as the Assemblies could not make permanent Laws without his Assent, so neither could he make a Law for them without theirs. He assur'd me I was totally mistaken. I did not think so however. And his Lordship's Conversation having a little alarm'd me as to what might be the Sentiments of the Court concerning us, I wrote it down as soon as I return'd to my Lodgings.—I recollected that about 20 Years before, a Clause in a Bill brought into Parliament by the Ministry, had propos'd to make the King's Instructions Laws in the Colonies; but the Clause was thrown out by the Commons, for which we ador'd them as our Friends & Friends of Liberty, till by their Conduct towards us in 1765, it seem'd that they had refus'd that Point of Sovereignty to the King, only that the might reserve it for themselves.

After some Days, Dr Fothergill having spoken to the Proprietaries, they agreed to a Meeting with me at Mr J. Penn's* House in Spring Garden. The Conversation at first consisted of mutual Declarations of Disposition to reasonable Accommodation; but I suppose each Party had its own Ideas of what should be meant by *reasonable*. We then went into Consideration of our several Points of Complaint which I enumerated. The Proprietaries justify'd their Conduct as

well as they could, and I the Assembly's. We now appeared
very wide, and so far from each other in our Opinions, as
to discourage all Hope of Agreement. However, it was
concluded that I should give them the Heads of our Complaints in Writing, and they promis'd then to consider
them.—I did so soon after; but they put the Paper into the
Hands of their Solicitor Ferdinando John Paris,* who
manag'd for them all their Law Business in their great Suit
with the neighbouring Proprietary of Maryland, Lord Baltimore, which had subsisted 70 Years, and wrote for them
all their Papers & Messages in their Dispute with the
Assembly. He was a proud angry Man; and as I had
occasionally in the Answers of the Assembly treated his
Papers with some Severity, they being really weak in point
of Argument, and haughty in Expression, he had conceiv'd
a mortal Enmity to me. which discovering itself whenever
we met, I declin'd the Proprietary's Proposal that he and I
should discuss the Heads of Complaint between our two
selves, and refus'd treating with any one but them. They
then by his Advice put the Paper into the Hands of the
Attorney and Solicitor General for their Opinion and Counsel upon it, where it lay unanswered a Year wanting eight
Days, during which time I made frequent Demands of an
Answer from the Proprietaries but without obtaining any
other than that they had not yet receiv'd the Opinion of the
Attorney & Solicitor General: What it was when they did
receive it I never learnt, for they did not communicate it
to me, but sent a long Message to the Assembly drawn &
signed by Paris reciting my Paper, complaining of its want
of Formality as a Rudeness on my part, and giving a flimsey
Justification of their Conduct, adding that they should be
willing to accomodate Matters, if the Assembly would send
over *some Person of Candour* to treat with them for that
purpose, intimating thereby that I was not such. The want
of Formality or Rudeness, was probably my not having
address'd the Pager to them with their assum'd Titles of
true and absolute Proprietaries of the Province of Pensilvania, wch I omitted as not thinking it necessary in a Paper

the Intention of which was only to reduce to a Certainty by writing what in Conversation I had delivered *vivâ voce*. But during this Delay, the Assembly having prevail'd with Govr Denny to pass an Act taxing the Proprietary Estate in common with the Estates of the People, which was the grand Point in Dispute, they omitted answering the Message.

When this Act however came over, the Proprietaries counsell'd by Paris determin'd to oppose its receiving the Royal Assent. Accordingly they petition'd the King in Council, and a Hearing was appointed, in which two Lawyers were employ'd by them against the Act, and two by me in Support of it. They alledg'd that the Act was intended to load the Proprietary Estate in order to spare those of the People, and that if it were suffer'd to continue in force, & the Proprietaries who were in Odium with the People, left to their Mercy in proportioning the Taxes, they would inevitably be ruined. We reply'd that the Act had no such Intention and would have no such Effect. That the Assessors were honest & discreet Men, under an Oath to assess fairly & equitably, & that any Advantage each of them might expect in lessening his own Tax by augmenting that of the Proprietaries was too trifling to induce them to perjure themselves. This is the purport of what I remember as urg'd by both Sides, except that we insisted strongly on the mischievous Consequences that must attend a Repeal; for that the Money, 100,000£, being printed and given to the King's Use, expended in his Service, & now spread among the People, the Repeal would strike it dead in their Hands to the Ruin of many, & the total Discouragement of future Grants, and the Selfishness of the Proprietors in soliciting such a general Catastrophe, merely from a groundless Fear of their Estate being taxed too highly, was insisted on in the strongest Terms. On this Lord Mansfield,* one of the Council rose, & beckoning to me, took me into the Clerk's Chamber, while the Lawyers were pleading, and ask'd me if I was really of Opinion that no Injury would be done the Proprietary Estate in the Execution of the Act. I said, Certainly. Then says he, you can have little Objection to enter into an Engagement to assure that Point. I answer'd None, at all. He then call'd in Paris, and after som Discourse his Lordship's Proposition was accepted on both Sides; a Paper to the purpose was drawn up by the Clerk of the Council, which I sign'd with Mr Charles,* who was also an Agent of the Province for their ordinary Affairs; when Lord Mansfield return'd to the Council Chamber where finally the Law was allowed to pass. Some Changes were however recommended and we also engag'd they should be made by a subsequent Law; but the Assembly did not think them necessary, For one Year's Tax having been levied by the Act before the Order of Council arrived, they appointed a Committee to examine the Percedings of the Assessors, & On this Committee they put several particular Friends of the Proprietaries. After a full Enquiry they unanimously sign'd a Report that they found the Tax had been assess'd with perfect Equity. The Assembly look'd on my entring into the first Part of the Engagement as an essential Service to the Province, since it secur'd the Credit of the Paper Money then spread over all the Country; and they gave me their Thanks in form when I return'd.——But the Proprietaries were enrag'd at Governor Denny for having pass'd the Act, & turn'd him out, with Threats of suing him for Breach of Instructions which he had given Bond to observe. He however having done it the Instance of the General & for his Majesty's Service, and having some powerful Interest at Court, despis'd the Threats, and they were never put in Execution

FRANKLIN'S OUTLINE FOR THE AUTOBIO-GRAPHY

My writing. Mrs.. Dogoods Letters—Differences arise between my Brother and me (his temper and mine) their Cause in general. His News Paper. The Prosecution he suffered. My Examination. Vote of Assembly. His Manner of evading it. Whereby I became free. My Attempt to get employ with other Printers. He prevents me. Our frequent pleadings

before our Father. The final Breach. My Inducements to
quit Boston. Manner of coming to a Resolution. My leaving
him & going to New York. (return to eating Flesh.) thence
to Pennsylvania, The Journey, and its Events on the Bay,
at Amboy, the Road, meet with Dr. Brown. his Character.
his great work. At Burlington. The Good Woman. On the
River. My Arrival at Philada... First Meal and first Sleep.
Money left. Employment. Lodging. First Acquaintance with
my Afterwards Wife, with J. Ralph. with Keimer. their
Characters. Osborne. Watson. The Governor takes Notice
of me. the Occasion and Manner. his Character. Offers to
set me up. My return to Boston. Voyage and Accidents.
Reception. My Father dislikes the proposal. I return to New
York and Philada... Governor Burnet. J. Collins. the
Money for Vernon. The Governors Deceit. Collins not
finding Employment goes to Barbados much in my Debt.
Ralph and I go to England. Disappointment of Governors
Letters. Col. French his Friend. Cornwallis's Letters. Cab-
bin. Denham. Hamilton, Arrival in England. Get Employ-
ment. Ralph not. He is an Expence to me. Adventures in
England. Write a Pamphlet and print 100. Schemes. Lyons.
Dr Pemberton. My Diligence and yet poor thro Ralph. My
Landlady. her Character. Wygate. Wilkes. Cibber. Plays.
Books I borrowed. Preachers I heard. Redmayne. At
Watts's— Temperance. Ghost,. Conduct and Influence
among the Men, persuaded by Mr Denham to return with
him to Philada.. & be his Clerk. Our Voyage. and Arrival.
My resolutions in Writing. My Sickness. His Death. Found
D. R married. Go to work again with Keimer. Terms. His
ill Usage of me. My Resentment. Saying of Decow. My
Friends at Burlington. Agreement with H Meredith to set
up in Partnership. Do so. Success with the Assembly.
Hamiltons Friendship. Sewells History. Gazette. Paper
Money. Webb. Writing Busy Body. Breintnal. Godfrey. his
Character. Suit against us. Offer of my Friends Coleman
and Grace. continue the Business and M. goes to Carolina.
Pamphlet on Paper Money. Gazette from Keimer. Junto
erected, its plan. Marry. Library erected. Manner of

conducting the Project. Its plan and Utility. Children. Almanack. The Use I made of it. Great Industry. Constant Study. Fathers Remark and Advice upon Diligence. Carolina Partnership. Learn French and German. Journey to Boston after 10 years. Affection of my Brother. His Death and leaving me his Son. Art of Virtue. Occasion. City Watch. amended. Post Office. Spotswood. Bradfords Behaviour. Clerk of Assembly. Lose one of my Sons. Project of subordinate Junto's. Write occasionally in the papers. Success in Business. Fire Companys. Engines. Go again to Boston in 1743. See Dr Spence. Whitefield. My Connection with him. His Generosity to me. my returns. Church Differences. My part in them. Propose a College. not then prosecuted. Propose and establish a Philosophical Society. War. Electricity. my first knowledge of it. Partnership with D Hall &c. Dispute in Assembly upon Defence. Project for it. Plain Truth. its Success. 10,000 Men raised and Disciplined. Lotteries. Battery built. New Castle. My Influence in the Council. Colours, Devices and Motto's.—Ladies. Military Watch. Quakers. chosen of the common council. Put in the Commission of the Peace. Logan fond of me. his Library. Appointed post Master General. Chosen Assembly Man. Commissioner to treat with Indians at Carlisle. and at Easton. Project and establish Academy. Pamphlet on it. Journey to Boston. At Albany. Plan of Union of the Colonies. Copy of it. Remarks upon it. It fails and how. (Journey to Boston in 1754.) Disputes about it in our Assembly. My part in them. New Governor. Disputes with him. His Character and Sayings to me. Chosen Alderman. Project of Hospital my Share in it. Its Success. Boxes. Made a Commissioner of the treasury My Commission to defend the Frontier Counties. Raise Men & build Forts. Militia Law of my drawing. Made Colonel. Parade of my Officers. Offence to Proprietor. Assistance to Boston Ambassadors— Journey with Shirley &c.. Meet with Braddock. Assistance to him. To the Officers of his Army. Furnish him with Forage. His Concessions to me and Character of me. Success of my Electrical Experiments. Medal sent me per Royal

Society and Speech of President. Dennys Arrival & Courtship to me. his Character. My Service to the Army in the
Affair of Quarters. Disputes about the Proprietors Taxes
continued. Project for paving the City. I am sent to England.]* Negociation there. Canada delenda est.* My Pamphlet. Its reception and Effect. Projects drawn from me
concerning the Conquest. Acquaintance made and their
Services to me Mrs.. S.., Mr Small. Sir John P. Mr Wood.
Sargent Strahan and others. their Characters. Doctorate
from Edinburg St. Andrews Doctorate from Oxford. Journey to Scotland. Lord Leicester. Mr. Prat.—DeGrey. Jack-
son. State of Affairs in England. Delays. Event. Journey
into Holland and Flanders. Agency from Maryland. Sons
Appointment. My Return. Allowance and thanks. Journey
to Boston. John Penn Governor. My Conduct towards him.
The Paxton Murders. My Pamphlet Rioters march to Philada. . . Governor retires to my House. My Conduct, Sent
out to the Insurgents—Turn them back. Little Thanks.
Disputes revived. Resolutions against continuing under Proprietary Government. Another Pamphlet. Cool Thoughts.
Sent again to England with Petition. Negociation there.
Lord H. his Character. Agencies from New Jersey, Georgia,
Massachusets. Journey into Germany 1766. Civilities re-
ceived there. Gottingen Observations. Ditto into France in
1767. Ditto in 1769. Entertainment there at the Academy.
Introduced to the King and the Mesdames. Mad. Victoria
and Mrs. Lamagnon. Duc de Chaulnes, M Beaumont. Le
Roy. Dalibard. Nollet. See Journals. Holland. Reprint my
papers and add many. Books presented to me from many
Authors. My Book translated into French. Lightning Kite.
various Discoveries. My Manner of prosecuting that Study.
King of Denmark invites me to Dinner. Recollect my
Fathers Proverb. Stamp Act. My Opposition to it. Recom-
mendation of J. Hughes. Amendment of it. Examination in
Parliament. Reputation it gave me. Caress'd by Ministry.
Charles Townsends Act. Opposition to it. Stoves and Chim-
ney plates. Armonica. Accquaintance with Ambassadors.
Russian Intimation. Writing in Newspapers. Glasses from

Germany. Grant of Land in Nova Scotia. Sicknesses. Letters to America returned hither. the Consequences. Insurance Office. My Character. Costs me nothing to be civil to inferiors, a good deal to be submissive to superiors &c &c. .

Farce of perpetl. Motion

Writing for Jersey Assembly.

Hutchinson's Letters. Temple. Suit in Chancery, Abuse before the Privy Council.—Lord Hillsborough's Character. & Conduct. Lord Dartmouth. Negotiation to prevent the War.—Return to America. Bishop of St Asaph. Congress, Assembly. Committee of Safety. Chevaux de Frize.—Sent to Boston, to the Camp. To Canada. to Lord Howe.— To France, Treaty, &c

Silence Dogood, 4

In the *Autobiography* Franklin describes how in his turbulent apprenticeship with his brother he submitted a contribution to his brother's newspaper *The New-England Courant* anonymously so it would get a fair reading from the overbearing James Franklin. The submission purported to be a letter from one Silence Dogood, the widow of a Puritan clergyman. James Franklin and his associates at the *Courant* immediately recognized that the *persona* alluded to Cotton Mather, the leading spokesman for American Puritanism at the time, the Franklins' adversary on a number of issues, and the author of a treatise known as *Essays to do Good*. Benjamin Franklin had already written two ballads which James Franklin had published and which have long disappeared, but Mistress Dogood's letter is Franklin's first published prose. Not long before, Franklin had worked to perfect his own prose by imitation of Joseph Addison's *Spectator*, an English series of periodical letters which served as the model for aspiring English writers throughout the century.

In printing the first Silence Dogood letter, James Franklin solicited the anonymous author for further contributions, so the first important series of periodical letters in America was begun. Here in the fourth letter, Silence considers whether her son should be sent to Harvard College and is urged to send him there by the local minister, who boards with her. After hearing his arguments she goes off by herself and has a dream vision about a place called the Temple of Learning, which can only be entered by permission of the porter named *Riches*. One of Benjamin Franklin's significant adaptations of Addison is his expansion of the audience for his periodical letters to include, in the words of the first letter, '*poor* or *rich*, *old* or *young*, a *Schollar* or a *Leather Apron Man*, &c.'; while Addison's *persona* was more clearly a member of a sort of literary establishment. The prejudices of the Leather Apron Man against the frivolousness and possibly the fraudulence of college education are vividly depicted in Silence Dogood's dream. As the dream accurately reflects, the largest number of Harvard graduates in 1722 went into the Puritan ministry, and Franklin indicates that the route to advancement was through plagiarism of published English sermons, such as those of Archbishop John Tillotson.

Late in his life, in a letter to Samuel Mather, Cotton Mather's son, Franklin describes how as a boy 'I met with a book, entitled "*Essays to do Good*," which I think was written by your father . . . [The book] gave me such a turn of thinking, as to have an influence on my conduct through life; for I have always set a greater value on the character of a *doer of good*, than on any other kind of reputation; and if I have been, as you seem to think, a useful citizen, the public owes the advantage of it to that book. . . . The last time I saw your father was in the beginning of 1724, when I visited him after my first trip to Pennsylvania. He received me in his library, and on my taking leave showed me a shorter way out of the house through a narrow passage, which was crossed by a beam over head. We were still talking as I withdrew, he accompanying me behind, and I turning partly towards him, when he said hastily, "*Stoop, stoop!*" I did not understand him, till I felt my head hit against the beam. He was a man that never missed any occasion of giving instruction, and upon this he said to me, "*You are young, and have the world before you;* STOOP *as you go through it, and you will miss many hard thumps*" ' (*Writings*, 1092). The 78-year-old Franklin could look back with fondness at Cotton Mather as a sort of inspiration for the sort of humbling practical advice he himself had dispensed in quantity in his life. The 16-year-old Franklin who knew he would never go to Harvard had little compunction about ridiculing the Mathers.

An sum etiam nunc vel Græcè loqui vel Latinè docendus? * Cicero.

To the Author of the New-England Courant.

Sir, [No 4

Discoursing the other Day at Dinner with my Reverend Boarder, formerly mention'd, (whom for Distinction sake we will call by the Name of *Clericus*,) concerning the Education of Children, I ask'd his Advice about my young Son *William*, whether or no I had best bestow upon him Academical Learning, or (as our Phrase is) *bring him up at our College*: He perswaded me to do it by all Means, using many weighty Arguments with me, and answering all the Objections that I could form against it; telling me withal, that he did not doubt but that the Lad would take his

Learning very well, and not idle away his Time as too many there now-a-days do. These Words of *Clericus* gave me a Curiosity to inquire a little more strictly into the present Circumstances of that famous Seminary of Learning; but the Information which he gave me, was neither pleasant, nor such as I expected.

As soon as Dinner was over, I took a solitary Walk into my Orchard, still ruminating on *Clericus*'s Discourse with much Consideration, until I came to my usual Place of Retirement under the *Great Apple-Tree*; where having seated my self, and carelesly laid my Head on a verdant Bank, I fell by Degrees into a soft and undisturbed Slumber. My waking Thoughts remained with me in my Sleep, and before I awak'd again, I dreamt the following DREAM.

I fancy'd I was travelling over pleasant and delightful Fields and Meadows, and thro' many small Country Towns and Villages; and as I pass'd along, all Places resounded with the Fame of the Temple of LEARNING: Every Peasant, who had wherewithal, was preparing to send one of his Children at least to this famous Place; and in this Case most of them consulted their own Purses instead of their Childrens Capacities: So that I observed, a great many, yea, the most part of those who were travelling thither, were little better than Dunces and Blockheads. Alas! alas!

At length I entred upon a spacious Plain, in the Midst of which was erected a large and stately Edifice: It was to this that a great Company of Youths from all Parts of the Country were going; so stepping in among the Crowd, I passed on with them, and presently arrived at the Gate.

The Passage was kept by two sturdy Porters named *Riches* and *Poverty*, and the latter obstinately refused to give Entrance to any who had not first gain'd the Favour of the former; so that I observed, many who came even to the very Gate, were obliged to travel back again as ignorant as they came, for want of this necessary Qualification. However, as a Spectator I gain'd Admittance, and with the rest entred directly into the Temple.

In the Middle of the great Hall stood a stately and magnificent Throne, which was ascended to by two high and difficult Steps. On the Top of it sat LEARNING in awful State; she was apparelled wholly in Black, and surrounded almost on every Side with innumerable Volumes in all Languages. She seem'd very busily employ'd in writing something on half a Sheet of Paper, and upon Enquiry, I understood she was preparing a Paper, call'd, *The New-England Courant.* On her Right Hand sat *English*, with a pleasant smiling Countenance, and handsomely attir'd; and on her left were seated several *Antique Figures* with their Faces vail'd. I was considerably puzzl'd to guess who they were, until one informed me, (who stood beside me,) that those Figures on her left Hand were *Latin, Greek, Hebrew*, &c. and that they were very much reserv'd, and seldom or never unvail'd their Faces here, and then to few or none, tho' most of those who have in this Place acquir'd so much Learning as to distinguish them from *English*, pretended to an intimate Acquaintance with them. I then enquir'd of him, what could be the Reason why they continued vail'd, in this Place especially: He pointed to the Foot of the Throne, where I saw *Idleness*, attended with *Ignorance*, and these (he informed me) were they, who first vail'd them, and still kept them so.

Now I observed, that the whole Tribe who entred into the Temple with me, began to climb the Throne; but the Work proving troublesome and difficult to most of them, they withdrew their Hands from the Plow, and contented themselves to sit at the Foot, with Madam *Idleness* and her Maid *Ignorance*, until those who were assisted by Diligence and a docible Temper, had well nigh got up the first Step: But the Time drawing nigh in which they could no way avoid ascending, they were fain to crave the Assistance of those who had got up before them, and who, for the Reward perhaps of a *Pint of Milk*, or a *Piece of Plumb-Cake*, lent the Lubbers a helping Hand, and sat them in the Eye of the World, upon a Level with themselves.

The other Step being in the same Manner ascended, and

the usual Ceremonies at an End, every Beetle-Scull seem'd well satisfy'd with his own Portion of Learning, tho' perhaps he was *e'en just* as ignorant as ever. And now the Time of their Departure being come, they march'd out of Doors to make Room for another Company, who waited for Entrance: And I, having seen all that was to be seen, quitted the Hall likewise, and went to make my Observations on those who were just gone out before me.

Some I perceiv'd took to Merchandizing, others to Travelling, some to one Thing, some to another, and some to Nothing; and many of them from henceforth, for want of Patrimony, liv'd as poor as Church Mice, being unable to dig, and asham'd to beg, and to live by their Wits it was impossible. But the most Part of the Crowd went along a large beaten Path, which led to a Temple at the further End of the Plain, call'd, *The Temple of Theology*. The Business of those who were employ'd in this Temple being laborious and painful, I wonder'd exceedingly to see so many go towards it; but while I was pondering this Matter in my Mind, I spy'd *Pecunia* behind a Curtain, beckoning to them with her Hand, which Sight immediately satisfy'd me for whose Sake it was, that a great Part of them (I will not say all) travel'd that Road. In this Temple I saw nothing worth mentioning, except the ambitious and fraudulent Contrivances of *Plagius*, who (notwithstanding he had been severely reprehended for such Practices before) was diligently transcribing some eloquent Paragraphs out of *Tillotson*'s *Works*, *&c.** to embellish his own.

Now I bethought my self in my Sleep, that it was Time to be at Home, and as I fancy'd I was travelling back thither, I reflected in my Mind on the extream Folly of those Parents, who, blind to their Childrens Dulness, and insensible of the Solidity of their Skulls, because they think their Purses can afford it, will needs send them to the Temple of Learning, where, for want of a suitable Genius, they learn little more than how to carry themselves handsomely, and enter a Room genteely, (which might as well be acquir'd at a Dancing-School,) and from whence they return, after

Abundance of Trouble and Charge, as great Blockheads as
ever, only more proud and self-conceited.

While I was in the midst of these unpleasant Reflections,
Clericus (who with a Book in his Hand was walking under
the Trees) accidentally awak'd me; to him I related my
Dream with all its Particulars, and he, without much Study,
presently interpreted it, assuring me, *That it was a lively
Representation of* HARVARD COLLEGE, *Etcetera.*

> *I remain, Sir,*
>
> *Your Humble Servant,*
>
> SILENCE DOGOOD.

The New-England Courant, 14 May 1722

To 'Your Honour': Defense of James Franklin to Samuel Sewall

This short piece appeared in the *New-England Courant* with a preface signed 'Juba' describing it as a rough draft of a letter found in the street, but as J. A. Leo Lemay points out, it must have been composed in the *Courant* office while Benjamin Franklin was serving as its editor (Lemay, *Canon*, 35–7). The letter unmistakably refers to Judge Samuel Sewall, who had led the counter-attack by the Boston authorities against James Franklin and the *Courant*, to the point where James was forbidden by decree from publishing it. It is quite possible that Benjamin had already attacked Sewall in one of the Dogood letters (Lemay, "Benjamin Franklin", 208), though the subject of 'Dogood', 9 may also be the late governor Joseph Dudley, who was certainly on Franklin's mind a few years later in the 1726 Journal. In the fourth and fifth paragraphs, Benjamin Franklin refers to Sewall's involvement as a judge in the Salem witchcraft trials. Nowhere else in his writings is Franklin so openly defiant toward authority as he is in this piece, and he looks back in his *Autobiography* to this period as one in which his 'Turn for Libelling and Satyr' was getting him into trouble in Boston.

In fact, Sewall had long since repented publicly for his role in the Salem trials, as Franklin notes in the last words of the essay. As he would later do in his writings before the American Revolution, Franklin makes no sharp distinction between personal conflicts and intellectual or legal issues: here Judge Sewall had threatened the Franklins, and the younger brother was fighting back. Characteristically, Franklin also includes arguments he himself probably thought little of but which he knew many of his readers would accept: one danger of persecuting James Franklin is that 'our Religion may suffer extreamly hereafter'. The *Autobiography* and own writings from this period indicate that he was not particularly tender about the fate of Boston Puritanism. 'S——y' in the fourth paragraph may refer to a contemporary usage of stationery or stationer: an official charged with supervision of published works.

SIR,

I am inform'd that your Honour was a leading Man in the late Extraordinary procedure against *F——n* the Printer: And inasmuch as it cannot be long before you must appear at *Christ*'s enlightned Tribunal, where every Man's work shall be tryed, I humbly beseech you, in the Fear of GOD, to consider & Examine, whether that Procedure be according to *the strict Rules of Justice and Equity*? It is manifest, that this Man had broke no *Law*; and you know, Sir, that where there is no Law, there can be no Transgression: And, Sir, methinks you cannot but know, that it is highly *unjust* to punish a Man by a *Law*, to which the Fact committed is *Antecedent*. The Law ever looks *forward*, but never *backward*; but if once we come to punish Men, by vertue of Laws *Ex post Facto*, Farewel *Magna Charta*, and *English Liberties*, for no Man can ever be *safe*, but may be punished for every Action he does by Laws made afterwards. This in my humble Opinion, both the Light of Nature and Laws of Justice abhor, and is what ought to be detested by all Good Men.

Summum jus, est summa injuria.*

Moreover, this is not according to the procedure of the *supream Judge of all the Earth*, (who cannot but do right) which is the most perfect Rule for *Humane Gods* to copy after. You know, Sir, that he will Judge and punish Men, according to that *Light and Law* they were favour'd with; And that he will not punish the *Heathen* for disobeying the Gospel, of which they were intirely ignorant.

The end of Humane Law is to fix the boundaries within which Men ought to keep themselves; But if any are so hardy and presumptuous as to break through them, doubtless they deserve punishment. Now, If this *Printer* had transgress'd any Law, he ought to have been presented by a Grand Jury, and a fair Tryal brought on.

I would further observe to your Honour the danger of ill Precedents, and that this Precedent *will not sleep*; And, Sir, can you bear to think that Posterity will have Reason to

Curse you on the Account hereof! By this our Religion may suffer extreamly hereafter; for, whatever those Ministers (if any such there were) who have push'd on this matter, may think of it, they have made a Rod for themselves in times to come, Blessed be God, we have a good King at present; but if it should please him for our Sins to punish us with a bad one, we may have a *S——y* that will so *Supervise* our Ministers Sermons, as to suffer them to print none at all.

I would also humbly remind your Honour, that you were formerly led into an Error, which you afterwards Publickly and Solemnly (and I doubt not, Sincerely) Confess'd and repented of; and Sir, ought not this to make you the more Cautious & Circumspect in your Actions which relate to the publick all your Days?

The New-England Courant, 4 February 1722/3

1726 Journal

The following piece of writing presents Franklin in a role in which he can seldom be found, writing for himself with no expectation of publication. One of Franklin's most perceptive recent critics has characterized the journal as 'the most intriguing and mysterious of Franklin's writings' (Breitwieser, 302). When Franklin concluded that his first stay in England was leading him nowhere, he decided to accompany Thomas Denham, a Quaker merchant who had befriended him during his voyage to London, as Denham returned to Philadelphia. Denham served as a sort of mentor to Franklin in the years in London and thereafter in Philadelphia. The high spirits Franklin displays in this journal suggest that he returned to Philadelphia not as a young man who had been made a fool of, but as someone who could still have a good time even in potentially boring circumstances.

The *Berkshire* encountered unfavourable winds for some time after entering the English Channel, so it spent a while along the south coast of England and in various anchorages on the Isle of Wight. In the journal entry for 8 August, Franklin leaves a blank space for an omitted name: the name is most likely that of Joseph Dudley, the unpopular governor of Massachusetts in Franklin's childhood (*Papers*, i. 78). Mr Denham was one of the owners of the ship, which may account for some of the leeway for impromptu explorations and shipboard horseplay young Franklin, his protégé, enjoyed. Later in the voyage, the *Berkshire* encounters ('speaks' is the nautical term Franklin uses) a small vessel bound for New York, called a snow, a modification of the brig.

Franklin himself considered the 1726 journal sufficiently noteworthy to refer to it in the first part of his *Autobiography*, so the journal is in an important sense a necessary appendix to his life story, though it is scarcely ever printed except in collected editions of his writings. The original journal in Franklin's own hand has been lost. But at some point between 1726 and 1817 a copyist transcribed the original manuscript. The journal was first printed by Franklin's grandson William Temple Franklin in 1817 as part of Temple Franklin's edition of his grandfather's papers. Temple Franklin, as he often did, made various changes in the copyist's manuscript as he prepared his edition. The copyist's transcript is evidently the closest thing we have to Franklin's original journal, but the editors of the great edition of *The Papers of Benjamin Franklin* have printed instead the Temple Franklin version on the basis that the handwritten transcript is insufficiently legible. The editors were working with photostatic copies of the transcript when they made that decision, though they consulted the transcript photostats as a partial check on the Temple Franklin version (and in fact some of the editors' corrections based on the photostats are incorrect). The photostats of the transcript are particularly difficult to read, but the original version is written in a clear copyist's hand with only a few holes in the pages or unclear passages. The transcript is among the Franklin papers in the Manuscript Division of the Library of Congress. This Oxford World's Classics edition is the first since Franklin's time to use the text of the copyist's transcript as the basis of the printed version. In the few places where the transcript is unclear, the absent wording has been supplied from *Memoirs of the Life and Writings of Benjamin Franklin, LL.D. F.R.S. &c. Minister Plenipotentiary from the United States of America at the Court of France, and for the Treaty of Peace and Independence with Great Britain, &c. &c. Written by Himself to a Late Period, and continued to the Time of His Death by His Grandson, William Temple Franklin. Comprising the Private Correspondence and Public Negociations of Dr. Franklin. And His Select Political, Philosophical, and Miscellaneous Works. Published from the Original MSS.*, 3rd edn. ii (London: Printed for Henry Colburn, Conduit Street, 1818).

Journal of occurrences in my voyage to Philadelphia aboard the Berkshire Henry Clarke, Master, from London

Friday July 22nd 1726

Yesterday in the afternoon we left London and came to anchor at Gravesend about eleven at night. I lay ashore all night and this morning took a walk up to the Windmill Hill, from whence I had an agreeable prospect of the country for above twenty miles round, and two or three reaches of the river with ships and boats sailing both up and down, and Tilbury Fort in the other side which commands the River and passage to London. This Gravesend is a *cursed biting* place. The chief dependence of the people being the advantage they make of imposing upon strangers. If you buy any thing of them, and give half what they ask, you pay twice as much as the thing is worth. Thank God we shall leave it tomorrow.

Saturday July 23

This day we weighed anchor and fell down with the tide, there being little or no wind. In the afternoon we had a fresh gale that brought us down to Margate, where we shall lie at anchor this night. Most of the passengers are very sick. Saw several porpusses &c.

Sunday July 24

This morning we weighed anchor and coming to the Downs, we set our pilot ashore at Deal and passed through. And now whilst I write this sitting upon the quarter deck I have methinks one of the pleasantest scenes in the world before me. Tis a fine clear day, and we are going away before the wind with an easy pleasant gale. We have near fifteen sail of ships in sight and I may say in company. On the left hand appears the coast of France at a distance, and on the right is the town and castle of Dover with the green hills and chalky cliffs of England, to which we must now bid farewell.—Albion, farewell!—

Monday July 25

All the morning calm. After noon sprung up a gale at East; blew very hard all night. Saw the Isle of Wight at a distance.

Tuesday July 26

Contrary winds all days blowing pretty hard. Saw the Isle of Wight again in the evening.

Wednesday July 27

This morning the wind blowing very hard at West, we stood for the land, in order to make some harbour. About noon we took onboard a pilot out of a fishing shallop, who brought the ship in to Spithead off Portsmouth. The Captain, Mr Denham and myself went on shore and during the little time we stayed I made some observations on the place.

Portsmouth has a fine harbour. The entrance is so narrow that you may throw a stone from Fort to Fort, yet it is near ten fathom deep and bold close to; but within there is room enough for five hundred or for aught I know a thousand sail of ships. The town is strongly fortified being encompassed with a high wall and a deep and broad ditch, and two gates that are entered over draw bridges; besides several forts, batteries of large cannon, and other outworks, the names of which I know not, nor had I time to take so strict a view as to be able to describe them. In war time the town has a garrison of 1000 men, but at present tis only manned by about 100 Invalids. Notwithstanding, the English have so many fleets of menofwar at sea at this time[†] I counted in this harbour above thirty sail of 2nd 3rd & 4th Rates that lay by unrigged, but easily fitted out upon occasion, all their masts and rigging, lying marked and numbered in storehouses at hand. The King's yards and docks employ abundance of men, who even in peace time are constantly building and refitting menofwar for the King's Service. Gosport lies opposite to Portsmouth, and is near as big if not bigger, but except the fort at the mouth of the harbour and a small outwork before the main street of the town, it is only defended by a mud wall which surrounds it, and a trench or dry ditch of about ten foot depth and breadth. Portsmouth is a place of very little trade in peace time, it depending chiefly on fitting out men of war. Spithead is the place where the Fleet commonly anchor, and is a very good riding place. The people of Portsmouth tell strange stories of the Severity of one *Gibson** who was governor of this place in the Queen's time, to his soldiers, and show you a miserable dungeon by the town gate, which they call *Johnny Gibson's hole*, where for trifling misdemeanours he used to confine his soldiers till they were almost starved to

[†] One gone to the Baltic one to the Mediterranean, and one to the W. Indies

death. Tis a common maxim that without severe discipline, tis impossible to govern the licentious rabble of soldiery. I own indeed that if a commander finds he has not those qualities in him that will make him beloved by his people, he ought by all means to make use of such methods as will make them fear him, since one or the other (or both) is absolutely necessary; but Alexander and Caesar those renowned generals received more faithful service, and performed greater actions by means of the love their soldiers bore them, than they could possibly have done, if instead of being beloved and respected they had been hated and feared by those they commanded.

Thursday July 28

This morning we came on board having been on shore all night. We weighed anchor and with a moderate gale stood in for Cowes in the Isle of Wight, and came to an anchor before the town about eleven o'clock. Six of the passengers went on shore and diverted themselves till about 12 at night and then got a boat, and came on board again—expecting to sail early in the morning.

Friday July 29

But the wind continuing adverse still, we went ashore again this morning, and took a walk to Newport which is about four miles distant from Cowes, and is the metropolis of the island. From thence we walked to Carisbrook, about a mile farther, out of curiosity to see that castle which King Charles the First was confined in; and so returned to Cowes in the afternoon and went on board, in expectation of sailing.—

Cowes is but a small town, and lies close to the sea side, pretty near opposite to Southampton on the main shore of England. It is divided into two parts by a small river that runs up within a quarter of a mile of Newport, and is distinguished by East and West Cowes. There is a fort built in an oval form, on which there is eight or ten guns mounted for the defence of the road. They have a post office, a custom-house and a chappel of ease. And a good harbour for ships to ride in easterly and westerly winds.

All this day I spent agreeably enough at the draft board. It is a game I much delight in, but it requires a clear head and undisturbed and the persons playing if they would play well ought not much to regard the *consequence* of the game, for that diverts and withdraws the attention of the mind from the game itself, and makes the player liable to make many false open moves; and I will venture to lay it down for an infallible rule, that if two persons *equal* in judgment play for a considerable sum, he that loves money most shall lose; his anxiety for the success of the game confounds him. Courage is almost as requisite for the good conduct of this game as in a real battle; for if the player imagines himself opposed by one that is much his Superior in Skill his mind is so intent on the defensive part that an advantage passes unobserved.

Newport makes a pretty prospect enough from the hills that surround it; (for it lies down in a bottom). The houses are beautifully intermixed with trees, and a tall old fashioned steeple rises in the midst of the town, which is very ornamental to it. The name of the church I could not learn, but there is a very neat markethouse paved with square stone, and consisting of eleven arches. There are several pretty handsome streets, and many well built houses and shops well stored with goods. But I think Newport is chiefly remarkable for oysters, which they send to London and other places, where they are very much esteemed, being thought the best in England. The oyster merchants fetch them as I am informed from other places, and lay them upon certain beds in the river, (the water of which is it seems excellently adapted for that purposes) a fattening, and when they have laid a suitable time they are taken up again and made fit for sale.

When we came to Carisbrook, which, as I said before, is a little village about a mile beyond Newport, we took a view of an ancient Church that had formerly been a priory in Romish times, and is the first church, or the mother church

of the island. It is an elegant building, after the old Gothic
manner, with a very high tower, and looks very venerable
in its ruins. There are several ancient monuments about it,
but the stone of which they are composed is of such a soft
crumbling nature, that the inscriptions are none of them
legible. Of the same stone are almost all the tombstones &c
that I observed in the island. From this church, (having
crossed over the brook that gives name to the village, and
got a little boy for a guide) we went up a very steep hill
through several narrow lanes and avenues, till we came to
the castle gate. We entered over the ditch (which is now
almost filled up, partly by the ruins of the mouldering walls
that have tumbled into it, and partly by the washing down
of the earth from the hill by the rain) upon a couple of
brick arches where I suppose formerly there was a draw-
bridge. An old woman who lives in the castle, seeing us as
strangers, walk about sent and offered to show us the rooms
if we pleased, which we accepted. This castle as she informed us has for many years been the Seat of the governors
of the island, and the rooms and hall which are very large
and handsome with high arched roofs, have all along been
kept handsomely furnished, every succeeding governor
buying the furniture of his predecessor, but Cadogan* the
last Governor who succeeded General Webb,* refusing to
purchase it, Webb stripped it clear of all, even the hangings,
and left nothing but bare walls. The floors are several of
them of plaster of Paris,* the art of making which, the
woman told us, was now lost: The castle stands upon a very
high and steep hill, and there is the remains of a deep ditch
round it; the walls are thick and seemingly well contrived;
and certainly it has been a very strong hold in its time, at
least before the invention of great guns. There are several
breaches in the ruinous walls, which are never repaired (I
suppose they are purposely neglected) and the ruins are
almost every where overspread with ivy. It is divided into
the tower, and the upper castle, the tower enclosing the
upper which is of a round form, and stands upon a pro-
montory to which you must ascend by near an hundred

stone steps; this upper castle was designed for a retreat in case the lower castle should be won, and is the least ruinous of any part except the stairs beforementioned which are so broken and decayed that I was almost afraid to come down again when I was up, they being but narrow and no rails to hold by. From the battlements of this upper castle (which they call the Coop) you have a fine prospect of the greatest part of the island, of the sea on one side, of Cowes road at a distance, and of newport as it were just below you. There is a well in the middle of the Coop which they called the bottomless well, because of its great depth; but it is now half filled up with stones and rubbish and is covered with two or three loose planks; yet a stone, as we tried, is near a quarter of a minute in falling before you hear it strike. But the well that supplies the inhabitants at present with water is in the lower castle and is thirty fathoms deep. They draw this water with a great wheel, and with a bucket that holds near a barrel. It makes a great sound if you speak in it, and ecchoed the flute which we played over it very sweetly. There are but seven pieces of ordnance mounted upon the walls, and those in no very good order; and the old man who is the gunner and keeper of the castle and who sells ale in a little house at the gate, has in his possession but six muskets (which hang up at his wall) and one of them wants a lock. He told us that the castle which had now been built 1203 years, was first founded by one Whitgert a Saxon who conquered the island, and that it was called Whitgertsburg, for many ages. That particular piece of building which King Charles lodged in during his confinement here is suffered to go entirely to ruin, there being nothing standing but the walls. The island is about sixty miles in circumference and produces plenty of corn and other provisions, and wool as fine as Cotswold; its militia having the credit of equalling the soldiery and being the best disciplined in England.   was once in King William's time entrusted with the government of this island.* At his death it appeared he was a great villain, and a great politician; there was no crime so damnable which he would stick at in the execution of his designs and yet he had the art of covering all so thick, that with almost all men in general while he lived he passed for a saint. What surprized me was, that the silly old fellow, the keeper of the castle, who remembered him governor should have so true a notion of his character as I perceived he had. In short, I believe it is impossible for a man, though he has all the cunning of a devil to live and die a villain, and yet conceal it so well, as to carry the name of an honest fellow to the grave with him, but some one by some accident or other shall discover him. Truth and sincerity have a certain distinguishing native lustre about them which cannot be perfectly counterfeited, they are like fire and flame that cannot be painted.

The whole castle was repaired and beautified by Queen Elizabeth and strengthened by a breast work all round without the walls as appears by this inscription in one or two places upon it.

1598
E.   R
40

Saturday July 30

This morning about eight o'clock we weighed anchor and turned to windward till we came to Yarmouth, another little town upon this island, and there cast anchor again, the wind blowing hard and full westerly. Yarmouth is a smaller town than Cowes yet the buildings being better it makes a handsomer prospect at a distance, and the streets are clean and neat. There is one monument in the church which the inhabitants are very proud of, and which we went to see. It was erected to the memory of Sir Robert Holmes,* who had formerly been governor of the island. It is his statue in armour somewhat bigger than the life, standing on his tomb with a truncheon in his hand, between two pillars of porphyry. Indeed all the marble about it is very fine and good; and they say it was designed by the French King for his palace at Versailles, but was cast away upon this island, and by Sir Robert himself in his life time applied to this use and that the whole monument was finished long before he died (though not fixed up in that place) The inscription likewise (which is very much to his honour) being written by himself. One would think either that he had no defect at all or had a very ill opinion of the world, seeing he was so careful to make sure of a monument to record his good actions and transmit them to posterity.

Having taken a view of the church town and fort (on which there is seven large guns mounted) three of us took a walk up further into the island, and having gone about two miles we headed a creek that runs up one end of the town, and then went to Freshwater church about a mile nearer the town but on the other side of the creek. Having stayed here some time it grew dark, and my companions were desirous to be gone, lest those whom we had left drinking where we dined in the town, should go on board and leave us. We were told that it was our best way to go strait down to the mouth of the creek, and that there was a ferry boy that would carry us over to the town. But when we came to the house the lazy whelp was in bed, and refused to rise and put us over, upon which we went down to the water side, with a design to take his boat and go over by ourselves. We found it very difficult to get the boat, it being fastened to a stake and the tide risen near fifty yards beyond it. I stripped all to my shirt to wade up to it, but missing the causeway which was under water, I got up to my middle in mud. At last I came to the stake, but to my great disappointment found she was locked and chained. I endeavoured to draw the staple with one of the thole pins, but in vain: I tried to pull up the stake but to no purpose; so that after an hour's fatigue and trouble in the wet and mud, I was forced to return without the boat. We had no money in our pockets, and therefore began to conclude to pass the night in some haystack, though the wind blew very cold and very hard. In the midst of these troubles one of us recol-

lected that he had a horseshoe in his pocket which he found
in his walk, and asked me if I could not wrench the staple
out with that. I took it, went, tried and succeeded, and
brought the boat ashore to them. Now we rejoiced and all
got in, and when I had dressed myself we put off. But the
worst of all our troubles was to come yet; for, it being high
water and the tide over all the banks, though it was moon-
light we could not discern the channel of the creek, but
rowing heedlessly straight forward, when we were got about
half way over, we found ourselves aground on a mud bank,
and striving to row her off by putting our oars in the mud,
we broke one and there struck fast not having four inches
water. We were now in the utmost perplexity, not knowing
what in the world to do; we could not tell whether the tide
was rising or falling, but at length we plainly perceived it
was ebb, and we could feel no deeper water within the reach
of our oar. It was hard to lie in an open boat all night
exposed to the wind and weather, but it was worse to think
how foolish we should look in the morning, when the owner
of the boat should catch us in that condition, where we
must be exposed to the view of all the town. After we had
strove and struggled for half an hour and more, we gave all
over, and sat down with our hands before us, despairing to
get off, for if the tide had left us we had been never the
nearer, we must have sat in the boat, as the mud was too
deep for us to walk ashore through it, being up to our necks.
At last we bethought ourselves of some means of escaping
and two of us stripped and got out, and thereby lightening
the boat we drew her upon our knees near fifty yards into
deeper water & then with much ado having but one oar, we
got safe ashore under the fort, and having dressed ourselves
and tied the man's boat we went with great joy to the
Queen's Head, where we left our companions, whom we
found waiting for us, though it was very late. Our boat
being gone on board, we were obliged to lie ashore all night;
and thus ended our walk.

Sunday July 31

This morning the wind being moderated, our pilot designed to weigh, and taking advantage of the tide got a little further to windward. Upon which the boat came ashore to hasten us onboard. We had no sooner returned and hoisted in our boat but the wind began again to blow very hard at West, insomuch that instead of going any farther we were obliged to weigh and run down again to Cowes for the sake of more secure riding, where we came to an anchor again in a very little time; and the pudding which our mess made and put into the pot at Yarmouth we dined upon at Cowes.

Monday August 1st

This morning all the vessels in the harbour put out their colours in honour of the day, and it made a very pretty appearance. The wind continuing to blow hard westerly, our mess resolved to go on shore though all our loose corks were gone already. We took with us some goods to dispose of, and walked to Newport to make our market, where we sold for three shillings in the pound less than the prime cost in London, and having dined at Newport we returned in the evening to Cowes, and concluded to lodge on shore.

Tuesday August 2nd

This day we passed on shore diverting ourselves as well as we could; and the wind continuing still westerly, we stayed on shore this night also.

Wednesday August 3rd

This morning we were hurried on board having scarce time to dine, weighed anchor, and stood away for Yarmouth again, though the wind is still westerly; but meeting with a hoy* when we were near half way there that had some goods onboard for us to take in, we tacked about for Cowes, and came to anchor there a third time about four in the afternoon.

Thursday August 4

Stayed on board till about five in the afternoon, and then went on shore and stopped all night.

Friday August 5

Called up this morning and hurried aboard, the wind
being Northwest. About noon we weighed and left Cowes
a third time, and sailing by Yarmouth we came into the
channel through the Needles, which passage is guarded by
Hurst Castle, standing on a spit of land which runs out
from the main land of England within a mile of the Isle of
Wight. Towards night the wind veered to the Westward
which put us under apprehensions of being forced into port
again: but presently after it fell a flat calm, and then we
had a small breeze that was fair for half an hour, when it
was succeeded by a calm again.

Saturday August 6

This morning we had a fair breeze for some hours, and
then a calm that lasted all day. In the afternoon I leaped
overboard and swam around the ship to wash myself. Saw
several porpuses this day. About eight o'clock we came to
an anchor in forty fathom water against the tide of flood,
somewhere below Portland, and weighed again about eleven
having a small breeze.

Sunday August 7

Gentle breezes all this Day. Spoke with a ship, the Ruby
bound for London from Nevis, off the Start of Plymouth.
This afternoon spoke with Capt Homans in a ship bound
for Boston, who came out of the River when we did, and
had been beating about in the Channel all the time we lay
at Cowes in the Wight.

Monday August 8

Fine weather but no wind worth mentioning, all this day;
in the afternoon saw the Lizard.*

Tuesday August 9

Took our leave of the land this morning. Calms the
forepart of the day: In the afternoon a small gale fair. Saw
a Grampus.*

Wednesday August 10

Wind NW. Course SW about four knots. By observation in Latitude 48°50′ Nothing remarkable happened.

Thursday August 11

Nothing remarkable. Fresh gale all day.

Calms & fair breezes alternately.	Friday August	12
	Saturday ——	13
	Sunday ——	14
No contrary winds but calms and fair breezes alternately	Monday ——	15
	Tuesday ——	16
	Wednesday ——	17

Thursday —— 18

Four dolphins followed the ship for some hours, we struck at them with the fizgig,* but took none.

Friday August 19

This day we have had a pleasant breeze at East. In the morning we spied a sail upon our larboard bow about two leagues distance. About noon the boat put out English colours, and we answered with our ensign and in the afternoon we spoke with her. She was a ship of New York Walter Kippen Master, bound from Rochelle in France to Boston with salt. Our captain and M^r. D. went onboard and stayed till evening it being fine weather. Yesterday complaints being made that M^r. G——n one of the passengers had with a fraudulent design marked the cards; a Court of Justice was called immediately and he was brought to his trial in form. A Dutchman who could speak no English deposed by his interpreter that when our mess was on shore at Cowes the prisoner at the bar marked all the Court cards on the back with a pen. [I have sometimes observed that we are apt to fancy the person that cannot speak intelligibly to us, proportionably stupid in understanding, and when we speak two or three words of English to a foreigner it is louder than ordinary as if we thought him deaf and that he had lost the use of his ears as well as his tongue. Something like this I imagine might be the case of M^r. G——n; he fancied the Dutchman could not see what he was about because he could not understand English and therefore boldly did it before his face

The evidence was plain and positive the prisoner could not deny the fact but replied in his defence that the cards he marked were not those we commonly played with, but an imperfect pack, which he afterwards gave to the cabbin boy. The Attorney General observed to the Court that it was not likely he should take the pains to mark the cards without some ill design, or some farther intention than just to give them to the boy when he had done, who understood nothing at all of cards. But another evidence being called deposed that he saw the prisoner in the main top one day when he thought himself unobserved, marking the backs some with the print of a dirty thumb, others with the top of his finger &c. Now there being but two packs on board and the prisoner having just confessed the marking of one, the Court perceived the case was plain. In fine the jury brought him in guilty, and he was condemned to be carried up to the round top, and made fast there in view of all the ships company during the space of three hours, that being the place where the fact was committed, and to pay a fine of two bottles of brandy. But the prisoner resisting authority, and refusing to submit to punishment, one of the sailors stepped up aloft and let down a rope to us which we with much struggling made fast about his middle and hoisted him up into the air sprawling, by main force. We let him hang cursing and swearing for near a quarter of an hour, but at length he crying out murder! and looking black in the face, the rope being overtort about his middle, we thought proper to let him down again; and our mess have excommunicated him till he pays his fine, refusing either to play, eat, drink or converse with him.

Saturday August 20th

We shortened sail all last night and all this day to keep company with the other ship. About noon Captain Kippen and one of his passengers came on board and dined with us; they stayed till evening. When they were gone we made sail and left them.

Sunday August 21st

This morning we lost sight of the Yorker, having a brisk gale of wind at East. Towards night a poor little bird came on board us being almost tired to death, and suffered itself to be taken by the hand. We reckon ourselves near two hundred leagues from land, so that no doubt a little rest was very acceptable to the unfortunate wanderer, who tis like was blown off the coast in thick weather, and could not find its way back again. We receive it hospitably and tender it victuals and drink, but he refuses both and I suppose will not live long. There was one came on board some days ago in the same circumstances with this, which I think the cat destroyed.

Monday August 22nd

This morning I saw several flying fish, but they were small. A favourable wind all day.

	Tuesday August 23
Fair winds, nothing remarkable	Wednesday 24
	Thursday —— 25

Our excommunicated ship mate thinking proper to comply with the sentence the court passed upon him, and expressing himself willing to pay the fine, we have this morning received him into unity again. Man is a sociable being, and it is for aught I know one of the worst of punishments to be excluded from society. I have read abundance of fine things on the subject of solitude, and I know tis a common boast in the mouths of those that affect to be thought wise, *that they are never less alone than when alone*. I acknowledge solitude an agreeable refreshment to a busy mind, but were these thinking people obliged to be always alone, I am apt to think they would quickly find their very being insupportable to them. I have heard of a gentleman who underwent seven years close confinement in the Bastile at Paris. He was a man of sense, he was a thinking man, but being deprived of all conversation, to what purpose should he think; for he was denied even the instruments of expressing his thoughts in writing. There is no burden so grievous to man as time that he knows not how to dispose of. He was forced at last to have recourse to this invention. He daily scattered pieces of paper about the floor of his little room, and then employed himself in picking them up again, and sticking them in rows and figures on the arm of his elbow chair; and he used to tell his friends after his release that he verily believed if he had not taken this method he should have lost his senses. One of the philosophers, I think it was Plato, used to say that he had rather be the veriest stupid block in nature, than the possessor of all knowledge without some intelligent being to communicate it to.

What I have said may in a measure account for some particulars in my present way of living here onboard. Our company is in general very unsuitably mixed, to keep up the pleasure and spirit of conversation: and if there are one or two pair of us that can sometimes entertain one another for half an hour agreeably, yet perhaps we are seldom in the humour for it together. I rise in the morning and read for an hour or two perhaps, and then reading grows tiresome. Want of exercise occasions want of appetite so that eating and drinking affords but little pleasure. I tire myself with playing at Draughts, then I go to cards, nay there is no play so trifling or childish, but we fly to it for entertainment. A contrary wind, I know not how, puts us all out of good humour; we grow sullen, silent and reserved, and fret at each other upon every little occasion. 'Tis a common opinion among the ladies, that if a man is illnatured he infallibly discovers it when he is in liquor. But I who have known many instances to the contrary will teach them a more effectual method to discover the natural temper and disposition of their humble servants. Let the ladies make one long sea voyage with them, and if they have the least spark of ill nature in them and conceal it to the end of the voyage I will forfeit all my pretensions to their favour—The wind continues fair—

Friday August 26

The wind and weather fair till night came on, and then the wind came about, and we had hard squalls with rain and lightning till morning.

Saturday August 27

Cleared up this morning and the wind settled westerly. Two dolphins followed us this afternoon: we hooked one and struck the other with the fizgig, but they both escaped us, and we saw them no more.——

Sunday August 28

The wind still continues westerly and blows hard. We are under a reefed mainsail and foresail.——

Monday August 29

Wind still hard west. Two dolphins followed us this day. We struck at them, but they both escaped.

Tuesday August 30

Contrary wind still. This evening the moon being near full, as she ran after eight o'clock, there appeared a rainbow in a western cloud to windward of us. The first time I ever saw a rainbow in the night caused by the moon.

Wednesday August 31

Wind still west, nothing remarkable.

Thursday Sept. 1

Bad weather and contrary winds.

Friday Sept. 2

This morning the wind changed, a little fair. We caught a couple of dolphins and fried them for dinner. They eat indifferent well. These fish make a glorious appearance in the water; their bodies are of a bright green, mixed with a silver colour, and their tails of a shining golden yellow, but all this vanishes presently after they are taken out of their element and they change all over to a light grey. I observed that cutting off pieces of a just caught living dolphin for bait, those pieces did not lose their lustre and fine colours when the dolphin die, but retained them perfectly.——— Everyone takes notice of that vulgar error of the painters, who always represent this fish monstrously crooked and deformed, when it is in reality as beautiful and well shaped a fish as any that swims. I cannot think what should be the original of this chimera of their's (since there is not a creature in nature that in the least resembles their dolphin) unless it proceeded at first from a false imitation of a fish in the posture of leaping, which they have since improved into a crooked monster with a head and eyes like a bull, a hog's snout, and a tail like a blown tulip. But the sailors give me another reason, though a whimsical one, viz. that as this most beautiful fish is only to be caught at sea, and that very far to the Southward, they say the painters wilfully deform it in their representations lest pregnant women should long for what it is impossible to procure for them———

Wind still westerly nothing remarkable.	Saturday September 3 Sunday 4 Monday 5

Tuesday Sept. 6

This afternoon the wind continuing still in the same quarter, increased till it blew a storm, and raised the Sea to a greater height than I had ever seen it before.———

Wednesday Sept. 7

The wind is somewhat abated, but the sea is very high still. A dolphin kept us company all this afternoon. We struck at him several times but could not take him.———

Thursday Sept. 8

This day nothing remarkable has happened, but I am so indolent that——— Contrary wind.

Friday Sept. 9

This afternoon we took four large dolphins, three with a hook and line, and the fourth we struck with a fizgig. The bait was a candle with two feathers stuck in it one on each side in imitation of a flying fish, which are the common prey of the dolphins. They appeared extremely eager and hungry, and snapped up the hook as soon as ever it touched the water. When we came to open them, we found in the belly of one a small dolphin half digested. Certainly they were half famished, or are naturally very savage to devour those of their own species.

Saturday Sept. 10

This day we dined upon the dolphins we caught yesterday, three of them sufficing the whole ship being twenty-one persons——

Sunday Sept. 11

We have had a hard gale of wind all this day, accompanied with showers of rain. Tis uncomfortable being upon deck, and though we have been alltogether all day below, yet the long continuance of these contrary winds have made us so dull, that scarce three words have passed between us.

Nothing remarkable. Wind contrary $\begin{cases} \text{Monday Sept 12} \\ \text{Tuesday} \quad 13 \\ \text{Wednesday} \quad 14 \end{cases}$

This afternoon about two o'clock, it being fair weather and almost calm, as we sat playing drafts upon deck, we were surprized with a sudden and unusual darkness of the sun, which as we could perceive was only covered with a small thin cloud; when that was passed by, we discovered that that glorious luminary laboured under a very great eclipse. At least ten parts out of twelve of him were hid from our eyes and we were apprehensive he would have been totally darkened.

Thursday Sept. 15

For a week past we have fed ourselves with the hopes

that the change of the moon (which was yesterday) would bring us a fair wind; but to our great mortification and disappointment, the wind seems now settled in the westward, and shews as little signs of an alteration as it did a fortnight ago.——

Friday September 16

Calm all this day. This morning we saw a *Tropic bird*,* which flew round our vessel several times. It is a white fowl with short wings, but one feather appears in his tail, and does not fly very fast. We reckon our selves about half our voyage Latitude 38 and odd minutes. These birds are said never to be seen further north that the Latitude of 40.—— ——

Saturday September 17

All the forenoon the calm continued, the rest of the day some light breezes easterly, and we are in great hopes the wind will settle in that quarter.

Sunday September 18

We have had the finest weather imaginable all this day accompanied with what is still more agreeable a fair wind. Every one puts on a clean shirt and a chearful countenance, and we begin to be very good company. Heaven grant, that this favourable gale may continue; for we have had so much of turning to windward, that the word *helm-a-lee* is become almost as disagreeable to our ears as the sentence of a judge to a convicted malefactor.——

Monday September 19

The weather looks a little uncertain, and we begin to fear the loss of our fair wind. We see Tropic birds every day, sometime five or six together; they are about as big as pigeons.——

Tuesday September 20

The wind is now westerly again to our great mortification; and we are come to an allowance of bread, two biscuits and a half a day.

Wednesday Sept. 21.

This morning our Steward was brought to the geers and whipped for making an extravagant Use of flour to the puddings, and for several other misdemeanors. It has been perfectly calm all this day, and very hot. I was determined to wash myself in the sea to-day, and should have done so had not the appearance of a shark that mortal foe to swimmers deterred me; he seemed to be about five foot long, moves round the ship at some distance in a slow majestic manner attended by near a dozen of those they call Pilot fish, of different sizes; the largest of them is not so big as a small mackerell, and the smallest not bigger than my little finger. Two of these diminutive Pilots keep just before his nose, and he seems to govern himself in his motions by their direction, while the rest surround him on every side indifferently. A shark is never seen without a retinue of these, who are his purveyors, discovering and distinguishing his prey for him; while he in return gratefully protects them from the ravenous hungry dolphin. They are commonly counted a very greedy fish, yet this refuses to meddle with the bait we have thrown out for him. Tis likely he has lately made a full meal

Thursday Sept. 22ⁿᵈ

A fresh gale at West all this day. The Shark has left us.

Friday September 23ʳᵈ

This morning we spied a sail to windward of us about two leagues. We showed our jack upon the ensign staff, and shortened sail for them till about noon when she came up with us. She was a snow from Dublin bound for New York, having upwards of fifty servants onboard of both sexes; they all appeared upon deck, and seemed very much pleased at the sight of us. There is really something strongly chearing to the spirits in the meeting of a ship at sea, containing a society of creatures of the same species and in the same circumstances with ourselves, after we had been long separated and excommunicated as it were from the rest of mankind. My heart fluttered in my breast with joy when I saw so many human countenances, and I could scarce refrain from that kind of laughter which proceeds from some degree of inward pleasure. When we have been for a considerable time tossing on the vast waters far from the sight of any land or ships, or any mortal creature but ourselves; (except a few fish and sea birds) the whole world for aught we know, may be under a second deluge, and we (like Noah and his company in the ark) the only surviving remnant of the human race. The two Captains have mutually promised to keep each other company, but this I look upon to be only matter of course, for if ships are unequal in their sailing they seldom stay for one another, especially strangers. This afternoon the wind that has been so long contrary to us, came about to the eastward (and looks as if it would hold) to our no small satisfaction; I find our mess mates in a better humour, and more pleased with their present condition than they have been since we came out, which I take to proceed from the contemplation of the miserable circumstances of the passengers onboard our neighbour, and making the comparison. We reckon ourselves in a kind of paradise, when we consider how they live confined and stifled up with such a lousy stinking rabble in this hot sultry latitude.——

Saturday Sept 24

Last night we had a very high wind, and very thick weather, in which we lost our consort. This morning early we saw a sail ahead of us, which we took to be her; but presently after we ˢpied another, and then we plainly perceived that neither of them could be the snow for one of them stemmed with us, and the other bore down directly upon us, having the weather gage of us. As the latter drew near we were a little surprized, not knowing what to make of her, for by the course she steered she did not seem designed for any port, but looked as if she intended to clap us aboard* immediately. I could perceive concern in every face onboard, but she presently eased us of our apprehensions by bearing away astern of us. When we hoisted our

jack* she answered with French colours, and presently took
them down again; and we soon lost sight of her. The other
ran by us in less than half an hour and answered our jack
with an English ensign; she stood to the Eastward, but the
wind was too high to speak with either of them. About nine
o'clock we spied our consort who had got a great way ahead
of us. She it seems had made sail in the night while we lay
by with our main yard down during the hard gale. She very
civilly shortened sail for us, and this afternoon we came up
with her, and now we are running along very amicably
together side by side having a most glorious fair wind.

> On either side the parted billows flow
> While the black ocean foams and roars below.*

Sunday September 25

Last night we shot ahead of our consort pretty far. About
midnight having lost sight of each other we shortened sail
for them: But this morning they were got as far ahead of
us as we could see having run by us in the dark unperceived.
We made sail and came up with them about noon; and if
we chance to be ahead of them again in the night we are
to show them a light, that we may not lose company by
any such accident for the future. The wind still continues
fair, and we have made a greater run these last four and
twenty hours, than we have done since we came out. All
our discourse now is of Philadelphia, and we begin to
fancy ourselves ashore already. Yet a small change of
weather attended by a westerly wind is sufficient to blast
all our blooming hopes, and quite spoil our present good
humour.

Monday September 26

The wind continued fair all night. In the twelve o'clock
watch our consort who was about a league ahead of us
showed us a light and we answered with another. About six
o'clock this morning we had a sudden hurry of wind at all
points of the compass accompanied with the most violent
shower of rain I ever saw, insomuch that the sea looked like

a *cream dish*. It surprized us with all our sails up, and was so various, uncertain, and contrary that the mizin topsail was full wile the head sails were all a-back, and before the men could run from one end of the ship to the other 'twas about again. But this did not last long 'ere the wind settled to the North East again to our great satisfaction. Our consort fell astern of us in the Storm, but made sail and came up with us again after it was over. We hailed one another on the morrow, congratulating upon the continuance of the fair wind, and both ran on very lovingly together.

Tuesday Sept 27:

The fair wind continues still. I have laid a bowl of punch that we are in Philadelphia next Saturday sen'night, for we reckon ourselves not above 150 leagues from land. The snow keeps us company still.——

Wednesday Sept. 28

We had very variable winds and weather last night accompanied with abundance of rain; and now the wind is come about westerly again, but we must bear it with patience. This afternoon we took up several bunches of gulfweed;* (with which the sea is spread all over from the Western Isles to the coast of America) but one of these branches had something peculiar on it. In common with the rest it had a leaf about three quarters of an inch long, indented like a saw, and a small yellow berry filled with nothing but wind; besides which it bore a fruit of the animal kind very surprising to see. It was a small shell fish like a heart. the stalk by which it proceeded from the branch being partly of a gristly kind. Upon this one branch of the weed there were near forty of these vegetable animals; the smallest of them near the end contained a substance somewhat like an oyster, but the larger were visibly animated, opening their shells every moment, and thrusting out a set of unformed claws not unlike those of crab; but the inner part was still a kind of soft jelly. Observing the weed more narrowly, I spied a very small crab crawling among it, about as big as the head of a tenpenny nail, and of a yellowish colour like the weed itself. This gave me some reason to think that he was a native of the branch, that he had not long since been in the same condition with the rest of those little embrios that appeared in the shells, this being the method of their generation, and that consequently all the rest of this odd kind of fruit might be crabs in due time. To strengthen my conjecture, I have resolved to keep the weed in salt water, renewing it every day till we come ashore, by this experiment to see whether any more crabs will be produced or not in this manner. I remember that the last calm we had, we took notice of a large crab upon the surface of the sea, swimming from one bunch of weed to another, which he seemed to prey upon; and I likewise recollect that in Boston in New England I have often seen small crabs with a shell like a snail shell upon their backs* crawling about in the salt water; and likewise at Portsmouth in England. It is like nature has provided this hard shell to secure them till their own proper shell has acquired a sufficient hardness, which once perfected, they quit their old habitation and venture abroad safe in their own strength. The various changes that silkworms, butterflies, and several other insects go through makes such alterations and meta-morphoses not improbable. This day the captain of the snow with one of his passengers came on board us, but the wind beginning to blow, they did not stay dinner, but returned to their own vessel.——

Thursday Sept. 29

Upon shifting the water in which I had put the weed yesterday, I found another crab, much smaller than the former, who seemed to have newly left his habitation. But the weed begins to wither, and the rest of the embrios are dead. This new comer fully convinces me that at least this sort of crabs are generated in this manner. The snow's captain dined on board us this day. Little or no wind.——

Friday Sept 30

I sat up last night to observe an eclipse of the moon, which the calendar calculated for London informed us would appear at five o'clock in the morning Sept 30. It began with us about eleven last night and continued till near two this morning, darkening her body about six digits, or one half; the middle of it being about half an hour after twelve, by which we may discover that we are in a meridian of about four hours and a half from London or 67½ degrees of Longitude, and consequently have not much above one hundred leagues to run. This is the second eclipse we have had within these fifteen days. We lost our consort in the night, but saw him again this morning near two leagues to windward. This afternoon we spoke with him again. We have had abundance of dolphins about us these three or four days, but we have not taken any more than one they being very shy of the bait. I took in some more gulfweed to day with the boat hook, with shells upon it like that beforementioned, and three living perfect crabs, each less than the nail of my little finger. One of them had something particularly observable to wit, a thin piece of the white shell which I before noticed as their covering while they remained in the condition of embrios, sticking close to his natural shell upon his back. This sufficiently confirms me in my opinion of the manner of their generation. I have put this remarkable crab with a piece of the gulf weed, shells &c into a glass phial, filled with salt water (for want of spirits of wine) in hopes to preserve the curiosity till I come ashore. The wind is SouthWest.——

Saturday October 1ˢᵗ

Last night our consort who goes incomparably better upon a wind than our vessel got so far to windward and ahead of us that this morning we could see nothing of him, and tis like shall see him no more. These South Wests are hot damp winds and bring abundance of rain and dirty weather with them.

Sunday October 2nd

Last night we prepared our line with a design to sound this morning at four o'clock but the wind coming about again to the Northwest we let it alone. I cannot help fancying the water is changed a little, as usual when a ship comes within soundings, but 'tis like I am mistaken, for there is but one besides myself of my opinion, and we are very apt to believe whatever we wish to be true.——

Monday October 3rd

The water is now very visibly changed to the eye of all except the Captain and Mate, and they will by no means allow it; I suppose because they did not see it first. Abundance of dolphins are about us, but they are very shy, and keep a distance. Wind North West——

Tuesday October 4

Last night we struck a dolphin, and this morning we found a flying-fish dead under the windlass. He is about the bigness of a small mackerel, a sharp head, a small mouth and a tail forked somewhat like a dolphin, but the lowest branch much larger and longer than the other and tinged with yellow. His back and sides of a darkish blue, his belly white, and his skin very thick. His wings are of a finny substance about a span long reaching when close to his body from an inch below his gills to an inch above his tail. When they fly it is strait forward, (for they cannot readily turn) a yard or two above the water, and perhaps fifty yards is the furthest before they dip into the water again, for they cannot support themselves in the air any longer than while their wings continue wet. These flying fish are the common prey of the dolphin, who is their mortal enemy. When he pursues them they rise and fly, and he keeps close under them till they drop, and then snaps them up immediately. They generally fly in flocks four or five or perhaps a dozen together, and a dolphin is seldom caught without one or more in his belly. We put this flying fish upon the hook in hopes of catching one, but in a few minutes they got it off without hooking themselves; and they will not meddle with any other bait.——

Since eleven o'clock we have struck three fine dolphins which are a great refreshment to us. This afternoon we have seen abundance of grampuses, which are seldom far from land; but towards evening we had a more evident token, to wit, a little tired bird something like a lark, came on board us, who certainly is an American, and tis likely was ashore this day. It is now calm. We hope for a fair wind next.

Wednesday October 5

This morning we saw a heron, who had lodged aboard last night. Tis a long legged long-necked bird, having, as they say but one gut. They live upon fish, and will swallow a living eel thrice sometimes before it will remain in their body. The wind is West again The ship's crew was brought to a short allowance of water

Thursday October 6th

This morning abundance of grass, rockweed &c passed by us; evident tokens that land is not far off. We hooked a dolphin this morning that made us a good breakfast. A sail passed by us about twelve o'clock and nobody saw her till she was too far astern to be spoke with. Tis very near calm. We saw another sail ahead this afternoon; but night coming on we could not speak with her, though we very much desired it; She stood to the northward and it is possible might have informed us how far we are from land. Our artists onboard are much at a loss. We hoisted our jack to him but he took no notice of it.

Friday October 7

Last night about nine o'clock sprung up a fine gale at North East which run us in our course at the rate of seven miles an hour all night. We were in hopes of seeing land this morning but cannot. The water which we thought was changed is now as blue as the sky, so that unless at that

time we were running over some unknown shoal our eyes
strangely deceived us. All the reckonings have been out
these several days; though the captain says 'tis his opinion
we are yet an hundred leagues from land: for my part I
know not what to think of it, we have run all this day at a
great rate; and now night is come on we have no soundings.
Sure the American continent is not all sunk under water
since we left it.————

Saturday October 8

The fair wind continues still; we ran all night in our
course, sounding every four hours, but can find no ground
yet, nor is the water changed by all this day's run. This
afternoon we saw an *Irish Lord,** and a bird which flying
looked like a yellow duck. These they say are not seen far
from the coast. Other signs of land have we none. Abundance of large porpusses ran by us this afternoon, and we
were followed by a shoal of small ones, leaping out of the
water, as they approached. Towards evening we spied a sail
and spoke with her just before dark. She was bound from
New York for Jamaica and left Sandy Hook yesterday about
noon, from whence they reckon themselves forty five leagues
distant. By this we compute that we are not above thirty
leagues from our Capes and hope to see land tomorrow.————

Sunday October 9——

We have had the wind fair all the morning; at twelve
o'clock we sounded, perceiving the water visibly changed
and struck ground at twenty five fathoms, to our universal
joy. After dinner one of our mess went up aloft to look out,
and presently pronounced the long-wished-for sound *Land!
Land!* In less than an hour we could descry it from the
deck, appearing like tufts of trees. I could not discern it so
soon as the rest, my eyes were dimmed with the suffusion
of two small drops of joy. By three o'clock we were run in
within two leagues of the land, and spied a small sail
standing along shore. We would gladly have spoke with her,
for our captain was unacquainted with the Coast, and knew

not what land it was that we saw. We made all the sail we could to speak with her. We made a signal of distress; but all would not do, the illnatured Dog would not come near us. Then we stood off again till morning not caring to venture too near.

Monday October 10

This morning we stood in again for the land, and we that had been here before all agreed that it was Cape Henlopen. About noon we came very near, and to our great joy saw the pilot-boat come off to us, which was exceeding welcome. He brought onboard about a peck of apples with him; they seemed the most delicious I ever tasted in my life: the salt provisions we had been used to gave them a relish. We had an extraordinary fair wind all the afternoon and ran above an hundred miles up the Delaware before ten at night. The country appears very pleasant to the eye, being covered with woods, except here and there an house and plantation. We cast anchor when the tide turned, about two miles below Newcastle and there lay till the morning tide.——

Tuesday October 11—

This morning we weighed anchor with a gentle breeze, and passed by Newcastle, from whence they hailed us and bade us welcome. Tis extreme fine weather. The sun enlivens our stiff limbs with his glorious rays of warmth and brightness. The sky looks gay with here and there a silver cloud. The fresh breezes from the woods refresh us, the immediate prospect of liberty after so long and irksome a confinement ravishes us. In short all things conspire to make this the most joyful day I ever knew. As we passed by Chester some of the company went on shore, impatient once more to tread on terra firma and designing for Philadelphia by land. Four of us remained onboard not caring for the fatigue of travel when we knew the voyage had much weakened us. About eight at night the wind failing us we cast anchor at Redbank, five miles from Philadelphia and thought we must be obliged to lie aboard that night; but some young Philadelphians happening to be out upon their pleasure in a boat they came onboard and offered to take us up with them, we accepted of their kind proposal and about ten o'clock landed at Philadelphia heartily congratulating each other upon our having happily completed so tedious and dangerous a voyage.———

Thank God.

Busy-Body, 3

When Franklin began his own printing establishment in Philadelphia he was immediately in competition with two established printers, his old employer Samuel Keimer and Andrew Bradford. For some years Bradford had been publishing an undistinguished newspaper, *The American Weekly Mercury*. With his own experience as a newspaper publisher in Boston, Franklin planned to set up his own rival journal, but Keimer got wind of the idea and pre-empted Franklin by beginning the *Universal Instructor in all Arts and Sciences: and Pennsylvania Gazette*. Franklin's countermove was to liven up the pages of the *American Weekly Mercury* with a series of periodical letters under the *persona* of the Busy-Body, who would 'take *no Body's Business* wholly into my own Hands'. Bruce Granger has pointed out that the Busy-Body is a more Addisonian character than Silence Dogood had been (Granger, 41); the character of the Busy-Body, in the numbers Franklin wrote, is not so fully developed as Silence Dogood's. Here in the third letter, the Busy-Body considers the question of virtue, a major preoccupation of the eighteenth century. How is virtue to be taught, and how can public virtue be preserved? Later in the century when public virtue would seem the only assurance for the safe continuance of an American republic, the question would surface again with particular urgency. The figure of 'Cato' resembles Franklin's own characterization of his father in the *Autobiography*, suggesting a continuity in his preoccupation with such a figure of mature wisdom (Seavey 149). The opposing figure of 'Cretico', despite Franklin's disclaimer that he lives in a neighbouring province, is obviously modelled on Samuel Keimer.

> *Non vultus instantis Tyranni*
> *Mente quatit solida—neque Auster*
> *Dux inquieti turbidus Adriæ,*
> *Nec fulminantis magna Jovis manus.** Hor.

It is said that the *Persians* in their ancient Constitution, had publick Schools in which Virtue was taught as a Liberal Art or Science; and it is certainly of more Consequence to a

Man that he has learnt to govern his Passions; in spite of Temptation to be just in his Dealings, to be Temperate in his Pleasures, to support himself with Fortitude under his Misfortunes, to behave with Prudence in all Affairs and in every Circumstance of Life; I say, it is of much more real Advantage to him to be thus qualified, than to be a Master of all the Arts and Sciences in the World beside.

Virtue alone is sufficient to make a Man Great, Glorious and Happy.—He that is acquainted with *CATO*, as I am, cannot help thinking as I do now, and will acknowledge he deserves the Name without being honour'd by it. *Cato* is a Man whom Fortune has plac'd in the most obscure Part of the Country. His Circumstances are such as only put him above Necessity, without affording him many Superfluities; Yet who is greater than *Cato*?—I happened but the other Day to be at a House in Town, where among others were met Men of the most Note in this Place: *Cato* had Business with some of them, and knock'd at the Door. The most trifling Actions of a Man, in my Opinion, as well as the smallest Features and Lineaments of the Face, give a nice Observer some Notion of his Mind. Methought he rapp'd in such a peculiar Manner, as seem'd of itself to express, there was One who deserv'd as well as desir'd Admission. He appear'd in the plainest Country Garb; his Great Coat was coarse and looked old and thread-bare; his Linnen was homespun; his Beard perhaps of Seven Days Growth, his Shoes thick and heavy, and every Part of his Dress corresponding. Why was this Man receiv'd with such concurring Respect from every Person in the Room, even from those who had never known him or seen him before? It was not an exquisite Form of Person, or Grandeur of Dress that struck us with Admiration. I believe long Habits of Virtue have a sensible Effect on the Countenance: There was something in the Air of his Face that manifested the true Greatness of his Mind; which likewise appear'd in all he said, and in every Part of his Behaviour, obliging us to regard him with a Kind of Veneration. His Aspect is sweetned with Humanity and Benevolence, and at the same

Time emboldned with Resolution, equally free from a diffident Bashfulness and an unbecoming Assurance. The Consciousness of his own innate Worth and unshaken Integrity renders him calm and undaunted in the Presence of the most Great and Powerful, and upon the most extraordinary Occasions. His strict Justice and known Impartiality make him the Arbitrator and Decider of all Differences that arise for many Miles around him, without putting his Neighbours to the Charge, Perplexity and Uncertainty of Law-Suits. He always speaks the Thing he means, which he is never afraid or asham'd to do, because he knows he always means well; and therefore is never oblig'd to blush and feel the Confusion of finding himself detected in the Meanness of a Falshood. He never contrives Ill against his Neighbour, and therefore is never seen with a lowring suspicious Aspect. A mixture of Innocence and Wisdom makes him ever seriously chearful. His generous Hospitality to Strangers according to his Ability, his Goodness, his Charity, his Courage in the Cause of the Oppressed, his Fidelity in Friendship, his Humility, his Honesty and Sincerity, his Moderation and his Loyalty to the Government, his Piety, his Temperance, his Love to Mankind, his Magnanimity, his Publickspiritedness, and in fine, his *Consummate Virtue*, make him justly deserve to be esteem'd the Glory of his Country.

> ——*The Brave do never shun the Light,*
> *Just are their Thoughts and open are their Tempers;*
> *Freely without Disguise they love and hate;*
> *Still are they found in the fair Face of Day,*
> *And Heaven and Men are Judges of their Actions.*
>
> Rowe.

Who would not rather chuse, if it were in his Choice, to merit the above Character, than be the richest, the most learned, or the most powerful Man in the Province without it?

Almost every Man has a strong natural Desire of being valu'd and esteem'd by the rest of his Species; but I am concern'd and griev'd to see how few fall into the Right and only infallible Method of becoming so. That laudable Ambition is too commonly misapply'd and often ill employ'd. Some to make themselves considerable pursue Learning, others grasp at Wealth, some aim at being thought witty, and others are only careful to make the most of an handsome Person; But what is Wit, or Wealth, or Form, or Learning when compar'd with Virtue? 'Tis true, we love the handsome, we applaud the Learned, and we fear the Rich and Powerful; but we even Worship and adore the Virtuous.—Nor is it strange; since Men of Virtue, are so rare, so very rare to be found. If we were as industrious to become Good, as to make ourselves Great, we should become really Great by being Good, and the Number of valuable Men would be much increased; but it is a Grand Mistake to think of being Great without Goodness; and I pronounce it as certain, *that there was never yet a truly Great Man that was not at the same Time truly Virtuous*.

O *Cretico*! Thou sowre Philosopher! Thou cunning Statesman! Thou art crafty, but far from being Wise. When wilt thou be esteem'd, regarded and belov'd like *Cato*? When wilt thou, among thy Creatures meet with that unfeign'd Respect and warm Good-will that all Men have for him? Wilt thou never understand that the cringing, mean, submissive Deportment of thy Dependants, is (like the Worship paid by *Indians* to the Devil) rather thro' Fear of the Harm thou may'st do to them, than out of Gratitude for the Favours they have receiv'd of thee?—Thou art not wholly void of Virtue; there are many good Things in thee, and many good Actions reported of thee. Be advised by thy Friend: Neglect those musty Authors; let them be cover'd with Dust, and moulder on their proper Shelves; and do thou apply thy self to a Study much more profitable, The Knowledge of Mankind, and of thy Self.

This is to give Notice that the BUSY-BODY strictly forbids all Persons, from this Time forward, of what Age, Sex, Rank, Quality, Degree or Denomination soever, on any Pretence to enquire who is the Author of this Paper, on Pain of his Displeasure, (his own near and Dear Relations only excepted).

'Tis to be observ'd that if any bad Characters happen to be drawn in the Course of these Papers, they mean no particular Person, if they are not particularly apply'd.

Likewise that the Author is no Partyman, but a general Meddler.

N. B. Cretico *lives in a neighbouring Province.*
The American Weekly Mercury, 18 February 1728/9

Epitaph

In the *Autobiography* Franklin describes a period of serious illness shortly after returning to Philadelphia; Thomas Denham, the merchant who had befriended him and for whom Franklin was then working, took sick about the same time and died. Franklin says of his own ailment, 'My Distemper was a Pleurisy, which very nearly carried me off:—I suffered a good deal, gave up the Point in my own mind, & was rather disappointed when I found my self recovering; regretting in some degree that I must now sometime or other have all that disagreeable Work to do over again.' For young Franklin death was a kind of work that had to be done. But part of his achievement in life was the transformation of work into various kinds of games. Probably about a year after his illness, when he had gone back to work as a printer, he composed this humorous epitaph for himself. 'When the individual existence inevitably falls into disrepair, according to Franklin's vision of things, it will be brought out in a new and more beautiful edition by a God who, like Franklin, is not only an author but a printer. He will both correct the errata of the first edition and make the new edition typographically elegant. In Franklin's epitaph salvation by faith in the regenerating grace of God becomes faith in the grammatical and verbal skills and in the printing shop know-how of a Deity who is both Man of Letters and Master Printer' (Simpson, 4). Franklin made copies of the epitaph for friends years after the probable date of composition in 1728, and the image of *errata*, mistakes in typesetting, as the metaphor for what others would call sins or mistakes came to be incorporated in the writing of his *Autobiography*. In fact there appears to be a pattern in Franklin's revisions of the *Autobiography* text of including specific references to *errata* where appropriate (Zall, 'Portrait of the Autobiographer', 57–8).

The Body of
B. Franklin,
Printer;
Like the Cover of an old Book,
Its Contents torn out,
And stript of its Lettering and Gilding,
Lies here, Food for Worms.
But the Work shall not be wholly lost:
For it will, as he believ'd, appear once more,
In a new & more perfect Edition,
Corrected and amended
By the Author.
He was born Jan. 6. 1706.
Died   17

On Simplicity

The Enlightenment, Franklin's intellectual milieu, set a high value on simplicity, in language, art, and ideology (Lovejoy, 7–8). Franklin was not in fact a simple person, nor were his times uncomplicated, but he and his contemporaries valued the sort of simplicity which he had earlier identified as the distinguishing mark of 'Cato' in *Busy-Body 3* (Lemay, *Canon*, 60–1). According to this view, it was simplicity that characterized the writings of the great Greek and Roman authors of antiquity, so the recovery of a comparable simplicity would link modern people like Franklin with the immortal ancients. Thus the praise of simplicity is related to an entire theory of history. The essay is also a consideration of the distinction between cunning and wisdom, one of much importance in the *Autobiography*, where Franklin contrasts his own behaviour with that of men of mere cunning like Governor Keith or Samuel Keimer.

There is in Humane Nature a certain charming Quality, innate and original to it, which is called SIMPLICITY. In latter Ages, this has been almost universally exploded, and banished from amongst Men, as the Characteristic of Folly; whilst *Cunning* and *Artifice* have prevailed in its stead, and with equal Justice been dignified with the Titles of Wisdom and Understanding. But I believe the juster Account of the Matter is, that Simplicity is the homespun Dress of Honesty, and Chicanery and Craft are the Tinsel Habits and the false Elegance which are worn to cover the Deformity of Vice and Knavery.

In the first Ages of the World, when Men had no Wants but what were purely natural, before they had refin'd upon their Necessities, and Luxury and Ambition had introduced a Thousand fantastick Forms of Happiness, Simplicity was the Dress and Language of the World, as Nature was its Law. The little Cunning which was then in use, only taught them to ensnare, or to make tame such Animals as were necessary to their Support or their Convenience, and were otherwise too swift or too strong for them; but since these Arts have attain'd their utmost Perfection, Men have practised the same low Stratagems upon one another, and by an infinite Variety of Disguises and well-covered Treacheries, have long since instituted those little Basenesses among the necessary Arts and Knowledges of Life, and practised without Scruple, that which they have long owned without Shame.

But if we look into the History of the World, and into the Characters of those who have had the greatest Names in it, we shall find, that this original Simplicity of Mind has gradually been worn off in every Age, down to the present Time, when there is hardly any Characters of it remaining undefaced. The old Greeks and Romans, whose unperishable Writings have preserved to us the Actions and Manners of their Countrymen, and who were so well studied in all the Forms and reasonable Happinesses of Life, are so full of that just and beautiful Stile and Sentiment, as seems to have been the only proper Method of transcribing the frank and open Characters of the Heroes they celebrate, and of making them and their Writers immortal.

To prove the natural Charm and Beauty there is in this Simplicity, we need only, at this Day, as false as the World is grown, retire but far enough from great Cities, the Scenes of all worldly Business and Action; and, I believe; the most cunning Man will be obliged to own, the high and sincere Pleasure there is in conversing from the Heart, and without Design. What Relief do we find in the simple and unaffected Dialogues of uncorrupted Peasants, after the tiresome Grimace of the Town! The veriest Double-Dealer in the World is ever hankering after an Opportunity to open his own Heart, tho' perhaps he curses himself after he has done it. We are all forward enough to protest and complain against the Falshood and Treachery of Mankind, tho' the Remedy be always in our own Power, and each is at Liberty to reform himself.

But perhaps we need not be forced always to go into the Country in search of this amiable Complexion of Mind,

Simplicity; for I believe it will be found sometimes, that the Men of the truest Genius and highest Characters in the Conduct of the World, (as few of them as rise in any Age) are observed to possess this Quality in the highest Degree. They are Pretenders only, to Policy and Business, who have recourse to Cunning, and the little Chicaneries thereof: for Cunning is but the Ape of Wisdom, as Sheepishness is of Modesty, Impudence of Courage, and Pedantry of Learning.—Cunning, says my Lord *Bacon*, is a sinister or crooked Wisdom, and Dissimulation but a faint kind of Policy; for it asks a strong Wit and a strong Heart, to know when to tell Truth and to do it; therefore they are the weaker sort of Politicians, that are the greatest Dissemblers. And certainly there is a great Difference between a cunning Man and a wise One, not only in point of Honesty but in point of Ability; as there are those that can pack the Cards, who cannot play the Game well.

Cunning is a Vice purely personal, and is with the greatest Difficulty practised in free and mixed Assemblies. A cunning Man is obliged to hunt his Game alone, and to live in the dark; he is uncapable of Counsel and Advice, for his dishonest Purpose dies upon Discovery. A vertuous and an honourable Action only, will bear a Conference and Freedom of Debate. And this is the Part of true Wisdom, to be busy and assistant in a fair and worthy Design. None but Fools are Knaves, for wise Men cannot help being honest. Cunning therefore is the Wisdom of a Fool; one who has Designs that he dare not own.

To draw these loose Thoughts towards an End. If Cunning were any real Excellence in Human Nature, how comes it that the greatest and ablest, the most amiable and worthy of Mankind, are often entirely without it, and vastly above it; while Numbers of the weaker Part are observed to be very expert therein; sordid and ignorant Servants, and dishonest idle Vagabonds, often attain to the highest Perfection in it. Simplicity we are sure is natural, and the highest Beauty of Nature; and all that is excellent in Arts which Men have invented, is either to demonstrate this native

Simplicity and Truth in Nature, or to teach us to transcribe and copy in every Thing from it. Simplicity of Speech and Manners is the highest Happiness as well as the greatest Ornament of Life; whereas nothing is so tiresome to one's self, as well as so odious to others, as Disguise and Affectation. Who was ever cunning enough to conceal his being so? No Mask ever hid it self. In a Word, those cunning Men, tho' they are not declared Enemies to the World, yet they are really Spies upon it, and ought in the Justice of Things to be considered and treated as such, whenever they are caught. And to what purpose is all this Craft? To make themselves suspected and avoided by the World in return, and to have never a Friend in it. A Knave cannot have a Friend, any more than he can be one: An honest Man must discover him, a Rascal will betray him. And by this Time I hope my Reader and I are agreed, that Wisdom and Vertue are the same Thing, as Knavery and Cunning are generally so too; and that for the future, we shall resolve to be what we would seem, which is the only sure way not to be afraid to seem what we really are.

Perhaps it is not necessary to add here, that by Simplicity is not at all meant the Pretences to it, which are made now a-days, by many good People, who I believe very honestly mistake the Thing, and while they aim at Simplicity are guilty of very gross Affectation. The Plainness and Integrity of Mind, which is here recommended, is very little concerned in any Quaintness of Habit, or Oddness of Behaviour: Nor is it at all of Importance to Vertue and Simplicity, that great care is taken to appear unfashionable. Again, on the other side, I know very well that the Word *Cunning* did in the ancient Sense of it imply Knowledge. The Word Ken may perhaps be akin to it; it is of Saxon Original, and we are told the Word King is derived from it. I have no Quarrel to this Construction of it; but only against (what it now comes to signify) the little Subtilty of base Minds, who are incapable of great and honest Actions; in which Sense the Word is now commonly used.

After all, I am sensible this crooked Wisdom has established itself by the Force of an unhappy Fashion, too firmly to be immediately exploded; and though I could wish my Reader would be ashamed to live in the World by such a wretched Method, yet I would warn him to be well aware of those that do; and to be sure to arm against them, not with the same Weapons, but those which are of much better Proof, the Integrity of a wise Man, and the Wisdom of an honest one.

The Pennsylvania Gazette, 13 April 1732

The Death of Infants

The following essay which appeared in the *Pennsylvania Gazette* in 1734 is interesting for a variety of reasons. It demonstrates for one thing the interconnection in Franklin's mind of such seemingly disparate considerations as religion and demography. The strong possibility of early death suggests arguments for life after death, including eternal punishment. Even the favourite image of the eighteenth-century Deists, the universe as a divinely created clock, is employed here to suggest that the universe looks rather like what revealed religion would dictate.

The extended meditation on the divine workmanship in the body of an infant leads Franklin to speculation about the design in creating such perfect beings and then destroying them. There must be some otherworldly use these children then serve, he speculates. But in case a reader should conclude from this piece that Franklin was a believer in some version of traditional religion, a little over a month later he introduces into the *Pennsylvania Gazette* a letter parodying religious lamentations as no different from the complaints of children that they cannot have their cake and eat it too: 'All the few Cakes we have are puffed up with Yeast; and the nicest Gingerbread is spotted with Flyshits!' (*Writings*, 231).

There is a poignant sequel to Franklin's lament over the death of an infant. Two years later his own 4-year-old son Francis Folger Franklin died of smallpox.

> *Ostendunt Terris hunc tantum Fata, neque ultra*
> *Esse sinunt.*——*   Virgil.

It has been observ'd Sir *William Petty* in his *Political Arithmetick*, that one half of Mankind, which are born into this World, die, before they arrive to the age of *Sixteen*, and that an half of the remaining part never measure out the short Term of *Thirty* Years. That this Observation is pretty just, every inquisitive Person may be satisfied by comparing the several Bills of Mortality, published in *Europe*, for some Years past; even a cursory View of any common Burial-place may, in a great measure evidence the Truth of it.

Many Arguments, to prove a *Future State*, have been drawn from the unequal Lot of good and bad Men upon Earth, but no one seems to carry a greater Degree of Probability in it, than the foregoing Observation.—, To see Virtue languish and repine, to see Vice prosperous and triumphant, to see a *Dives* faring deliciously every Day, and rioting in all the Excess of Luxury and Wantonness; to see a *Lazarus* poor, hungry, naked, and full of Sores,* lying at his Door, and denied even the Crumbs that fall from his Table, the Portion of his Dogs, which Dogs are more charitable, more human than their Master: Such a View, I confess, raises in us a violent Presumption that there is another State of Retribution, where the Just and the Unjust will be equally punished or rewarded by an impartial Judge. On the other hand, when we reflect on the vast Numbers of Infants, that just struggle into Life, then weep and die, and at the same time consider, that it can be in no wise consistent with the Justice and Wisdom of an infinite Being, to create to no end, we may very reasonably conclude, that those animated Machines, those *Men* in *miniature*, who know no Difference between Good and Evil, who are incapable of any good Offices towards their Fellow-Creatures, or of serving their Maker, were made for good and wise Designs and Purposes, which Purposes, and Designs transcend all the Limits of our Ideas and all our present Capacities to conceive. Should an able and expert Artificer employ all his Time and his Skill in contriving and framing an exquisite Piece of *Clock-work*, which, when he had brought it to the utmost Perfection Wit and Art were capable of, and just set it a-going, he should suddenly dash it to pieces; would not every wise Man naturally infer, that his intense Application had disturb'd his Brain and impair'd his Reason?

Let us now contemplate the Body of an Infant, that curious Engine of Divine Workmanship. What a rich and artful Structure of Flesh upon the solid and well compacted Foundation of Bones! What curious Joints and Hinges, on which the Limbs are moved to and fro! What an inconceivable Variety of Nerves, Veins, Arteries, Fibres and little invisible parts are found in every Member! What various Fluids, Blood and Juices run thro' and agitate the innumerable slender Tubes, the hollow Strings and Strainers of the Body! What millions of folding Doors are fixed within, to stop those red or transparent Rivulets in their course, either to prevent their Return backwards, or else as a Means to swell the Muscles and move the Limbs! What endless contrivances to secure Life, to nourish Nature, and to propagate the same to future Animals! Can we now imagine after such a Survey, that so wise, so good and merciful a Creator should produce *Myriads* of such exquisite Machines to no other End or Purpose, but to be deposited in the dark Chambers of the Grave, where each of the Dead lie in their cold Mansions, in Beds of Darkness and Dust. The Shadows of a long Evening are stretch'd over them, the Curtains of a deep Midnight are drawn around them, *The Worm lies under them, and the Worm covers them.* No! the Notion of Annihilation has in it something so shocking and absurd, Reason should despise it; rather let us believe, that when they drop this earthly Vehicle they assume an Ætherial one, and become the Inhabitants of some more glorious Region. May they not help to people that infinite Number of *Starry* and *Planetary* Worlds that roll above us: may they not become our better *Genii*, our Guardian Angels, watch round our Bed and our Couch, direct our wandring Paths thro' the Maze and Labyrinth of Life, and at length conduct us safe, even us, who were the Instruments of their passing thro' this *Valley* of Sorrow and Death, to a Land of Peace and the Mountains of *Paradise*?—But these are things that belong to the Provinces of Light and immortality, and lie far beyond our mortal Ken.—

I was led into this Train of thinking by the Death of a desireable Child, whose Beauty is now turning a-pace into Corruption, and all the Loveliness of its Countenance fled for ever. Death sits heavy upon it, and the Sprightliness and Vigour of Life is perished in every Feature and in every

Limb. If the foregoing Reflections should urge any one forward in the Paths of Vertue, or yield any Consolation to those in the like Circumstances, and help to divert the Stream of their Sorrow into a better Channel, I shall hope my Thoughts have been employ'd to good Purpose. When Nature gave us Tears, she gave us leave to weep. A long Separation from those who are so near a-kin to us in Flesh and Blood, will touch the Heart in a painful Place, and awaken the tenderest Springs of Sorrow. The Sluices must be allowed to be held open a little; *Nature* seems to demand it as a Debt to *Love*. When *Lazarus* died, *Jesus* groaned and wept.*

I shall only add by way of Conclusion an *Epitaph* upon an Infant: It is taken from a Tombstone in a little obscure Village in *England*, that seems to have very little Title to any thing so elegantly poetical, which renders it the more remarkable.

> *Read this and weep—but not for me;*
> *Lament thy longer Misery:*
> *My Life was short, my Grief the less;*
> *Blame not my Hast to Happiness!*

The Pennsylvania Gazette, 20 June 1734

Letter to Josiah and Abiah
Franklin, 13 April 1738

In the *Autobiography* Franklin indicates the importance religion had for his father, since he came to New England for the sake of worshipping in the Congregational way, leaving a profitable trade in England and having to resort to a less lucrative one in Boston. It is not surprising therefore that his son's spiritual state should be a matter of concern to Josiah Franklin. We know less about Franklin's mother, but the internal evidence of this letter indicates that she shared his father's views and could articulate them in a sophisticated religious vocabulary. Evidently both parents had written to Benjamin from Boston to register concern about his religious opinions. Another recent occurrence which their letters refer to is a bizarre fatal occurrence in which Franklin was peripherally involved in a mock-masonic ritual, as reported in the Boston newspapers (*Papers*, ii. 204). The previous year a group of Philadelphia men played a trick on a gullible apprentice on the pretence of inducting him into freemasonry. The mock initiation was later described to Franklin, who claimed later to have been at first amused and then disturbed by the story. A later stage of initiation was then proposed, which eventuated in the apprentice's death from burning brandy spilled over him. Franklin's adversaries accused him of complicity in the apprentice's death, which he in turn denied in the *Pennsylvania Gazette* (*Papers*, ii. 198–202).

An earlier draft of the letter exists which takes a more defiant tone than this one does, but characteristically Franklin did not send that version. Here he does not deny his unorthodoxy; rather he implies that the possibility of perfectly correct doctrine is beyond human reach. And he associates assertions of orthodoxy with Roman Catholic claims of papal infallibility. He concludes his discussion of religious positions with an allusion to the gospels, though the passage he appears to be referring to comes from Matthew 25: 31–46, not from Matthew 26. Judging from subsequent letters to his parents from Franklin, his profession satisfied them.

Honour'd Father and Mother   April 13. 1738

I have your Favour of the 21st of March in which you both
seem concern'd lest I have imbib'd some erroneous Opinions. Doubtless I have my Share, and when the natural
Weakness and Imperfection of Human Understanding is
considered, with the unavoidable Influences of Education,
Custom, Books and Company, upon our Ways of thinking,
I imagine a Man must have a good deal of Vanity who
believes, and a good deal of Boldness who affirms, that all
the Doctrines he holds, are true; and all he rejects, are false.
And perhaps the same may be justly said of every Sect,
Church and Society of men when they assume to themselves
that Infallibility which they deny to the Popes and Councils.
I think Opinions should be judg'd of by their Influences
and Effects; and if a Man holds none that tend to make
him less Virtuous or more vicious, it may be concluded he
holds none that are dangerous; which I hope is the Case
with me. I am sorry you should have any Uneasiness on my
Account, and if it were a thing possible for one to alter his
Opinions in order to please others, I know none whom I
ought more willingly to oblige in that respect than your
selves: But since it is no more in a Man's Power *to think*
than *to look* like another, methinks all that should be
expected from me is to keep my Mind open to Conviction,
to hear patiently and examine attentively whatever is offered
me for that end; and if after all I continue in the same
Errors, I believe your usual Charity will induce you rather
to pity and excuse than blame me. In the mean time your
Care and Concern for me is what I am very thankful for.

As to the Freemasons, unless she will believe me when I
assure her that they are in general a very harmless sort of
People; and have no principles or Practices that are inconsistent with Religion or good Manners, I know no Way of
giving my Mother a better Opinion of them than she seems
to have at present, (since it is not allow'd that Women
should be admitted into that secret Society). She has, I must
confess, on that Account, some reason to be displeas'd with
it; but for any thing else, I must entreat her to suspend her

Judgment till she is better inform'd, and in the mean time exercise her Charity.

My Mother grieves that one of her Sons is an Arian, another an Arminian. What an Arminian or an Arian is, I cannot say that I very well know; the Truth is, I make such Distinctions very little my Study; I think vital Religion has always suffer'd, when Orthodoxy is more regarded than Virtue. And the Scripture assures me, that at the last Day, we shall not be examin'd what we *thought*, but what we *did*; and our Recommendation will not be that we said *Lord, Lord*, but that we did GOOD to our Fellow Creatures. See Matth. 26.

We have had great Rains here lately, which with the Thawing of Snow in the Mountains back of our Country has made vast Floods in our Rivers, and by carrying away Bridges, Boats, &c. made travelling almost impracticable for a Week past, so that our Post has entirely mist making one Trip.

I know nothing of Dr. Crook, nor can I learn that any such Person has ever been here.

I hope my Sister Janey's Child is by this time recovered. I am Your dutiful Son

Apology for the Young Man in Goal

This short poem refers to a news item which had recently appeared in Franklin's *Pennsylvania Gazette*, though the poem itself was published anonymously, as was common in eighteenth-century newspapers, in the *American Weekly Mercury*, the principal competitor to the *Gazette* in Philadelphia. The 'Apology' has only recently been identified as Franklin's work. Professor Leo Lemay, who discovered it, notes that Franklin 'did not, in fact, publish his own best hoaxes and satires in the *Gazette*. He gradually came to think the *Pennsylvania Gazette* was unsuitable for grotesque or bawdy pieces' (Lemay, *Canon*, 107). Obviously Franklin has created a literary *persona* in this piece, as he often did, and is not expressing his own attitudes. Lemay commends Franklin for 'the witty, ironic, Olympian, contemptuous, and disgusted anonymous persona' (*Canon*, 135) in the poem. Certainly one critical question which must occur to readers of the 'Apology' is whether the piece invites the reader to feel disgust for the young man in jail ('goal' is an alternative spelling) or whether it invites sympathetic participation in the crime as a sort of madcap stunt. People of the eighteenth century would visit the Hospital of St Mary of Bethlehem (or Bedlam), London's insane asylum, in order to laugh at the antics of the inmates confined there. The noble sentiments in the Declaration of Independence have to be seen in conjunction with other attitudes of the eighteenth century which are less likely to be inscribed in marble on American public buildings.

An Apology *for the young Man in Goal, and in Shackles, for ravishing an old Woman of 85 at* Whitemarsh, *who had only one Eye, and that a red one.*

> Unhappy Youth, that could not longer stay,
> Till by old Age thy Choice had dy'd away;
> A few Days more had given to thy Arms,
> Free from the Laws, her aged Lump of Charms,
> Which, tho' defunct, might feel not less alive

Than we imagine Maids of Eighty-five;
Or hadst thou staid till t'other Eye was gone,
Thou mightst have lov'd and jogg'd securely on.
Yet may thy Council urge this prudent Plea,
That by one Crime, thou has avoided three;
For had a Mare or Sow attack'd thy Love,
No human Form to save thy Life would move;
Or had thy Lust been offer'd to a Male,
All Vindications would and ought to fail;
Or hadst thou sought a blooming Virgin's Rape,
Thou shouldst not from the Penalty escape:
But when the Object is long past her Flow'r,
And brings no County-Charge, and wants no Dow'r;
Who, slighted all her Life, would fain be ravish'd,
Thou shouldst be pity'd for thy Love so lavish'd.

The American Weekly Mercury, 15 September 1743

Old Mistresses Apologue

This piece of satirical advice remained unpublished in full for any general audience until the twentieth century. Nineteenth-century Franklinists knew of it but felt it unsuitable for general publication, though it was printed a few times in limited editions intended to be read only by men. According to Paul Leicester Ford, the great Franklin bibliographer of the late nineteenth century, when an edition of Franklin writings was to be edited by John Bigelow in 1887–9, permission to include the letter was refused by the Secretary of State (copies of the letter had turned up in the State Department library) (*Papers*, iii. 27–9).

Readers of the 1990s may find their own reasons to object to the frankly sexist message of this letter, a message hardly palliated by the introductory paragraph's recommendations of marriage. Needless to say, Franklin himself made no effort to publish this piece in his lifetime, though he definitely wrote it and even revised a copy that was made from it. But the reader of today may find it even more shocking to consider how long a conspiracy of literary gentlemen kept the piece suppressed.

My dear Friend,   June 25. 1745

I know of no Medicine fit to diminish the violent natural Inclinations you mention; and if I did, I think I should not communicate it to you. Marriage is the proper Remedy. It is the most natural State of Man, and therefore the State in which you are most likely to find solid Happiness. Your Reasons against entring into it at present, appear to me not well-founded. The circumstantial Advantages you have in View by postponing it, are not only uncertain, but they are small in comparison with that of the Thing itself, the being *married and settled*. It is the Man and Woman united that make the compleat human Being. Separate, she wants his Force of Body and Strength of Reason; he, her Softness, Sensibility and acute Discernment. Together they are more likely to succeed in the World. A single Man has not nearly the Value he would have in that State of Union. He is an incomplete Animal. He resembles the odd Half of a Pair of Scissars. If you get a prudent healthy Wife, your Industry in your Profession, with her good Œconomy, will be a Fortune sufficient.

But if you will not take this Counsel, and persist in thinking a Commerce with the Sex inevitable, then I repeat my former Advice, that in all your Amours you should *prefer old Women to young ones*. You call this a Paradox, and demand my Reasons. They are these:

1. Because as they have more Knowledge of the World and their Minds are better stor'd with Observations, their Conversation is more improving and more lastingly agreable.

2. Because when Women cease to be handsome, they study to be good. To maintain their Influence over Men, they supply the Diminution of Beauty by an Augmentation of Utility. They learn to do a 1000 Services small and great, and are the most tender and useful of all Friends when you are sick. Thus they continue amiable. And hence there is hardly such a thing to be found as an old Woman who is not a good Woman.

3. Because there is no hazard of Children, which irregularly produc'd may be attended with much Inconvenience.

4. Because thro' more Experience, they are more prudent and discreet in conducting an Intrigue to prevent Suspicion. The Commerce with them is therefore safer with regard to your Reputation. And with regard to theirs, if the Affair should happen to be known, considerate People might be rather inclin'd to excuse an old Woman who would kindly take care of a young Man, form his Manners by her good Counsels, and prevent his ruining his Health and Fortune among mercenary Prostitutes.

5. Because in every Animal that walks upright, the Deficiency of the Fluids that fill the Muscles appears first in the highest Part: The Face first grows lank and wrinkled; then the Neck; then the Breast and Arms; the lower Parts continuing to the last as plump as ever: So that covering

all above with a Basket, and regarding only what is below the Girdle, it is impossible of two Women to know an old from a young one. And as in the dark all Cats are grey, the Pleasure of corporal Enjoyment with an old Woman is at least equal, and frequently superior, every Knack being by Practice capable of Improvement.

6. Because the Sin is less. The debauching a Virgin may be her Ruin, and make her for Life unhappy.

7. Because the Compunction is less. The having made a young Girl *miserable* may give you frequent bitter Reflections; none of which can attend the making an old Woman *happy*.

8thly and Lastly They are *so grateful!!*

Thus much for my Paradox. But still I advise you to marry directly; being sincerely Your affectionate Friend.

The Speech of Miss Polly Baker

Like the 'Apology for the Young Man in Goal', 'The Speech of
Miss Polly Baker' appeared first in a place where it could not
readily be traced to Franklin, the *General Advertiser* in London in
April 1747. No one knows exactly how the piece got from Franklin's hand to London, and it was of course published without
attribution, but once published, it developed a significant history
of its own (Hall, 16–75). It is a literary hoax, a form Franklin
employed several times in his life (see also, for example, his 'Edict
by the King of Prussia'). At the time the piece was written and
published, Franklin was still several years from the sort of achievements that would eventually bring him international fame. Many
of its first readers took the piece to be genuine, though a careful
reading indicates clearly that it is at least in part satirical. For one
thing, as the leading textual scholar of Franklin has pointed out,
there are unmistakable references in the text to the eighteenth
century's most outrageous satire, 'A Modest Proposal' by Jonathan
Swift (Lemay, 'Text . . . and Themes', 99–100). The satire in 'A
Modest Proposal' is clearly directed at the *persona* himself, who
advocates cannibalism as a solution to the problems of Ireland,
and in part 'The Speech of Miss Polly Baker' makes Polly Baker
also look ridiculous, with her claim that she deserves a statue in
her name for repeatedly giving birth to illegitimate children. But
many of Franklin's own ideas are voiced by Polly Baker, such as
her defiant individualism or the notion that abortion is wrong
because it destroys future generativity (Breitwieser, 220). Also,
Polly Baker's casual attitude toward legitimacy of birth reflects a
comparable casualness in Franklin, whose son William was born
out of wedlock and who later took charge of raising William's own
illegitimate son William Temple Franklin.

The SPEECH of Miss Polly Baker, *before a Court of
Judicature, at* Connecticut *in* New England, *where she was
prosecuted the fifth Time for having a Bastard Child; which
influenced the Court to dispense with her Punishment, and
induced one of her Judges to marry her the next Day.*

May it please the Honourable Bench to indulge me a few Words: I am a poor unhappy Woman; who have no Money to Fee Lawyers to plead for me, being hard put to it to get a tolerable Living. I shall not trouble your Honours with long Speeches; for I have not the presumption to expect, that you may, by any Means, be prevailed on to deviate in your Sentence from the Law, in my Favour. All I humbly hope is, that your Honours would charitably move the Governor's Goodness on my Behalf, that my Fine may be remitted. This is the Fifth Time, Gentlemen, that I have been dragg'd before your Courts on the same Account; twice I have paid heavy Fines, and twice have been brought to public Punishment, for want of Money to pay those Fines. This may have been agreeable to the Laws; I do not dispute it: But since Laws are sometimes unreasonable in themselves, and therefore repealed; and others bear too hard on the Subject in particular Circumstances; and therefore there is left a Power somewhere to dispense with the Execution of them; I take the Liberty to say, that I think this Law, by which I am punished, is both unreasonable in itself, and particularly severe with regard to me, who have always lived an inoffensive Life in the Neighbourhood where I was born, and defy my Enemies (if I have any) to say I ever wrong'd Man, Woman, or Child. Abstracted from the Law, I cannot conceive (may it please your Honours) what the Nature of my Offence is. I have brought Five fine Children into the World, at the Risque of my Life: I have maintained them well by my own Industry, without burthening the Township, and could have done it better, if it had not been for the heavy Charges and Fines I have paid. Can it be a Crime (in the Nature of Things I mean) to add to the Number of the King's Subjects, in a new Country that really wants People? I own I should think it rather a Praise worthy, than a Punishable Action. I have debauch'd no other Woman's Husband, nor inticed any innocent Youth: These Things I never was charged with; nor has any one the least cause of Complaint against me, unless, perhaps the Minister, or the Justice, because I have had Children without being Married, by which they have miss'd a Wedding Fee. But, can even this be a Fault of mine? I appeal to your Honours. You are pleased to allow I don't want Sense; but I must be stupid to the last Degree, not to prefer the honourable State of Wedlock, to the Condition I have lived in. I always was, and still am, willing to enter into it; I doubt not my Behaving well in it, having all the Industry, Frugality, Fertility, and Skill in Oeconomy, appertaining to a good Wife's Character. I defy any Person to say I ever Refused an Offer of that Sort: On the contrary, I readily Consented to the only Proposal of Marriage that ever was made me, which was when I was a Virgin; but too easily confiding in the Person's Sincerity that made it, I unhappily lost my own Honour, by trusting to his; for he got me with Child, and then forsook me: That very Person you all know; he is now become a Magistrate of this County; and I had hopes he would have appeared this Day on the Bench, and have endeavoured to moderate the Court in my Favour; then I should have scorn'd to have mention'd it; but I must Complain of it as unjust and unequal, that my Betrayer and Undoer, the first Cause of all my Faults and Miscarriages (if they must be deemed such) should be advanced to Honour and Power, in the same Government that punishes my Misfortunes with Stripes and Infamy. I shall be told, 'tis like, that were there no Act of Assembly in the Case, the Precepts of Religion are violated by my Transgressions. If mine, then, is a religious Offence, leave it, Gentlemen, to religious Punishments. You have already excluded me from all the Comforts of your Church Communion: Is not that sufficient? You believe I have offended Heaven, and must suffer eternal Fire: Will not that be sufficient? What need is there, then, of your additional Fines and Whippings? I own, I do not think as you do; for, if I thought, what you call a Sin, was really such, I would not presumptuously commit it. But how can it be believed, that Heaven is angry at my having Children, when, to the little done by me towards it, God has been pleased to add his divine Skill and admirable Workmanship in the Formation of their Bodies, and crown'd it by furnishing them with rational and immortal Souls? Forgive me Gentlemen, if I talk a little extravagantly on these Matters; I am no Divine: But if you, great Men,[†] must be making Laws, do not turn natural and useful Actions into Crimes, by your Prohibitions. Reflect a little on the horrid Consequences of this Law in particular: What Numbers of procur'd Abortions! and how many distress'd Mothers have been driven, by the Terror of Punishment and public Shame, to imbrue, contrary to Nature, their own trembling Hands in the Blood of their helpless Offspring! Nature would have induc'd them to nurse it up with a Parent's Fondness. 'Tis the Law therefore, 'tis the Law itself that is guilty of all these Barbarities and Murders. Repeal it then, Gentlemen; let it be expung'd for ever from your Books: And on the other hand, take into your wise Consideration, the great and growing Number of Batchelors in the Country, many of whom, from the mean Fear of the Expence of a Family, have never sincerely and honourably Courted a Woman in their Lives; and by their Manner of Living, leave unproduced (which I think is little better than Murder) Hundreds of their Posterity to the Thousandth Generation. Is not theirs a greater Offence against the Public Good, than mine? Compel them then, by a Law, either to Marry, or pay double the Fine of Fornication every Year. What must poor young Women do, whom Custom has forbid to sollicit the Men, and who cannot force themselves upon Husbands, when the Laws take no Care to provide them any, and yet severely punish if they do their Duty without them? Yes, Gentlemen, I venture to call it a Duty; 'tis the Duty of the first and great Command of Nature, and of Nature's God, *Increase and multiply*: A Duty, from the steady Performance of which nothing has ever been able to deter me; but for it's Sake, I have hazarded the Loss of the public Esteem, and frequently incurr'd public Disgrace and Punishment; and therefore ought, in my humble Opinion,

---

[†] *Turning to some Gentlemen of the Assembly, then in Court.*

instead of a Whipping, to have a Statue erected to my Memory.

The Maryland Gazette, 11 August 1747; first printed 15 April 1747

Observations Concerning the Increase of Mankind

Franklin's age saw the emergence of what we would call the social sciences as coherent, cumulative bodies of knowledge, and Franklin himself both witnessed and contributed to that development, perhaps especially in his 'Observations Concerning the Increase of Mankind, Peopling of Countries, &c.', which he wrote in 1751 and at first circulated among various friends. The title trails off into '&c.' because it was only published four years later as an addition to a Boston pamphlet on another subject. In the late years of the twentieth century when we worry about overpopulation, it is not easy to recognize that economic theorists of the eighteenth century considered growth in population one of the distinguishing marks of a healthy state. Franklin argues that America was specially suited for increases in population.

As Franklin points out, the possibility for large increases in population had passed for Europe because that continent was fully settled. In America however the land was still occupied primarily by a native population engaged mostly in hunting. These hunters could easily dispense with some of their lands to prospective farmers, Franklin asserts. He also foresees the eventual complete displacement of the native Americans by people who would occupy the land in a more concentrated way. But he anticipates that 'it will require many Ages to settle it fully'. In the mean time land and labour would remain cheap in America and manufacturers in the colonies would find it difficult to compete with English manufacturers, since American labourers would readily move on to other, more independent situations. As a result restrictions on colonial manufacturers would be inappropriate and unnecessary.

Calculating that the population simply by natural increase in America would double every twenty-five years, Franklin predicted that the American population would exceed the population of Great Britain in 100 years—a remarkably accurate prediction. The prospect of such an increase brings out a burst of British imperial patriotism in Franklin. 'What an Accession of Power to the *British* Empire by Sea as well as Land! What Increase of Trade and

Navigation!' Especially important to Franklin's analysis is the conclusion that natural increase without any supplementary immigration would bring about the desired increase in population.

At the end of the essay Franklin's English patriotism evolves into negative reflections on other potential sources of American population, including a reference to the '*Palatine Boors*', the Pennsylvania Dutch immigrants from the Palatinate (a region in Germany near the Rhine). The term 'Boor' denominates a small farmer, such as many of the Pennsylvania Dutch were, but it carried then as it does now the connotation of 'hick'. In fact the essay concludes with a paragraph suggesting that the English are virtually the only white people on earth. Franklin concludes this racist meditation with one of his characteristically slippery half-denials. 'But perhaps I am partial to the Complexion of my Country, for such Kind of Partiality is natural to Mankind.' Perhaps anticipating that these summary reflections had exposed him to the sort of criticism he normally was careful to avoid, Franklin eliminated paragraph 24 from later reprintings of the essay. After he returned to Philadelphia in 1762–4, though, his political enemies made his negative references to the Pennsylvania Dutch a campaign issue in the election to the Assembly, and Franklin lost.

1. Tables of the Proportion of Marriages to Births, of Deaths to Births, of Marriages to the Numbers of Inhabitants, &c. form'd on Observations made upon the Bills of Mortality, Christnings, &c. of populous Cities, will not suit Countries; nor will Tables form'd on Observations made on full settled old Countries, as *Europe*, suit new Countries, as *America*.

2. For People increase in Proportion to the Number of Marriages, and that is greater in Proportion to the Ease and Convenience of supporting a Family. When Families can be easily supported, more Persons marry, and earlier in Life.

3. In Cities, where all Trades, Occupations and Offices are full, many delay marrying, till they can see how to bear the Charges of a Family; which Charges are greater in Cities, as Luxury is more common: many live single during Life, and continue Servants to Families, Journeymen to Trades,

&c. hence Cities do not by natural Generation supply themselves with Inhabitants; the Deaths are more than the Births.

4. In Countries full settled, the Case must be nearly the same; all Lands being occupied and improved to the Heighth; those who cannot get Land, must Labour for others that have it; when Labourers are plenty, their Wages will be low; by low Wages a Family is supported with Difficulty; this Difficulty deters many from Marriage, who therefore long continue Servants and single.—Only as the Cities take Supplies of People from the Country, and thereby make a little more Room in the Country; Marriage is a little more incourag'd there, and the Births exceed the Deaths.

5. *Europe* is generally full settled with Husbandmen, Manufacturers, &c. and therefore cannot now much increase in People: *America* is chiefly occupied by Indians, who subsist mostly by Hunting.—But as the Hunter, of all Men, requires the greatest Quantity of Land from whence to draw his Subsistence, (the Husbandman subsisting on much less, the Gardner on still less, and the Manufacturer requiring least of all), The *Europeans* found *America* as fully settled as it well could be by Hunters; yet these having large Tracks, were easily prevail'd on to part with Portions of Territory to the new Comers, who did not much interfere with the Natives in Hunting, and furnish'd them with many Things they wanted.

6. Land being thus plenty in *America*, and so cheap as that a labouring Man, that understands Husbandry, can in a short Time save Money enough to purchase a Piece of new Land sufficient for a Plantation, whereon he may subsist a Family; such are not afraid to marry; for if they even look far enough forward to consider how their Children when grown up are to be provided for, they see that more Land is to be had at Rates equally easy, all Circumstances considered.

7. Hence Marriages in *America* are more general, and more generally early, than in *Europe*. And if it is reckoned

there, that there is but one Marriage per Annum among 100 Persons, perhaps we may here reckon two; and if in *Europe* they have but 4 Births to a Marriage (many of their Marriages being late) we may here reckon 8, of which if one half grow up, and our Marriages are made, reckoning one with another at 20 Years of Age, our People must at least be doubled every 20 Years.

8. But notwithstanding this Increase, so vast is the Territory of *North-America*, that it will require many Ages to settle it fully; and till it is fully settled, Labour will never be cheap here, where no Man continues long a Labourer for others, but gets a Plantation of his own, no Man continues long a Journeyman to a Trade, but goes among those new Settlers, and sets up for himself, &c. Hence Labour is no cheaper now, in *Pennsylvania*, than it was 30 Years ago, tho' so many Thousand labouring People have been imported.

9. The Danger therefore of these Colonies interfering with their Mother Country in Trades that depend on Labour, Manufactures, &c. is too remote to require the Attention of *Great-Britain*.

10. But in Proportion to the Increase of the Colonies, a vast Demand is growing for British Manufactures, a glorious Market wholly in the Power of *Britain*, in which Foreigners cannot interfere, which will increase in a short Time even beyond her Power of supplying, tho' her whole Trade should be to her Colonies: Therefore *Britain* should not too much restrain Manufactures in her Colonies. A wise and good Mother will not do it. To distress, is to weaken, and weakening the Children, weakens the whole Family.

11. Besides if the Manufactures of *Britain* (by Reason of the *American* Demands) should rise too high in Price, Foreigners who can sell cheaper will drive her Merchants out of Foreign Markets; Foreign Manufactures will thereby be encouraged and increased, and consequently foreign Nations, perhaps her Rivals in Power, grow more populous and more powerful; while her own Colonies, kept too low, are unable to assist her, or add to her Strength.

12. 'Tis an ill-grounded Opinion that by the Labour of Slaves, *America* may possibly vie in Cheapness of Manufactures with *Britain*. The Labour of Slaves can never be so cheap here as the Labour of working Men is in *Britain*. Any one may compute it. Interest of Money is in the Colonies from 6 to 10 per Cent. Slaves one with another cost 30 £. Sterling per Head. Reckon then the Interest of the first Purchase of a Slave, the Insurance or Risque on his Life, his Cloathing and Diet, Expences in his Sickness and Loss of Time, Loss by his Neglect of Business (Neglect is natural to the Man who is not to be benefited by his own Care or Diligence), Expence of a Driver to keep him at Work, and his Pilfering from Time to Time, almost every Slave being *by Nature* a Thief, and compare the whole Amount with the Wages of a Manufacturer of Iron or Wool in *England*, you will see that Labour is much cheaper there than it ever can be by Negroes here. Why then will *Americans* purchase Slaves? Because Slaves may be kept as long as a Man pleases, or has Occasion for their Labour; while hired Men are continually leaving their Master (often in the midst of his Business,) and setting up for themselves. §. 8.

13. As the Increase of People depends on the Encouragement of Marriages, the following Things must diminish a Nation, *viz.* 1. The being conquered; for the Conquerors will engross as many Offices, and exact as much Tribute or Profit on the Labour of the conquered, as will maintain them in their new Establishment, and this diminishing the Subsistence of the Natives discourages their Marriages, & so gradually diminishes them, while the Foreigners increase. 2. Loss of Territory. Thus the *Britons* being driven into *Wales*, and crowded together in a barren Country insufficient to support such great Numbers, diminished 'till the People bore a Proportion to the Produce, while the *Saxons* increas'd on their abandoned Lands; 'till the Island became full of *English*. And were the *English* now driven into *Wales* by some foreign Nation, there would in a few Years be no more Englishmen in *Britain*, than there are now People in *Wales*. 3. Loss of Trade. Manufactures exported, draw

Subsistence from Foreign Countries for Numbers; who are thereby enabled to marry and raise Families. If the Nation be deprived of any Branch of Trade, and no new Employment is found for the People occupy'd in that Branch, it will also be soon deprived of so many People. 4. Loss of Food. Suppose a Nation has a Fishery, which not only employs great Numbers, but makes the Food and Subsistence of the People cheaper: If another Nation becomes Master of the Seas, and prevents the Fishery, the People will diminish in Proportion as the Loss of Employ, and Dearness of Provision, makes it more difficult to subsist a Family. 5. Bad Government and insecure Property. People not only leave such a Country, and settling Abroad incorporate with other Nations, lose their native Language, and become Foreigners; but the Industry of those that remain being discourag'd, the Quantity of Subsistence in the Country is lessen'd, and the Support of a Family becomes more difficult. So heavy Taxes tend to diminish a People. 6. The Introduction of Slaves. The Negroes brought into the *English* Sugar *Islands*, have greatly diminish'd the Whites there; the Poor are by this Means depriv'd of Employment, while a few Families acquire vast Estates; which they spend on Foreign Luxuries, and educating their Children in the Habit of those Luxuries; the same Income is needed for the Support of one that might have maintain'd 100. The Whites who have Slaves, not labouring, are enfeebled, and therefore not so generally prolific; the Slaves being work'd too hard, and ill fed, their Constitutions are broken, and the Deaths among them are more than the Births; so that a continual Supply is needed from *Africa*. The Northern Colonies having few Slaves increase in Whites. Slaves also pejorate the Families that use them; the white Children become proud, disgusted with Labour, and being educated in Idleness, are rendered unfit to get a Living by Industry.

14. Hence the Prince that acquires new Territory, if he finds it vacant, or removes the Natives to give his own People Room; the Legislator that makes effectual Laws for promoting of Trade, increasing Employment, improving

Land by more or better Tillage; providing more Food by
Fisheries; securing Property, &c. and the Man that invents
new Trades, Arts or Manufactures, or new Improvements
in Husbandry, may be properly called *Fathers* of their
Nation, as they are the Cause of the Generation of
Multitudes, by the Encouragement they afford to Marriage.

15. As to Privileges granted to the married, (such as the
Jus trium Liberorum among the *Romans*), they may hasten
the filling of a Country that has been thinned by War or
Pestilence, or that has otherwise vacant Territory; but can-
not increase a People beyond the Means provided for their
Subsistence.

16. Foreign Luxuries & needless Manufactures imported
and used in a Nation, do, by the same Reasoning, increase
the People of the Nation that furnishes them, and diminish
the People of the Nation that uses them.—Laws therefore
that prevent such Importations, and on the contrary promote
the Exportation of Manufactures to be consumed in Foreign
Countries, may be called (with Respect to the People that
make them) *generative Laws*, as by increasing Subsistence
they encourage Marriage. Such Laws likewise strengthen a
Country, doubly, by increasing its own People and diminishing its Neighbours.

17. Some *European* Nations prudently refuse to consume
the Manufactures of *East-India*:—They should likewise
forbid them to their Colonies; for the Gain to the Merchant,
is not to be compar'd with the Loss by this Means of People
to the Nation.

18. Home Luxury in the Great, increases the Nation's
Manufacturers employ'd by it, who are many, and only
tends to diminish the Families that indulge in it, who are
few. The greater the common fashionable Expence of any
Rank of People, the more cautious they are of Marriage.
Therefore Luxury should never be suffer'd to become common.

19. The great Increase of Offspring in particular Families,
is not always owing to greater Fecundity of Nature, but
sometimes to Examples of Industry in the Heads, and

industrious Education; by which the Children are enabled to provide better for themselves, and their marrying early, is encouraged from the Prospect of good Subsistence.

20. If there be a Sect therefore, in our Nation, that regard Frugality and Industry as religious Duties, and educate their Children therein, more than others commonly do; such Sect must consequently increase more by natural Generation, than any other Sect in *Britain.*—

21. The Importation of Foreigners into a Country that has as many Inhabitants as the present Employments and Provisions for Subsistence will bear; will be in the End no Increase of People; unless the New Comers have more Industry and Frugality than the Natives, and then they will provide more Subsistence, and increase in the Country; but they will gradually eat the Natives out.—Nor is it necessary to bring in Foreigners to fill up any occasional Vacancy in a Country; for such Vacancy (if the Laws are good, § 14, 16) will soon be filled by natural Generation. Who can now find the Vacancy made in *Sweden, France* or other Warlike Nations, by the Plague of Heroism 40 Years ago; in *France*, by the Expulsion of the Protestants; in *England*, by the Settlement of her Colonies; or in *Guinea*, by 100 Years Exportation of Slaves, that has blacken'd half *America?*— The thinness of Inhabitants in *Spain*, is owing to National Pride and Idleness, and other Causes, rather than to the Expulsion of the *Moors*, or to the making of new Settlements.

22. There is in short, no Bound to the prolific Nature of Plants or Animals, but what is made by their crowding and interfering with each others Means of Subsistence. Was the Face of the Earth vacant of other Plants, it might be gradually sowed and overspread with one Kind only; as, for Instance, with Fennel; and were it empty of other Inhabitants, it might in a few Ages be replenish'd from one Nation only; as, for Instance, with *Englishmen*. Thus there are suppos'd to be now upwards of One Million *English* Souls in *North-America*, (tho' 'tis thought scarce 80,000 have been brought over Sea) and yet perhaps there is not one the fewer

in *Britain*, but rather many more, on Account of the Employment the Colonies afford to Manufacturers at Home. This Million doubling, suppose but once in 25 Years, will in another Century be more than the People of *England*, and the greatest Number of *Englishmen* will be on this Side the Water. What an Accession of Power to the *British* Empire by Sea as well as Land! What Increase of Trade and Navigation! What Numbers of Ships and Seamen! We have been here but little more than 100 Years, and yet the Force of our Privateers in the late War, united, was greater, both in Men and Guns, than that of the whole *British* Navy in Queen *Elizabeth*'s Time.——How important an Affair then to *Britain*, is the present Treaty for settling the Bounds between her Colonies and the *French*, and how careful should she be to secure Room enough, since on the Room depends so much the Increase of her People?

23. In fine, A Nation well regulated is like a Polypus; take away a Limb, its Place is soon supply'd; cut it in two, and each deficient Part shall speedily grow out of the Part remaining. Thus if you have Room and Subsistence enough, as you may be dividing, make ten Polypes out of one, you may of one make ten Nations, equally populous and powerful; or rather, increase a Nation ten fold in Numbers and Strength.

And since Detachments of *English* from *Britain* sent to *America*, will have their Places at Home so soon supply'd and increase so largely here; why should the *Palatine Boors* be suffered to swarm into our Settlements, and by herding together establish their Language and Manners to the Exclusion of ours? Why should *Pennsylvania*, founded by the *English*, become a Colony of *Aliens*, who will shortly be so numerous as to Germanize us instead of our Anglifying them, and will never adopt our Language or Customs, any more than they can acquire our Complexion.

24. Which leads me to add one Remark: That the Number of purely white People in the World is proportionably very small. All *Africa* is black or tawny. *Asia* chiefly tawny. *America* (exclusive of the new Comers) wholly so. And in

Europe, the *Spaniards, Italians, French, Russians* and *Swedes*, are generally of what we call a swarthy Complexion; as are the *Germans* also, the *Saxons* only excepted, who with the *English*, make the principal Body of White People on the Face of the Earth. I could wish their Numbers were increased. And while we are, as I may call it, *Scouring* our Planet, by clearing *America* of Woods, and so making this Side of our Globe reflect a brighter Light to the Eyes of Inhabitants in *Mars* or *Venus*, why should we in the Sight of Superior Beings, darken its People? why increase the Sons of *Africa*, by Planting them in *America*, where we have so fair an Opportunity, by excluding all Blacks and Tawneys, of increasing the lovely White and Red? But perhaps I am partial to the Complexion of my Country, for such Kind of Partiality is natural to Mankind.

The Kite Experiment

Colonial Americans were engaged in scientific investigation from the first settlement of New England and Virginia, and several Americans, including Benjamin Franklin, were admitted as Fellows of the Royal Society, the leading British scientific organization. None of these early American students of science specialized in one particular field of inquiry in the manner of the nineteenth or twentieth centuries. Rather the whole realm of scientific study seemed open to them all. So we find Franklin interested in the design of a flexible catheter, in the pattern of movement in hurricanes, in waterspouts and whirlwinds, and in arithmetic curiosities called magic squares, just to name a few. But there was one area of science where Franklin went beyond the limits of an amateur interest in science. His research into the nature of electricity really made all subsequent understanding of the phenomenon possible.

Peter Collinson, an English Quaker correspondent of Franklin's, sent an early electrical generator to the Library Company around 1746. In the first of his reports back to Collinson, Franklin writes on 28 March 1747, 'For my own part, I never was before engaged in any study that so totally engrossed my attention and my time as this has lately done' (*Papers*, iii. 118–19). In the following few years Franklin correctly discovered that electricity consists of a current which can be directed in certain ways and repelled from certain things. As he expresses it in 1750, 'The Electrical Matter consists of Particles extreamly subtile, since it can permeate common Matter, even the densest Mettals, with such Ease and Freedom, as not to receive any perceptible Resistance' (*Papers*, iv. 10). With his discovery of electricity as a current came as well his discovery of a ground: 'Thus common Matter is a Kind of Spunge to the Electrical Fluid' (*Papers*, iv. 10). Franklin's written reports on his findings, conducted along with a group of fellow experimenters in Philadelphia, were read and admired in English scientific circles largely through letters to Peter Collinson, who eventually arranged for the publication in London of Franklin's *Experiments and Observations on Electricity, Made at Philadelphia in America*, published in 1751 and eventually going through five editions by 1774.

This newspaper account of the kite experiment appeared in the *Pennsylvania Gazette* and exemplifies the clarity and elegance of both Franklin's experimental and literary styles. After the basic scientific work on electricity that he and his friends had accomplished, Franklin sought for a means of turning their experimentation to some practical use. Since one of the results of his work was the identification of lightning as an electrical discharge, Franklin went on to invent the lightning rod. In *Poor Richard Improved* for 1753, Franklin included directions for protecting houses by lightning rods.

As frequent Mention is made in the News Papers from *Europe*, of the Success of the *Philadelphia* Experiment for drawing the Electric Fire from Clouds by Means of pointed Rods of Iron erected on high Buildings, &c. it may be agreeable to the Curious to be inform'd, that the same Experiment has succeeded in *Philadelphia*, tho' made in a different and more easy Manner, which any one may try, as follows.

Make a small Cross of two light Strips of Cedar, the Arms so long as to reach to the four Corners of a large thin Silk Handkerchief when extended; tie the Corners of the Handkerchief to the Extremities of the Cross, so you have the Body of a Kite; which being properly accommodated with a Tail, Loop and String, will rise in the Air, like those made of Paper; but this being of Silk is fitter to bear the Wet and Wind of a Thunder Gust without tearing. To the Top of the upright Stick of the Cross is to be fixed a very sharp pointed Wire, rising a Foot or more above the Wood. To the End of the Twine, next the Hand, is to be tied a silk Ribbon, and where the Twine and the silk join, a Key may be fastened. This Kite is to be raised when a Thunder Gust appears to be coming on, and the Person who holds the String must stand within a Door, or Window, or under some Cover, so that the Silk Ribbon may not be wet; and Care must be taken that the Twine does not touch the Frame of the Door or Window. As soon as any of the Thunder Clouds come over the Kite, the pointed Wire will draw the Electric Fire from them, and the Kite, with all the Twine, will be electrified, and the loose Filaments of the Twine will stand out every Way, and be attracted by an approaching Finger. And when the Rain has wet the Kite and Twine, so that it can conduct the Electric Fire freely, you will find it stream out plentifully from the Key on the Approach of your Knuckle. At this Key the Phial may be charg'd; and from Electric Fire thus obtain'd, Spirits may be kindled, and all the other Electric Experiments be perform'd, which are usually done by the Help of a rubbed Glass Globe or Tube; and thereby the *Sameness* of the Electric Matter with that of Lightning compleatly demonstrated.

The Pennsylvania Gazette, 19 October 1752

The Way to Wealth

The title given here to the Preface to *Poor Richard Improved* for 1758 was not chosen by Franklin, though he uses the phrase elsewhere in his writings. Next to the *Autobiography* this work has been the most widely read piece of Franklin's writings, and during the eighteenth century it was the single most notable product of his pen, translated into numerous other languages and going through multiple editions.

By the time Franklin wrote the Preface to *Poor Richard Improved*, 1758, he had been retired from the active business of printing for nine years, though he continued to produce the almanacs. This final preface was written at sea while Franklin was under way to his period of service in England as colonial agent for the Pennsylvania Assembly, so it can be seen as a sort of valediction to Americans, whom he was leaving behind for the time being (Seavey, 180–2). Referring to the reception of the piece in the *Autobiography*, Franklin notes, 'The Piece being universally approv^{ed} was copied in all the Newspapers of the Continent, reprinted in Britain on a Broadside to be stuck up in Houses . . . In Pennsylvania, as it discouraged useless Expence in foreign Superfluities, some thought it had its share of Influence in producing that growing Plenty of Money which was observable for several Years after its Publication.' In his eighties, recalling the piece, Franklin sets aside the deliberate ambiguities which the text of the piece contains. There the audience which hears Father Abraham's exhortations to industry and frugality 'approved the Doctrine, and immediately practised the contrary, just as if it had been a common Sermon'. Only Poor Richard himself, the source of the wisdom, is persuaded. Franklin's own attitude toward the sermon as a rhetorical form was complicated all his life. He describes in part 2 of the *Autobiography* his frustration with a Philadelphia Presbyterian whose sermon on a text from Philippians focused on dogma rather than morality, and in part 3 he describes his efforts in support of the plagiarizing minister Samuel Hemphill, whose sermons Franklin liked despite discovering their lack of originality. The efforts Franklin took on Hemphill's behalf show how committed he was to the presentation of morality in sermon form. But his writing is also full of examples of the reluctance of readers or hearers to heed good advice.

COURTEOUS READER,

I have heard that nothing gives an Author so great Pleasure, as to find his Works respectfully quoted by other learned Authors. This Pleasure I have seldom enjoyed; for tho' I have been, if I may say it without Vanity, an *eminent Author* of Almanacks annually now a full Quarter of a Century, my Brother Authors in the same Way, for what Reason I know not, have ever been very sparing in their Applauses; and no other Author has taken the least Notice of me, so that did not my Writings produce me some solid *Pudding*, the great Deficiency of *Praise* would have quite discouraged me.

I concluded at length, that the People were the best Judges of my Merit; for they buy my Works; and besides, in my Rambles, where I am not personally known, I have frequently heard one or other of my Adages repeated, with, *as Poor Richard says*, at the End on't; this gave me some Satisfaction, as it showed not only that my Instructions were regarded, but discovered likewise some Respect for my Authority; and I own, that to encourage the Practice of remembering and repeating those wise Sentences, I have sometimes *quoted myself* with great Gravity.

Judge then how much I must have been gratified by an Incident I am going to relate to you. I stopt my Horse lately where a great Number of People were collected at a Vendue of Merchant Goods. The Hour of Sale not being come, they were conversing on the Badness of the Times, and one of the Company call'd to a plain clean old Man, with white Locks, *Pray, Father* Abraham, *what think you of the Times? Won't these heavy Taxes quite ruin the Country? How shall we be ever able to pay them? What would you advise us to?*—Father *Abraham* stood up, and reply'd, If you'd have my Advice, I'll give it you in short, for a *Word to the Wise is enough*, and *many Words won't fill a Bushel*, as Poor Richard says. They join'd in desiring him to speak his Mind, and gathering round him, he proceeded as follows;

"Friends, says he, and Neighbours, the Taxes are indeed very heavy, and if those laid on by the Government were the only Ones we had to pay, we might more easily discharge them; but we have many others, and much more grievous to some of us. We are taxed twice as much by our *Idleness*, three times as much by our *Pride*, and four times as much by our *Folly*, and from these Taxes the Commissioners cannot ease or deliver us by allowing an Abatement. However let us hearken to good Advice, and something may be done for us; *God helps them that help themselves*, as *Poor Richard* says, in his Almanack of 1733.

It would be thought a hard Government that should tax its People one tenth Part of their *Time*, to be employed in its Service. But *Idleness* taxes many of us much more, if we reckon all that is spent in absolute *Sloth*, or doing of nothing, with that which is spent in idle Employments or Amusements, that amount to nothing. *Sloth*, by bringing on Diseases, absolutely shortens Life. *Sloth, like Rust, consumes faster than Labour wears, while the used Key is always bright*, as *Poor Richard* says. But *dost thou love Life, then do not squander Time, for that's the Stuff Life is made of*, as *Poor Richard* says.—How much more than is necessary do we spend in Sleep! forgetting that *The sleeping Fox catches no Poultry*, and that *there will be sleeping enough in the Grave*, as *Poor Richard* says. If Time be of all Things the most precious, *wasting Time* must be, as *Poor Richard* says, *the greatest Prodigality*, since, as he elsewhere tells us, *Lost Time is never found again*; and what we call *Time-enough, always proves little enough*: Let us then up and be doing, and doing to the Purpose; so by Diligence shall we do more with less Perplexity. *Sloth makes all Things difficult, but Industry all easy*, as *Poor Richard* says; and *He that riseth late, must trot all Day, and shall scarce overtake his Business at Night*. While *Laziness travels so slowly, that Poverty soon overtakes him*, as we read in *Poor Richard*, who adds, *Drive thy Business, let not that drive thee*; and *Early to Bed, and early to rise, makes a Man healthy, wealthy and wise*.

So what signifies *wishing* and *hoping* for better Times. We may make these Times better if we bestir ourselves. *Industry need not wish*, as *Poor Richard* says, and *He that lives upon Hope will die fasting*. *There are no Gains, without Pains*; then *Help Hands, for I have no Lands*, or if I have, they are smartly taxed. And, as *Poor Richard* likewise observes, *He that hath a Trade hath an Estate*, and *He that hath a Calling hath an Office of Profit and Honour*; but then the *Trade* must be worked at, and the *Calling* well followed, or neither the *Estate*, nor the *Office*, will enable us to pay our Taxes.—If we are industrious we shall never starve; for, as *Poor Richard* says, *At the working Man's House* Hunger *looks in, but dares not enter*. Nor will the Bailiff or the Constable enter, for *Industry pays Debts, while Despair encreaseth them*, says *Poor Richard*.—What though you have found no Treasure, nor has any rich Relation left you a Legacy, *Diligence is the Mother of Good-luck*, as *Poor Richard* says, *and God gives all Things to Industry*. Then *plough deep, while Sluggards sleep, and you shall have Corn to sell and to keep*, says *Poor Dick*. Work while it is called To-day, for you know not how much you may be hindered To-morrow, which makes *Poor Richard* say, *One To-day is worth two To-morrows*; and farther, *Have you somewhat to do To-morrow, do it To-day*. If you were a Servant, would you not be ashamed that a good Master should catch you idle? Are you then your own Master, *be ashamed to catch yourself idle*, as *Poor Dick* says. When there is so much to be done for yourself, your Family, your Country, and your gracious King, be up by Peep of Day; *Let not the Sun look down and say, Inglorious here he lies*. Handle your Tools without Mittens; remember that *the Cat in Gloves catches no Mice*, as *Poor Richard* says. 'Tis true there is much to be done, and perhaps you are weak handed, but stick to it steadily, and you will see great Effects, for *constant Dropping wears away Stones*, and by *Diligence and Patience the Mouse ate in two the Cable*; and *little Strokes fell great Oaks*, as *Poor Richard* says in his Almanack, the Year I cannot just now remember.

Methinks I hear some of you say, *Must a Man afford himself no Leisure?*—I will tell thee, my Friend, what *Poor Richard* says, *Employ thy Time well if thou meanest to gain Leisure*; and, *since thou art not sure of a Minute, throw not away an Hour*. Leisure, is Time for doing something useful; this Leisure the diligent Man will obtain, but the lazy Man never; so that, as *Poor Richard* says, a *Life of Leisure and a Life of Laziness are two Things*. Do you imagine that Sloth will afford you more Comfort than Labour? No, for as *Poor Richard* says, *Trouble springs from Idleness, and grievous Toil from needless Ease. Many without Labour, would live by their* WITS *only, but they break for want of Stock*. Whereas Industry gives Comfort, and Plenty, and Respect: *Fly Pleasures, and they'll follow you. The diligent Spinner has a large Shift*; and *now I have a Sheep and a Cow, every Body bids me Good morrow*; all which is well said by *Poor Richard*.

But with our Industry, we must likewise be *steady, settled* and *careful*, and oversee our own Affairs *with our own Eyes*, and not trust too much to others; for, as *Poor Richard* says,

> *I never saw an oft removed Tree,*
> *Nor yet an oft removed Family,*
> *That throve so well as those that settled be.*

And again, *Three Removes is as bad as a Fire*; and again, *Keep thy Shop, and thy Shop will keep thee*; and again, *If you would have your Business done, go; If not, send*. And again,

> *He that by the Plough would thrive,*
> *Himself must either hold or drive.*

And again, *The Eye of a Master will do more Work than both his Hands*; and again, *Want of Care does us more Damage than Want of Knowledge*; and again, *Not to oversee Workmen, is to leave them your Purse open*. Trusting too much to others Care is the Ruin of many; for, as the *Almanack* says, *In the Affairs of this World, Men are saved, not by Faith, but by the Want of it*; but a Man's own Care is profitable; for, saith *Poor Dick, Learning is to the Studious*, and *Riches to the*

Careful, as well as *Power to the Bold*, and *Heaven to the Virtuous*. And farther, *If you would have a faithful Servant, and one that you like, serve yourself*. And again, he adviseth to Circumspection and Care, even in the smallest Matters, because sometimes *a little Neglect may breed great Mischief*; adding, *For want of a Nail the Shoe was lost; for want of a Shoe the Horse was lost; and for want of a Horse the Rider was lost*, being overtaken and slain by the Enemy, all for want of Care about a Horse-shoe Nail.

So much for Industry, my Friends, and Attention to one's own Business; but to these we must add *Frugality*, if we would make our *Industry* more certainly successful. A Man may, if he knows not how to save as he gets, *keep his Nose all his Life to the Grindstone*, and die not worth a *Groat* at last. *A fat Kitchen makes a lean Will*, as *Poor Richard* says; and,

> *Many Estates are spent in the Getting,*
> *Since Women for Tea forsook Spinning and Knitting,*
> *And Men for Punch forsook Hewing and Splitting.*

If you would be wealthy, says he, in another Almanack, *think of Saving as well as of Getting: The* Indies *have not made* Spain *rich, because her* Outgoes *are greater than her* Incomes. Away then with your expensive Follies, and you will not have so much Cause to complain of hard Times, heavy Taxes, and chargeable Families; for, as *Poor Dick* says,

> *Women and Wine, Game and Deceit,*
> *Make the Wealth small, and the Wants great.*

And farther, *What maintains one Vice, would bring up two Children*. You may think perhaps, That a *little* Tea, or a *little* Punch now and then, Diet a *little* more costly, Clothes a *little* finer, and a *little* Entertainment now and then, can be no *great* Matter; but remember what *Poor Richard* says, *Many a Little makes a Mickle*; and farther, *Beware of little Expences; a small Leak will sink a great Ship*; and again, *Who Dainties love, shall Beggars prove*; and moreover, *Fools make Feasts, and wise Men eat them*.

Here you are all got together at this Vendue of *Fineries*
and *Knicknacks.* You call them *Goods,* but if you do not take
Care, they will prove *Evils* to some of you. You expect they
will be sold *cheap,* and perhaps they may for less than they
cost; but if you have no Occasion for them, they must be
dear to you. Remember what *Poor Richard* says, *Buy what
thou hast no Need of, and ere long thou shalt sell thy Necessaries.* And again, *At a great Pennyworth pause a while*: He
means, that perhaps the Cheapness is *apparent* only, and not
real; or the Bargain, by straitning thee in thy Business, may
do thee more Harm than Good. For in another Place he
says, *Many have been ruined by buying good Pennyworths.*
Again, *Poor Richard* says, *'Tis foolish to lay out Money in a
Purchase of Repentance*; and yet this Folly is practised every
Day at Vendues, for want of minding the Almanack. *Wise
Men,* as *Poor Dick* says, *learn by others Harms, Fools scarcely
by their own*; but, *Felix quem faciunt aliena Pericula cautum.*
Many a one, for the Sake of Finery on the Back, have gone
with a hungry Belly, and half starved their Families; *Silks
and Sattins, Scarlet and Velvets,* as *Poor Richard* says, *put
out the Kitchen Fire.* These are not the *Necessaries* of Life;
they can scarcely be called the *Conveniencies,* and yet only
because they look pretty, how many *want* to *have* them. The
artificial Wants of Mankind thus become more numerous
than the *natural*; and, as *Poor Dick* says, *For one* poor *Person,
there are an hundred* indigent. By these, and other Extrava-
gancies, the Genteel are reduced to Poverty, and forced to
borrow of those whom they formerly despised, but who
through *Industry* and *Frugality* have maintained their Standing; in which Case it appears plainly, that a *Ploughman on
his Legs is higher than a Gentleman on his Knees,* as *Poor
Richard* says. Perhaps they have had a small Estate left them,
which they knew not the Getting of; they think *'tis Day,
and will never be Night*; that a little to be spent out of *so
much,* is not worth minding; (*a Child and a Fool,* as *Poor
Richard* says, *imagine* Twenty Shillings *and Twenty Years
can never be spent*) but, *always taking out of the Meal-tub,
and never putting in, soon comes to the Bottom*; then, as *Poor*

Dick says, *When the Well's dry, they know the Worth of Water*.
But this they might have known before, if they had taken
his Advice; *If you would know the Value of Money, go and
try to borrow some*; for, *he that goes a borrowing goes a
sorrowing*; and indeed so does he that lends to such People,
when he goes *to get it in again.*—*Poor Dick* farther advises,
and says,

> *Fond* Pride of Dress, *is sure a very Curse*;
> E'er Fancy *you consult, consult your Purse*.

And again, *Pride is as loud a Beggar as Want, and a great
deal more saucy*. When you have bought one fine Thing you
must buy ten more, that your Appearance may be all of a
Piece; but *Poor Dick* says, *'Tis easier to* suppress *the first
Desire, than to* satisfy *all that follow it*. And 'tis as truly
Folly for the Poor to ape the Rich, as for the Frog to swell,
in order to equal the Ox.

> *Great Estates may venture more,*
> *But little Boats should keep near Shore.*

'Tis however a Folly soon punished; for *Pride that dines on
Vanity sups on Contempt*, as *Poor Richard* says. And in
another Place, *Pride breakfasted with Plenty, dined with Poverty, and supped with Infamy*. And after all, of what Use is
this *Pride of Appearance*, for which so much is risked, so
much is suffered? It cannot promote Health, or ease Pain;
it makes no Increase of Merit in the Person, it creates Envy,
it hastens Misfortune.

> *What is a Butterfly? At best*
> *He's but a Caterpillar drest.*
> *The gaudy Fop's his Picture just,*

as *Poor Richard* says.

But what Madness must it be to *run in Debt* for these
Superfluities! We are offered, by the Terms of this Vendue,
Six Months Credit; and that perhaps has induced some of
us to attend it, because we cannot spare the ready Money,
and hope now to be fine without it. But, ah, think what

you do when you run in Debt; *You give to another Power over your Liberty*. If you cannot pay at the Time, you will be ashamed to see your Creditor; you will be in Fear when you speak to him; you will make poor pitiful sneaking Excuses, and by Degrees come to lose your Veracity, and sink into base downright lying; for, as *Poor Richard* says, *The second Vice is Lying, the first is running in Debt*. And again, to the same Purpose, *Lying rides upon Debt's Back*. Whereas a freeborn *Englishman* ought not to be ashamed or afraid to see or speak to any Man living. But Poverty often deprives a Man of all Spirit and Virtue: *'Tis hard for an empty Bag to stand upright*, as *Poor Richard* truly says. What would you think of that Prince, or that Government, who should issue an Edict forbidding you to dress like a Gentleman or a Gentlewoman, on Pain of Imprisonment or Servitude? Would you not say, that you are free, have a Right to dress as you please, and that such an Edict would be a Breach of your Privileges, and such a Government tyrannical? And yet you are about to put yourself under that Tyranny when you run in Debt for such Dress! Your Creditor has Authority at his Pleasure to deprive you of your Liberty, by confining you in Goal for Life, or to sell you for a Servant, if you should not be able to pay him! When you have got your Bargain, you may, perhaps, think little of Payment; but *Creditors*, *Poor Richard* tells us, *have better Memories than Debtors*; and in another Place says, *Creditors are a superstitious Sect, great Observers of set Days and Times*. The Day comes round before you are aware, and the Demand is made before you are prepared to satisfy it. Or if you bear your Debt in Mind, the Term which at first seemed so long, will, as it lessens, appear extreamly short. *Time* will seem to have added Wings to his Heels as well as Shoulders. *Those have a short Lent*, saith *Poor Richard, who owe Money to be paid at Easter*. Then since, as he says, *The Borrower is a Slave to the Lender, and the Debtor to the Creditor*, disdain the Chain, preserve your Freedom; and maintain your Independency: Be *industrious* and *free*; be *frugal* and *free*. At present, perhaps, you may think yourself in thriving Circumstances, and that you can bear a little Extravagance without Injury; but,

> *For Age and Want, save while you may;*
> *No Morning Sun lasts a whole Day,*

as *Poor Richard* says.—Gain may be temporary and uncertain, but ever while you live, Expence is constant and certain; and *'tis easier to build two Chimnies than to keep one in Fuel*, as *Poor Richard* says. So *rather go to Bed supperless than rise in Debt*.

> *Get what you can, and what you get hold;*
> *'Tis the Stone that will turn all your Lead into Gold,*

as *Poor Richard* says. And when you have got the Philosopher's Stone, sure you will no longer complain of bad Times, or the Difficulty of paying Taxes.

This Doctrine, my Friends, is *Reason* and *Wisdom*; but after all, do not depend too much upon your own *Industry*, and *Frugality*, and *Prudence*, though excellent Things, for they may all be blasted without the Blessing of Heaven; and therefore ask that Blessing humbly, and be not uncharitable to those that at present seem to want it, but comfort and help them. Remember *Job* suffered, and was afterwards prosperous.

And now to conclude, *Experience keeps a dear School, but Fools will learn in no other, and scarce in that*; for it is true, *we may give Advice, but we cannot give Conduct*, as *Poor Richard* says: However, remember this, *They that won't be counselled, can't be helped*, as *Poor Richard* says: And farther, That *if you will not hear Reason, she'll surely rap your Knuckles*."

Thus the old Gentleman ended his Harangue. The People heard it, and approved the Doctrine, and immediately practised the contrary, just as if it had been a common Sermon; for the Vendue opened, and they began to buy extravagantly, notwithstanding all his Cautions, and their own Fear of Taxes.—I found the good Man had thoroughly studied my Almanacks, and digested all I had dropt on those Topicks

during the Course of Five-and-twenty Years. The frequent
Mention he made of me must have tired any one else, but
my Vanity was wonderfully delighted with it, though I was
conscious that not a tenth Part of the Wisdom was my own
which he ascribed to me, but rather the *Gleanings* I had
made of the Sense of all Ages and Nations. However, I
resolved to be the better for the Echo of it; and though I
had at first determined to buy Stuff for a new Coat, I went
away resolved to wear my old One a little longer. *Reader*,
if thou wilt do the same, thy Profit will be as great as mine.

I am, as ever,

Thine to serve thee,

RICHARD SAUNDERS.

Poor Richard's Maxims

Franklin made his own anthology of maxims from *Poor Richard's Almanack* and *Poor Richard Improved* in the Preface to *Poor Richard Improved* for 1758, a preface which also came to be known as *The Way to Wealth*, but that anthology collects only maxims concerned with industry and frugality. After turning the *Pennsylvania Gazette* into a successful publication, Franklin began to produce *Poor Richard's Almanack*, his other successful serial. As in the *Silence Dogood* and *Busy-Body* series, Franklin began with a *persona*, Richard Saunders, a hen-pecked astrologer. Almanacs, which contained information on hours of daylight and tides through the year, were of interest to a reading public even barely literate, since fishermen and farmers would need that information. The principal rival in Philadelphia to Franklin's almanac was one published by Titan Leeds. In the introductory preface Poor Richard the astrologer predicts the death of Titan Leeds, a joke Jonathan Swift had played thirty years earlier, but Franklin did not lay claim to originality in *Poor Richard*. As he describes it in the *Autobiography* he 'filled all the little Spaces that occur'd between the Remarkable Days in the Calendar, with Proverbial Sentences . . .'.

In later years he also included little instructive essays on the uses of the microscope or 'How to Get Riches' or references to the births of figures he or his readers would consider great—Newton, Locke, Calvin, Luther, and others. In the Preface to *Poor Richard Improved* for 1752, in the year that Great Britain and the colonies were to shift from the Julian calendar to the Gregorian calendar used in most of Europe and still used today, Poor Richard writes a lengthy essay on the history of calendars. Franklin took some justifiable pride in the educational value of his almanacs.

Most of the maxims included were adapted or even taken directly from other anthologies of maxims. Franklin in fact never claimed originality; in *The Way to Wealth* Poor Richard refers to the maxims as 'the *Gleanings* I had made of the Sense of all Ages and Nations'. The confession is, of course, in part a sort of boast. In avoiding originality, that peculiarly modern preoccupation, Franklin resorts to the accumulated wisdom of all human cultures.

There is also an implicit denial of authorship in Franklin's confession—an appropriate denial, since many of the maxims express the conventional Protestant piety which Franklin himself felt more ambiguous about. Others express concerns about princes, courts, and courtiers—concerns which are proverbial in a civic humanist intellectual tradition, and of which Franklin would only later discover the experiential truth.

1733

A house without woman & Fire-light, is like a body without soul or sprite.

Kings & Bears often worry their keepers.

Great Talkers, little Doers.

Eat to live, and not live to eat.

The favour of the Great is no inheritance.

Fools make feasts and wise men eat 'em.

Beware of the young Doctor & the old Barber.

The poor have little, beggars none, the rich too much, *enough* not one.

He that lies down with Dogs, shall rise up with fleas.

A fat kitchin, a lean Will.

Men & Melons are hard to know.

He's the best physician that knows the worthlessness of the most medicines.

He that lives carnally, won't live eternally.

1734

Where there's Marriage without Love, there will be Love without Marriage.

Lawyers, Preachers, and Tomtits Eggs, there are more of them hatch'd than come to perfection.

Neither a Fortress nor a Maidenhead will hold out long after they begin to parly.

Teach your child to hold his tongue, he'l learn fast enough to speak.

He that cannot obey, cannot command.

An innocent *Plowman* is more worthy than a vicious *Prince*.

An Egg to day is better than a Hen to-morrow.

Drink Water, Put the Money in your Pocket, and leave the *Dry-bellyach* in the *Punchbowl*.

Necessity has no Law; I know some Attorneys of the name.

1735

The Family of Fools is ancient.

Be slow in chusing a Friend, slower in changing.

The King's cheese is half wasted in parings: But no matter, 'tis made of the peoples milk.

Three may keep a Secret, if two of them are dead.

Deny Self for Self's sake.

To be humble to Superiors is Duty, to Equals Courtesy, to Inferiors Nobleness.

An old young man, will be a young old man.

1736

Fish & Visitors stink in 3 days.

He that lives upon Hope, dies farting.

In a discreet man's mouth, a publick thing is private.

There's more old Drunkards than old Doctors.

He that lives well, is learned enough.

Poverty, Poetry, and new Titles of Honour, make Men ridiculous.

> He that would live in peace & at ease,
> Must not speak all he knows, nor judge all he sees.

1737

He that can compose himself, is wiser than he that composes books.

There are no ugly Loves, nor handsome Prisons.

If you want a neat wife, chuse her on a Saturday.

If you have time dont wait for time.

Don't go to the doctor with every distemper, nor to the lawyer with every quarrel, nor to the pot for every thirst.

1738

There are three faithful friends, an old wife, an old dog, and ready money.

Read much, but not many Books.

Write with the learned, pronounce with the vulgar.

> If you wou'd not be forgotten
> As soon as you are dead and rotten,
> Either write things worth reading,
> or do things worth the writing.

Keep your eyes wide open before marriage, half shut afterwards.

The ancients tell us what is best; but we must learn of the moderns what is fittest.

If you do what you should not, you must hear what you would not.

Defer not thy well-doing; be not like St. *George*, who is always a horseback, and never rides on.

Wish not so much to live long as to live well.

Time is an herb that cures all Diseases.

Drive thy business; let not that drive thee.

Wink at small faults; remember thou hast great ones.

Eat to please thyself, but dress to please others.

1739

He that pays for Work before it's done, has but a pennyworth for twopence.

Historians relate, not so much what is done, as what they would have believed.

He that falls in love with himself, will have no Rivals.

Blessed is he that expects nothing, for he shall never be disappointed.

Let thy Discontents be Secrets.

Hear no ill of a Friend, nor speak any of an Enemy.

Pay what you owe, and you'll know what's your own.

Thirst after Desert, not Reward.

Beware of him that is slow to anger: He is angry for something, and will not be pleased for nothing.

No longer virtuous no longer free; is a Maxim as true with regard to a private Person as a Common-wealth.

Proclaim not all thou knowest, all thou owest, all thou hast, nor all thou canst.

1740

To bear other Peoples Afflictions, every one has Courage enough, and to spare.

Happy that nation, fortunate that age, whose history is not diverting.

None are deceived but they that confide.

There are lazy Minds as well as lazy Bodies.

Tricks and Treachery are the Practice of Fools, that have not Wit enough to be honest.

> The Man who with undaunted toils,
> sails unknown seas to unknown soils,
> With various wonders feasts his Sight:
> What stranger wonders does he write?

Fear not Death; for the sooner we die, the longer shall we be immortal.

When you speak to a man, look on his eyes; when he speaks to thee, look on his mouth.

Observe all men; thy self most.

> Seek Virtue, and, of that possest,
> To Providence, resign the rest.

Marry above thy match, and thou'll get a Master.

Employ thy time well, if thou meanest to gain leisure.

1741

Learn of the skilful: He that teaches himself, hath a fool for his master.

No wood without Bark.

Let thy discontents be thy Secrets;—if the world knows them, 'twill despise *thee* and increase *them*.

At 20 years of age the Will reigns; at 30 the Wit; at 40 the Judgment.

Christianity commands us to pass by Injuries; Policy, to let them pass by us.

If you would keep your Secret from an enemy, tell it not to a friend.

Up, Sluggard, and waste not life; in the grave will be sleeping enough.

Honours change Manners.

There are no fools so troublesome as those that have wit.

1742

Strange! that a Man who has wit enough to write a Satyr; should have folly enough to publish it.

> The painful Preacher, like a candle bright,
> Consumes himself in giving others Light.

Speak and speed: the close mouth catches no flies.

Late Children, early Orphans.

> *Ben* beats his Pate, and fancys wit will come;
> But he may knock, there's no body at home.

One good Husband is worth two good Wives; for the scarcer things are the more they're valued.

1743

Men differ daily, about things which are subject to Sense, is it likely then they should agree about things invisible.

The church the state, and the poor, are 3 daughters which we should maintain, but not portion off.

Let all Men know thee, but no man know thee thoroughly: Men freely ford that see the shallows.

The sleeping Fox catches no poultry. Up! up!

1744

Who is strong? He that can conquer his bad Habits. Who is rich? He that rejoices in his Portion.

He that has not got a Wife, is not yet a compleat Man.

If you'd lose a troublesome Visitor, lend him Money.

Drive thy Business, or it will drive thee.

Epitaph on a Scolding Wife by her Husband.

Here my poor *Bridget's* Corps doth lie,
she is at rest,—and so am I.

1745

He's a Fool that cannot conceal his Wisdom.

Great spenders are bad lenders.

All blood is alike ancient.

A man without ceremony has need of great merit in its place.

Many complain of their Memory, few of their Judgment.

'Tis easier to prevent bad habits than to break them.

He that resolves to mend hereafter, resolves not to mend now.

1746

A quarrelsome Man has no good Neighbours.

Dost thou love Life? then do not squander Time; for that's the Stuff Life is made of.

What's proper, is becoming: See the Blacksmith with his white Silk Apron!

The most exquisite Folly is made of Wisdom spun too fine.

A true great Man will neither trample on a Worm, nor sneak to an Emperor.

1747

Pride and the *Gout*,
are seldom cur'd throughout.

A good Example is the best sermon.

He that won't be counsell'd, can't be help'd.

What is Serving God? 'Tis doing Good to Man.

A Slip of the Foot you may soon recover:
But a Slip of the Tongue you may never get over.

d. wise, l. foolish.

Time enough, always proves *little enough*.

He that cannot bear with other People's Passions, cannot govern his own.

1748

Lost Time is never found again.

Sell-cheap kept shop on *Goodwin Sands*, and yet had Store of Custom.

Liberality is not giving much but giving wisely.

When you're good to others, you are best to yourself.

Most Fools think they are only ignorant.

Pardoning the Bad, is injuring the Good.

He is not well-bred, that cannot bear Ill-Breeding in others.

1749

The end of Passion is the beginning of Repentance.

Words may shew a man's Wit, but *Actions* his Meaning.

'Tis a well spent penny that saves a groat.

Many Foxes grow grey, but few grow good.

A cold April,
   The Barn will fill.

Drink does not drown *Care*, but waters it, and makes it grow faster.

Who dainties love, shall Beggars prove.

Different Sects like different clocks, may be all near the matter, 'tho they don't quite agree.

Having been poor is no shame, but being ashamed of it, is.

The wise Man draws more Advantage from his Enemies, than the Fool from his Friends.

All would live long, but none would be old.

Declaiming against Pride, is not always a Sign of Humility.

9 Men in 10 are suicides.

Doing an Injury puts you below your Enemy; *Revenging* one makes you *even* with him; *Forgiving* it sets you *above* him.

Most of the Learning in use, is of no great Use.

1750

There are three Things extreamly hard, Steel, a Diamond and to know one's self.

Hunger is the best Pickle.

He is a Governor that governs his Passions, and he a Servant that serves them.

Those that have much Business must have much Pardon.

> Little Strokes,
> Fell great Oaks.

1751

We may give Advice, but we cannot give Conduct.

There are lazy Minds as well as lazy Bodies.

Talking against Religion is unchaining a Tyger; The Beast let loose may worry his Deliverer.

> Great Estates may venture more;
> Little Boats must keep near Shore.

Cunning proceeds from Want of Capacity.

1752

Observe old *Vellum*; he praises former Times, as if he'd a mind to sell'em.

The busy Man has few idle Visitors; to the boiling Pot the Flies come not.

'Tis more noble to forgive, and more manly to despise, than to revenge an Injury.

Mankind are very odd Creatures: One Half censure what they practise, the other half practise what they censure; the rest always say and do as they ought.

Children and Princes will quarrel for Trifles.

Praise to the undeserving, is severe Satyr.

Success has ruin'd many a Man.

1753

'Tis against some Mens Principle to pay Interest, and seems against others Interest to pay the Principal.

A great Talker may be no Fool, but he is one that relies on him.

When Reason preaches, if you won't hear her she'll box your Ears.

The Good-will of the Governed will be starv'd, if not fed by the good Deeds of the Governors.

Haste makes Waste.

Sudden Power is apt to be insolent, *Sudden Liberty* saucy; that behaves best which has grown gradually.

He that best understands the World, least likes it.

A lean Award is better than a fat Judgment.

God, *Parents*, and *Instructors* can never be requited.

If you have no Honey in your Pot, have some in your Mouth.

A Pair of good Ears will drain dry an hundred Tongues.

Serving God is Doing Good to Man, but Praying is thought an easier Service, and therefore more generally chosen.

Nothing humbler than *Ambition*, when it is about to climb.

1754

The Cat in Gloves catches no Mice.

Love your Neighbour; yet don't pull down your Hedge.

In the Affairs of the World Men are saved, not by Faith, but by the Want of it.

1755

Where there is Hunger, Law is not regarded; and where Law is not regarded, there will be Hunger.

The Day is short, the Work great, the Workmen lazy, the Wages high, the Master urgeth; Up, then, and be doing.

1756

Love your Enemies, for they tell you your Faults.

Be civil to *all*; serviceable to *many*; familiar with *few*; Friend to *one*; Enemy to *none*.

Laws *too gentle* are seldom *obeyed*; *too severe*, seldom executed.

Get what you can, and what you get, hold;
'Tis the *Stone* that will turn all your Lead into Gold.

1757

He that would rise at Court, must begin by Creeping.

Nothing dries sooner than a Tear.

'Tis easier to build two Chimneys, than maintain one in Fuel.

One *To-day* is worth two *To-morrows*.

The way to be safe, is never to be secure.

Work as if you were to live 100 Years, Pray as if you were to die To-morrow.

Act uprightly, and despise Calumny; Dirt may stick to a Mud Wall, but not to polish'd Marble.

1758

Silence is not always a Sign of Wisdom, but Babbling is ever a Mark of Folly.

Great Modesty often hides great Merit.

Virtue may not always make a Face handsome, but *Vice* will certainly make it ugly.

He that's content, hath enough; He that complains, has too much.

The first Mistake in publick Business, is the going into it.

A full Belly makes a dull Brain: The Muses starve in a Cook's Shop.

In a corrupt Age, the putting the World in order would breed Confusion; then e'en mind your own Business.

'Homespun's' Further Defense of Indian Corn

During his years as colonial agent in London for Pennsylvania and other colonies (1757–62, 1764–75), Franklin was the leading spokesman for the American cause in England. He advanced that cause both by the normal quasi-diplomatic functions of the colonial agent and also by a newspaper campaign conducted anonymously through Franklin's well-developed contacts in the London press. The extent of Franklin's newspaper campaign has only been recognized in the twentieth century as scholars have reviewed eighteenth-century newspapers in search of his contributions. Often Franklin's English newspaper items would be reprinted or excerpted in American newspapers, as this one was. This letter is a sequel to an earlier response, also signed 'HOMESPUN', to a writer designating himself as 'VINDEX PATRIÆ' (protector of the homeland), who defends the ministry of George Grenville and the Stamp Act. Franklin obviously perceived the conflict between the British ministry and the colonies as more than a political struggle: it was necessarily a clash of cultures. The overt occasion for Homespun to write is the defence of Indian corn as a staple of the American diet. Homespun by implication defends the institution of slavery, saying that there is nothing wrong with feeding slaves corn since their purpose is to make money for their owners. Much later in his life Franklin would become a strong advocate for the abolition of slavery, but here he feels he must defend even features of American life which he had criticized while in America, such as the resemblance between the Puritan Americans and the Scotch Presbyterians. Franklin also takes on Vindex Patriæ's defence of the concept of virtual representation in Parliament: according to that concept, although representation in the House of Commons did not accurately reflect the distribution of population in England in the eighteenth century, people who could not elect members, like the Americans, or who were under-represented were 'virtually' represented in Parliament regardless of the apparent inequity. The concept of virtual representation was basic to the British system of government in the eighteenth century, so for Franklin to assault it showed a real breach with the mother country as early as 1766. Instead he proposes a union between Great Britain and America similar to the union between England and Scotland which had been completed in 1707.

To the PRINTER.

JOHN BULL shews in nothing more his great veneration for good eating, and how much he is always thinking of his belly, than in his making it the constant topic of his contempt for other nations, that *they do not eat so well as himself.* The *roast beef of Old England* he is always exulting in, as if no other country had beef to roast;—reproaching, on every occasion, the *Welsh* with their leeks and toasted cheese, the *Irish* with their potatoes, and the *Scotch* with their oatmeal. And now that we are a little out of favour with him, he has begun, by his attorney VINDEX PATRIÆ, to examine our eating and drinking, in order, I apprehend, to fix some horrible scandal of the same kind upon us poor *Americans*.

I did but say a word or two in favour of *Indian corn*, which he had treated as "disagreable and indigestible," and this vindictive gentleman grows angry. "Let him tell the world, IF HE DARES (says he) that the Americans prefer it to a place at their own tables." Ah, Sir, I see the dilemma you have prepared for me. If I should not *dare* to say, that we do prefer it to a place at our tables, then you demonstrate, that we must come to England for tea, or go without our breakfasts: and if I do *dare* to say it, you fix upon me and my countrymen for ever, the indelible disgrace of being *Indian corn-eaters*.

I am afraid, Mr. Printer, that you will think this too trifling a dispute to deserve a place in your paper: but pray, good Sir, consider, as you are yourself an Englishman, that we Americans, who are allowed even by Mr. VINDEX to have some English blood in our veins, may think it a very serious thing to have the honour of our eating impeached in any particular whatsoever.

"Why doth he not deny the fact (says VINDEX) that it is assigned to the slaves for their food? To proclaim the *wholesomeness* of this corn, without assigning a reason why white men give it to their slaves, when they can get other food, is only satirizing the good sense of their brethren in America." In truth I cannot deny the fact, though it should reflect ever so much on the *good sense* of my countrymen. I own we do give food made of Indian corn to our slaves, as well as eat it ourselves; not, as you suppose, because it is "*indigestible* and *unwholesome*;" but because it keeps them healthy, strong and hearty, and fit to go through all the labour we require of them. Our slaves, Sir, cost us money, and we buy them to make money by their labour. If they are sick, they are not only unprofitable, but expensive. Where then was your *English good sense*, when you imagined we gave the slaves our Indian corn, because we knew it to be *unwholesome*?

In short, this is only another of Mr. VINDEX's paradoxes, in which he is a great dealer. The first endeavoured to persuade us, that we were represented in the British Parliament *virtually*, and by *fiction*:—Then that we were *really* represented there, because the Manor of East Greenwich in Kent is represented there, and all the Americans live in East Greenwich. And now he undertakes to prove to us, that taxes are the most profitable things in the world to those that pay them; for that Scotland is grown rich since the Union, by paying English taxes. I wish he would accommodate himself a little better to our dull capacities. We Americans have a great many heavy taxes of our own, to support our several governments, and pay off the enormous debt contracted by the war; we never conceived ourselves the richer for paying taxes, and are willing to leave all new ones to those that like them. At least, if we must with Scotland, participate in your taxes, let us likewise, with Scotland, participate in the Union, and in all the privileges and advantages of commerce that accompanied it.

VINDEX, however, will never consent to this. He has made us partakers in all the odium with which he thinks fit to load Scotland:—"They resemble the Scots in sentiments (says he) their religion is Scottish; their customs and *laws* are Scottish; like the Scotch they Judaically observe what *they call* the Sabbath, persecute old women for witches, are intolerant to other sects, &c." But we must not, like the Scots, be admitted into Parliament; for that, he thinks, would increase "the Scotch interest in England, which is equally hostile to the cause of liberty, and the cause of our church."

Pray, Sir, who informed you that our "*laws* are Scottish?" The same, I suppose, that told you our Indian corn is unwholesome. Indeed, Sir, your information is very imperfect. The common law of England, is, I assure you, the common law of the colonies: and if the civil law is what you mean by the Scottish law, we have none of it but what is forced upon us by England, in its courts of Admiralty, depriving us of that inestimable part of the common law, trials by juries. And do you look upon keeping the *Sabbath*, as part of the Scottish law? "The Americans, like the Scots, (you say,) observe what *they call* the Sabbath." Pray, Sir, you who are so zealous for your church (in abusing other Christians) what *do you call* it? and where the harm of their *observing* it? If you look into your prayer-book, or over your altars, you will find these words written, *Remember to keep holy the* SABBATH *Day*. This law, tho' it may be observed in Scotland, and has been *countenanced* by some of your statutes, is, Sir, originally one of *God's Commandments*: a body of laws still in force in America, tho' they may have become *obsolete* in *some other* countries.

Give me leave, Master JOHN BULL, to remind you, that you are *related to all mankind*; and therefore it less becomes you than any body, to affront and abuse other nations. But you have mixed with your many virtues, a pride, a haughtiness, and an insolent contempt for all but yourself, that, I am afraid, will, if not abated, procure you one day or other a handsome drubbing. Besides your rudeness to foreigners, you are far from being civil even to your own family. The Welch you have always despised for submitting to your government: But why despise your own English, who conquered and settled Ireland for you; who conquered and settled America for you? Yet these you now think you may treat as you please, because, forsooth, they are a *conquered* people. Why dispise the Scotch, who fight and die for you all over the world? Remember, you courted Scotland for one hundred years, and would fain have had your *wicked will* of her. She virtuously resisted all your importunities, but at length kindly consented to become your lawful wife. You then solemnly promised to *love, cherish*, and *honour* her, as long as you both should live; and yet you have ever since treated her with the utmost contumely, which you now begin to extend to your common children. But, pray, when your enemies are uniting in a *Family Compact* against you, can it be discreet in you to kick up in your own house a *Family Quarrel?* And at the very time you are inviting foreigners to settle on your lands, and when you have more to settle than ever you had before, is it prudent to suffer your lawyer, VINDEX, to abuse those who have settled there already, because they cannot yet speak "Plain English?"—It is my opinion, Master BULL, that the Scotch and Irish, as well as the colonists, are capable of speaking much *plainer English* than they have ever yet spoke, but which I hope they will never be provoked to speak.

To be brief, Mr. VINDEX, I pass over your other accusations of the Americans, and of the Scotch, that we "Persecute old women for witches, and are intolerant to other sects," observing only, that we were wise enough to leave off both those foolish tricks, long before Old England made the act of toleration, or repealed the statute against witchcraft; so that even *you yourself* may safely travel through all Scotland and the Colonies, without the least danger of being persecuted as a churchman, or taken (up) for a conjurer. And yet I own myself so far of an intolerant spirit, that though I thank you for the box-in-the-ear you have given TOM HINT, as being, what you justly call him, "a futile calumniator," I cannot but wish he would give you another—for the same reason.

One word more, however, about the *Indian corn*, which I began and must end with, even though I should hazard your remarking, that it is certainly "indigestible," as it plainly appears to *stick in my stomach*. "Let him tell the world, IF HE DARES, (you say) that the Americans prefer it to a place at their tables."—And, pray, if I should DARE,—what then?—Why then—"You will enter upon a discussion of its salubrity and pleasant taste."—Really?—Would you venture to write on the salubrity and *pleasant taste* of Indian corn, when you never in your life have tasted a *single grain* of it?—But why should that hinder your writing on it? Have you not written even on *politics*?   Your's,

HOMESPUN.

The Gazetteer and New Daily Advertiser, January 15 1766

An Edict by the King of Prussia

Possibly the best of Franklin's newspaper contributions is this hoax, which a letter of Franklin's to his son of 6 October 1773 indicates fooled some fairly sophisticated readers. In fact that letter is an excellent contemporary record of how eighteenth-century satire was actually read in its own time. Franklin was visiting a prominent friend, Francis Dashwood, Lord Le Despencer when the mail brought the day's newspapers; Paul Whitehead, a minor satirist and one of Le Despencer's hangers-on, would always read through them first and report on anything of special interest. 'He had them in another room, and we were chatting in the breakfast parlour, when he came running into us, out of breath, with the paper in his hand. Here! says he, here's news for ye! *Here's the king of Prussia, claiming a right to this kingdom!* All stared, and I as much as any body; and he went on to read it. When he had read two or three paragraphs, a gentleman present said, *Damn his impudence, I dare say, we shall hear by next post that he is upon his march with one hundred thousand men to back this.* Whitehead, who is very shrewd, soon after began to smoke it, and looking in my face said, *I'll be hanged if this is not some of your American jokes upon us.* The reading went on, and ended with abundance of laughing, and a general verdict that it was a fair hit: and the piece was cut out of the paper and preserved in my lord's collection' (*Writings*, 887).

Part of the humour in the 'Edict' derives from Franklin's analogy between the Anglo-Saxon settlement of England in the fifth century and the settlement of America. The 'Edict' alleges that Frederick II, known as Frederick the Great, King of Prussia, was making the same demands on the formerly German colonists in England that England made in the 1770s on the American colonies. Frederick was known also both as a king who cared little what pretext could be found for military aggression and as the only really brilliant thinker and wit among European rulers in his day. As Franklin indicates, the language of the 'Edict' echoes the legal language of specific decrees from England regarding the colonies.

For the Public Advertiser.

The SUBJECT of the following Article of
FOREIGN INTELLIGENCE
being exceeding EXTRAORDINARY, is the Reason of its
being separated from the usual Articles of *Foreign News.*

Dantzick, September 5.

WE have long wondered here at the Supineness of the
English Nation, under the Prussian Impositions upon its
Trade entering our Port. We did not till lately know the
Claims, antient and modern, that hang over that Nation, and
therefore could not suspect that it might submit to those
Impositions from a Sense of *Duty,* or from Principles of
Equity. The following *Edict,* just made public, may, if
serious, throw some Light upon this Matter.

'FREDERICK, by the Grace of God, King of *Prussia,* &c.
&c. &c. to all present and to come,[†] HEALTH. The Peace
now enjoyed throughout our Dominions, having afforded us
Leisure to apply ourselves to the Regulation of Commerce,
the Improvement of our Finances, and at the same Time
the easing our *Domestic Subjects* in their Taxes: For these
Causes, and other good Considerations us thereunto moving,
We hereby make known, that after having deliberated these
Affairs in our Council, present our dear Brothers, and other
great Officers of the State, Members of the same, WE, of
our certain Knowledge, full Power and Authority Royal,
have made and issued this present Edict, viz.

'WHEREAS it is well known to all the World, that the
first German Settlements made in the Island of *Britain,* were
by Colonies of People, Subjects to our renowned Ducal
Ancestors, and drawn from *their* Dominions, under the
Conduct of *Hengist, Horsa, Hella, Uffa, Cerdicus, Ida,* and
others; and that the said Colonies have flourished under the
Protection of our august House, for Ages past, have never
been *emancipated* therefrom, and yet have hitherto yielded
little Profit to the same. And whereas We Ourself have in

[†] *A tous presens & à venir.* Orig.

the last War fought for and defended the said Colonies against the Power of *France*, and thereby enabled them to make Conquests from the said Power in *America*, for which we have not yet received adequate Compensation. And whereas it is just and expedient that a Revenue should be raised from the said Colonies in *Britain* towards our Indemnification; and that those who are Descendants of our antient Subjects, and thence still owe us due Obedience, should contribute to the replenishing of our Royal Coffers, as they must have done had their Ancestors remained in the Territories now to us appertaining: WE do therefore hereby ordain and command, That from and after the Date of these Presents, there shall be levied and paid to our Officers of the Customs, on all Goods, Wares and Merchandizes, and on all Grain and other Produce of the Earth exported from the said Island of *Britain*, and on all Goods of whatever Kind imported into the same, a *Duty* of *Four and an Half* per Cent. *ad Valorem*, for the Use of us and our Successors.—And that the said Duty may more effectually be collected, We do hereby ordain, that all Ships or Vessels bound from *Great Britain* to any other Part of the World, or from any other Part of the World to *Great Britain*, shall in their respective Voyages touch at our Port of KONINGS-BERG, there to be unladen, searched, and charged with the said Duties.

'AND WHEREAS there have been from Time to Time discovered in the said Island of *Great Britain* by our Colonists there, many Mines or Beds of Iron Stone; and sundry Subjects of our antient Dominion, skilful in converting the said Stone into Metal, have in Times past transported themselves thither, carrying with them and communicating that Art; and the Inhabitants of the said Island, *presuming* that they had a natural Right to make the best Use they could of the natural Productions of their Country for their own Benefit, have not only built Furnaces for smelting the said Stone into Iron, but have erected Plating Forges, Slitting Mills, and Steel Furnaces, for the more convenient manufacturing of the same, thereby endangering a Diminution of the said Manufacture in our antient Dominion. WE *do therefore* hereby farther ordain, that from and after the Date hereof, no Mill or other Engine for Slitting or Rolling of Iron, or any Plating Forge to work with a Tilt-Hammer, or any Furnace for making Steel, shall be erected or continued in the said Island of *Great Britain*: And the Lord Lieutenant of every County in the said Island is hereby commanded, on Information of any such Erection within his County, to order and by Force to cause the same to be abated and destroyed, as he shall answer the Neglect thereof to Us at his Peril.——But We are nevertheless graciously pleased to permit the Inhabitants of the said Island to transport their Iron into *Prussia*, there to be manufactured, and to them returned, they paying our Prussian Subjects for the Workmanship, with all the Costs of Commission, Freight and Risque coming and returning, any Thing herein contained to the contrary notwithstanding.

'WE do not however think fit to extend this our Indulgence to the Article of *Wool*, but meaning to encourage not only the manufacturing of woollen Cloth, but also the raising of Wool in our antient Dominions, and to prevent *both*, as much as may be, in our said Island, We do hereby absolutely forbid the Transportation of Wool from thence even to the Mother Country *Prussia*; and that those Islanders may be farther and more effectually restrained in making any Advantage of their own Wool in the Way of Manufacture, We command that none shall be carried *out of one Country into another*, nor shall any Worsted-Bay, or Woollen-Yarn, Cloth, Says, Bays, Kerseys, Serges, Frizes, Druggets, Cloth-Serges, Shalloons, or any other Drapery Stuffs, or Woollen Manufactures whatsoever, made up or mixt with Wool in any of the said Counties, be carried into any other County, or be Water-borne even across the smallest River or Creek, on Penalty of Forfeiture of the same, together with the Boats, Carriages, Horses, &c. that shall be employed in removing them. *Nevertheless* Our loving Subjects there are hereby permitted, (if they think proper) to use all their Wool as *Manure for the Improvement of their Lands*.

'AND WHEREAS the Art and Mystery of making *Hats* hath arrived at great Perfection in *Prussia*, and the making of Hats by our remote Subjects ought to be as much as possible restrained. And forasmuch as the Islanders beforementioned, being in Possession of Wool, Beaver, and other Furs, have *presumptuously* conceived they had a Right to make some Advantage thereof, by manufacturing the same into Hats, to the Prejudice of our domestic Manufacture, WE do therefore hereby strictly command and ordain, that no Hats or Felts whatsoever, dyed or undyed, finished or unfinished, shall be loaden or put into or upon any Vessel, Cart, Carriage or Horse, to be transported or conveyed *out of one County* in the said Island *into another County*, or to *any other Place whatsoever*, by any Person or Persons whatsoever, on Pain of forfeiting the same, with a Penalty of *Five Hundred Pounds* Sterling for every Offence. Nor shall any Hat-maker in any of the said Counties employ more than two Apprentices, on Penalty of *Five Pounds* Sterling per Month: We intending hereby that such Hat-makers, being so restrained both in the Production and Sale of their Commodity, may find no Advantage in continuing their Business.—But lest the said Islanders should suffer Inconveniency by the Want of Hats, We are farther graciously pleased to permit them to send their Beaver Furs to *Prussia*; and We also permit Hats made thereof to be exported from *Prussia* to *Britain*, the People thus favoured to pay all Costs and Charges of Manufacturing, Interest, Commission to Our Merchants, Insurance and Freight going and returning, as in the Case of Iron.

'And lastly, Being willing farther to favour Our said Colonies in *Britain*, We do hereby also ordain and command, that all the Thieves, Highway and Street-Robbers, Housebreakers, Forgerers, Murderers, So——tes, and Villains of every Denomination, who have forfeited their Lives to the Law in *Prussia*, but whom We, in Our great Clemency, do not think fit here to hang, shall be emptied out of our Gaols into the said Island of *Great Britain for the* BETTER PEOPLING *of that Country*.

'We flatter Ourselves that these Our Royal Regulations and Commands will be thought *just* and *reasonable* by Our much-favoured Colonists in *England*, the said Regulations being copied from their own Statutes of 10 and 11 Will. III. C. 10—5 Geo. II. C. 22—23 Geo. II. C. 29—4 Geo. I. C. 11. and from other equitable Laws made by their Parliaments, or from Instructions given by their Princes, or from Resolutions of both Houses entered into for the GOOD *Government* of their own Colonies in *Ireland* and *America*.

'And all Persons in the said Island are hereby cautioned not to oppose in any wise the Execution of this Our Edict, or any Part thereof, such Opposition being HIGH TREASON, of which all who are *suspected* shall be transported in Fetters from *Britain* to *Prussia*, there to be tried and executed according to the *Prussian Law*.

'Such is our Pleasure.

'Given at *Potsdam* this twenty-fifth Day of the Month of August, One Thousand Seven Hundred and Seventy-three, and in the Thirty-third Year of our Reign.

'By the KING in his Council.

'RECHTMÆSSIG, *Secr.*'

Some take this Edict to be merely one of the King's *Jeux d'Esprit*: Others suppose it serious, and that he means a Quarrel with England: But all here think the Assertion it concludes with, "that these Regulations are copied from Acts of the English Parliament respecting their Colonies," a very *injurious* one: it being impossible to believe, that a People distinguished for their *Love of Liberty*, a Nation so *wise*, so *liberal in its Sentiments*, so *just and equitable* towards its *Neighbours*, should, from mean and *injudicious* Views of *petty immediate Profit*, treat *its own Children* in a Manner so *arbitrary* and TYRANNICAL!

The Public Advertiser, 22 September 1773

Letter to William Strahan,
5 July 1775

Franklin probably had no closer friend in England during his long stay there in 1757–62 and 1764–75 than William Strahan. Like Franklin, the Scottish-born Strahan was a printer by trade and a self-made man. Franklin had come to know Strahan at first by correspondence when Franklin was actively a printer in Philadelphia. As this angry letter indicates, Strahan was also by 1775 a Member of Parliament and a supporter of Lord North's efforts to squelch the incipient American rebellion. It is noteworthy both that Franklin should have felt the anger and indignation that this letter expresses, after the opening hostilities of the Revolution, and that, as the editors of the Franklin *Papers* (xxii, 85) point out, he did not send the letter to Strahan. In fact Franklin was careful not to burn his bridges and resumed soon after a cordial correspondence with Strahan.

Mr. Strahan,   Philada. July 5. 1775

    You are a Member of Parliament, and one of that Majority which has doomed my Country to Destruction. You have begun to burn our Towns, and murder our People. Look upon your Hands! They are stained with the Blood of your Relations! You and I were long Friends: You are now my Enemy, and I am, Yours,

Letter to Benjamin Vaughan, 9 November 1779

Franklin was considered by the Enlightenment to be a philosopher, but at the time the term embraced what was called natural philosophy (or what we would call natural science) and did not necessarily include some of the preoccupations we would associate with the philosopher. Benjamin Vaughan, the recipient of this letter and the author of one of the letters introduced into the text of the *Autobiography* after part 1, was an English radical and minor man of letters. He had completed an English edition of Franklin's letters shortly before receiving this letter. His devotion to Franklin, acknowledged in this letter, shows clearly in the *Autobiography* letter. The details of the publication of Franklin's one philosophical attempt agree with the account in his *Autobiography*, except that his life story does not go on to describe his later argument to the contrary. The attitude Franklin declares toward philosophical speculation was one widely though not universally shared by thinkers of the eighteenth century—partly as they reacted against both the theological and the systematic philosophical thought of the previous century: 'The great uncertainty I found in metaphysical reasonings disgusted me, and I quitted that kind of reading and study for others more satisfactory.'

DEAR SIR,   Passy, Nov. 9. 1779.
I have received several kind Letters from you, which I have not regularly answered. They gave me however great Pleasure, as they acquainted me with your Welfare, and that of your Family and other Friends; and I hope you will continue writing to me as often as you can do it conveniently.

I thank you much for the great Care and Pains you have taken in regulating and correcting the Edition of those Papers. Your Friendship for me appears in almost every Page; and if the Preservation of any of them should prove of Use to the Publick, it is to you that the Publick will owe the Obligation. In looking them over, I have noted some Faults of Impression that hurt the Sense, and some other little Matters, which you will find all in a Sheet under the title of *Errata*. You can best judge whether it may be worth while to add any of them to the Errata already printed, or whether it may not be as well to reserve the whole for Correction in another Edition, if such should ever be. Inclos'd I send a more perfect copy of the *Chapter*.

If I should ever recover the Pieces that were in the Hands of my Son, and those I left among my Papers in America, I think there may be enough to make three more such Volumes, of which a great part would be more interesting.

As to the *Time* of publishing, of which you ask my Opinion I am not furnish'd with any Reasons, or Ideas of Reasons, on which to form any Opinion. Naturally I should suppose the Bookseller to be from Experience the best Judge, and I should be for leaving it to him.

I did not write the Pamphlet you mention. I know nothing of it. I suppose it is the same, concerning which Dr. Priestley formerly asked me the same Question. That for which he took it was intitled, *A Dissertation on Liberty and Necessity, Pleasure and Pain*, with these Lines in the Title-Page.

> "Whatever is, is right. But purblind Man
> Sees but a part o' the Chain, the nearest Link;
> His eye not carrying to that equal Beam,
> That poises all above."
>
> DRYDEN.
>
> *London, Printed M.D.C.C.X.X.V.*

It was addressed to Mr. J. R., that is, James Ralph, then a youth of about my age, and my intimate friend; afterwards a political writer and historian. The purport of it was to prove the doctrine of fate, from the supposed attributes of God; in some such manner as this: that in erecting and governing the world, as he was infinitely wise, he knew what would be best; infinitely good, he must be disposed, and infinitely powerful, he must be able to execute it: consequently all is right. There were only an hundred copies printed, of which I gave a few to friends, and afterwards disliking the piece, as conceiving it might have an ill tendency, I burnt the rest, except one copy, the margin of which was filled with manuscript notes by Lyons, author of the Infallibility of Human Judgment, who was at that time another of my acquaintance in London. I was not nineteen years of age when it was written. In 1730, I wrote a piece on the other side of the question, which began with laying for its foundation this fact: "That almost all men in all ages and countries, have at times made use of prayer." Thence I reasoned, that if all things are ordained, prayer must among the rest be ordained. But as prayer can produce no change in things that are ordained, praying must then be useless and an absurdity. God would therefore not ordain praying if everything else was ordained. But praying exists, therefore all things are not ordained, etc. This pamphlet was never printed, and the manuscript has been long lost. The great uncertainty I found in metaphysical reasonings disgusted me, and I quitted that kind of reading and study for others more satisfactory.

I return the Manuscripts you were so obliging as to send me; I am concern'd at your having no other copys, I hope these will get safe to your hands. I do not remember the Duke de Chaulnes showing me the Letter you mention. I have received Dr. Crawford's book, but not your Abstract, which I wait for as you desire.

I send you also M. Dupont's *Table Economique*, which I think an excellent Thing, as it contains in a clear Method all the principles of that new sect, called here *les Economistes*.

Poor Henley's dying in that manner is inconceivable to me. Is any Reason given to account for it, besides insanity?

Remember me affectionately to all your good Family, and believe me, with great Esteem, my dear Friend, yours, most sincerely,

The Whistle

After arriving as the principal American ambassador to France in 1776, Franklin was immediately enmeshed in a diplomatic and publicity campaign to secure French aid to the new American government. His success there remains probably the greatest achievement of any American diplomat. But he also managed to sustain a diverting personal life based in Passy, at the time on the outskirts of Paris. Madame Anne-Catherine de Ligneville Helvetius, the widow of a *philosophe*, who was not much younger than Franklin, and Madame Anne-Louise d'Hardancourt Brillon de Jouy, a pious and sprightly young matron in the neighbourhood, became the leading members of a circle of fascinating women whom Franklin developed around him.

Franklin played chess with Madame Brillon and tried to marry his feckless grandson William Temple Franklin to Madame Brillon's daughter. To the still attractive Madame Helvetius he even proposed marriage, though a bagatelle was the medium by which he made his proposal. Franklin had set up a printing press at his residence in Passy, partly to print up copies of the bagatelles he wrote for his friends. 'The Whistle' was written in part as an exercise in perfecting his written French with the guidance of Madame Brillon and in part as a contribution to his literary collaboration with her. 'Always a realist,' writes Claude-Anne Lopez, the most perceptive student of Franklin's literary romances, 'Franklin accepted the fact that Madame Brillon would never offer him more than her particular blend of chastity and exaltation. Still, her presence stimulated his mind and his pen' (Lopez, 69).

As in the *Autobiography* Franklin's early life contains the truths by which later human experiences are to be measured. Giving too much for our whistles is the failing of the courtier, the man of pleasure or of appearance, the woman who marries unwisely. But even in the end Franklin knows how attractive the whistle can be, as it had been to him at 7 years old.

Passy, November 10 1779.

I received my dear Friend's two Letters, one for Wednesday

& one for Saturday. This is again Wednesday. I do not deserve one for to day, because I have not answered the former. But indolent as I am, and averse to Writing, the Fear of having no more of your pleasing Epistles, if I do not contribute to the Correspondance, obliges me to take up my Pen: And as M. B. has kindly sent me Word,* that he sets out to-morrow to see you; instead of spending this Wednesday Evening as I have long done its Name-sakes, in your delightful Company, I sit down to spend it in thinking of you, in writing to you, & in reading over & over again your Letters.

I am charm'd with your Description of Paradise, & with your Plan of living there. And I approve much of your Conclusion, that in the mean time we should draw all the Good we can from this World. In my Opinion we might all draw more Good, from it than we do, & suffer less Evil, if we would but take care *not to give too much for our Whistles*. For to me it seems that most of the unhappy People we meet with, are become so by Neglect of that Caution.

You ask what I mean?—You love Stories, and will excuse my telling you one of my self. When I was a Child of seven Years old, my Friends on a Holiday fill'd my little Pocket with Halfpence. I went directly to a Shop where they sold Toys for Children; and being charm'd with the Sound of a Whistle that I met by the way, in the hands of another Boy, I voluntarily offer'd and gave all my Money for it. When I came home, whistling all over the House, much pleas'd with my Whistle, but disturbing all the Family, my Brothers, Sisters & Cousins, understanding the Bargain I had made, told me I had given four times as much for it as it was worth, put me in mind what good Things I might have bought with the rest of the Money, & laught at me so much for my Folly that I cry'd with Vexation; and the Reflection gave me more Chagrin than the Whistle gave me Pleasure.

This however was afterwards of use to me, the Impression continuing on my Mind; so that often when I was tempted to buy some unnecessary thing, I said to my self, *Do not give too much for the Whistle*; and I sav'd my Money.

As I grew up, came into the World, and observed the Actions of Men, I thought I met many *who gave too much for the Whistle*.—When I saw one ambitious of Court Favour, sacrificing his Time in Attendance at Levees, his Repose, his Liberty, his Virtue and perhaps his Friend, to obtain it; I have said to my self, *This Man gives too much for his Whistle*.—When I saw another fond of Popularity, constantly employing himself in political Bustles, neglecting his own Affairs, and ruining them by that Neglect, *He pays*, says I, *too much for his Whistle*.—If I knew a Miser, who gave up every kind of comfortable Living, all the Pleasure of doing Good to others, all the Esteem of his Fellow Citizens, & the Joys of benevolent Friendship, for the sake of Accumulating Wealth, *Poor Man*, says I, *you pay too much for your Whistle*.—When I met with a Man of Pleasure, sacrificing every laudable Improvement of his Mind or of his Fortune, to mere corporeal Satisfactions, & ruining his Health in their Pursuit, *Mistaken Man*, says I, *you are providing Pain for your self instead of Pleasure, you pay too much for your Whistle*.—If I see one fond of Appearance, of fine Cloaths, fine Houses, fine Furniture, fine Equipages, all above his Fortune, for which he contracts Debts, and ends his Career in a Prison; *Alas*, says I, *he has paid too much for his Whistle*.—When I saw a beautiful sweet-temper'd Girl, marry'd to an ill-natured Brute of a Husband; *What a Pity*, says I, *that she should pay so much for a Whistle!*—In short, I conceiv'd that great Part of the Miseries of Mankind, were brought upon them by the false Estimates they had made of the Value of Things, and by their *giving too much for the Whistle*.

Yet I ought to have Charity for these unhappy People, when I consider that with all this Wisdom of which I am boasting, there are certain things in the World so tempting; for Example the Apples of King John, which happily are not to be bought, for if they were put to sale by Auction, I might very easily be led to ruin my self in the Purchase, and find that I had once more *given too much for the Whistle*.

Adieu, my dearest Friend, and believe me ever yours very sincerely and with unalterable Affection.

Letter to George Washington, 5 March 1780

In general, Franklin wrote letters primarily in response to letters he received. This letter's pretext is that it responds to a routine letter of recommendation General George Washington wrote to Franklin for the Marquis de Lafayette when the young French commander returned to France from service in America. In fact the letter is clearly an occasion for Franklin to commend Washington for his successes as commander-in-chief and to reflect on the promising future for the new nation the two of them had collaborated in founding. The concluding image of America as a field of corn after a thunderstorm has long been admired for its eloquence.

SIR,   Passy, March 5 1780.

I have received but lately the Letter your Excellency did me the honour of writing to me in Recommendation of the Marquis de la Fayette. His modesty detained it long in his own Hands. We became acquainted, however, from the time of his Arrival at Paris; and his Zeal for the Honour of our Country, his Activity in our Affairs here, and his firm Attachment to our Cause and to you, impress'd me with the same Regard and Esteem for him that your Excellency's Letter would have done, had it been immediately delivered to me.

Should peace arrive after another Campaign or two, and afford us a little Leisure, I should be happy to see your Excellency in Europe, and to accompany you, if my Age and Strength would permit, in visiting some of its ancient and most famous Kingdoms. You would, on this side of the Sea, enjoy the great Reputation you have acquir'd, pure and free from those little Shades that the Jealousy and Envy of a Man's Countrymen and Cotemporaries are ever endeavouring to cast over living Merit. Here you would know, and enjoy, what Posterity will say of Washington. For 1000 Leagues have nearly the same Effect with 1000 Years. The feeble Voice of those grovelling Passions cannot extend so far either in Time or Distance. At present I enjoy that Pleasure for you, as I frequently hear the old Generals of this martial Country, (who study the Maps of America, and mark upon them all your Operations,) speak with sincere Approbation and great Applause of your conduct; and join in giving you the Character of one of the greatest Captains of the Age.

I must soon quit the Scene, but you may live to see our Country flourish, as it will amazingly and rapidly after the War is over. Like a Field of young Indian Corn, which long Fair weather and Sunshine had enfeebled and discolored, and which in that weak State, by a Thunder Gust, of violent Wind, Hail, and Rain, seem'd to be threaten'd with absolute Destruction; yet the Storm being past, it recovers fresh Verdure, shoots up with double Vigour, and delights the Eye, not of its Owner only, but of every observing Traveller.

The best Wishes that can be form'd for your Health, Honour, and Happiness, ever attend you from your Excellency's most obedient and most humble servant

Letter to Joseph Priestley,
7 June 1782

Joseph Priestley, the recipient of this letter, was an English radical clergyman and one of the most distinguished scientists of his time, the first person to separate oxygen from water. Franklin had come to know him well during his long stay in England, even spending his last day in England with Priestley reading American newspaper reactions to the Boston Port Bill, the most recent repressive act of the North ministry (Zall, *Ben Franklin Laughing*, 1980, 90–1). During his years in France he maintained a correspondence with Priestley in which Franklin expressed to his younger and more hopeful associate a fairly grim view of the human condition. Priestley was a genuine eighteenth-century optimist, so it is significant to note that Franklin is in part baiting him by his suggestion that human beings are badly constructed and might appropriately be substituted for the mice Priestley had used in his laboratory experiments. But in fact Franklin clearly likes Priestley and after describing the imaginary visit of the two angels to one of the sea battles in the continuing war between France and England, he laments the loss of his contact with his scientific friends in England. The letter is also of interest in relation to the history of science, because in the last paragraph Franklin refers to the interest in recent chemical research of Antoine Lavoisier, the man who would advance beyond Priestley in the understanding of oxygen as a component of air.

DEAR SIR,   Passy near Paris, June 7, 1782.

I received your kind Letter of the 7th of April, also one of the 3d of May. I have always great Pleasure in hearing from you, in learning that you are well, and that you continue your Experiments. I should rejoice much, if I could once more recover the Leisure to search with you into the Works of Nature; I mean the *inanimate*, not the *animate* or moral part of them, the more I discover'd of the former, the more I admir'd them; the more I know of the latter, the more I am disgusted with them. Men I find to be a Sort of Beings very badly constructed, as they are generally more easily provok'd than reconcil'd, more disposed to do Mischief to each other than to make Reparation, much more easily deceiv'd than undeceiv'd, and having more Pride and even Pleasure in killing than in begetting one another; for without a Blush they assemble in great armies at NoonDay to destroy, and when they have kill'd as many as they can, they exaggerate the Number to augment the fancied Glory; but they creep into Corners, or cover themselves with the Darkness of night, when they mean to beget, as being asham'd of a virtuous Action. A virtuous Action it would be, and a vicious one the killing of them, if the Species were really worth producing or preserving; but of this I begin to doubt.

I know you have no such Doubts, because, in your zeal for their welfare, you are taking a great deal of pains to save their Souls. Perhaps as you grow older, you may look upon this as a hopeless Project, or an idle Amusement, repent of having murdered in mephitic air so many honest, harmless mice, and wish that to prevent mischief, you had used Boys and Girls instead of them. In what Light we are viewed by superior Beings, may be gathered from a Piece of late West India News, which possibly has not yet reached you. A young Angel of Distinction being sent down to this world on some Business, for the first time, had an old courier-spirit assigned him as a Guide. They arriv'd over the Seas of Martinico, in the middle of the long Day of obstinate Fight between the Fleets of Rodney and De Grasse. When, thro' the Clouds of smoke, he saw the Fire of the Guns, the Decks covered with mangled Limbs, and Bodies dead or dying; the ships sinking, burning, or blown into the Air; and the Quantity of Pain, Misery, and Destruction, the Crews yet alive were thus with so much Eagerness dealing round to one another; he turn'd angrily to his Guide, and said, "You blundering Blockhead, you are ignorant of your Business; you undertook to conduct me to the Earth, and you have brought me into Hell!" "No, Sir," says the Guide,

"I have made no mistake; this is really the Earth, and these are men. Devils never treat one another in this cruel manner; they have more Sense, and more of what Men (vainly) call *Humanity*."

But to be serious, my dear old Friend, I love you as much as ever, and I love all the honest Souls that meet at the London Coffee-House. I only wonder how it happen'd, that they and my other Friends in England came to be such good Creatures in the midst of so perverse a Generation. I long to see them and you once more, and I labour for Peace with more Earnestness, that I may again be happy in your sweet society.

I show'd your letter to the Duke de Larochefoucault, who thinks with me, the new Experiments you have made are extremely curious; and he has given me thereupon a Note, which I inclose, and I request you would furnish me with the answer desired.

Yesterday the Count du Nord was at the Academy of Sciences, when sundry Experiments were exhibited for his Entertainment; among them, one by M. Lavoisier, to show that the strongest Fire we yet know, is made in a Charcoal blown upon with dephlogisticated air. In a Heat so produced, he melted Platina presently, the Fire being much more powerful than that of the strongest burning mirror. Adieu, and believe me ever, yours most affectionately,

Remarks Concerning the Savages of North-America

During Franklin's long stay in France, he was accepted as an authority on wild America even though his own first-hand experience of native Americans or the natural American habitat was rather limited by contemporary American standards. Still, like nearly every other American of his time, he had had personal contacts with American Indians, some of which are reported in the *Autobiography. Remarks Concerning the Savages of North-America* was written in Paris in 1783. Like many other Franklin writings, it occupies a shifting ground between conflicting modes of writing. It purports to be an accurate and neutral characterization of Indian culture. But one does not read far before encountering some of Franklin's and the Enlightenment's favourite ideas. Franklin's Indians are employed as Montesquieu's Persians were in *The Persian Letters*, as a satiric contrast to white Western Christians.

Franklin's introduction suggests that he will consider whether the so-called savages of North America are savage at all, but before long they are seen to meet very neatly a white male standard of civilization. In fact, so admirable by that standard are the Indians that it is the society of white Christians that the essay truly focuses on. Indian society is so perfect that 'all their Government is by the Counsel or Advice of the Sages; there is no Force, there are no Prisons, no Officers to compel Obedience, or inflict Punishment. . . . The Indian Women till the Ground, dress the Food, nurse and bring up the Children, and preserve and hand down to Posterity the Memory of Public Transactions. These Employments of Men and Women are accounted natural and honorable.' Farming, food preparation, child care, and historical record-keeping are the natural and honourable activities of women. To men fall hunting, war, oratory, and diplomacy.

It is the diplomatic capacities of the Indians which receive the most attention in this little essay. The Indians observe perfect decorum in their public proceedings, never speaking out of turn. Franklin himself had experienced the bad effects of disregard of orderly proceedings while in London before the war. In fact a major part of his grievance about the 1774 Privy Council hearing in which he was baited by Alexander Wedderburn came from the denial there of the respect he was entitled to as 'a public Messenger, whose Character in all Nations, savage as well as civilized, used to be deemed sacred, and his Person under public Protection' (*Papers*, xxi. 112–13).

On three occasions in the essay the Indians reverse white Christian expectations. Offered the opportunity to send their youths to William and Mary College, they respond by offering to educate young Virginia gentlemen in Indian skills 'and make *Men* of them'; after hearing from a missionary about the fall of man in Genesis, they reply with a creation myth of their own accounting for the beginnings of agriculture. When the missionary reacts angrily to their story, they appeal to 'the Rules of common Civility'; a Mohawk who had travelled to Albany to trade beaver skins for goods finds that after the traders have attended church services they lower the price of beaver. 'You see they have not yet learnt those little *good things*, that we need no Meetings to be instructed in, because our Mothers taught them to us when we were Children. And therefore it is impossible their Meetings should be as they say for any such purpose, or have any such Effect; they are only to contrive *the Cheating of Indians in the Price of Beaver.*'

Savages we call them, because their manners differ from ours, which we think the Perfection of Civility; they think the same of theirs.

Perhaps if we could examine the manners of different Nations with Impartiality, we should find no People so rude as to be without any Rules of Politeness; nor any so polite as not to have some remains of Rudeness.

The Indian Men, when young, are Hunters and Warriors; when old, Counsellors; for all their Government is by the Counsel or Advice of the Sages; there is no Force, there are no Prisons, no Officers to compel Obedience, or inflict Punishment. Hence they generally study Oratory; the best Speaker having the most Influence. The Indian Women till the Ground, dress the Food, nurse and bring up the Children, and preserve and hand down to Posterity the Memory of Public Transactions. These Employments of Men and

Women are accounted natural and honorable. Having few Artificial Wants, they have abundance of Leisure for Improvement by Conversation. Our laborious manner of Life compared with theirs, they esteem slavish and base; and the Learning on which we value ourselves; they regard as frivolous and useless. An Instance of this occurred at the Treaty of Lancaster in Pennsylvania, Anno 1744, between the Government of Virginia & the Six Nations. After the principal Business was settled, the Commissioners from Virginia acquainted the Indians by a Speech, that there was at Williamsburg a College with a Fund for Educating Indian Youth, and that if the Chiefs of the Six-Nations would send down half a dozen of their Sons to that College, the Government would take Care that they should be well provided for, and instructed in all the Learning of the white People. It is one of the Indian Rules of Politeness not to answer a public Proposition the same day that it is made; they think it would be treating it as a light Matter; and that they show it Respect by taking time to consider it, as of a Matter important. They therefore deferred their Answer till the day following; when their Speaker began by expressing their deep Sense of the Kindness of the Virginia Government, in making them that Offer; for we know, says he, that you highly esteem the kind of Learning taught in those Colleges, and that the Maintenance of our Young Men while with you, would be very expensive to you. We are convinced therefore that you mean to do us good by your Proposal, and we thank you heartily. But you who are wise must know, that different Nations have different Conceptions of things; and you will therefore not take it amiss, if our Ideas of this Kind of Education happen not to be the same with yours. We have had some Experience of it: Several of our Young People were formerly brought up at the Colleges of the Northern Provinces; they were instructed in all your Sciences; but when they came back to us, they were bad Runners, ignorant of every means of living in the Woods, unable to bear either Cold or Hunger, knew neither how to build a Cabin, take a Deer, or kill an Enemy, spoke our Language

imperfectly; were therefore neither fit for Hunters, Warriors, or Counsellors; they were totally good for nothing.
We are however not the less obliged by your kind Offer,
tho' we decline accepting it; and to show our grateful Sense
of it, if the Gentlemen of Virginia will send us a dozen of
their Sons, we will take great Care of their Education,
instruct them in all we know, and make *Men* of them.

Having frequent Occasions to hold public Councils, they
have acquired great Order and Decency in conducting them.
The old Men sit in the foremost Ranks, the Warriors in the
next, and the Women and Children in the hindmost. The
Business of the Women is to take exact notice of what
passes, imprint it in their Memories, for they have no
Writing, and communicate it to their Children. They are
the Records of the Council, and they preserve Tradition of
the Stipulations in Treaties a hundred Years back, which
when we compare with our Writings we always find exact.
He that would speak, rises. The rest observe a profound
Silence. When he has finished and sits down, they leave
him five or six Minutes to recollect, that if he has omitted
any thing he intended to say, or has any thing to add, he
may rise again and deliver it. To interrupt another, even in
common Conversation, is reckoned highly indecent. How
different this is from the Conduct of a polite British House
of Commons, where scarce a Day passes without some
Confusion that makes the Speaker hoarse in calling *to order*;
and how different from the mode of Conversation in many
polite Companies of Europe, where if you do not deliver
your Sentence with great Rapidity, you are cut off in the
middle of it by the impatient Loquacity of those you
converse with, & never suffer'd to finish it.

The Politeness of these Savages in Conversation is indeed
carried to excess, since it does not permit them to contra-
dict, or deny the Truth of what is asserted in their Presence.
By this means they indeed avoid Disputes, but then it
becomes difficult to know their Minds, or what Impression
you make upon them. The Missionaries who have attempted
to convert them to Christianity, all complain of this as one

of the great Difficulties of their Mission. The Indians hear with Patience the Truths of the Gospel explained to them, and give their usual Tokens of Assent and Approbation: you would think they were convinced. No such Matter. It is mere Civility.

A Suedish Minister having assembled the Chiefs of the Sasquehanah Indians, made a Sermon to them, acquainting them with the principal historical Facts on which our Religion is founded, such as the Fall of our first Parents by Eating an Apple, the Coming of Christ to repair the Mischief, his Miracles and Suffering, &c. When he had finished, an Indian Orator stood up to thank him. What you have told us, says he, is all very good. It is indeed bad to eat Apples. It is better to make them all into Cyder. We are much obliged by your Kindness in coming so far to tell us those things which you have heard from your Mothers. In Return I will tell you some of those we have heard from ours.

In the Beginning our Fathers had only the Flesh of Animals to subsist on, and if their Hunting was unsuccessful, they were starving. Two of our young Hunters having killed a Deer, made a Fire in the Woods to broil some Parts of it. When they were about to satisfy their Hunger, they beheld a beautiful young Woman descend from the Clouds, and seat herself on that Hill which you see yonder among the blue Mountains. They said to each other, it is a Spirit that perhaps has smelt our broiling Venison, & wishes to eat of it: let us offer some to her. They presented her with the Tongue: She was pleased with the Taste of it, & said, your Kindness shall be rewarded. Come to this Place after thirteen Moons, and you shall find something that will be of great Benefit in nourishing you and your Children to the latest Generations. They did so, and to their Surprise found Plants they had never seen before, but which from that ancient time have been constantly cultivated among us to our great Advantage. Where her right Hand had touch'd the Ground, they found Maize; where her left Hand had touch'd it, they found Kidney-beans; and where her Back-

side had sat on it, they found Tobacco. The good Missionary, disgusted with this idle Tale, said, what I delivered to
you were sacred Truths; but what you tell me is mere Fable,
Fiction & Falsehood. The Indian offended, reply'd, my
Brother, it seems your Friends have not done you Justice
in your Education; they have not well instructed you in the
Rules of common Civility. You saw that we who understand
and practise those Rules, believed all your Stories; why do
you refuse to believe ours?

When any of them come into our Towns, our People are
apt to croud round them, gaze upon them, and incommode
them where they desire to be private; this they esteem great
Rudeness, and the Effect of want of Instruction in the Rules
of Civility and good Manners. We have, say they, as much
Curiosity as you, and when you come into our Towns we
wish for Opportunities of looking at you; but for this
purpose we hide ourselves behind Bushes where you are to
pass, and never intrude ourselves into your Company.

Their Manner of entring one anothers Villages has like-
wise its Rules. It is reckon'd uncivil in travelling Strangers
to enter a Village abruptly, without giving Notice of their
Approach. Therefore as soon as they arrive within hearing,
they stop and hollow, remaining there till invited to enter.
Two old Men usually come out to them, and lead them in.
There is in every Village a vacant Dwelling, called the
Strangers House. Here they are placed, while the old Men
go round from Hut to Hut acquainting the Inhabitants that
Strangers are arrived, who are probably hungry and weary;
and every one sends them what he can spare of Victuals
and Skins to repose on. When the Strangers are refresh'd,
Pipes & Tobacco are brought; and then, but not before,
Conversation begins, with Enquiries who they are, whither
bound, what News, &c. and it usually ends with Offers of
Service, if the Strangers have Occasion of Guides or any
Necessaries for continuing their Journey; and nothing is
exacted for the Entertainment.

The same Hospitality, esteemed among them as a principal Virtue, is practised by private Persons; of which *Conrad*

Weiser, our Interpreter, gave me the following Instance. He had been naturaliz'd among the Six-Nations, and spoke well the Mohock Language. In going thro' the Indian Country, to carry a Message from our Governor to the Council at *Onondaga*, he called at the Habitation of *Canassetego*, an old Acquaintance, who embraced him, spread Furs for him to sit on, placed before him some boiled Beans and Venison, and mixed some Rum and Water for his Drink. When he was well refresh'd, and had lit his Pipe, Canassetego began to converse with him, ask'd how he had fared the many Years since they had seen each other, whence he then came, what occasioned the Journey, &c. &c. Conrad answered all his Questions; and when the Discourse began to flag, the Indian, to continue it, said, Conrad, you have liv'd long among the white People, and know something of their Customs; I have been sometimes at Albany, and have observed that once in seven Days, they shut up their Shops and assemble all in the great House; tell me, what it is for? what do they do there? They meet there, says Conrad, to hear & learn *good things*. I do not doubt, says the Indian, that they tell you so; they have told me the same; but I doubt the Truth of what they say, & I will tell you my Reasons. I went lately to Albany to sell my Skins, & buy Blankets, Knives, Powder, Rum, &c. You know I used generally to deal with Hans Hanson; but I was a little inclined this time to try some other Merchants. However I called first upon Hans, and ask'd him what he would give for Beaver; He said he could not give more than four Shillings a Pound; but, says he, I cannot talk on Business now; this is the Day when we meet together to learn *good things*, and I am going to the Meeting. So I thought to myself since I cannot do any Business to day, I may as well go to the Meeting too; and I went with him. There stood up a Man in black, and began to talk to the People very angrily. I did not understand what he said; but perceiving that he looked much at me, & at Hanson, I imagined he was angry at seeing me there; so I went out, sat down near the House, struck Fire & lit my Pipe; waiting till the

Meeting should break up. I thought too, that the Man had mentioned something of Beaver, and I suspected it might be the Subject of their Meeting. So when they came out I accosted any Merchant; well Hans, says I, I hope you have agreed to give more than four Shillings a Pound. No, says he, I cannot give so much. I cannot give more than three Shillings and six Pence. I then spoke to several other Dealers, but they all sung the same Song, three & six Pence, three & six Pence. This made it clear to me that my Suspicion was right; and that whatever they pretended of Meeting to learn *good things*, the real Purpose was to consult, how to cheat Indians in the Price of Beaver. Consider but a little, Conrad, and you must be of my Opinion. If they met so often to learn *good things*, they would certainly have learnt some before this time. But they are still ignorant. You know our Practice. If a white Man in travelling thro' our Country, enters one of our Cabins, we all treat him as I treat you; we dry him if he is wet, we warm him if he is cold, and give him Meat & Drink that he may allay his Thirst and Hunger, & we spread soft Furs for him to rest & sleep on: We demand nothing in return[†]. But if I go into a white Man's House at Albany, and ask for Victuals & Drink, they say, where is your Money? and if I have none, they say, get out, you Indian Dog. You see they have not yet learnt those little *good things*, that we need no Meetings to be instructed in, because our Mothers taught them to us when we were Children. And therefore it is impossible their Meetings should be as they say for any such purpose, or have any such Effect; they are only to contrive *the Cheating of Indians in the Price of Beaver.*

[†] *It is remarkable that in all Ages and Countries, Hospitality has been allowed as the Virtue of those, whom the civiliz'd were pleased to call Barbarians; the Greeks celebrated the Scythians for it. The Saracens possess'd it eminently; and it is to this day the reigning Virtue of the wild Arabs. S. Paul too, in the Relation of his Voyage & Shipwreck, on the Island of Melita, says,* The Barbarous People shew'd us no little Kindness; for they kindled a Fire, and received us every one, because of the present Rain & because of the Cold.

Information to Those Who Would Remove to America

In the months following the successful peace treaty Franklin assisted in negotiating to end the war, he received numerous requests for letters of recommendation from people who looked forward to emigrating to the United States. In some cases he wrote back recommending that his correspondents read Hector St John de Crevecoeur's *Letters from an American Farmer*, probably anticipating that Crevecoeur's depiction of a predominantly rustic America would prove less inviting to people whose talents required an urban scene. In many cases he complied by supplying rather vaguely worded letters. His ultimate response to these correspondents, though, is this essay (written at Passy in February 1784), which describes an America not indifferent to the talents of European artists or writers but simply unable to support those talents.

In fact Franklin writes here in praise of a favourite American mystique, the all-inclusive middle class: 'The Truth is, that tho' there are in that Country few People so miserable as the Poor of Europe, there are also very few that in Europe would be called rich: it is rather a general happy Mediocrity that prevails.' The term 'mediocrity' carried for Franklin's age no negative connotations.

In fact, although the supposed audience for the essay is prospective European emigrants to America, the essay is really part of a concerted attempt by Franklin to define the American character as it was taking shape in the first years of independence. He includes a reference from the constitution of Pennsylvania which he had helped to draft which dictated that there should be no offices of profit under the new state government. (A few years later, at the Constitutional Convention of 1787, Franklin even proposed that officials of the new national government serve without pay.) Having turned himself into a sort of gentleman in American terms, Franklin was trying to institute an ethic of *noblesse oblige*.

Americans, he writes, have little regard for hereditary honours and do not ask 'concerning a Stranger, *What IS he?* but *What can he DO?*' Americans are always busy, writes Franklin—specifying also that he means white Americans. Interestingly enough, one of the criticisms raised against Franklin in his later years was that he appeared to be indolent. The volume of writing he produced into old age is part of the answer to that, and the older Franklin found ways of being productive while appearing to be having a good time.

Many Persons in Europe having directly or by Letters, express'd to the Writer of this, who is well acquainted with North-America, their Desire of transporting and establishing themselves in that Country; but who appear to him to have formed thro' Ignorance, mistaken Ideas & Expectations of what is to be obtained there; he thinks it may be useful, and prevent inconvenient, expensive & fruitless Removals and Voyages of improper Persons, if he gives some clearer & truer Notions of that Part of the World than appear to have hitherto prevailed.

He finds it is imagined by Numbers that the Inhabitants of North-America are rich, capable of rewarding, and dispos'd to reward all sorts of Ingenuity; that they are at the same time ignorant of all the Sciences; & consequently that strangers possessing Talents in the Belles-Letters, fine Arts, &c. must be highly esteemed, and so well paid as to become easily rich themselves; that there are also abundance of profitable Offices to be disposed of, which the Natives are not qualified to fill; and that having few Persons of Family among them, Strangers of Birth must be greatly respected, and of course easily obtain the best of those Offices, which will make all their Fortunes: that the Governments too, to encourage Emigrations from Europe, not only pay the expence of personal Transportation, but give Lands gratis to Strangers, with Negroes to work for them, Utensils of Husbandry, & Stocks of Cattle. These are all wild Imaginations; and those who go to America with Expectations founded upon them, will surely find themselves disappointed.

The Truth is, that tho' there are in that Country few People so miserable as the Poor of Europe, there are also very few that in Europe would be called rich: it is rather a general happy Mediocrity that prevails. There are few great Proprietors of the Soil, and few Tenants; most People cultivate their own Lands, or follow some Handicraft or Merchandise; very few rich enough to live idly upon their Rents or Incomes; or to pay the high Prices given in Europe, for Paintings, Statues, Architecture and the other Works of Art that are more curious than useful. Hence the natural Geniuses that have arisen in America, with such Talents, have uniformly quitted that Country for Europe, where they can be more suitably rewarded. It is true that Letters and mathematical Knowledge are in Esteem there, but they are at the same time more common than is apprehended; there being already existing nine Colleges or Universities, viz. four in New-England, and one in each of the Provinces of New-York, New-Jersey, Pensilvania, Maryland and Virginia, all furnish'd with learned Professors; besides a number of smaller Academies: These educate many of their Youth in the Languages and those Sciences that qualify Men for the Professions of Divinity, Law or Physick. Strangers indeed are by no means excluded from exercising those Professions, and the quick Increase of Inhabitants every where gives them a Chance of Employ, which they have in common with the Natives. Of civil Offices or Employment. there are few; no superfluous Ones as in Europe; and it is a Rule establish'd in some of the States, that no Office should be so profitable as to make it desirable. The 36 Article of the Constitution of Pensilvania, runs expresly in these Words: *As every Freeman, to preserve his Independance, (if he has not a sufficient Estate) ought to have some Profession, Calling, Trade or Farm, whereby he may honestly subsist, there can be no Necessity for, nor Use in, establishing Offices of Profit; the usual Effect of which are Dependance and Servility, unbecoming Freemen, in the Possessors and Expectants; Faction, Contention, Corruption, and Disorder among the People. Wherefore whenever an Office, thro' Increase of Fees or otherwise, becomes so profitable as to occasion many to apply for it, the Profits ought to be lessened by the Legislature.*

These Ideas prevailing more or less in all the United States, it cannot be worth any Man's while, who has a means of Living at home, to expatriate himself in hopes of obtaining a profitable civil Office in America; and as to military Offices, they are at an End with the War; the Armies being disbanded. Much less is it adviseable for a Person to go thither who has no other Quality to recommend him but his Birth. In Europe it has indeed its Value, but it is a Commodity that cannot be carried to a worse Market than to that of America, where People do not enquire concerning a Stranger, *What* IS he? but *What can he* DO? If he has any useful Art, he is welcome; and if he exercises it and behaves well, he will be respected by all that know him; but a mere Man of Quality, who on that Account wants to live upon the Public, by some Office or Salary, will be despis'd and disregarded. The Husbandman is in honor there, & even the Mechanic, because their Employments are useful. The People have a Saying, that God Almighty is himself a Mechanic, the greatest in the Universe; and he is respected and admired more for the Variety, Ingenuity and Utility of his Handiworks, than for the Antiquity of his Family. They are pleas'd with the Observation of a Negro, and frequently mention it, that *Boccarorra* (meaning the Whiteman) make de Blackman workee, make de Horse workee, make de Ox workee, make ebery ting workee; only de Hog. He de Hog, no workee; he eat, he drink, he walk about, he go to sleep when he please, *he libb like a Gentleman.* According to these Opinions of the Americans, one of them would think himself more oblig'd to a Genealogist, who could prove for him that his Ancestors & Relations for ten Generations had been Ploughmen, Smiths, Carpenters, Turners, Weavers, Tanners, or even Shoemakers, & consequently that they were useful Members of Society; than if he could only prove that they were Gentlemen, doing nothing of Value, but living idly on the Labour of others, mere *fruges consumere nati*[†],

---

[†]   There are a Number of us born
       Merely to eat up the Corn.   WATTS.

and otherwise *good* for *nothing*, till by their Death, their Estates like the Carcase of the Negro's Gentleman-Hog, come to be *cut up*.

With Regard to Encouragements for Strangers from Government, they are really only what are derived from good Laws & Liberty. Strangers are welcome because there is room enough for them all, and therefore the old Inhabitants are not jealous of them; the Laws protect them sufficiently, so that they have no need of the Patronage of great Men; and every one will enjoy securely the Profits of his Industry. But if he does not bring a Fortune with him, he must work and be industrious to live. One or two Years Residence give him all the Rights of a Citizen; but the Government does not at present, whatever it may have done in former times, hire People to become Settlers, by Paying their Passages, giving Land, Negroes, Utensils, Stock, or any other kind of Emolument whatsoever. In short America is the Land of Labour, and by no means what the English call *Lubberland*, and the French *Pays de Cocagne*, where the Streets are said to be pav'd with half-peck Loaves, the Houses til'd with Pancakes, and where the Fowls fly about ready roasted, crying, *Come eat me!*

Who then are the kind of Persons to whom an Emigration to America may be advantageous? and what are the Advantages they may reasonably expect?

Land being cheap in that Country, from the vast Forests still void of Inhabitants, and not likely to be occupied in an Age to come, insomuch that the Propriety of an hundred Acres of fertile Soil full of Wood may be obtained near the Frontiers in many Places for eight or ten Guineas, hearty young Labouring Men, who understand the Husbandry of Corn and Cattle, which is nearly the same in that Country as in Europe, may easily establish themselves there. A little Money sav'd of the good Wages they receive there while they work for others, enables them to buy the Land and begin their Plantation, in which they are assisted by the Good Will of their Neighbours and some Credit. Multitudes of poor People from England, Ireland, Scotland and Germany, have by this means in a few Years become wealthy Farmers, who in their own Countries, where all the Lands are fully occupied, and the Wages of Labour low, could never have emerged from the mean Condition wherein they were born.

From the Salubrity of the Air, the Healthiness of the Climate, the Plenty of good Provisions, and the Encouragement to early Marriages, by the certainty of Subsistance in cultivating the Earth, the Increase of Inhabitants by natural Generation is very rapid in America, and becomes still more so by the Accession of Strangers; hence there is a continual Demand for more Artisans of all the necessary and useful kinds, to supply those Cultivators of the Earth with Houses, and with Furniture & Utensils of the grosser Sorts which cannot so well be brought from Europe. Tolerably good Workmen in any of those mechanic Arts, are sure to find Employ, and to be well paid for their Work, there being no Restraints preventing Strangers from exercising any Art they understand, nor any Permission necessary. If they are poor, they begin first as Servants or Journeymen; and if they are sober, industrious & frugal, they soon become Masters, establish themselves in Business, marry, raise Families, and become respectable Citizens.

Also, Persons of moderate Fortunes and Capitals, who having a Number of Children to provide for, are desirous of bringing them up to Industry, and to secure Estates for their Posterity, have Opportunities of doing it in America, which Europe does not afford. There they may be taught & practice profitable mechanic Arts, without incurring Disgrace on that Account; but on the contrary acquiring Respect by such Abilities. There small Capitals laid out in Lands, which daily become more valuable by the Increase of People, afford a solid Prospect of ample Fortunes thereafter for those Children. The Writer of this has known several Instances of large Tracts of Land, bought on what was then the Frontier of Pensilvania, for ten Pounds per hundred Acres, which, after twenty Years, when the Settlements had been extended far beyond them, sold readily, without any Improvement made upon them, for three Pounds per Acre. The Acre in America is the same with the English Acre or the Acre of Normandy.

Those who desire to understand the State of Government in America, would do well to read the Constitutions of the several States, and the Articles of Confederation that bind the whole together for general Purposes under the Direction of one Assembly called the Congress. These Constitutions have been printed by Order of Congress in America; two Editions of them have also been printed in London, and a good Translation of them into French has lately been published at Paris.

Several of the Princes of Europe having of late Years, from an Opinion of Advantage to arise by producing all Commodities & Manufactures within their own Dominions, so as to diminish or render useless their Importations, have endeavoured to entice Workmen from other Countries, by high Salaries, Privileges, &c. Many Persons pretending to be skilled in various great Manufactures, imagining that America must be in Want of them, and that the Congress would probably be dispos'd to imitate the Princes above mentioned, have proposed to go over, on Condition of having their Passages paid, Lands given, Salaries appointed, exclusive Privileges for Terms of Years, &c. Such Persons on reading the Articles of Confederation will find that the Congress have no Power committed to them, or Money put into their Hands, for such purposes; and that if any such Encouragement is given, it must be by the Government of some separate State. This however has rarely been done in America; and when it has been done it has rarely succeeded, so as to establish a Manufacture which the Country was not yet so ripe for as to encourage private Persons to set it up; Labour being generally too dear there, & Hands difficult to be kept together, every one desiring to be a Master, and the Cheapness of Land enclining many to leave Trades for Agriculture. Some indeed have met with Success, and are carried on to Advantage; but they are generally such as require only a few Hands, or wherein great Part of the Work is perform'd by Machines. Goods that are bulky, & of so small Value as not well to bear the Expence of Freight, may often be made cheaper in the Country than they can be imported; and the Manufacture of such Goods will be profitable wherever there is a sufficient Demand. The Farmers in America produce indeed a good deal of Wool & Flax; and none is exported, it is all work'd up; but it is in the Way of Domestic Manufacture for the Use of the Family. The buying up Quantities of Wool & Flax with the Design to employ Spinners, Weavers, &c. and form great Establishments, producing Quantities of Linen and Woollen Goods for Sale, has been several times attempted in different Provinces; but those Projects have generally failed, Goods of equal Value being imported cheaper. And when the Governments have been solicited to support such Schemes by Encouragements, in Money, or by imposing Duties on Importation of such Goods, it has been generally refused, on this Principle, that if the Country is ripe for the Manufacture, it may be carried on by private Persons to Advantage; and if not, it is a Folly to think of forceing Nature. Great Establishments of Manufacture, require great Numbers of Poor to do the Work for small Wages; these Poor are to be found in Europe, but will not be found in America, till the Lands are all taken up and cultivated, and the excess of People who cannot get Land, want Employment. The Manufacture of Silk, they say, is natural in France, as that of Cloth in England, because each Country produces in Plenty the first Material: But if England will have a Manufacture of Silk as well as that of Cloth, and France one of Cloth as well as that of Silk, these unnatural Operations must be supported by mutual Prohibitions or high Duties on the Importation of each others Goods, by which means the Workmen are enabled to tax the home-Consumer by greater Prices, while the higher Wages they receive makes them neither happier nor richer, since they only drink more and work less. Therefore the Governments in America do nothing to encourage such Projects. The People by this Means are not impos'd on, either by the Merchant or

Mechanic; if the Merchant demands too much Profit on imported Shoes, they buy of the Shoemaker: and if he asks too high a Price, they take them of the Merchant: thus the two Professions are Checks on each other. The Shoemaker however has on the whole a considerable Profit upon his Labour in America, beyond what he had in Europe, as he can add to his Price a Sum nearly equal to all the Expences of Freight & Commission, Risque or Insurance, &c. necessarily charged by the Merchant. And the Case is the same with the Workmen in every other Mechanic Art. Hence it is that Artisans generally live better and more easily in America than in Europe, and such as are good Œconomists make a comfortable Provision for Age, & for their Children. Such may therefore remove with Advantage to America.

In the old longsettled Countries of Europe, all Arts, Trades, Professions, Farms, &c. are so full that it is difficult for a poor Man who has Children, to place them where they may gain, or learn to gain a decent Livelihood. The Artisans, who fear creating future Rivals in Business, refuse to take Apprentices, but upon Conditions of Money, Maintenance or the like, which the Parents are unable to comply with. Hence the Youth are dragg'd up in Ignorance of every gainful Art, and oblig'd to become Soldiers or Servants or Thieves, for a Subsistance. In America the rapid Increase of Inhabitants takes away that Fear of Rivalship, & Artisans willingly receive Apprentices from the hope of Profit by their Labour during the Remainder of the Time stipulated after they shall be instructed. Hence it is easy for poor Families to get their Children instructed; for the Artisans are so desirous of Apprentices, that many of them will even give Money to the Parents to have Boys from ten to fifteen Years of Age bound Apprentices to them till the Age of twenty one; and many poor Parents have by that means, on their Arrival in the Country, raised Money enough to buy Land sufficient to establish themselves, and to subsist the rest of their Family by Agriculture. These Contracts for Apprentices are made before a Magistrate, who regulates the

Agreement according to Reason and Justice; and having in view the Formation of a future useful Citizen, obliges the Master to engage by a written Indenture, not only that during the time of Service stipulated, the Apprentice shall be duly provided with Meat, Drink, Apparel, washing & Lodging, and at its Expiration with a compleat new suit of Clothes, but also that he shall be taught to read, write & cast Accompts, & that he shall be well instructed in the Art or Profession of his Master, or some other, by which he may afterwards gain a Livelihood, and be able in his turn to raise a Family. A Copy of this Indenture is given to the Apprentice or his Friends, & the Magistrate keeps a Record of it, to which Recourse may be had, in case of Failure by the Master in any Point of Performance. This Desire among the Masters to have more Hands employ'd in working for them, induces them to pay the Passages of young Persons, of both Sexes, who on their Arrival agree to serve them one, two, three or four Years; those who have already learnt a Trade agreeing for a shorter Term in Proportion to their Skill and the consequent immediate Value of their Service; and those who have none, agreeing for a longer Term, in Consideration of being taught an Art their Poverty would not permit them to acquire in their own Country.

The almost general Mediocrity of Fortune that prevails in America, obliging its People to follow some Business for Subsistance, those Vices that arise usually from Idleness are in a great Measure prevented. Industry and constant Employment are great Preservatives of the Morals and Virtue of a Nation. Hence bad Examples to Youth are more rare in America, which must be a comfortable Consideration to Parents. To this may be truly added, that serious Religion under its various Denominations, is not only tolerated but respected and practised. Atheism is unknown there, Infidelity rare & secret, so that Persons may live to a great Age in that Country without having their Piety shock'd by meeting with either an Atheist or an Infidel. And the Divine Being seems to have manifested his Approbation of the mutual Forbearance and Kindness with which the different Sects treat each other, by the remarkable Prosperity with which he has been pleased to favour the whole Country.

Letter to Samuel Mather, 12 May 1784

Franklin had a long history of contact with the Mather family,
going back to his early youth, when his brother James edited the
New-England Courant and used his newspaper to attack Increase
and Cotton Mather, who were the self-conscious defenders of a
somewhat beleaguered Puritan establishment. The principal area
of early controversy centred around Cotton Mather's proposed
introduction of a form of inoculation against smallpox, which the
Courant and its writers ridiculed. Among the participants in the
controversy in the 1720s was Cotton Mather's son Samuel, who
at the time was a Harvard undergraduate. Sixty years later these
quarrels had long since been set aside. Samuel Mather was an
advocate of American independence. Benjamin Franklin came to
be a strong defender of the practice of inoculation, and as this
letter and his *Autobiography* indicate, he himself had been
inspired by ideas he had read in writings of Cotton Mather. In
fact the recollection of Samuel Mather's father in this letter
describes Cotton Mather as dispensing just the sort of practical advice Franklin had been dispensing through a long writing
career.

REV^d SIR,   Passy, May 12, 1784.
I received your kind letter, with your excellent advice to
the people of the United States, which I read with great
pleasure, and hope it will be duly regarded. Such writings,
though they may be lightly passed over by many readers,
yet, if they make a deep impression on one active mind in
a hundred, the effects may be considerable. Permit me to
mention one little instance, which, though it relates to
myself, will not be quite uninteresting to you. When I was
a boy, I met with a book, entitled *"Essays to do Good,"*
which I think was written by your father. It had been so
little regarded by a former possessor, that several leaves of

it were torn out; but the remainder gave me such a turn of thinking, as to have an influence on my conduct through life; for I have always set a greater value on the character of a *doer of good*, than on any other kind of reputation; and if I have been, as you seem to think, a useful citizen, the public owes the advantage of it to that book.

You mention your being in your 78th year; I am in my 79th; we are grown old together. It is now more than 60 years since I left Boston, but I remember well both your father and grandfather, having heard them both in the pulpit, and seen them in their houses. The last time I saw your father was in the beginning of 1724, when I visited him after my first trip to Pennsylvania. He received me in his library, and on my taking leave showed me a shorter way out of the house through a narrow passage, which was crossed by a beam over head. We were still talking as I withdrew, he accompanying me behind, and I turning partly towards him, when he said hastily, "*Stoop, stoop!*" I did not understand him, till I felt my head hit against the beam. He was a man that never missed any occasion of giving instruction, and upon this he said to me, "*You are young, and have the world before you;* STOOP *as you go through it, and you will miss many hard thumps.*" This advice, thus beat into my head, has frequently been of use to me; and I often think of it, when I see pride mortified, and misfortunes brought upon people by their carrying their heads too high.

I long much to see again my native place, and to lay my bones there. I left it in 1723; I visited it in 1733, 1743, 1753, and 1763. In 1773 I was in England; in 1775 I had a sight of it, but could not enter, it being in possession of the enemy. I did hope to have been there in 1783, but could not obtain my dismission from this employment here; and now I fear I shall never have that happiness. My best wishes however attend my dear country. *Esto perpetua.* It is now blest with an excellent constitution; may it last for ever!

This powerful monarchy continues its friendship for the United States. It is a friendship of the utmost importance to our security, and should be carefully cultivated. Britain has not yet well digested the loss of its dominion over us, and has still at times some flattering hopes of recovering it. Accidents may increase those hopes, and encourage dangerous attempts. A breach between us and France would infallibly bring the English again upon our backs; and yet we have some wild heads among our countrymen, who are endeavouring to weaken that connexion! Let us preserve our reputation by performing our engagements; our credit by fulfilling our contracts; and friends by gratitude and kindness; for we know not how soon we may again have occasion for all of them. With great and sincere esteem, I have the honour to be, &c.

Letter to William Franklin,
16 August 1784

In this letter Benjamin Franklin shows, while denying it, the depth
of his anger at his son. During the American Revolution William
Franklin not only stayed on the king's side but led and organized
Loyalist forces. After the war was lost, William Franklin left New
York for London and joined the American Loyalist settlement
there. During the negotiations for a peace treaty with the English,
Benjamin Franklin was the American who took the most intransigent stand against Loyalist claims. In one of the bagatelles he
wrote in Paris he refers to Tories as 'a mongrel race, derived from
a mixture with wolves and foxes, corrupted by royal promises of
great rewards' (*Writings*, 967). During a brief stop in England after
leaving France, Benjamin Franklin visited his son. But the ill
feelings persisted. In his final will, he left to his son the books
and papers of his already in William's possession and some worthless property in Nova Scotia. 'The part he acted against me in the
late war, which is of public notoriety, will account for my leaving
him no more of an estate he endeavoured to deprive me of'
(*Writings*, ed. Smyth, x. 494).

DEAR SON,   Passy, Aug. 16, 1784.
I received your Letter of the 22d past, and am glad to find
that you desire to revive the affectionate Intercourse, that
formerly existed between us. It will be very agreable to me;
indeed nothing has ever hurt me so much and affected me
with such keen Sensations, as to find myself deserted in my
old Age by my only Son; and not only deserted, but to find
him taking up Arms against me, in a Cause, wherein
my good Fame, Fortune and Life were all at Stake. You
conceived, you say, that your Duty to your King and Regard
for your Country requir'd this. I ought not to blame you
for differing in Sentiment with me in Public Affairs. We
are Men, all subject to Errors. Our Opinions are not in our

own Power; they are form'd and govern'd much by Circumstances, that are often as inexplicable as they are irresistible. Your Situation was such that few would have censured your remaining Neuter, *tho' there are Natural Duties which precede political ones, and cannot be extinguish'd by them.*

This is a disagreable Subject. I drop it. And we will endeavour, as you propose mutually to forget what has happened relating to it, as well as we can. I send your Son over to pay his Duty to you. You will find him much improv'd. He is greatly esteem'd and belov'd in this Country, and will make his Way anywhere. It is my Desire, that he should study the Law, as a necessary Part of Knowledge for a public Man, and profitable if he should have occasion to practise it. I would have you therefore put into his hands those Law-books you have, viz. Blackstone, Coke, Bacon, Viner, &c. He will inform you, that he received the Letter sent him by Mr. Galloway, and the Paper it enclosed, safe.

On my leaving America, I deposited with that Friend for you, a Chest of Papers, among which was a Manuscript of nine or ten Volumes, relating to Manufactures, Agriculture, Commerce, Finance, etc., which cost me in England about 70 Guineas; eight Quire Books, containing the Rough Drafts of all my Letters while I liv'd in London. These are missing. I hope you have got them, if not, they are lost. Mr. Vaughan has publish'd in London a Volume of what he calls my Political Works. He proposes a second Edition; but, as the first was very incompleat, and you had many Things that were omitted, (for I used to send you sometimes the Rough Drafts, and sometimes the printed Pieces I wrote in London,) I have directed him to apply to you for what may be in your Power to furnish him with, or to delay his Publication till I can be at home again, if that may ever happen.

I did intend returning this year; but the Congress, instead of giving me Leave to do so, have sent me another Commission, which will keep me here at least a Year longer; and perhaps I may then be too old and feeble to bear the Voyage. I am here among a People that love and respect me, a most amiable Nation to live with; and perhaps I may conclude to die among them; for my Friends in America are dying off, one after another, and I have been so long abroad, that I should now be almost a Stranger in my own Country.

I shall be glad to see you when convenient, but would not have you come here at present. You may confide to your son the Family Affairs you wished to confer upon with me, for he is discreet. And I trust, that you will prudently avoid introducing him to Company, that it may be improper for him to be seen with. I shall hear from you by him and any letters to me afterwards, will come safe under Cover directed to Mr. Ferdinand Grand, Banker at Paris. Wishing you Health, and more Happiness than it seems you have lately experienced, I remain your affectionate father,

The Art of Procuring Pleasant Dreams

Throughout his mature life Franklin found it easy to make friends with intelligent young women, often the daughters of his friends; his correspondence with Catharine Ray Greene, Mary Stevenson Hewson, Georgiana and Catherine Shipley, and Madame Anne-Louise Boivin d'Hardancourt Brillon de Jouy provided Franklin occasions to display a certain avuncular charm all his own. This little essay (1786) addressed to Kitty Shipley, the daughter of his host on the vacation when he began his *Autobiography*, is a bagatelle and thus falls in the same category as writings like 'The Whistle'. Frivolity never prevented Franklin from venturing on to serious subjects, though. The exhortation to exercise and temperance is consistent with the preoccupations of the *Autobiography* or other Franklin writings. The importance of fresh air while sleeping had been a long-standing belief of Franklin's; John Adams's journal describes an occasion during the winter of 1776 when the two of them shared a room in New Jersey and Franklin insisted on keeping the windows open and explained his reasons to Adams, who fell asleep during the explanation (*The Diary and Autobiography of John Adams*, iii. 418). Franklin is particularly emphatic in this essay on the necessity of fresh air while sleeping, even inventing a Biblical precedent for it from the life of Methusaleh. (Miss Shipley wrote back in reply that she had failed to find such a story about Methusaleh in her Bible.) This was not the first time that Franklin had rewritten the Bible to corroborate his own views.

It is also clear that the anxieties or fears that disturb the sleep of many people seem to Franklin avoidable by various simple procedures involving diet and the arrangement of the bed and bedclothes. And for Franklin the ultimate requisite, 'A GOOD CONSCIENCE', also seems well within reach of us all.

As a great part of our life is spent in sleep during which we have sometimes pleasant and sometimes painful dreams, it becomes of some consequence to obtain the one kind and avoid the other; for whether real or imaginary, pain is pain and pleasure is pleasure. If we can sleep without dreaming, it is well that painful dreams are avoided. If while we sleep we can have any pleasing dream, it is, as the French say, *autant de gagné*, so much added to the pleasure of life.

To this end it is, in the first place, necessary to be careful in preserving health, by due exercise and great temperance; for, in sickness, the imagination is disturbed, and disagreeable, sometimes terrible, ideas are apt to present themselves. Exercise should precede meals, not immediately follow them; the first promotes, the latter, unless moderate, obstructs digestion. If, after exercise, we feed sparingly, the digestion will be easy and good, the body lightsome, the temper cheerful, and all the animal functions performed agreeably. Sleep, when it follows, will be natural and undisturbed; while indolence, with full feeding, occasions nightmares and horrors inexpressible; we fall from precipices, are assaulted by wild beasts, murderers, and demons, and experience every variety of distress. Observe, however, that the quantities of food and exercise are relative things; those who move much may, and indeed ought to eat more; those who use little exercise should eat little. In general, mankind, since the improvement of cookery, eat about twice as much as nature requires. Suppers are not bad, if we have not dined; but restless nights naturally follow hearty suppers after full dinners. Indeed, as there is a difference in constitutions, some rest well after these meals; it costs them only a frightful dream and an apoplexy, after which they sleep till doomsday. Nothing is more common in the newspapers, than instances of people who, after eating a hearty supper, are found dead abed in the morning.

Another means of preserving health, to be attended to, is the having a constant supply of fresh air in your bed-chamber. It has been a great mistake, the sleeping in rooms exactly closed, and in beds surrounded by curtains. No outward air that may come in to you is so unwholesome as the unchanged air, often breathed, of a close chamber. As boiling water does not grow hotter by longer boiling, if the particles that receive greater heat can escape; so living bodies do not putrefy, if the particles, so fast as they become putrid, can be thrown off. Nature expels them by the pores of the skin and the lungs, and in a free, open air they are carried off; but in a close room we receive them again and again, though they become more and more corrupt. A number of persons crowded into a small room thus spoil the air in a few minutes, and even render it mortal, as in the Black Hole at Calcutta. A single person is said to spoil only a gallon of air per minute, and therefore requires a longer time to spoil a chamber-full; but it is done, however, in proportion, and many putrid disorders hence have their origin. It is recorded of Methusalem, who, being the longest liver, may be supposed to have best preserved his health, that he slept always in the open air; for, when he had lived five hundred years, an angel said to him; "Arise, Methusalem, and build thee an house, for thou shalt live yet five hundred years longer." But Methusalem answered, and said, "If I am to live but five hundred years longer, it is not worth while to build me an house; I will sleep in the air, as I have been used to do." Physicians, after having for ages contended that the sick should not be indulged with fresh air, have at length discovered that it may do them good. It is therefore to be hoped, that they may in time discover likewise, that it is not hurtful to those who are in health, and that we may be then cured of the *aërophobia*, that at present distresses weak minds, and makes them choose to be stifled and poisoned, rather than leave open the window of a bed-chamber, or put down the glass of a coach.

Confined air, when saturated with perspirable matter, will not receive more; and that matter must remain in our bodies, and occasion diseases; but it gives some previous notice of its being about to be hurtful, by producing certain uneasiness, slight indeed at first, which as with regard to the lungs is a trifling sensation, and to the pores of the skin a kind of restlessness, which is difficult to describe, and few that feel it know the cause of it. But we may recollect, that sometimes on waking in the night, we have, if warmly covered, found it difficult to get asleep again. We turn often without finding repose in any position. This fidgettiness (to use a vulgar expression for want of a better) is occasioned wholly by an uneasiness in the skin, owing to the retention of the perspirable matter—the bed-clothes having received their quantity, and, being saturated, refusing to take any more. To become sensible of this by an experiment, let a person keep his position in the bed, but throw off the bed-clothes, and suffer fresh air to approach the part uncovered of his body; he will then feel that part suddenly refreshed; for the air will immediately relieve the skin, by receiving, licking up, and carrying off, the load of perspirable matter that incommoded it. For every portion of cool air that approaches the warm skin, in receiving its part of that vapour, receives therewith a degree of heat that rarefies and renders it lighter, when it will be pushed away with its burthen, by cooler and therefore heavier fresh air, which for a moment supplies its place, and then, being likewise changed and warmed, gives way to a succeeding quantity. This is the order of nature, to prevent animals being infected by their own perspiration. He will now be sensible of the difference between the part exposed to the air and that which, remaining sunk in the bed, denies the air access: for this part now manifests its uneasiness more distinctly by the comparison, and the seat of the uneasiness is more plainly perceived than when the whole surface of the body was affected by it.

Here, then, is one great and general cause of unpleasing dreams. For when the body is uneasy, the mind will be disturbed by it, and disagreeable ideas of various kinds will in sleep be the natural consequences. The remedies, preventive and curative, follow:

1. By eating moderately (as before advised for health's sake) less perspirable matter is produced in a given time; hence the bed-clothes receive it longer before they are saturated, and we may therefore sleep longer before we are made uneasy by their refusing to receive any more.

2. By using thinner and more porous bed-clothes, which will suffer the perspirable matter more easily to pass through them, we are less incommoded, such being longer tolerable.

3. When you are awakened by this uneasiness, and find you cannot easily sleep again, get out of bed, beat up and turn your pillow, shake the bed-clothes well, with at least twenty shakes, then throw the bed open and leave it to cool; in the meanwhile, continuing undrest, walk about your chamber till your skin has had time to discharge its load, which it will do sooner as the air may be dried and colder. When you begin to feel the cold air unpleasant, then return to your bed, and you will soon fall asleep, and your sleep will be sweet and pleasant. All the scenes presented to your fancy will be too of the pleasing kind. I am often as agreeably entertained with them, as by the scenery of an opera. If you happen to be too indolent to get out of bed, you may, instead of it, lift up your bed-clothes with one arm and leg, so as to draw in a good deal of fresh air, and by letting them fall force it out again. This, repeated twenty times, will so clear them of the perspirable matter they have imbibed, as to permit your sleeping well for some time afterwards. But this latter method is not equal to the former.

Those who do not love trouble, and can afford to have two beds, will find great luxury in rising, when they wake in a hot bed, and going into the cool one. Such shifting of beds would also be of great service to persons ill of a fever, as it refreshes and frequently procures sleep. A very large bed, that will admit a removal so distant from the first situation as to be cool and sweet, may in a degree answer the same end.

One or two observations more will conclude this little piece. Care must be taken, when you lie down, to dispose your pillow so as to suit your manner of placing your head, and to be perfectly easy; then place your limbs so as not to bear inconveniently hard upon one another, as, for instance, the joints of your ankles; for, though a bad position may at first give but little pain and be hardly noticed, yet a continuance will render it less tolerable, and the uneasiness may come on while you are asleep, and disturb your imagination. These are the rules of the art. But, though they will generally prove effectual in producing the end intended, there is a case in which the most punctual observance of them will be totally fruitless. I need not mention the case to you, my dear friend, but my account of the art would be imperfect without it. The case is, when the person who desires to have pleasant dreams has not taken care to preserve, what is necessary above all things,

A GOOD CONSCIENCE.

The Internal State of America

Among Franklin's late writings concerned with forming the character and perceptions of Americans, this essay has special importance, though it has never before been printed in a text edition of Franklin's writings. While in France Franklin had become sensitive to disparaging characterizations of the new republic which insinuated that the United States would soon self-destruct or submit to colonial rule again. On his return to Philadelphia in 1785 he plunged immediately into the political life of his home state and energetically defended the new country in letters to his European acquaintances. In this piece he begins like other New England-born writers with a mythicized account of the psychological state of the first New England settlers and asserts in the words of his hypothetical spokesman, 'a farmer of plain sense', that instead of lamentation over the country's deficiencies, they should instead proclaim a day of thanksgiving.

Instead of disunion, the new states presented a picture of prosperity shared by all. Though he himself had lived his whole life in cities, he depicts America as a place primarily agrarian in nature, and he contrasts rural life in America with the squalor and poverty of the peasants of Europe. When he speaks of 'the happy Mediocrity, that so generally prevails throughout these States', the term mediocrity is not pejorative. Rather it refers honorifically to the middle-class status which he asserts Americans generally enjoy. In fact the promotion of middle-class status had been a preoccupation of Franklin's since his earliest writings (Conner, 33–4). America, in his depiction, is a place where no class fails to prosper: farmers continue to produce high yields at steadily high prices; in cities, land values are rising; American fisheries will be readily able to adjust to the loss of their British markets, possibly by substituting French customers (the French, who tend to stay up late at night, may well provide a demand for spermaceti candles provided by the whaling industry). The only real danger Franklin hints at for America is the possibility of farmers seeking to become merchants or shopkeepers. Franklin had been a spokesman or guide for so-called simple farmers so long that he sounds at times like a more ideologically driven agrarian such as Thomas Jefferson. Of course, latent in this optimistic view of America as a place where everyone should naturally thrive is the vulnerability to economic realities in which there are necessarily both winners and losers.

Franklin also confronts one of the new nation's great concerns, 'that in some of the states there are parties and discords'. After a war which had required an ideology of national unity, the presence of faction in America appeared to many as a threat (Wood, 58–60, 402–3). Franklin's view, however, is that political liberty inevitably fosters the existence of parties, and by the 'collision of different sentiments, sparks of truth are struck out, and political light is obtained'. A related national concern was the growth of luxury; classical republican theory had dictated that luxury and republican virtue were incompatible (Wood, 416–21; Pocock, 430–3). But Franklin dismisses the appearances of luxury as insignificant.

There is a tradition, that in the planting of New-England, the first settlers met with many difficulties and hardships, as is generally the case when a civilized people attempt establishing themselves in a wilderness country. Being piously disposed, they sought relief from heaven, by laying their wants and distresses before the Lord in frequent set days of Fasting and Prayer. Constant meditation and discourse on these subjects kept their minds gloomy and discontented; and, like the children of Israel, there were many disposed to return to that Egypt, which persecution had induced them to abandon. At length, when it was proposed in the Assembly to proclaim another fast, a farmer of plain sense rose, and remarked that the inconveniences they suffered, and concerning which they had so often wearied heaven with their complaints, were not so great as they might have expected, and were diminishing every day as the colony strengthened; that the earth began to reward their labour, and to furnish liberally for their subsistence; that the seas and rivers were found full of fish, the air sweet, the climate healthy; and above all, that they were there in the full enjoyment of liberty, civil and religious: He therefore thought that reflecting and conversing on these subjects would be more comfortable, as tending more to make them contented with their situation; and that it would be more becoming the gratitude they owed to the divine being, if, *instead of a* FAST, *they should proclaim a* THANKSGIVING. His advice was taken, and from that day to this, they have in every year observed circumstances of public felicity sufficient to furnish employment for a THANKSGIVING DAY, which is therefore constantly ordered and religiously observed.

I see in the public news-papers of different states, frequent complaints of *hard times, deadness of trade, scarcity of money, &c. &c.* It is not my intention to assert or maintain that these complaints are entirely without foundation. There can be no country or nation existing, in which there will not be some people so circumstanced as to find it hard to gain a livelihood, people who are not in the way of any profitable trade, and with whom money is scarce because they have nothing to give in exchange for it. And it is always in the power of a small number to make a great clamour. But let us take a cool view of the general state of our affairs, and perhaps the prospect will appear less gloomy than has been imagined.

The great business of the continent is agriculture. For one artizan or merchant, I suppose we have at least 100 farmers, by far the greatest part cultivators of their own fertile lands, from whence many of them draw not only the food necessary for their subsistence, but the materials of their cloathing, so as to need very few foreign supplies; while they have a surplus of productions to dispose of, whereby wealth is gradually accumulated. Such has been the goodness of divine providence to these regions, and so favourable the climate, that since the three or four years of hardship in the first settlement of our fathers here, a famine or scarcity has never been heard of among us; on the contrary, though some years may have been more, and others less plentiful, there has always been provision enough for ourselves, and a quantity to spare for exportation. And although the crops of last year were generally good, never was the farmer better paid for the part he can spare to commerce, as the published price currents abundantly testify. The lands he possesses are also continually rising in value with the increase of population. And on the whole he is enabled to give such good wages to those who work for him, that all who are acquainted with the old world must agree, that in no part of it are the labouring poor so generally well fed, well cloathed, well lodged, and well paid, as in the United States of America.

If we enter the cities, we find that, since the revolution, the owners of houses and lots of ground have had their interest vastly augmented in value; rents have risen to an astonishing height, and thence encouragement to increase building, which gives employment to an abundance of workmen, as does also the increased luxury and splendor of living of the inhabitants thus made richer. These workmen all demand and obtain much higher wages than any other part of the world would afford them, and are paid in ready money. This rank of people therefore do not or ought not to complain of hard times, and they make a very considerable part of the city inhabitants.

At the distance I live from our American fisheries, I cannot speak of them with any certainty; but I have not heard that the labour of the valuable race of men employed in them is worse paid, or that they meet with less success than before the revolution. The whalemen indeed have been deprived of one market for their oil, but another I hear is opening for them, which it is hoped may be equally advantageous. And the demand is constantly increasing for their spermaceti candles, which therefore bear a much higher price than formerly.

There remain the merchants and shopkeepers. Of these, though they make but a small part of the whole nation, the number is considerable, too great indeed for the business they are employed in. For the consumption of goods in every country has its limits. The faculties of the people, that is, their ability to buy and pay, is equal only to a certain quantity of merchandize. If merchants calculate amiss on this proportion, and import too much, they will of course find the sale dull for the overplus, and some of them will say that trade languishes. They should, and doubtless will, grow wiser by experience, and import less. If too many artificers in town, and farmers from the country, flattering themselves with the idea of leading easier lives, turn shop-keepers, the whole natural quantity of that business divided among them all may afford too small a share for each, and occasion complaints that trading is dead; these may also suppose that it is owing to scarcity of money, while, in fact, it is not so much from the fewness of buyers, as from the excessive number of sellers, that the mischief arises; and if every shopkeeping farmer and mechanic would return to the use of his plough and working tools, there would remain of widows and other women shopkeepers sufficient for the business, which might then afford them a comfortable main-tenance.

Whoever has travelled through the various parts of Europe, and observed how small is the proportion of people in affluence or easy circumstances there, compared with those in poverty and misery; the few rich and haughty landlords, the multitude of poor, abject, rack-rented, tythe-paying tenants, and half paid and half starved ragged la-bourers; and views here the happy mediocrity that so generally prevails throughout these states, where the culti-vator works for himself, and supports his family in decent plenty, will, methinks, see abundant reason to bless divine providence for the evident and great difference in our favour, and be convinced that no nation known to us enjoys a greater share of human felicity.

It is true that in some of the states there are parties and discords; but let us look back, and ask if we were ever without them? Such will exist wherever there is liberty; and perhaps they help to preserve it. By the collision of different sentiments, sparks of truth are struck out, and political light is obtained. The different factions, which at present divide us, aim all at the public good; the differences are only about the various modes of promoting it. Things, actions, meas-ures and objects of all kinds, present themselves to the minds of men in such a variety of lights, that it is not possible we should all think alike at the same time on every subject, when hardly the same man retains at all times the same ideas of it. Parties are therefore the common lot of humanity, and ours are by no means more mischievous or less beneficial than those of other countries, nations and ages, enjoying in the same degree the great blessing of political liberty.

Some indeed among us are not so much grieved for the present state of our affairs, as apprehensive for the future. The growth of luxury alarms them, and they think we are from that alone in the high road to ruin. They observe, that no revenue is sufficient without economy, and that the most plentiful income of a whole people from the natural productions of their country may be dissipated in vain and needless expences, and poverty be introduced in the place of affluence. This may be possible. It however rarely happens: For there seems to be in every nation a greater proportion of industry and frugality, which tend to enrich, than of idleness and prodigality, which occasion poverty, so that upon the whole there is a continual accumulation. Reflect what Spain, Gaul, Germany and Britain were in the time of the Romans, inhabited by people little richer than our savages, and consider the wealth they at present possess, in numerous well-built cities, improved farms, rich moveables, magazines stocked with valuable manufactures, to say nothing of plate, jewels and coined money; and all this notwithstanding their bad, wasteful, plundering governments, and their mad destructive wars; and yet luxury and extravagant living has never suffered much restraint in those countries. Then consider the great proportion of industrious frugal farmers inhabiting the interior parts of these American states, and of whom the body of our nation consists; and judge whether it is possible that the luxury of our sea ports can be sufficient to ruin such a country. If the importation of foreign luxuries could ruin a people, we should probably have been ruined long ago: For the British nation claimed a right, and practised it, of importing among us not only the superfluities of their own production, but those of every nation under heaven; we bought and consumed them, and yet we flourished and grew rich. At present our independent governments may do what we could not then do, discourage by heavy duties, or prevent by prohibitions, such importations, and thereby grow richer; if indeed, which may admit of dispute, the desire of adorning ourselves with fine clothes, possessing fine furniture, with elegant houses, &c. is not, by strongly inciting to labour and industry, the occasion of producing a greater value than is consumed in the gratification of that desire.

The agriculture and fisheries of the United States are the great sources of our encreasing wealth. He that puts a seed into the earth is recompenced perhaps by receiving forty out of it; and he who draws a fish out of our waters draws up a piece of silver. Let us (and there is no doubt but we shall) be attentive to these; and then the power of rivals, with all their restraining and prohibiting acts, cannot much hurt us. We are sons of the earth and seas, and, like *Anteus* in the fable,* if in wrestling with a *Hercules* we now and then receive a fall, the touch of our parents will communicate to us fresh strength and vigour to renew the contest.

A. B.*

Speech in the Constitutional Convention at the Conclusion of its Deliberations

Naturally Franklin served in the Pennsylvania delegation to the 1787 Constitutional Convention. He was 81 but had completed a three-year term as president of the Supreme Executive Council of Pennsylvania after returning from France. During the deliberations of the Convention he served as host to the younger men who were principally engaged in drafting the Constitution. Because he was a politician by training and not a lawyer, Franklin's preoccupations were somewhat out of step with those of James Madison, James Wilson, and Alexander Hamilton, the dominant intellectual figures in the Convention. At one point where the delegates had been at a long-standing impasse, Franklin even moved that sessions be opened with prayer, though his colleagues ignored the motion. Later he conceived of the central compromise needed in the design of the new Congress, having one house represent the states equally and the other proportioned to population.

His final speech is far short of the unqualified endorsement of the Constitution that Madison, Hamilton, and John Jay would soon draft in the *Federalist*, but the understated approval registered here was well calculated to appeal to the undecided. The reference to the 'certain French Lady' who believed herself always right was also a reminder of the extent of his own acquaintance with the world. Since his period of service as an American diplomat, Franklin had been aware of the predictions of doom for the United States that appeared frequently in the English press, so he argues for unanimous approval of the Constitution as a means of contradicting those reports.

I confess that I do not entirely approve of this Constitution at present, but Sir, I am not sure I shall never approve it: For having lived long, I have experienced many Instances of being oblig'd, by better Information or fuller Consideration, to change Opinions even on important Subjects, which I once thought right, but found to be otherwise. It is therefore that the older I grow the more apt I am to doubt my own Judgment and to pay more Respect to the Judgment of others. Most Men indeed as well as most Sects in Religion, think themselves in Possession of all Truth, and that wherever others differ from them it is so far Error. Steele, a Protestant, in a Dedication tells the Pope, that the only Difference between our two Churches in their Opinions of the Certainty of their Doctrine, is, the Romish Church is infallible, and the Church of England is never in the Wrong. But tho' many private Persons think almost as highly of their own Infallibility, as that of their Sect, few express it so naturally as a certain French lady, who in a little Dispute with her Sister, said, I don't know how it happens, Sister, but I meet with no body but myself that's *always* in the right. *Il n'y a que moi qui a toujours raison.*

In these Sentiments, Sir, I agree to this Constitution, with all its Faults, if they are such: because I think a General Government necessary for us, and there is no *Form* of Government but what may be a Blessing to the People if well administred; and I believe farther that this is likely to be well administred for a Course of Years, and can only end in Despotism as other Forms have done before it, when the People shall become so corrupted as to need Despotic Government, being incapable of any other. I doubt too whether any other Convention we can obtain, may be able to make a better Constitution: For when you assemble a Number of Men to have the Advantage of their joint Wisdom, you inevitably assemble with those Men all their Prejudices, their Passions, their Errors of Opinion, their local Interests, and their selfish Views. From such an Assembly can a perfect Production be expected? It therefore astonishes me, Sir, to find this System approaching so near to Perfection as it does; and I think it will astonish our Enemies, who are waiting with Confidence to hear that our Councils are confounded, like those of the Builders of Babel, and that our States are on the Point of Separation, only to meet hereafter for the Purpose of cutting one another's Throats. Thus I consent, Sir, to this Constitution because I expect no better, and because I am not sure that it is not the best. The Opinions I have had of its Errors, I sacrifice to the Public Good. I have never whisper'd a Syllable of them abroad. Within these Walls they were born, & here they shall die. If every one of us in returning to our Constituents were to report the Objections he has had to it, and endeavour to gain Partizans in support of them, we might prevent its being generally received, and thereby lose all the salutary Effects & great Advantages resulting naturally in our favour among foreign Nations, as well as among ourselves, from our real or apparent Unanimity. Much of the Strength and Efficiency of any Government, in procuring & securing Happiness to the People depends on Opinion, on the general Opinion of the Goodness of that Government as well as of the Wisdom & Integrity of its Governors. I hope therefore that for our own Sakes, as a Part of the People, and for the Sake of our Posterity, we shall act heartily & unanimously in recommending this Constitution, wherever our Influence may extend, and turn our future Thoughts and Endeavours to the Means of having it well administred.—

On the whole, Sir, I cannot help expressing a Wish, that every Member of the Convention, who may still have Objections to it, would with me on this Occasion doubt a little of his own Infallibility, and to make *manifest* our *Unanimity*, put his Name to this Instrument.—

Then the Motion was made for adding the last Formula, viz Done in Convention by the unanimous Consent &c— which was agreed to and added—accordingly.

17 September 1787

Letter to Ezra Stiles, 9 March 1790

Many of Franklin's American correspondents were people he never met but whose interests or political persuasions coincided with his, and by the end of his life few of his correspondents were of his own generation. Ezra Stiles and Franklin had written to each other for twenty years on a variety of topics before this final letter. Stiles, the Calvinist president of Yale College, had written to the aged Franklin asking about his religious views early in 1790. Only a month before his death Franklin sent this careful reply. Needless to say, the portrait of himself that Franklin volunteers to sit for in the first paragraph was never done from life. He reiterates here the all-purpose creed described in the *Autobiography*. On the crucial question in Stiles's mind, Franklin's belief or unbelief in the divinity of Jesus, Franklin aligns himself with English Unitarians but says 'it is a question I do not dogmatize upon, having never studied it, and think it needless to busy myself with it now, when I expect soon an Opportunity of knowing the Truth with less Trouble.' To say he had never studied the question does not really reflect the extensive history of Franklin's reflections on religion, but Franklin knew that this letter would be read at Yale, the stronghold of Calvinist theology in America, and he phrases his letter so that a religious well-wisher like Stiles might be satisfied by this last Franklin letter.

REVEREND AND DEAR SIR,   Philad^a, March 9. 1790.

I received your kind Letter of Jan'y 28, and am glad you have at length received the portrait of Gov'r Yale from his Family, and deposited it in the College Library. He was a great and good Man, and had the Merit of doing infinite Service to your Country by his Munificence to that Institution. The Honour you propose doing me by placing mine in the same Room with his, is much too great for my Deserts; but you always had a Partiality for me, and to that it must be ascribed. I am however too much obliged to Yale College, the first learned Society that took Notice of me and adorned me with its Honours, to refuse a Request that comes from it thro' so esteemed a Friend. But I do not think any one of the Portraits you mention, as in my Possession, worthy of the Place and Company you propose to place it in. You have an excellent Artist lately arrived. If he will undertake to make one for you, I shall cheerfully pay the Expence; but he must not delay setting about it, or I may slip thro' his fingers, for I am now in my eighty-fifth year, and very infirm.

I send with this a very learned Work, as it seems to me, on the antient Samaritan Coins, lately printed in Spain, and at least curious for the Beauty of the Impression. Please to accept it for your College Library. I have subscribed for the Encyclopædia now printing here, with the Intention of presenting it to the College. I shall probably depart before the Work is finished, but shall leave Directions for its Continuance to the End. With this you will receive some of the first numbers.

You desire to know something of my Religion. It is the first time I have been questioned upon it. But I cannot take your Curiosity amiss, and shall endeavour in a few Words to gratify it. Here is my Creed. I believe in one God, Creator of the Universe. That he governs it by his Providence. That he ought to be worshipped. That the most acceptable Service we render to him is doing good to his other Children. That the soul of Man is immortal, and will be treated with Justice in another Life respecting its Conduct in this. These I take to be the fundamental Principles of all sound Religion, and I regard them as you do in whatever Sect I meet with them.

As to Jesus of Nazareth, my Opinion of whom you particularly desire, I think the System of Morals and his Religion, as he left them to us, the best the World ever saw or is likely to see; but I apprehend it has received various corrupting Changes, and I have, with most of the present Dissenters in England, some Doubts as to his Divinity; tho' it is a question I do not dogmatize upon, having never studied it, and think it needless to busy myself with it now, when I expect soon an Opportunity of knowing the Truth with less Trouble. I see no harm, however, in its being believed, if that Belief has the good Consequence, as probably it has, of making his Doctrines more respected and better observed; especially as I do not perceive, that the Supreme takes it amiss, by distinguishing the Unbelievers in his Government of the World with any peculiar Marks of his Displeasure.

I shall only add, respecting myself, that, having experienced the Goodness of that Being in conducting me prosperously thro' a long life, I have no doubt of its Continuance in the next, though without the smallest Conceit of meriting such Goodness. My Sentiments on this Head you will see in the Copy of an old Letter enclosed, which I wrote in answer to one from a zealous Religionist, whom I had relieved in a paralytic case by electricity, and who, being afraid I should grow proud upon it, sent me his serious though rather impertinent Caution. I send you also the Copy of another Letter, which will shew something of my Disposition relating to Religion. With great and sincere Esteem and Affection, I am, Your obliged old Friend and most obedient humble Servant

P. S. Had not your College some Present of Books from the King of France? Please to let me know, if you had an Expectation given you of more, and the Nature of that Expectation? I have a Reason for the Enquiry.

I confide, that you will not expose me to Criticism and censure by publishing any part of this Communication to you. I have ever let others enjoy their religious Sentiments, without reflecting on them for those that appeared to me unsupportable and even absurd. All Sects here, and we have a great Variety, have experienced my good will in assisting them with Subscriptions for building their new Places of Worship; and, as I have never opposed any of their Doctrines, I hope to go out of the World in Peace with them all.

EXPLANATORY NOTES

3 *Twyford, at the Bishop of St Asaph's*: Twyford was the name of the country residence of Jonathan Shipley, Bishop of St Asaph, a friend and political ally of Franklin.

   some Degree of Reputation: Franklin first wrote the word 'Fame' but crossed it out and replaced it with 'Reputation'.

5 *1702 Jan. 6. old Stile*: Old Style refers to the Julian calendar in use in England and its American colonies until 1752. The year did not change at 1 January but on 25 March.

13 *and another of Dr Mather's*: Cotton Mather.

15 *the Spectator*: The *Spectator* was a series of periodical essays published in 1711 and 1712 written primarily by Joseph Addison and Richard Steele.

28 *He had been one of the French Prophets and could act their enthusiastic Agitations*: The French Prophets were refugee Huguenots who arrived in England in 1707 preaching in the London streets the imminent arrival of the millennium, a belief accompanied by expressions of religious ecstasy. (See Garrett, 21–3, 145–55.)

29 *New Castle*: Newcastle was the capital of the colony of Delaware in the early eighteenth century. Delaware and Pennsylvania shared a governor appointed by the descendants of William Penn, the Proprietaries.

30 *grum*: morose and surly.

45 *a pale Ale-House in   Lane, Cheapside*: Franklin leaves a blank in the manuscript before the word Lane.

48 *Riggite*: derived from the verb 'rig', which in English dialect usage could mean to play tricks or hoax.

50 *the College and Don Saltero's Curiosities*: Chelsea Hospital, built on the site of a former college, still one of London's most impressive architectural sites; James Salter, popularly called Don Saltero, maintained nearby an exhibit of odd items of doubtful origin.

53 *nuncupative Will*: oral will.

59   *Whatever is, is right . . . That poizes all, above*: Franklin mis-remembers the passage from John Dryden which he had cited accurately in his 1725 *Dissertation on Liberty and Necessity*. Here he transposes a famous line from Alexander Pope's *Essay on Man* in place of a similar line from Dryden's play *Oedipus*. In his 1779 letter to Benjamin Vaughan he similarly misquotes the original.

72   *Privileges.—*: Franklin's note to himself following the completed text of Part 1 reads: My Manner of acting to engage People in this & future Undertakings.

81   *"Seest thou . . . before mean Men."*: Proverbs 22: 29.

83   *"Finally . . . think on these Things;"*: Philippians 4: 8, not quite accurately recalled by Franklin.

86   *Advice of Pythagoras in his Golden Verses*: Franklin adds a note that the Golden Verses of Pythagoras should be inserted as a note to the text. The *Carmina aurea*, attributed apocryphally to Pythagoras, was the best-known text of the ancient Greek philosopher, translated numerous times into English from the Renaissance up to the eighteenth century. (See Heninger, 259–61.)

88   *"O Vitae Philosophia . . . immortalitati est anteponendus."*: Cicero, *Tusculan Disputations*, V. ii. 5. 'O Philosophy guide of life! O explorer of excellences and scourge of faults! One day spent well and according to thy rule is to be preferred before a sinning immortality.' Franklin has abridged the original considerably.

93   *James II*, 15, 16: 'If a brother or sister be naked, and destitute of daily food, And one of you say unto them, Depart in peace, be ye warmed and filled; notwithstanding ye give them not those things which are needful to the body; what doth it profit?' (King James Version).

112   *litera scripta manet*: 'the written word endures'.

117   *honourable & learned Mr Logan*: James Logan, learned and wealthy Quaker, who was an important patron of the young Franklin.

119   *Michael Welfare*: Michael Wohlfart, charismatic leader of a German Baptist group called the Brethren, known also as the Dunkers or Dunkards for their practice of initiating members through immersion in water.

135 *Look . . . pursue*: the opening lines of John Dryden's translation of Juvenal's tenth *Satire*.

139 *General Braddock*: Edward Braddock, commander of British forces in America, who led a large army of British regulars and American colonials with the intent of taking Fort Duquesne, now on the site of Pittsburgh, Pennsylvania, but the French and Indians repelled his advance in a battle known in American history as Braddock's Defeat, 9 July 1755.

149 *General Shirley*: William Shirley, governor of Massachusetts, the immediate successor to Braddock as commander of British North American forces.

151 *Moravians*: members of the Moravian Church, also known as the Renewed Church of the Brethren or Unitas Fratrum, spiritual followers of Count Nikolaus Ludwig von Zinzendorf. The group emigrated to the area around Bethlehem, Pennsylvania, from Saxony around 1740.

155 *Hautboys*: oboes.

160 *Dr Fothergill*: Dr John Fothergill, Quaker physician in London and patron of science, Fellow of the Royal Society.

Cave . . . his Gentleman's Magazine: Edward Cave, London printer of the *Gentleman's Magazine*.

the Count de Buffon: Georges-Louis Leclerc, comte de Buffon, French scientist, author of the influential and encyclopedic *Histoire naturelle*.

the Abbé Nollet: Jean-Antoine Nollet, French physicist whose explanation of the phenomenon of electricity was displaced by Franklin's.

161 *Mr B——*: Mathurin-Jacques Brisson.

162 *the celebrated Dr Watson*: Dr William Watson, physician and electrical theorist, winner of the Royal Society's Copley Medal for his electrical experiments in 1745 (*Papers*, iii. 457 n.).

Mr Canton: English electrical experimenter who succeeded in verifying Franklin's hypothesis about the identity of lightning and electricity as described in a letter by William Watson printed in the *Philosophical Transactions* of the Royal Society (*Papers*, iv. 390–1).

Lord Macclesfield: George Parker, Earl of Macclesfield, president of the Royal Society 1752–64.

164   *the Dispute between Prince Frederic and the King*: Frederick, Prince of Wales, became embroiled in a factional dispute with his father, George II.

      the Dunciad: Alexander Pope composed a long satiric denunciation of his literary rivals entitled the *Dunciad*.

      General Lord Loudon: John Campbell, Earl of Loudoun, Scottish peer and commander of British forces in North America 1756–7 (*Papers*, vi. 453–4 n.).

166   *Mr Pitt*: William Pitt the Elder, Prime Minister during the Seven Years War.

      Amherst and Wolf: General Lord Jeffrey Amherst and General James Wolfe, the commanders of the British forces in North America after Loudoun was relieved of command.

170   *the Log-Line*: a ship's log is a method of estimating speed at sea whereby a floating object connected to a log-line is released from the ship and reeled in so that the length of the log-line will indicate elapsed distance.

172   *Mr Peter Collinson*: Quaker merchant in London, long-time correspondent with Franklin and the original recipient of his letters describing experimentation in electricity.

      John Hanbury: one of a family of Quaker merchants involved in colonial affairs (*Papers*, vii. 249 n.).

      Lord Granville's: John Carteret, first Earl Granville, currently president of the Privy Council (*Papers*, vii. 249 n.).

173   *Mr J. Penn's*: John Penn, grandson of William Penn and nephew of the Proprietaries of Pennsylvania.

174   *Ferdinando John Paris*: Ferdinand John Paris, colonial agent for Pennsylvania in the 1730s and later the principal advisor and legal counsel to the Proprietaries.

175   *Lord Mansfield*: William Murray, Baron Mansfield, chief justice of the King's Bench and member of the Privy Council.

176   *Mr Charles*: Robert Charles, colonial agent for New York and Pennsylvania at the time.

179   *England.]*: the editors of the *Genetic Text* of the *Autobiography* conclude that Franklin added this closed bracket to note that he had completed the writing up to this point, when two copies of the text thus far completed were sent to friends in England and France (Lemay and Zall, *Genetic Text*, 208).

179   *Canada delenda est*: Franklin paraphrases the famous pronouncement repeatedly made by Cato the Elder, statesman of the Roman republic, *Carthago delenda est*: Carthage must be destroyed.

182   *An sum . . . vel Latinè docendus?*: 'For am I even now to be taught to speak either Greek or Latin', Cicero, *De finibus*, 2. 5. Franklin has altered the thrust in the rhetorical question of Cicero, who would have known Latin and Greek already from his basic education.

185   *some eloquent Paragraphs out of Tillotson's Works*: John Tillotson, archbishop of Canterbury in the late seventeenth century, had been the leading spokesman for latitudinarian Anglicanism. His views were quite compatible with those of the mature Franklin, but more liberal than the orthodoxy of New England Puritanism, though Franklin's description suggests that orthodoxy was somewhat diluted by 1722.

188   *Summum jus, est summa injuria*: 'perfect justice brings on the worst injustice', Cicero, *De officiis*, 1. 10. 33. The statement appears in a context in which Cicero is describing inappropriate or too rigid observances of the law.

193   *Gibson*: Sir John Gibson, Lieutenant-Governor of Portsmouth, 1689–1717 (*Papers*, i. 74 n.).

196   *Cadogan*: Lieutenant-General William Cadogan, governor of the Isle of Wight, 1715–26 (*Papers*, i. 77 n.).

     General Webb: Lieutenant-General John Richmond Webb, governor of the Isle of Wight, 1710–15 (*Papers*, i. 77 n.).

     plaster of Paris: calcium sulphate, a paste of which is capable of being moulded and hardening.

197   *was once in King William's time entrusted with the government of this island*: Franklin leaves a blank space in place of the name, which almost certainly refers to Joseph Dudley, an unpopular governor of Massachusetts from 1702 to 1715.

198   *Sir Robert Holmes*: governor of the Isle of Wight, 1669–92 (*Papers*, i. 79 n.).

201   *a hoy*: a sloop-rigged coasting vessel.

202   *saw the Lizard*: Lizard Point in southern Cornwall, virtually the most southwesterly spot in Great Britain.

202   *a Grampus*: an aquatic mammal related to but smaller than a whale, sometimes identified by the puffing noise made in respiration.

203   *fizgig*: a barbed fishing-spear.

210   *Tropic bird*: the tropic bird (*phaeton lepturus*) is distinctive for its long, ribbon-like tail.

212   *clap us aboard*: to overtake and forcibly board another vessel.

213   *jack*: a small signal flag, or possibly the British flag (the Union Jack).

    On either side . . . and roars below: Franklin is quoting, not quite accurately but evidently from memory, from Alexander Pope's translation of Homer's *Odyssey*, 13. 102–3 (Zall, *Franklin's Autobiography*, 103).

214   *gulfweed*: seaweed common in the south Atlantic (*sargassum bacciferum*).

215   *small crabs . . . backs*: possibly hermit crabs.

219   *Irish Lord*: probably a sculpin, a spiny, large-mouthed fish.

222   *Non vultus . . . magna Jovis manus*: 'Not the face of the pressing tyrant, nor the north wind, ruler of the restless whirling Adriatic, nor the mighty hand of thundering Jove shakes the firm mind', Horace, *Odes*, 3–6.

234   *Ostendunt Terris . . . Esse sinunt*: 'The Fates show him only so much, nor do they permit more', Virgil, *Aeneid*, 6. 869–70. Virgil is describing the abbreviated life of Marcellus, son-in-law of Augustus, who is the prototype of Virgil's hero Aeneas.

235   *to see a Dives faring deliciously every Day . . . to see a Lazarus poor, hungry, naked, and full of Sores*: Luke 16: 19–21.

237   *When Lazarus died, Jesus groaned and wept*: John 11: 35.

303   *And as M. B. has kindly sent me Word*: M. B. is Monsieur Brillon, the husband of Madame Brillon, to whom this bagatelle is addressed.

348   *like Anteus in the fable*: Antaeus, a mythological giant, was the child of the earth and famous for wrestling. When wrestled to the earth, Antaeus gained strength from it; he was only defeated by Hercules, who held him away from contact with the earth.

348 *A. B.*: like most writers on political questions in eighteenth-century periodicals, Franklin commonly used pseudonyms or initials which were not his own. In fact, such pseudonymous initials in some cases could even be identifying marks for a polemical writer. Verner W. Crane discovered a number of Franklin contributions to the press signed A. B. (Crane, *Letters*, 7, 22, 112, 183, 248).

THE WORLD'S CLASSICS

A Select List

HANS ANDERSEN: Fairy Tales
Translated by L. W. Kingsland
Introduction by Naomi Lewis
Illustrated by Vilhelm Pedersen and Lorenz Frølich

ARTHUR J. ARBERRY (Transl.): The Koran

LUDOVICO ARIOSTO: Orlando Furioso
Translated by Guido Waldman

ARISTOTLE: The Nicomachean Ethics
Translated by David Ross

JANE AUSTEN: Emma
Edited by James Kinsley and David Lodge

Mansfield Park
Edited by James Kinsley and John Lucas

Persuasion
Edited by John Davie

HONORÉ DE BALZAC: Père Goriot
Translated and Edited by A. J. Krailsheimer

CHARLES BAUDELAIRE: The Flowers of Evil
Translated by James McGowan
Introduction by Jonathan Culler

WILLIAM BECKFORD: Vathek
Edited by Roger Lonsdale

R. D. BLACKMORE: Lorna Doone
Edited by Sally Shuttleworth

KEITH BOSLEY (Transl.): The Kalevala

JAMES BOSWELL: Life of Johnson
The Hill/Powell edition, revised by David Fleeman
Introduction by Pat Rogers

MARY ELIZABETH BRADDON: Lady Audley's Secret
Edited by David Skilton

GIORGIO VASARI: The Lives of the Artists
Translated and Edited by Julia Conaway Bondanella and Peter Bondanella

JULES VERNE: Journey to the Centre of the Earth
Translated and Edited by William Butcher

IZAAK WALTON and CHARLES COTTON:
The Compleat Angler
Edited by John Buxton
Introduction by John Buchan

OSCAR WILDE: Complete Shorter Fiction
Edited by Isobel Murray